Fighting Words

Fighting Words

Working-Class Formation, Collective Action, and Discourse in Early Nineteenth-Century England

Marc W. Steinberg

Cornell University Press   ITHACA AND LONDON

Copyright © 1999 by Cornell University

All rights reserved. Except for brief quotations in a review, this book, or parts thereof, must not be reproduced in any form without permission in writing from the publisher. For information, address Cornell University Press, Sage House, 512 East State Street, Ithaca, New York 14850.

First published 1999 by Cornell University Press

Printed in the United States of America

Cornell University Press strives to use environmentally responsible suppliers and materials to the fullest extent possible in the publishing of its books. Such materials include vegetable-based, low-VOC inks and acid-free papers that are recycled, totally chlorine-free, or partly composed of nonwood fibers. Books that bear the logo of the FSC (Forest Stewardship Council) use paper taken from forests that have been inspected and certified as meeting the highest standards for environmental and social responsibility. For further information, visit our website at www.cornellpress.cornell.edu.

Library of Congress
Cataloging-in-Publication Data
Steinberg, Marc W. (Marc William), 1956–
Fighting words : working-class formation, collective action, and discourse in early nineteenth-century England / Marc W. Steinberg.
  p. cm.
Includes bibliographical references and index.
ISBN 0-8014-3582-X (cloth : alk. paper)
1. Working class—England—History—19th century. 2. Social conflict—England—History—19th century. I. Title.
HD8399.E52S73 1999
305.5′62′094209034—dc21   99-17936

Cloth printing
10 9 8 7 6 5 4 3 2 1

For my parents

At vero laborantes pervenimus

Contents

Tables	ix
Preface	xi
Abbreviations	xvii

PRELIMINARIES

Introduction: Theoretical and Historiographical Considerations		1
1	Patterns of English Labor Contention in the Early Nineteenth Century	23
2	A Tale of Two Areas	36

SPITALFIELDS

3	The Silk Trade: Memory, Market, and Means of Production	49
4	Local Political Culture: From Reciprocity to Hegemony	67
5	The Repeal of the Spitalfields Acts	87
6	Post-Repeal Collective Actions: Battling the Hydra of Degradation	101

ASHTON-STALYBRIDGE

7	King Cotton: Markets, Mills, and Mechanics	129
8	Class Structure, Class Cultures, and Social Lives	151
9	Local Political Culture: The Stranglehold of Wealth	167
10	The Vitriol of Conflict	187
11	Class War: The Spinners' Strikes of 1830–1831	206

CONCLUSION

12 Class Formation, Collective Action, and the Role of Discourse   229

Appendix 1. Spitalfields weavers' collective actions,
  c. 1825–1831   243
Appendix 2. Ashton and Stalybridge spinners' collective
  actions, April 1830–January 1831   247
References   249
Index   277

Tables

1. Adjudicated cases of silk embezzlement and theft in Spitalfields, 1828–1831 — 74
2. Punishments for adjudicated cases of silk embezzlement and theft in Spitalfields, 1828–1831 — 75
3. May/June 1829 cutting and destroying incidents, by firm — 123
4. Assessed value of mill property for sixteen Stalybridge firms, 1830 — 133
5. Distribution of mills, by height, for sixteen Stalybridge firms, 1830 — 135
6. Religious identification of heads of families in Ashton, Stalybridge, and Dukinfield, c. 1835 — 179

Preface

This book has linked subjects—the historical processes of class formation and the dynamics of contentious collective action. The principal thread tying them together is the role of discourse in each process. In both my theoretical statements and my historical case studies, I explain how the analysis of discourse provides more encompassing understandings of class formation and collective action. The volume opens with one theoretical and one historiographic chapter, but throughout most of the book analyses of discourse, collective action, and processes of class formation emerge in these histories of the early nineteenth century. The two subjects are intertwined in detailed historical accounts of the silk weavers of London's Spitalfields district and the cotton spinners of the towns of Ashton and Stalybridge in the northern industrial county of Lancashire. Before weaving this analytic whole cloth, let me outline the focuses and my purposes in studying them.

Most of us have found ourselves bleary-eyed in front of the TV at some point, watching a grade-B western. In virtually every one of these films, two cowboys at some critical juncture square off on Main Street outside the saloon, and an exchange between them heats up. Finally, hands perched on his gun handles, one makes a patented quick move, exclaiming, "Why, them's fightin' words!" Fighting words are the recurring objects of analysis in this study.

In my investigation of fighting words—what I also call discourses of contention—I hope to build an analytical bridge between what have been two somewhat divergent schools of thought in the study of collective action. Resource mobilization and political process models of collective action, those dominant in U.S. research, have in the past placed resources, social structures, organization, and strategies in the foreground in their analyses, while making less central issues of culture, consciousness, and language. The new social movements literature and allied trends in postmodernist/poststructuralist perspectives, prominent in European research, tend to reverse these theoretical and empirical priorities. Accepting many of the basic premises of the former, I demonstrate how the concerns of the latter must be brought into the analysis of collective action. We must analyze both the material and social dynamics of how people act collectively *and* the processes of culture and consciousness by which groups come to envision a changed world and to see their actions as necessary and efficacious. In the movie, the town may not be big enough for both cowboys, but they do not simply stride out into the street, guns blazing, in response to this structural constraint. Rather, the fighting words are necessary to define the inadequacy and provide justification for the showdown. These words themselves, however, do not create the conflict between the two gunslingers; its root is in their having opposed interests in a common social space. Structural position and fighting words thus conjoin to set the boundaries of the battle. And this is the case as well in the social drama of group struggles.

Through what I term a dialogic perspective on collective action and the discourses of contention, I demonstrate how subordinate groups develop discursive repertoires that articulate this sense of group purpose, efficacy, and vision of a better world. I also show how these discursive repertoires are reciprocally linked to the repertoires of collective actions that groups develop to realize their goals. In so doing, I hope to provide a more comprehensive analysis of purposive contentious action.

Some scholars will no doubt accuse me of fence sitting, of refusing to take a clear stand on the epistemological issues that seem to divide disciplines. I have two responses. First, I believe that the division of the social sciences into the contentious camps of materialism and post-materialism is a dualism that we must go beyond. My analysis is materialist, but it demonstrates that materialism need not and should not be reductionist. Social life is at once both material and symbolic; it is the welter of people's activities within complex social, economic, and political systems, their agency in responding to (and sometimes overcoming) them, and their representations of both. It is our task to grapple with how all of these processes fit into a dynamic system. Second, fence sitting provides a better vantage for judging the terrain on either side. Although I believe that a materialist account of collective action and class formation is still our most promising foundation, post-materialist analyses ask necessary and challenging questions that we must address.

I maintain that a dialogic perspective is a way of taking the concerns of both camps into account. This perspective looks at how people make sense of their life experiences through the collective (and often contentious) cultural processes of conveying their experiences in discourse. Discourse is a powerful mediating force in the structuring of group consciousness, but it neither creates this consciousness nor masters those who articulate it. A dialogic perspective focuses on how material experiences and their discursive representations exist in a larger interactive and dynamic system that is social life. My investigation of workers' struggles will detail the particular ways in which the material and discursive were tied for these groups in early nineteenth-century England.

> They tie you up and put you in a cage
> And wonder why you should be in a rage
> Then feed you on scraps, comes off their taxes too
> And say you've gotta
> Keep up with the age.
> But there goes the child of labourers
> Through the valley of the kings
> And demanding the birthright like all children should
> At the source of the liberty spring
> By the root of the liberty tree
> I'll meet you there in the dawning
> If you'd wait for me
> And I do hope you wait for me.
>   (Frank Tovey and the Pyros, "The Liberty Tree,"
>   from *Grand Union* [1992])

> You gave me my birth
> Then you made me pay
> What is it worth
> Cast me away
> You really done it now
> Dying in my arms
> You stand here with nothing
> But you've still got english charm . . .
> Why is it england
> I feel like rubbish on your streets
> Why is it when I care
> I feel so incomplete
> Why does our future
> Seem such a feat
> When will our consciousness
> Finally meet.
>   (The Levellers, "England My Home,"
>   from *A Weapon Called the Word*)

In 1963 E. P. Thompson published *The Making of the English Working Class* and fundamentally changed the way we now look at class formation. Thompson demonstrated that the working class was present at its own making, indeed was an active progenitor, and that part of working people's critical efforts was the cultural production of their class consciousness. The often-quoted passage from Thompson's preface bears repeating, for the core of its meaning seems to have been obscured by successive debates and commentaries:

> Class happens when some men, as a result of common experiences (inherited or shared), feel and articulate the identity of their interests as between themselves, and as against other men whose interests are different from (and usually opposed to) theirs. The class experience is largely determined by the productive relations into which men are born—or enter involuntarily. Class-consciousness is the way in which these experiences are handled in cultural terms: embodied in the traditions, value-systems, ideas, and institutional forms. If the experience appears as determined, class-consciousness does not. We can see a logic in the responses of similar occupational groups undergoing similar experiences, but we cannot predicate any law. Consciousness of class arises in the same way in different times and places, but never in just the same way. (1966, pp. 9–10)

Since the publication of these words, all historians and social scientists analyzing the English working class have had to acknowledge Thompson's thesis, even if only to critique or reject it. Those critiques have rippled across scholastic pages in waves. The first wave was from a school of staid historians who sought to reject any marxist analysis of class formation. After a time, they were followed by some marxists themselves, who argued that Thompson had emphasized working-class culture too much and did not pay enough attention to the economic forces that shaped it. The last and current wave has several aspects. One part of the criticism rightly takes Thompson to task for his relative neglect of the processes of gender and the role of women in the story. Another strand resembles the staid historians in its extremes, in that it proclaims that Thompson's work created a chimera, the semblance of class consciousness where in fact none existed. Based in what is often termed the "linguistic turn" in the history, these critics argue that the discourses used by workers over the course of the nineteenth and twentieth centuries reveal many kinds of consciousness, but none of them class consciousness.

In this book, I hope to convince the critics that they have miscast Thompson's argument in the form of a tired and reductionist marxism, which he never advocated, and that class consciousness was writ large in the language of the workers he studied. I do so by paying more systematic attention to this discourse and by taking seriously the critics' arguments that language had a powerful impact in the shaping of consciousness. That granted, I show how that language was born of class experiences and mediated and expressed a class consciousness. Fighting words were part of the logic of the class experience, though they were never just the same among different occupational groups. Far from discrediting *The Making*, the analysis of workers' discourse provides additional insight for appreciating the validity of its thesis.

As I sit hear finishing this preface and listening to English rock music, I can hear the echoes of those nineteenth-century workers in the lyrics. The Levellers and other contemporary groups sing of the material and psychic wounds of class, the furtive hopes that these wounds can inspire, and the determination to realize these visions of betterment. They are by no means alone. All across the face of England, working-class youths are composing and playing similar odes, even as many in the academy are singing the death knell of class. I think that the workers I study in this book would find great virtue in this music; I believe it would resonate with their class consciousness. This homage to the lessons from Wick Episcopi seeks to show that the words of today reverberate with the consciousness created by those of the past. *The Making* happened, as it does still, although not in just the same way.

My intellectual balance sheet is heavy with debits. Those who are familiar with Charles Tilly's work will undoubtedly see his guidance throughout these pages. What they will not see is something as consequential—his encouragement and support in the face of my uncertainty at exploring new directions. Those who have had the privilege of working with Chuck, particularly in the formative stages of their careers, well understand the importance of the respect he unflinchingly shows for the struggling young scholar. He is a master at helping a fledgling map out options without ever dictating direction. Through his mentorship he enacted and helped me realize in all the best ways a maxim repeatedly used by the subjects of my study throughout their many struggles, "knowledge is power." My appreciation for guidance and support extends also to Mayer Zald, Bill Sewell, Aldon Morris, and Geoff Eley. Bill Gamson provided inspiration in the early stages of this project. Peggy Somers has since been a constant wellspring of intellectual guidance. And more than she could possibly imagine, Sonya Rose has shepherded me through numerous intellectual and professional travails—in many critical ways, she helped this project toward its completion.

I was fortunate in my colleagues at Clark University. Stefan Tanaka schooled me in Bakhtin and enormously expanded my knowledge of linguistic and cultural theory. Countless conversations with Patty Ewick deeply inform my approach in this analysis—no one is a more astute analyst of the social. Bob Vitalis served as a critical partner in thinking through issues of political economy in the face of cultural theory. In addition, my colleagues in the sociology department provided critical support along the way.

At Smith College, Rick Fantasia and Nancy Whittier affably and deftly guided me. Mickey Glazer, Pat Miller, and Peter Rose were unflappable sources of cheer.

Other scholars have given good support and advice. Robert Hall freely offered suggestions for interpretation and sources for Ashton-under-Lyne. Phillip McCann generously provided counsel on sources for my research in Spitalfields. I also have benefited from exchanges with Anna Clark, John Hall, John Smail, Sid Tarrow, and the members of the Great Barrington theory group. My long sojourn in English history could not have begun without the patient and thoughtful guidance of David Spring.

I am grateful for financial assistance from several sources. Early research was supported by the Horace Rackham Graduate School at the University of Michigan. A Clark University faculty development grant allowed for the continuation of the research process. Support from Smith College was absolutely essential in seeing this book to publication.

Anyone who has engaged in historical research knows that nothing consequential gets accomplished without the assistance of savvy archivists and librarians. In England, generous help was provided by the staffs of the British Library, the Public Record Office, and the Lancashire County Record Office. The members of the public libraries of Tower Hamlets, Tameside, and Manchester, and those of the Goldsmith's Library, Bishopsgate Institute, the Guildhall Library, and the British Library for Economic and Political Science also offered essential assistance. Stateside, numerous librarians at the University of Michigan, Clark University, and Smith College were the backbone of my continuing research process. I also wish to thank the British Library and the Public Record Office for permission to quote from their collections, as well as Emile Music and Green Park Music for permission to reproduce lyrics for songs by Frank Tovey and The Levellers.

A project of this duration is not accomplished without friends, and I want to thank especially Kirsten Alscer, Janette Greenwood, Chalmers Knight, Irene Padavic, Angel Vargas, and the Vegtapeople, who provided me with special sustenance. In no small part, this project has been accomplished because of Jane Rafferty's effusive kindness and support.

No author could have more supportive and sagacious editors than Peter Agree and Carol Betsch at Cornell. Grey Osterud also provided insightful commentary for essential revisions of the final manuscript.

Finally, I owe my greatest debt to my family, my parents and my brother, Alan, who showed me their total support time and again throughout this long process. Above all, my parents' unflappable support, encouragement, and love have always seen me through. Whatever advantages I've had along the way, none have been any more important than to be their son.

MARC W. STEINBERG

Northampton, Massachusetts

Abbreviations

B.L.	British Library
CMPM	*Carpenter's Monthly Political Magazine*
Hans.	*Hansard's Parliamentary Debates*
H.O.	British Public Record Office, Home Office Papers
L.C.R.O.	Lancashire County Record Office, Preston
L.S.P.	House of Lords Select Committee Reports
MC	*Morning Chronicle* (London)
M.C.L.	Manchester Central Library, Manuscripts Collection
MG	*Manchester Guardian*
MM	*Manchester Mercury*
MT	*Manchester Times*
MC	*Morning Chronicle* (London)
P.C.	British Library, Francis Place Collection of Newspaper Clippings and Pamphlets
PMA	*Poor Man's Advocate*
PMG	*Poor Man's Guardian*
P.P.	House of Commons Select Committee Reports
SA	*Stockport Advertiser*
T.L.L.H.	Tameside Library (Stalybridge), Local History Collection
TN	*Trades' Newspaper and Mechanics' Weekly Journal*
TFP	*Trades' Weekly Free Press*
UPCI	*Union Pilot and Co-operative Intelligencer*

UTCJ	*United Trades' Co-operative Journal*
VP	*Voice of the People*
WFP	*Weekly Free Press*
WMC	*Wheelers' Manchester Chronicle*
Webb Coll.	London School of Economics, British Library of Political and Economic Science, Sidney and Beatrice Webb, Collected Papers

PRELIMINARIES

INTRODUCTION

Theoretical and Historiographical Considerations

This is a book about conjunctions and relations. Most concretely, it is about how two groups of working people—silk weavers and cotton spinners—facing difficult and sometimes tragic circumstances, combined to resist exploitation and oppression. These particular tales, however, illuminate a larger theoretical perspective on how structuring processes of inequality combine.

As people face conditions of inequality, they react simultaneously to a welter of circumstances that they did not create and yet sometimes seek to change. Analytically, social scientists and historians have tried to tease out and disaggregate these structuring processes to probe how each contributes to inequality and its transformation. Broadly speaking, the focus of much recent work has been to understand the conjoining and relations between the material and discursive structures of inequality. In focusing on the material structures, we analyze how the concrete processes of production and reproduction create durable patterns of interaction. We fix on how work and co-habitation, social and economic ties within communities, and the authoritative use of power in political bodies are systemically organized in enduring groups and networks. This focus on the discursive highlights how these patterned forms of interaction are infused with meaning and given enduring structures of intelligibility, purpose, and legitimacy. This task primarily involves the analysis of language; but it also encompasses how other forms of social action—such as collective gatherings and ways of dress and presentation—also speak of people's identities, social position, and scope for allowable action.

While many analysts have sought to clarify how the material and the discursive conjoin in processes of inequality, too often these analytical emphases have been made without demonstrating how these processes work together. Either discourse produces the meaning by which people understand and enact social inequality, or a material process structures it. Either discourse provides the collective identities that reveal inequality and motivate collective action, or evident disparities in material resources and systemic power catalyze conflict.

The thesis of this book is that we need to refine our understanding of how the discursive and the material conjoin in shaping and transforming processes of inequality—in this case class formation. We must analyze not only how shared material experiences underlie class formation, but also how discourse critically mediates and makes interpretable these patterned and enduring interactions of inequality. I argue that our understandings and depictions of materially structured inequalities and our reactions to them in the form of collective action are given form and substance through the discourses that contour social, political, and economic life.

Discourse matters because through it groups construct shared consciousnesses, making interpretable and sometimes confronting the systems of social organization in which their lives are rooted. This shared consciousness includes senses of agency, concepts of morality and social justice, and visions of a desired future. Group members do not automatically know when and why they should act to bring about their common material concerns. They do not always know how to formulate and express what those interests are. Shared understandings of oppression, redress, or collective purpose do not spring fully formed from a common position or a set of life experiences. Rather, through the production of discourses that articulate mutual experiences, group members construct these shared understandings of their world and the need for changes in it. And it is within these discourses—the fighting words of conflict—that collective actions can be framed with legitimacy and efficacy, both for the group itself and for other members of the society. Just as importantly, discursive analysis illuminates how groups collectively challenge and transform the symbolic structures of social life in order to change their material circumstances.

The succeeding chapters will closely scrutinize the lives and struggles of the silk weavers and cotton spinners, and the communities and industries of which they were a part. We will delve into how these workers and their families actively participated in the making of their own histories—as artisans and factory workers, class actors, community members, politicized citizens, and men and women. Much of the focus will be on the processes of class formation and collective action through which they partly shaped these histories, and the important mediating role discourse played. Such analysis requires us to investigate the gendered aspects of work, community life, and collective struggle. Before entering the bustling and gritty neighborhoods of working-class London, or the smoke-shrouded environs of Ashton and Stalybridge, however, we need to spell out the questions and theories on which our analyses depend.

Problems in the Analysis of Class Formation: Thompson's Legacy

What are the processes by which classes are formed? Under what conditions do working people form solidary ties to act for acknowledged collective interests? Can the experiences of the Spitalfields silk weavers and the Ashton-Stalybridge cotton spinners be understood as examples of such processes? Over the past decade, both social scientists and historians have focused with renewed vigor on the complex dynamics of class formation and its diverse components. The common foundation for many of these explorations, regardless of discipline, has been E. P. Thompson's *The Making of the English Working Class*. Thompson's work has been both a fertile seedbed for elaboration and, more recently, critique and re-evaluation. In the process, *The Making* (and the rest of his corpus) has become much like a dependable household appliance; we use it frequently but rarely if ever read the manual. The problem with this familiarity is that it can create inattention and neglect. Some recent critiques of Thompson's work suffer from such familiarity and needlessly abandon his perspective. To understand both how the critics have misrepresented Thompson's argument and how his thesis on class formation is compatible with discourse analysis, I briefly review his perspective.

Distinguishing his class analysis from older Marxist models, Thompson argued that class should be understood not so much as a formation of economic structures but as "an ever-changing and never-static *process* in our political and cultural life in which human agency is entailed at every level" (1960b, p. 24). Throughout the course of his work, Thompson investigated how working people (many of whom were artisans), facing common exploitation and oppression imposed upon them by the systems of productive and political relations into which they entered, created a shared culture and solidary ties to act collectively (1978, p. 250; 1978 [1965]; Kaye 1984; Meiksins Woods 1982). Rejecting a base-superstructure model, Thompson opted for Marx's metaphor in the *Grundrisse* that the mode of production is the "general illumination in which all other colours are plunged and which modifies specific tonalities" (1977a, p. 264; 1977b, pp. 240, 244). He argued that class analysis was the dissection of how historically specific *productive relations*, illuminated by the mode of production, provided the involuntary coloring of experience. Since "capitalist society was founded on forms of exploitation which are simultaneously economic, moral and cultural," *all* social relations and processes of *power* consequential to maintenance of the capitalist order—including inheritance patterns, the law, and the cake of custom—fell within this sphere (1978 [1965], p. 294; Thompson 1977a, pp. 261–264, 1976, 1975; Woods 1990, p. 116; Kaye 1984; Rose 1986, 1992; Sayer 1987; Spohn 1990).[1] As we will see, diverse relations, such as those between local magistrates and factory workers in Ashton and between a male weaver and his household workshop, were integral to the productive relations of each trade.

From this perspective, common experiences within these productive relations critically mediate between social being and social consciousness (1978, p. 8; 1981, p. 405; 1966, p. 11; 1957, p. 114; Wood 1982, pp. 49, 62; see also Meiksins 1987). Nineteenth-century English working people came to share a set of cultural dispositions—values, languages, traditions, ways of acting collectively—in resistance to systems of economic exploitation and political oppression that so powerfully shaped their lives. Through this shared experience and its cultural manifestations, they forged solidarity for class action. As he observed "class and class consciousness are always the last, not the first, stage in the real historical process" (1978, p. 149).[2] Silk weavers and cotton spinners can be said to have had a class consciousness because of their cultural repertoires, which in part translated local struggles into more encompassing class terms.

For Thompson then, culture is the forge of these common experiences. In *Customs in Common*, he defined culture as "a pool of diverse resources ... an arena of conflictual elements which requires some compelling pressure—as, for example, nationalism or prevalent religious orthodoxy or class consciousness—to take form as a 'system'" (1991, p. 6). Within any given cultural formation, rulers seek to exert hegemony, limiting understandings of the possible, while underlings seek to construct their own oppositional moral vision to create binding ties (1978b, p. 164). Thompson insisted that hegemony was never total and that the common sense of shared experience could rudely interrupt the pontifications of a dominant ideology (1978, p. 164).[3] Workers fought back, often through appro-

---

[1] Sewell argues that, for all his emphasis on culture, Thompson, in fact, replicates a base-superstructure model. Here I follow Ellen Meiksins Wood, who suggests that "Thompson is perhaps at his most materialist when he refuses to privilege the 'economy' over 'culture'" (1990, p. 139). Thompson emphasized the reciprocal causality between the material and the cultural. Reflecting on radical social history, he felt that "we've had an insufficient vocabulary for examining the structure of power relations through symbolism" (1994b, p. 362).

[2] Thompson argued that class consciousness always operates in tension with divisional fissures among working people; it is the pressures exerted by struggle that arise in the continually closer engagement of classes within existing institutions that creates the tendencies for a shared oppositional culture (1960b, p. 26; 1958, p. 57; 1960a, p. 6; 1978, pp. 149–50). Seed recently has made a parallel point on the development of shared consciousness among the bourgeoisie (1993, p. 29).

[3] In *Customs in Common*, Thompson draws on Gramsci to suggest that there is a common sense of lived experience that precedes the linguistic and can be used to question the meanings of life conveyed in a dominant language (1991, p. 11; for the relevant passages in Gramsci, see 1971, pp. 327, 333).

priating the past to construct their oppositional morality. The oppressed poached the rulers' ideology and theater of legitimation as well as their game (1991, p. 10). A significant part of this study demonstrates the ways in which silk weavers and cotton spinners artfully practiced such poaching in the process of building class solidarity.

A constellation of emphases emerge from Thompson's work on the ways we should analyze how working people articulate their common experiences of class and create solidary ties to act on them. First, the process only can be understood *historically* by watching the sparks and fusions of dialectical processes of struggle. "Class, in the Marxist tradition, is (or ought to be) *a historical category*, describing people in *relation over time*" (1977a, p. 264; 1978a, pp. 46, 103; 1978b, p. 150; Merrill 1976, p. 17; Wood 1982; Trimberger 1984). There are no "true" or model formations, no emblematic set of experiences; the process of class is *necessarily contingent and open-ended*. "Minds which thirst for a tidy platonism," he warned, "very soon become impatient with actual history" (1978 [1965], p. 257). In this sense, the struggles of the silk weavers and cotton spinners were distinct manifestations of a more general class process of the early nineteenth century.

Second, as stated above, the process of class is *relational*; a shared consciousness of interests and solidary ties can only arise in opposition to other formations (Thompson 1960b, p. 24; 1978a, p. 103). The cultural product of frictional relations, class consciousness, is temporally specific to those struggles. It can only be recognized in situ, within the times and spaces that are the spawning grounds of experience.

> When we employ a term, like *bourgeoisie* or "working-class" which covers a whole historical epoch, we should not expect the specific forms of class consciousness in any particular segment of this epoch to have any immediate relationship to those of any other segment. In this epochal sense, forms of "working class consciousness" may be found to differ as much from each other as the consciousness of Roundheads differed from Lancashire cotton masters. (1960b, p. 24)

Third, Thompson's focus on experience directs analysis to the dynamics of struggle within *concrete communities* (Koditschek 1990, pp. 3, 22; Calhoun 1982). It is within the lattice work of daily life that working people develop shared cultures and solidary ties. These then can be disseminated beyond the confines of the daily world of experience and struggle, potentially producing widening circles of common understandings. Nonetheless, the process of class is always locally stirred, as it was in the offal-filled alleys of London's East End and the smoky towns of the Lancashire valleys.

Grounded in this understanding of the process of class *The Making* charts the formation of the English working class from the 1790s to the 1830s as diverse groups of artisans and outworkers struggled against growing capitalist degradation and a repressive state. Starting with the trials of radical London artisans and the degraded Nottingham framework knitters, Thompson analyzes how disparate groups of working people constructed a class consciousness by stitching shared experiences into a common cultural quilt. The familiar recounting of Thompson's quilt focuses on the patches of common consciousness and solidarity crafted through participation in radical politics, particularly during the periodic campaigns for parliamentary reform from the 1810s to the Great Reform Bill of 1832. The fight against the degradation of honorable trades, however, and the chiliasm of religion are equally important to his whole cloth of class consciousness. Artisans and outworkers (such as the Spitalfields silk weavers) are the central collective actors in these protracted struggles, though factory workers such as Ashton and Stalybridge's spinners appear in significant roles. Most importantly, in Thompson's mind the process of working-class formation was never tidy or final (Merrill 1976, p. 16; Thompson 1960a, b, c; 1965).

Collective Action: Political Process and Resource Mobilization Theories

Critical examples of the formation of class recounted in *The Making* are contentious gatherings, from the vast public demonstrations for radical reform in the early 1830s to the furtive machine breaking of Nottingham's stealthy Luddites. For Thompson, these are examples of class struggle, and many social scientists focus on such happenings as forms of collective action. Currently influential perspectives in the analysis of collective action—the resource mobilization and political process models— evaluate the potential for contention through theoretical perspectives that see actors as rational and goal-oriented.[4] Such perspectives focus on the way challenging groups organize people and resources and act with deliberation to realize goals. Given this emphasis, these perspectives center on four features of collective action which are the template of analysis—interests, organization, mobilization and opportunity (Tilly 1978).

Rational action approaches focus on how and under what circumstances challenging groups will pursue a goal or claim that they see as being in their interests. As purposive models, these theories illuminate five key aspects of collective action, including (1) the importance of group solidarity and networks in facilitating action, (2) the temporal sequencing of organization and preparation necessary for sustained action and the cycles of action themselves, (3) the importance of explicit shared decision rules by which a group can adjudicate the costs and benefits of action and

---

[4] Both resource mobilization and political process theory offer similar formulations in this regard. For overviews of the former, see Tilly 1978, 1985, and Jenkins 1983; for political process, see McAdam 1982 and Tarrow 1994. For a recent integration, see McAdam, Tarrow, and Tilly 1996 and McAdam, McCarthy, and Zald 1996.

the form of action taken, (4) the necessity of resources for a group to engage in a sustained effort, and (5) windows of opportunity creating favorable conditions for action (Tilly 1978, 1985; Gamson et al. 1982; Jenkins 1983; McAdam et al. 1996; Tarrow 1994). The analyses of the collective actions by the silk weavers and cotton spinners in the pages to come will examine each group's relative success in terms of these dimensions.

Analysts broadly within this framework also have sought to address issues of consciousness and culture central to Thompson's class analysis, including the ways in which groups construct and articulate an understanding of shared interest; their shared senses of collective identity, efficacy and agency; and the ideologies through which all of these are collectively constructed (Gamson 1992; Klandermans 1992; Johnston and Klandermans 1995). Taking the lead, William Gamson, David Snow, and Robert Benford have argued that successful collective action is based partly on the process of *framing*. Frames are cognitive organizing schemes that allow people to analyze the events and forces that influence their lives and to make meaningful their involvement in action (Gamson 1985, p. 615; Zald 1996). A challenging group must cogently frame its grievances and goals to provide the efficacy for group action ideologically (Gamson et al. 1982, Gamson 1985, 1988; Snow, Benford et al. 1986, Snow and Benford 1988; Klandermans 1988; Tarrow 1992). A frame provides a relatively stable moral vision for grievances and action against authority. The moral vision through which a frame is constructed is forged from a group's memories and its members palpable experiences of power and justice (Gamson 1985, p. 616; Gamson et al. 1982, p. 123; Gamson 1992; Snow and Benford 1988, pp. 16–17; Snow and Benford 1992).

Frame analysis thus provides a conceptual scheme for the analysis of collective action ideologies, but it has paid insufficient attention to their dynamic structuring in collective action and to the ways in which their elements form loosely-coupled ensembles internally and in relation to dominant ideologies. I will argue that discourse analysis provides useful tools for such analyses. To move toward this answer, I review revisions, refinements, and refutations on these two basic perspectives, which in their own ways grapple with aspects of both problems simultaneously.

PERMUTATIONS AND COMBINATIONS

Taking on the impulses of agronomists, social scientists frequently see hybridization as a solution to many problems. Many scholars investigating working-class formation and collective action have created cross-pollinated perspectives, hoping to create sturdier theories and models. Analysts of collective action have crossed Thompson's thesis with further specification of the causal levels and contingencies of working-class formation, and the links between national politics and the construction of solidary ties. Sympathetic readers of Thompson have attempted combining rational actor models with more culturalist accounts of interest formulation. Since all concerned focus on the impetuses for solidarity, action, and change, these efforts have yielded important varieties.

In the analysis of working-class collective action, Rick Fantasia (1988) draws on Thompson's experiential model of class formation to tease out the dynamics of interest formulation. He demonstrates how a "culture of solidarity" is a contingent product of crisis and conflict, responsive to particular acts of oppression. Such cultures cut against the grain of assumed wisdom and illuminate the need for solidary ties and direct action (1988, pp. 19–20). He demonstrates both how such an action culture provides shared understandings for the formulation of concrete goals and how these understandings need not be tied to custom. The pages that follow show how the analysis of fighting words sharpens our understanding of how working people produce these cultures.

Accepting Thompson's precepts that class formation is open-ended, relational, and historically grounded, both Marxist and historical sociologists have sought to understand how organizational and resource capacities and structures of opportunity shape formation processes. Both Goran Therborn and Scott McNall contend that the specific regimes of capitalist accumulation and the spatial and organizational patterning of workers within such regimes create variations in the potential for class cohesion (1983, pp. 39–43; McNall 1988 pp. 10–12; cf. also Offe and Wiesenthal [1980] on organizational capacities). In his four-level model of class formation, Ira Katznelson distinguishes between the "structure of economic development" (the broad configuration of the organization of production and its markets) and "ways of life" (the more mundane and "experience-near" realities of capitalist social formations) (1986, pp. 14–16).[5] This distinction analytically separates the structure of the capitalist organization within which a trade or industry was embedded from the work-a-day realities of its effects. Capitalist organization, rationality, and control encroached very unevenly in different trades, and Thompson sometimes glossed these dynamics within his narrative on artisanal degradation (Sabel and Zeitlin 1985; Samuel 1977; Sewell 1988; Stedman Jones 1984). Analyzing the tribulations of the cotton spinners and silk weavers, I demonstrate how such macro- and micro-structural features of an emergent industrial capitalism created distinctive pressures and experiences. I also show how the analysis of fighting words adds analytical rigor to the links between the third and fourth levels of Katznelson's model—collective action and shared dispositions (the shared cognitive constructs that provide an evaluative map of experience). Indeed, it is through discourse that

---

[5] Katznelson carefully notes that these four levels are not rigidly linked by teleological priority. For critiques of his residual teleology, neglect of gender, and the construction of moral orders see Somers (1989), Canning (1992), and Spohn (1990) respectively.

working people can translate their wealth of local experience into the stuff of solidary ties for class action. Class consciousness in this extra-local sense is thoroughly wedded to discourse.

Both Therborn and Katznelson maintain that working-class formation is fundamentally a national political process in which consciousness and interests are constituted through collective action (Therborn 1983, p. 39; Katznelson 1986, pp. 19–20). In this claim, they not only follow Thompson, but also echo the work of historical sociologists who seek to distill patterns of capitalist development and state formation from the muddy waters of the historical record (Aminzade 1993a,b; Hanagan 1989; McNall 1988; Tilly 1978, 1986, 1992; Shorter and Tilly 1975, Tilly, Tilly, and Tilly 1974; Tilly and Tilly 1981). These scholars scrutinize the historical intertwining of two great transformations in Western societies: the growth of industrial capitalism (including the nationalization and globalization of markets and capital, proletarianization, and capital concentration) and the process of state-making (including its increased centralization, resource extraction, and expansion and penetration of power). They argue that particular conjunctures in these two processes created periodic opportunities for workers to construct broad inter-trade and regional alliances by providing institutional mechanisms, changes in the balance of power between classes and the state, and possibilities for historically bounded class alliances. Both the expansion of institutional politics and the development of new nonviolent repertoires of mass-based contention created opportunities for disparate groups of working people to define shared national interests for mobilization (Aminzade 1993b; Tarrow 1994; Tilly 1982, 1995).[6]

Such work provides a vantage on class formation from the perspective of organizational capacities and potentials independent of particular forms of consciousness (Cronin 1993, p. 72). Mobilization and collective action are important markers of class formation, since they demonstrate the creation and activation of solidary ties, although we should be careful not to rely exclusively on such behavioral indicators. Although this study focuses on community conflict, it draws on such approaches by connecting the roots of local struggles to their national dynamics. As we shall see, the growth of bourgeois political power within each community, the transformations of local labor markets within the context of increasing globalization of commodity markets, and the development of a national radical politics so central to Thompson's story, were foundations for local struggles. Class identities were a joint product of both struggles at the point of production and of autonomous politics from the immediate

---

[6] Others such as Geoff Eley (1990, 1992) and Christopher Johnson (1993) have argued that a Habermasian analysis of the public sphere provides the best means of understanding the intersection of national politics and class formation. For a class struggle analysis of state-making as a cultural revolution, see Corrigan and Sayer (1985).

world of labor. As I will detail, for the working people of early nineteenth-century England, this particular mating was often to bear strange and bitter fruit.

REFINEMENTS AND REFUTATIONS: COMMUNITY, GENDER, AND LANGUAGE

Although some theorists engaged in cross-fertilization, others came bearing pruning shears and scythes. A number of critics in the areas of working-class formation and collective action have argued that much of the work in these areas has failed to address important issues of consciousness and identity along with the bases of social solidarity. In the specific case of English working-class formation, questions concerning divergent experiences and fissures in cohesion have become the springboard for critiques of *The Making*. This is the focus of *The Question of Class Struggle* and a series of related essays by Craig Calhoun. He argues that artisans and factory workers produced two clearly disjointed oppositional cultures in response to their distinctive experiences with the growth of modern capitalism (1982, 1980, 1983, 1987). For artisans, the incursion of capitalism challenged their once-stable communities and the tradition that morally vivified their dense social ties. Responding to this threat to their very social existence, they produced a "reactionary radicalism," an anticapitalist and defensive radical politics articulated through community tradition. Factory workers, however, lacking these community ties and a sense of tradition, adopted a reformist consciousness, through which they accommodated themselves (albeit uneasily) to the emerging industrial society. Calhoun provides a picture of two working-class worlds, partitioned by differing (and sometimes divisive) collective experiences, cultures, and discourses of opposition.

Calhoun's emphasis on the multiplex solidary ties of community presents a valuable formalization of an analysis implicit in Thompson's work and echoes resource mobilization theory's focus on networks. His stark contrasts between the worlds of artisans and factory, however, provide an oversimplified picture of overlapping and complex working-class formations.[7] As I document in the cases of the silk weavers and cotton spinners, community networks were the transmitters of class solidarities, but not of the reactionary and reformist forms of consciousness that Calhoun depicts.

More generally, issues of identity construction and the bases of unity draw attention to gendering processes and the discursive roots of identity in working-class formation and collective action. A wealth of literature has demonstrated how Thompson and others systematically neglected not

---

[7] I have debated this matter with Calhoun at some length (Steinberg 1993; Calhoun 1993).

only the role of women in productive relations but also the social construction of class itself through the lens of gender. As Sonya Rose, Anna Clark, Catherine Hall, Sally Alexander, and many others have noted, gender—the process of socially creating differences of femininity and masculinity—saturates Thompson's category of lived experience.[8] Workshop and factory practices, concepts of worker rights and respectability, capacities for participation and mobilization were all illuminated through the coloring of gender difference.

In re-examining "the making," Anna Clark (1995) observes that gender practices and ideologies intersected with systems of productive relations to produce several types of working-class patriarchal orders in the early nineteenth century. Among domestic outworkers such as silk weavers, males exercised patriarchal control over women's and children's work and wages and in trade organizations. However, they pragmatically acknowledged women's essential contributions to household income and trade actions. Consequently, male weavers did not discursively highlight sexual difference in public debates on their trade. Male factory workers such as cotton spinners, however, seeking exclusive control over entrance to their employment, were more openly misogynistic. Through successive battles, they developed a strategy of limited patriarchal cooperation with women workers, recognizing their common community and class ties while successfully maintaining exclusionary barriers. In subsequent decades, the results of these actions in part led to the crystallization of the ideology of separate spheres and of the male breadwinner (Clark 1995, chap. 10, 1992; Rose 1992, 1993; Hall 1992). In the case studies below, I follow Clark in noting distinctive patterns of gender differences between the spinners and weavers in the social organization and cultural construction of paid labor and community life. Additionally, I explore how in both cases the construction of gender differences in discourses of contention may have been muted because of the essential role of women in community mobilization and class struggle.

In parallel fashion, recent critiques of the resource mobilization perspective on collective action explicate how gender mediates the dynamics of solidarity and decision making (Ferree 1992; Taylor and Whittier 1992, 1995). Myra Marx Ferree argues that a "pseudo-universal" concept of a self-interested individual who pursues concrete and finite goals is a "nar-

---

[8] In addition to these studies of gender and class, see the related discussions in Baron (1991), Davidoff (1986, and Davidoff and Hall 1987), Lown (1990), McClelland (1989), Poovey (1988), Seecombe (1986), B. Taylor (1983), Valenze (1995), and Walby (1990). Thompson acknowledged this neglect in small ways, such as noting that materialist definitions of needs tend "to enforce a hierarchy of causation which affords insufficient priority to other needs: the needs of identity, the needs of gender identity, the need for respect and status among working people themselves" (1994b, p. 362). Writing to Bryan Palmer concerning Joan Scott's critique of *The Making*, he observed, "She has a point about gendered class. I didn't do it . . . it *was* so gendered" (Palmer 1994, p. 16, n. 7).

row definition of what is rational exclud[ing] the principles, goals and means of expression that have been historically favored by subordinated groups" (1992, p. 47). Others have offered parallel critiques of the assumed wisdom of social movement organization dynamics and their cultural bases (Buechler 1993; Martin 1990; Taylor and Whittier 1992, 1995; Whittier 1995) and have focused on the particular dynamics of constructing feminist movement cultures. These critiques show that we need purposive models of collective action more grounded in the gendered cultural understandings of participants. I argue that a careful analysis of a challenging group's fighting words helps provide such a vantage.

The analysis of gendering has also brought the linguistic turn to prominence in debates on historical class formation. Broadly influenced by poststructuralist theories of meaning, many of those in the linguistic turn find the construction of hierarchies and conflict, indeed social life in general, not within the experiential realm of material practices, but in language (see Eley 1996 for an overview). As Joan Scott asserts, "Without meaning there is no experience; without processes of signification, there is no meaning" (1988, p. 38; cf. also 1991, p. 793).

Most historians within the linguistic turn have argued to varying degrees that Thompson's account of class formation is chimerical and based on preconceived categories of class not reflected in the languages of working people. In his foundational analysis for this revisionism, Gareth Stedman Jones (1982, 1983) argues that the political language of English radicals in the early nineteenth century crucially intervened between the experience of domination and exploitation, on the one hand, and working-class consciousness and action on the other. Politics became the foundation upon which shared consciousness was structured and in whose cause struggle was conducted.[9]

Operating on the shared ground of linguistic and institutional analysis, Margaret Somers (1992, 1993, 1994) argues that working people created long-standing narratives of justice in the early modern period by which they constructed identities as aggrieved rights holders. Such narratives were the vehicles for both local and collective action within the polity to press institutionally-based claims for common rights. Somers's concept of narrative identity provides an important window on how language was a conduit for solidarity.

Others, such as Patrick Joyce and James Vernon, press linguistic analysis still further by maintaining that workers constructed solidary ties and common identities through inclusive political languages. They relegate class structure, organization, and conflict to at most a peripheral role.

---

[9] Stedman Jones's revisionist interpretation has spawned considerable debate. For significant critiques and commentaries, see Epstein 1986; Foster 1985; Gray 1986; Kirk 1987; Mayfield and Thorne 1992; Meiksins Wood 1986; Palmer 1990; Scott 1987; and Steinberg 1996b.

Joyce in several recent studies broadly asserts that "meaning makes subjects and not subjects meaning" (1994, p. 13). In *Voices of the People* (1991), he maintains that the discourses through which workers constructed their consciousness were part of a family of many sorts of populism (including radical and liberal varieties), which were "extra-economic in character" (1991, pp. 8, 16–17). Through a series of linked studies in *Democratic Subjects*, he asserts that melodramatic political narratives created a democratic imaginary by which both rulers and ruled understood their political subjectivity and power. For Vernon, the melodramatic master narrative of popular constitutionalism was the vital constituent of common consciousness, with institutional politics providing the most stable foundation for shared identity (1993, pp. 328, 334–335; 1994, p. 90). Both view class as only one of many identities discursively constructed and transcended in a more socially encompassing and deep-seated popular politics. Additionally, Joyce argues that a collective consciousness of class emerged from political rather than economic processes: "Class identities were, therefore, a product of arguments about meanings, arguments which were primarily political in character. Class does not seem to have been the collective cultural experience of new economic classes produced by the Industrial Revolution" (1994, p. 161). Thus working people's collective identities far outstripped any process of class, and languages of people and nation were the narrative vehicles for mobilization and action.[10]

In parallel fashion, the rise of new social movements has focused attention on the discursive and cultural dynamics of collective action. Diverse but overlapping perspectives emphasize the construction of new collective identities as a focal point of collective action (Cohen 1985; Johnston, Laraña, and Gusfield 1994; Melucci 1989, 1996; Offe 1987; Whittier 1995). Movement activity is often defined as centering on the opening of social space and the production of alternative culture outside of the traditional polity, with mobilization often directed against state intrusion rather than toward institutional power. Some post-materialist theorists, such as Laclau and Mouffe (1982, 1985, 1987, Mouffe 1988, 1990), argue that new social movements are a form of radical pluralism fighting an elusive and never-final struggle over the symbolic resources of democratic politics.

The linguistic turn thus poses heady questions for students of class formation, challenging not only Thompson's thesis but the very bases of historical materialism. It also raises serious issues in the analysis of identity, ideology, and discourse, issues that are insufficiently addressed by resource mobilization and political process theories. This book accepts

[10] Both Joyce and Vernon begrudgingly admit that production-centered discourses existed, but claim their class inflections were lesser and unstable meanings within broader discourses of popular politics (Joyce 1991, pp. 57–58, 90–92, 94, 99, 100, 108–109, 336; Vernon 1993, pp. 297, 309–311, 330; 1994, p. 89).

these challenges and additional emphases but looks elsewhere for solutions. In the analyses to follow, I recount how the stories working people told about themselves—and particularly the fighting words they used in the process of collective action—critically mediated the allied processes of class formation and collective action. To provide such an alternative path let me first define discourse and then explain its role in the processes that are our focus.

The Role of Fighting Words in Class Formation and Collective Action

As we will see in the following studies, each group of working people constructed vivid collective characterizations of themselves and their opponents through their fighting words, the discourses of contention.[11] Discourse is the symbolic practice by which people create and reproduce their cultural codes for making sense of the world. Foremost, the stuff of discourse is language, and generally discourse is the social process of putting language in motion (Terdiman 1986, p. 55; Purvis and Hunt 1993, p. 485). "Language and power," notes Robert Stam, "intersect wherever the question of language becomes involved in asymmetrical power arrangements" (1988, p. 123). Class formation is the process of creating such asymmetries; contentious action is born from them; and discourse is thoroughly imbricated in both. From this perspective, discourse is both a mediator and a source of power. Discourse mediates power by facilitating the social action of control and exploitation. It is a form of power, for through it consciousness is shaped and the possibilities for action and change are culturally constituted. Fighting words are thus both a conduit and source of power.[12]

Discourse quintessentially involves dialogue situated in particular social contexts (Volosinov 1983, pp. 115–118; Pred 1989, pp. 212–213; Todorov 1984, pp. 60–61). The outcome of this process is the result of the meanings and usages of language that actors can bring to the situation and the power they can exercise vis-à-vis other actors to establish these as the standards for communication. As dialogic theory highlights, groups can develop competing meanings and inflections in discourse because of their distinctive experiences (Hirschkop 1986, p. 98, 1989, p. 16). The Bakhtin Circle emphasized that the production of meaning is necessarily *relational*, much as Thompson underscored this for the process of class. "The word

---

[11] This account draws heavily from my reading of Bakhtinian theory. For works by and on the Bakhtinian school, see Bakhtin 1981, 1986; Volosinov 1983, 1986; Bernard-Donals 1994; Gardiner 1992; Hirschkop 1986, 1989; Holquist 1990; and Todorov 1984.

[12] While claiming that discourse can be a form of power, following Stuart Hall I oppose tendencies in post-structuralist theory that claim power is foremost discursive. Such arguments are reductionist (Grossberg 1986, p. 57). Power and indeed all social practices cannot be reduced to discourse because they have conditions of existence not reducible to it (Purvis and Hunt 1993, p. 490).

in language," proclaimed Bakhtin, "is half someone else's" (1981, p. 293; 1986, pp. 65–71, 122–127; Bernard-Donals 1994, pp. 9–11; Gardiner 1992, pp. 86–87). Discourses are thus multivocal; i.e., the signs that convey meanings frequently are open to multiple meanings and interpretations and become contested terrains (Holquist 1990, p. 24; Evans 1990, p. 515; Hitchcock 1994, pp. 5–6). In this inherent instability lies the origins of fighting words.

An important facet of contention between groups—be it class struggle or some other form of collective action—is thus the attempt by each to have the elements of discourse speak with its voice. "Every discourse has its own selfish and biased proprietor; there are no words with meanings shared by all, no words 'belonging to no one'" (Bakhtin 1981, p. 401). Multivocality creates a condition for ongoing conflict, becoming both part of the ideological dimension of class formation and collective action. Even though much discourse is the familiar turf of routine patterns, as Marianne Valverde notes, "discourses themselves—even when containing some instructions on proper use—always have some ambiguity and instability at the level of form and content which can be utilized by those who interpret the status and meaning of discourses against the grain" (1991, p. 176). This quality of instability and ambiguity both establishes and necessitates human agency in the construction of meanings.

For any given context, there are always webs of discourses—discursive *formations* or *genres*—that contain the typical sets of vocabularies, meanings, and their rules for dialogue and create a particular naturalized view of social life (Bakhtin 1986, pp. 20, 65, 79; Gardiner 1992, pp. 74, 81; Hirschkop 1989, p. 21). Through genres, power holders seek to objectivize and generalize their partial and interested vision of the world into a more popular common sense, and in doing so they hold the instability of discourse at bay (Bakhtin 1986, pp. 65, 79; 1984, p. 202; Briggs and Bauman 1992, p. 148; Gardiner 1992, pp. 74, 81; Sampson 1993, pp. 117–122; Todorov 1984, pp. 80–85; Volosinov 1983, p. 116). Within any period and patterned social context, some genres are dominant, defined by the "social impossibility of their absence" and provide the most importantly recognized public ways of interpreting the world (Terdiman 1986, p. 61).

Discourse is critical to processes of class formation and collective action because it provides the ideological dimension of domination and resistance. As Volosinov remarked, "The word is the ideological phenomenon par excellence"; and he elaborated elsewhere, "Every word, spoken or thought, is not simply a point but an evaluating point of view" (1986, p. 13, 1983, p. 147; see also Bakhtin 1981, pp. 271–272; Bernard-Donals 1994, p. 92; Hirschkop 1989, pp. 18–22; Pred 1989, p. 220).[13] The evaluative

---

[13] Following Stuart Hall, I define ideologies as "frameworks of thinking and calculation about the world . . . which people use to figure out how the social world works, what their

talk and back talk of conflict, the fighting words of class struggle and contention, provide the moral and normative bases for collective evaluation of shared experiences. Through discourse, both power holders and challengers construct notions of justice, fairness, and possibility. These discourses elaborate a group's place within a social order, its relations to other groups, and thus its identity, thereby defining the limits of legitimate agency.

In both class formation and collective action, discourse is enacted as ideological practices of hegemony and counter-hegemony.[14] Successful hegemony involves power holders' capacity to limit dialogue and its clash of meanings in their interactions with subordinates, while naturalizing and universalizing their power-laden meanings and valuations of the world (Volosinov 1983, p. 147; Brandist 1966a; Ewick and Silbey 1995). Limiting what can be said, and how the said can be understood, creates critical boundaries in the way subordinates see their place in a system of power and how they act within it. Working people are unlikely to create cultures of solidarity, and potential challengers will languish in their possibilities, unless each collectively produce fighting words that deny the reasonableness of their conditions.

Fighting words alone cannot conjure class struggle or collective action through captivating prose or orations of belligerence. These words make evaluative sense of a group's world and help in the collective imagining of alternatives and the justification of a path to shared goals. It is because discourse is anchored to shared material realities *outside* of its own collage of meanings that some people can have advantage within it. As Alan Pred suggests, "It is largely through language that locally situated practices and projects are instituted. Yet, it is largely through locally present institutions that language is practised and given meaning" (1989, p. 212). The capacity of dominant groups to exercise power through discourse is clearly based on their ability to translate their accrued power from other spheres of social and material life into control over the production of meaning. "The bond between domination and appropriation," James Scott suggests, "means that it is impossible to separate the ideas and symbolism of subordination from a process of material exploitation" (1990, p. 188). Doing so, however, in turn provides dominant groups with leverage over the ways

---

place is in it and what they ought to do about it" (1985, p. 99). As Purvis and Hunt remark, we cannot collapse ideology and discourse. Rather, "ideological discourses contain forms of signification that are incorporated into lived experience where the basic mechanism of incorporation is one whereby sectional or specific interests are represented as universal interests" (1993, p. 497).

[14] Hegemony is the complex social process by which dominant groups seek to elicit consent from subordinates by determining the legitimate boundaries of social thought and action (Scott 1985, p. 326; Volosinov 1983, pp. 140, 145; see also Brandist 1996a, b; Femia 1981; Gramsci 1971; Hunt 1990). Hegemony involves the organization of social life beyond discourse, but cannot be accomplished except through discourse (Purvis and Hunt 1993).

subordinates conceive of themselves and their opponents, formulate their interests, and frame their conflict and their prescriptions for change. This is where the conduit of power gels into a force in its own right.

From a dialogic perspective, both class struggle and collective action involve discursive contests within specific dominant formations and genres, and are channeled by the ongoing communication. Working people and other subordinated groups seek to subvert the power holders' authoritative voice, first by questioning the accepted interpretations of dominant meanings. When challengers expose these as defined in the interests of power, they can attempt to appropriate and transform the genres into fighting words, which broadcast their shared sense of injustice and resolution (Hunt 1990, p. 314; Mouffe 1979, p. 192; Valverde 1991, pp. 178–180; Volosinov 1983; Pred 1992, pp. 111–113; Ewick and Silbey 1995; Scott 1990).[15] Such acts of resistance are piecemeal, complex, and often prolonged, for as Bakhtin noted, "many words stubbornly resist, others remain alien. . . . Expropriating it, forcing it to submit to one's own intentions and accents, is a difficult and complicated process" (1981, p. 294). Challengers generally do not attempt whole-sale changes in a discursive formation, but pragmatically engage in appropriation as they find its elements become more transparently vulnerable to questioning and transformation within specific contexts. Through this process, challengers construct the fighting words essential to class struggle and other forms of collective action (Bakhtin 1986, p. 143; 1984, pp. 106, 184, 188; Hitchcock 1994, p. 18; Pred 1989, p. 222; Valverde 1991, pp. 182–183).

In the case studies, I will demonstrate how this dialogic perspective is compatible with and adds to materialist perspectives on class formation. A major focus of this book is to illuminate how working people shared common experiences of exploitation and oppression through their fighting words; how the chatter of community and work and the clamor of collective action were integral to the process of class. Peering back at the struggles of the silk weavers and cotton spinners, we will find historical remnants of class formation and the effervescence of class consciousness in their discourse as they appropriated bourgeois language to make it a weapon of the weak.

In analyzing working-class consciousness, we need to concentrate on how working people appropriated pieces of dominant genres to construct a collective consciousness. A critical part of that struggle, as we will investigate, was the tussle over what was said and how it was articulated *within* the bourgeois discourse of political economy. That these silk weavers and

---

[15] For Bakhtin (1984), the inflection of irony or parody was central to dialogic struggle. More generally, if we accept the argument of Lackoff and Johnson (1980) that all language is essentially metaphorical, then a central part of hegemonic struggle involves the control over the way the meanings of words and utterances are related to one another in communication (see Gastil 1992).

cotton spinners could successfully expose political economy and allied discourses as class-interested reflected both its newness as a dominant genre and the conjoining with nondiscursive factors that tipped working people and capitalists over the precipice into chasm of open and sometimes bloody conflict. Most importantly, this was a shared process participated in by diverse groups of working people throughout the nation, which is precisely why, in Thompson's terms, it was part of a making. Similar experiences of degradation and oppression, and a common battle against hegemony jointly resulted in class consciousness. In this sense, the local happenings of class aggregated as national experiences, partly through the conduit of discourse, and then circulated back down to the local as oppositional genres.

Thompson's work, in fact, is infused with the scrutiny of discourse, which he considered to be the bearer of shared moral visions.[16] As he observed in *Whigs and Hunters* moral languages simultaneously "may modify, in profound ways, the behaviour of the powerful and mystify the powerless. They may disguise the true realities of power, but, at the same time, they may curb and check its intrusions. And it is often from within this very rhetoric that a radical critique of the practice of society is developed" (1975, p. 265).

It was often in moral language that he found the systemization of oppositional culture (1960b, p. 12; 1966, pp. 49–50; 1981b, p. 41). He predicated his analysis of the English radical tradition on this perspective: "From the Chartist camp meeting to the dockers' picket line, it has expressed itself most naturally in the language of moral revolt" (1960a, p. 9). In *The Making* and his many other historical writings, Thompson sketched the development of these moral languages from their germinal forms in plebeian moral economy to Chartism. A vital strand was the language of the free-born Englishman, appropriated from the constitutional rhetoric of the ruled and turned as a weapon against them (1975 p. 265; 1978b, p. 158). Moving beyond the language of political radicalism, he suggested that the moral battle of these years was against industrialization and more particularly "that one way of reading the working-class movement during the Industrial Revolution is as a movement of resistance to the annunciation of economic man" (1978 [1965], p. 294; see also 1960b, p. 25).[17] In part, the working classes reacted against the development of a political

---

[16] David Mayfield and Susan Thorne (1992, 1993) perceptively discuss Thompson's concern with language and culture, as a central point of material life, and the misplaced critiques of some in the linguistic turn. I concur with them that Thompson's reading of productive relations provides ample room for the role of language in the process of class, but find some problems with their equation of Thompson with deconstructionism (Steinberg 1996).

[17] In his defense of the notion of moral economy, Thompson noted, "There was a plebeian discourse here, almost beneath the level of articulation, appealing to the solidarities so deeply assumed that they were almost nameless" (1991, p. 350).

and moral language underwritten by the linguistic capital of Smithian political economy (1978 [1965], pp. 272–273; 1991, p. 269).[18] The silk weavers and cotton spinners were fierce combatants in these discursive struggles, and their stories illuminate the role of fighting words in the process of class formation.

In some senses then, those in the linguistic turn have been looking for class language and consciousness in its most unlikely forms—a working-class discourse *distinct from* the processes of hegemony and struggle that sat at the dynamic heart of nineteenth-century class formation. Class is often revealed in discourse, not by a separate vocabulary or formation of meanings, but by the ways in which working people actively contest the naturalness of the meanings provided by a dominant formation, seek to appropriate some of its terms, and recast these in oppositional ways. Class realized in discourse is thus generally the agency working people exhibit in creating their fighting words within the discourses of their oppressors (McNally 1995, pp. 21, 28–29). In part, historians such as Joyce and Vernon do not find class discourse because they are not attentive enough to these processes, particularly because these heated stirrings occur in the discourse of political economy; in part, I will maintain, that what they term "political" is a label sometimes misapplied, for it can mask the ways in which working people creatively use the multivocality of language and reify the flux of its meanings. As we will see, especially in the case of the cotton spinners, words that we might expect to have "political" connotations can be used as potent weapons against exploitive relations in production.

A dialogic perspective also complements the analyses of historians such as Rose and Clark who have demonstrated the changing patterns in which gender and class identities conjoined over the course of nineteenth-century class formation. It provides theoretical insight into the ways in which working men could deploy bourgeois language against their employers while reinforcing gender hierarchies of household and shop floor.

On the sociological side, contentious action brings ideological battles within discourse center-stage in the process of claims and counter-claims. Dialogic analysis permits us to modify the notion of frame, thinking instead of a repertoire of fighting words drawn upon by actors. The concept

---

[18] As Thompson observed in a relatively early essay, the uses of the language of political economy changed with the process of class: "We should reflect that ideas are handled roughly by parties, institutions, and social processes. The ideology of Victorian laissez-faire mill owners was not the same thing as the thought of Adam Smith or Bentham; the middle class seized on certain ideas only—and these often imperfectly understood—and adopted them to their own interests" (1957, p. 112). Ultimately it was the language of political economy, a flexible yet powerful moral language, which allowed for the construction of a hegemonic politics after the collapse of Chartism (Thompson 1978 [1965], p. 280; 1960b, p. 25; 1968, p. 937.) For a similar argument on the formation of the English working class and language, see Epstein 1990, 1994.

is parallel to Tilly's repertoires of contentious action, "a limited set of routines that are learned, shared, and acted out through a relatively deliberate process of choice. Repertoires are learned cultural creations, but they do not descend from abstract philosophy or take shape as a result of political propaganda; they emerge from struggle" (1995a, p. 26).[19] This concept refines the analysis of framing by highlighting the variation in the way discourses in a given formation are drawn upon to construct mobilizing and injustice frames. It also emphasizes the continual relational struggle over meaning in the framing process and portrays these structures of meaning as more loosely coupled and dynamic ensembles. A dialogic perspective also allows us to move analytically between micro and macro levels—to focus more clearly on how localized streams of communication become drawn into extra-local formations and how these in turn can be transformed in use.

The analysis of fighting words demonstrates the ways in which discursive repertoires are not only limited themselves but also limit possibilities for contention. These repertoires bound the set of meanings through which challengers can articulate claims, create enduring solidary ties, and ideologically mediate the decision to act. By mediating between consciousness and action, fighting words shape conceptions of just claims and their legitimate pursuit, the structure and scope of solidary networks, and the targets for their redress (Steinberg 1998). Discursive and instrumental action repertoires clearly interact and can be mutually reinforcing and therefore stabilizing. To the extent that the two repertoires are not mutually reinforcing during contention, groups may be pressed to re-examine the cogency and validity of their frames and actions.

Part of the inadequacy with new social movement theory rests in its peculiarly temporalized vision of the role of discourse. Much of this work creates a false dichotomy between the importance of collective identity in historical and contemporary contentious action (Calhoun 1995). The construction of a sense historicity and collective identity was as important to the silk weavers and cotton spinners in the early nineteenth century as it is to peace and ecology movements in the late twentieth century. A dialogic perspective suggests that *all* challenging groups are deeply engaged in the process of creating a collective identity, which legitimates their grievances and claims and provides license for action. It also argues that to understand how challenging groups fashion collective identities we must

---

[19] Repertoires are reasonably durable because (a) they result from processes of group interaction and thus depend on the actions of more than one group, (b) are constrained by the contexts of contention, and (c) as shared routines must be reasonably stable to be used collectively (Tilly 1995a, p. 26). For an extended discussion of repertoires of discourse, see Steinberg 1995a. For a critique of framing analysis and a dialogic alternative, see Steinberg 1998.

focus on how they dialogically develop discursive repertoires from the friction of conflict.

Where We Go from Here

Most of this volume is an extended of analysis class formation and collective action as it is revealed in the cases of the Spitalfields silk weavers and Ashton and Stalybridge cotton spinners. I put forward a case to conjoin Thompson's and other materialist theories of class formation with the dialogic analysis of discourse for a more encompassing understanding of the class process. Similarly, in the analyses of contentious collective action to follow, I demonstrate how discourse critically mediates both the organizational and decision-making processes of collective action. In extensive analyses of the silk weavers' and cotton spinners' conflicts, I explore how the discursive repertoires were fashioned from a dialogic process, and how they in turn bounded the ways in which working people articulated moral claims and conceived of redress.

Before submerging ourselves in the lives and struggles of these working people, however, a bit of context is necessary. Chapter 1 surveys the transformation in patterns of labor contention during the period from 1800 to 1830. My object is to illustrate how patterns of class struggle and collective action changed over these decades and how the theories of class formation and resource mobilization we have reviewed clarify these changes. After this overview, I introduce our two areas of interest, the Spitalfields and Ashton districts. Thompson insisted that class never happened in just the same way in different places because it occurred in particular communities, and these two regions are in some respects studies in contrast. Spitalfields lay in the working-class heart of a great metropolitan center, while Ashton and Stalybridge were small mill towns, the young offspring of the Industrial Revolution. It is partly for this reason that after this introduction I devote separate chapters in each study (4, 9, 10) to local class structure and to social and political life. Leisure activities, daily rounds of household life, the workings of the civil parish, religious practices, and local justice were all part of the dense tissue of class practices that Thompson's perspective on class formation so aptly highlights. We must analyze class formation in these particular practices and local structures as a relational, local, and historical process. We will see some broad commonalties in how institutions such as the legal system facilitated domination, but also some distinctions in these processes, as in the role of the local parish vestry in facilitating class alliances. But as I have noted class formation and the impetus for collective action were both embedded within national and processes. In the analyses of each trade (Chapters 3 and 7), I not only delineate the social relations of production—including its gendered aspects—and the histories of labor conflict, but the larger contexts for these trades as well. In analyzing the immediate social and technical relations of production, I focus on the ways class and gender were produced through daily practices in the workplace. There are significant contrasts for our two cases, since silk weaving was done in domestic workshops, while cotton spinning occurred in the confines of the factory. The Spitalfields silk industry was not only situated in a national market, but was also involved in a highly charged national political battle regarding the industrial protection by the state and international competition with the French. The cotton spinning industry was caught up in one of the most far-flung and integrated commodities markets the world had ever known. In the immediate context we will be analyzing, however, political debates had much fainter echoes in the daily machinations of its class relations.

I devote a separate chapter in each study (5 and 11) to the discursive formations within which class conflicts transpired. In each case, these conflicts and the discursive repertoires that emerge from them center around the discourses of political economy. The aim of each chapter is to provide a sense of the principal elements within the discursive formations and the ways in which working people were able to structure their resistance. As we will see, the particular contexts of struggle influenced the content of these discursive repertoires. We will also observe, however, that both groups developed broadly similar forms of appropriation and resistance to the genre of political economy. Finally, in Chapters 6 and 12 I provide extended analyses of each trade group's collective actions in the late 1820s. My goal is to examine how discursive and instrumental repertoires dynamically intertwined to shape the courses of contention. We will also investigate how the discourses of contention are both reflective and constitutive of processes of class struggle. In the conclusion, I revisit the issues that have provided our opening to assess what the stories of the silk weavers and cotton spinners have told us about class formation and collective action.

CHAPTER ONE

Patterns of English Labor Contention in the Early Nineteenth Century

*C*lass formation occurs in great measure because of struggle. This is part of the studied wisdom, found in both Marx and *The Making of the English Working Class*. In early nineteenth-century England, there were struggles aplenty, involving both the deeds and words of diverse groups of working people across the country. In this chapter I review the changing repertoires of labor struggle between 1800 and 1830, and chart the factors that prompted their transformation. The case studies focus on both the discursive and instrumental repertoires of the silk weavers and cotton spinners.

Changing patterns of labor contention show the happening of class conflict. Recent critics of class formation argue that political conflicts provided working people with their most central and definitive collective identities during this period. A review of the history, however, demonstrates the critical part labor conflict also played. The structural antinomies of productive relations brought capitalists and workers to loggerheads, cutting across specific trades and communities to create common patterns of antagonism and a shared consciousness. These fissures intersected with those of gender, combining to form notions of the skilled artisan and complicating (though not necessarily undermining) class cohesion within a trade or community.[1]

---

[1] These fissures also intersected with concepts of national identity and ethnicity, although these were less directly addressed by the workers who appear in this study. In terms of the for-

Gradually, but significantly, battles between capital and labor metamorphosed from frequently workplace-centered, informal, parochial, and sometimes violent affairs to more public, disciplined, and extra-local actions. The pace of this change varied by industry and region, but the change reflected a more general restructuring of capitalist control of the production process and workplace. Historians and sociologists who have questioned the validity of class analysis sometimes have returned to the history of a particular trade or community and discovered trade or community conflict, but no class struggle (Glenn 1984; Joyce 1991, 1992, 1995). The results, in a sense, are not surprising. To understand the struggles of the silk weavers and the cotton spinners as *class* conflict, broadly indicative of other struggles over degradation and exploitation, we must grasp the larger context of structural tensions and transformation within which their battles occurred.

In the early nineteenth century, the organized workers, in general terms, were male artisans, generally workshop-based, with some claim to skill. Artisans were typically journeymen who were destined to ply their trade for the profit of others (Rule 1986, pp. 387–388). At the turn of the century, capitalist reorganization had ensured that strikingly few skilled handworkers were truly independent petty producers. In London, the home of the silk weavers, only 5 to 6 percent of all artisans could be classified as self-employed (Rule 1985, p. 24).

As John Rule suggests, the rubric *artisan* "generally described those who through apprenticeship or its equivalent had come to possess a skill in a particular craft and the right to exercise it. This restriction on entry was crucial." In addition, the term generally meant the exclusion of women (1988, p. 102; see also Clark 1995). The meaning of skill was "as much rooted in social and gender distinctions as in technical aptitude" (Rule 1988, p. 108; see also Berg 1988, 1993). Battles over the "proprietary" control of pace and organization of work and regulation of entry into a trade often demarcated the skilled workers. This process gendered the happening of class (Morris 1980, p. 14; Sykes 1982, v. 1, p. 46; Rose 1992; Rule 1988).

Proprietary claims to skill were animated by a self-conscious artisanal collectivism, which defined the social moorings for a trade community and promoted male camaraderie. These claims distinguished the skilled

---

mer, working people such as the silk weavers fashioned a collective identity against the foreign labor with whom they were in competition. For further discussion of this, see Steinberg 1995b. Workers also sought to make claims for wages, protections, and freedoms in explicit contrast to other whites who were making freedom claims on behalf of African slaves, as was the case with the cotton spinners (see Hall 1992 for the development of racial identity). In this book, however, I concentrate on their class claims since they represented the most central component of their discourses, though I recognize that silence differentiates as well.

worker, with at least a modicum of independence, from the "hand," who was tethered to the commands of a master (Thompson 1966, pp. 424, 548). As we will see, the silk weavers' and cotton spinners' struggles against degradation and exploitation exemplified the ways in which collective notions of skill, craft, and respectability were defended by workers during these transformative years.

The increasing fissure between collective skill and capital pushed artisans to defend standing norms of pace, standards of craft, "just" rewards for labor, and inclusionary criteria of trade membership (Thompson 1966, p. 236; Prothero 1979, p. 38; Behagg 1990; Randall 1991). Such standards, however, were not solely "custom" or "tradition," if by that is meant vestigial encrustations of past practices. "Custom," at times, was an epithet of convenience, invoked to defend practices under pressure from capitalist reorganization (Behagg 1979, pp. 466, 470; Hobsbawm 1984, p. 361). In doing so, artisans were preservationists, but not therefore simply conservative. The standards themselves were the outcomes of previous struggles, many of which had occurred in the waning decades of the eighteenth century (Berg et al. 1983, pp. 10–13; Dobson 1980, chap. 4; George 1925, 1962). Their defense was part of an emerging class dynamic in which capitalists and workers sought to secure their positions in the trench warfare of trade control. The silk weavers and cotton spinners also faced these intrusive challenges in the 1820s and 1830s.

Artisans constructed their foundational defense of their collective "property" in the workshop or work group (Prothero 1979, p. 167). The ways in which the workshop was closed off from the outside world made it an alien environment, and employers intruded into it only in the most important circumstances (Behagg 1982, 1990). Moreover, given the legal prohibitions on the organization of workers until the repeal of the Combination Laws in 1824, the organizational culture of workers operated in a "twilight world of semi-legality" (Thompson 1966, p. 508). As we shall see, both the weavers and the spinners articulated notions of collective property, but in the changing context of their discursive battles with political economy.

Bonds of the workshop ensured solidarity against interlopers—be they masters, Irish, or women—and were maintained through status hierarchies and ceremonial practices (Palmer 1976, pp. 8–11; Rule 1985).[2] Linkages between shops often were accomplished through loosely knit trade societies or benefit clubs and houses of call (for tramping artisans), which often operated through public houses (Hobsbawm 1984, p. 361). In these precursors to unions, organizational structure was fluid, varying

---

[2] As Palmer reminds us, "this was a male culture, and it was often at woman's expense that the artisan articulated his implicit contempt for a genteel aristocracy or a pious bourgeoisie" (1976, p. 10).

with the legacies of experience in and between locales and even between shops. Leadership was a temporal crystallization produced by necessity (Behagg 1982, p. 171; Turner 1962, pp. 77, 82; Hobsbawm 1964; Randall 1991). Such informal networks, along with market cycles, changes in the structure of capital formation, and the ebbs and flows in public and magisterial sympathies—all contributed to organizational flux (Behagg 1979, pp. 462–463; see also 1990; Lees 1980, p. 35). As we shall see, the silk weavers were caught in such a whirlwind of change.

Early trade societies struggled to preserve the integrity of skill claims on two linked but distinct fronts, craft control and work control (Prothero 1979, p. 38; Behagg 1990, p. 5). Crafts had three defining characteristics. First, they were maintained in part by clearly defined handicraft standards that colored the culture of work. Second, a relative monopoly of technical knowledge or skill allowed for control over entry into the trade. Third, genuine inclusion was gained only through recognized avenues of training. Work control encompassed craft control and was the more general ability of a trade group to maintain collective independence in the labor process (Price 1980, p. 11). The lines between the honorable trade and the dishonorable, and between the producer and the nonproductive leech, were firmly etched in the artisanal consciousness (Thompson 1966, p. 258).

These distinctions are important in terms of the potential for class conflict and collective action. Trades with established support systems and substantive control over entry were strategically better positioned to fight the battle of control. In our cases, the silk weavers faced devastating trade degradation, while the cotton spinners tangled with manufacturers more over issues of control. Both questioned the roles of the capitalists who controlled their work. In the process, both groups developed a class consciousness, in part through particular discursive struggles.

From the end of the Napoleonic wars onward, an increasing number of trades fell to the scourge of degradation or doggedly fought to stave off its effects. The wars' aftereffects, culminating in a severe depression in 1816, left a large pool of the unemployed on the margins (Prothero 1979, pp. 62–67; Hilton 1975). Some trades could mount few defenses against this tide of reserve labor. In the most infamous cases of the cotton weavers and framework knitters (exemplars for the silk weavers), wages plunged, and work intensified (Bythell 1969; Hall 1988; Wells 1972).

By the 1820s, diverse trades were experiencing the swell of the "dishonorable" branch of labor, in which apprenticeship and trade rules no longer held sway and "slop shops" produced cheap goods for immediate sale to large warehousers. These "sweated" workers were frequently women denied access to the honorable branches and desperate males unable to find work in them (Alexander 1976; Prothero 1979, pp. 65, 214;

Thompson 1966, pp. 257–258; Berg 1993; Bythell 1978; Haynes 1977). As Thompson has remarked, "We may say that large-scale sweated outwork was as intrinsic to [the industrial] revolution as was factory production and steam" (1966, p. 261). When we examine the plight of the silk weavers, we will observe similar processes, which served to negate status distinctions within the trade. Cotton spinners also fiercely fought against wage reductions, the introduction of women into their trade, and the intensification of the labor process—all of which they believed undermined their special status as skilled workers of distinction in a sea of debased labor.

The reorganization of the labor process was a second plague on the honorable house of labor (Morris 1980, p. 14). Increasingly larger capitalist merchants and manufacturers, in an effort to secure their position in the market, transgressed the boundaries of the lair of labor in order to rationalize production (Behagg 1984, p. 15). Reorganization could be piecemeal or more systematic, but the demise of the small master and the rise of large master manufacturer created a transformation in labor relations (Rule 1988, p. 117).

In the 1820s, both silk weavers and cotton spinners fought such critical battles over reorganization. For the weavers, the struggle concerned the rising domination of large capitalist warehousers in the organization of production and their transformation of outwork relations. The cotton spinners struggled over issues of control over the labor market and intensification of the labor process.

The introduction of new technologies by capitalists intent on increasing productivity, in conjunction with female competition, created threats of intensification for a variety of trade groups. The technologies were not generally highly complex; many relied on hand rather than steam power. The pace of mechanization was often uneven, but for a few trades the actual supplanting of hand labor by steam was transforming production by the latter 1820s. The most famous instance of this was the spread of the power loom in cotton weaving—in which females initially dominated—but other more skilled artisans—such as printers and sawyers—were under severe pressure (Berg 1980, pp. 21, 27; Prothero 1979, p. 215; Yeo and Thompson 1975, p. 332). The piecemeal process of enlarging the cotton spinning mule, along with the possibility of replacing it altogether with a totally automatic machine, presented just such threats to the cotton spinners. The clatter of the power looms in the weaving rooms and sheds of the factory constantly reminded them of this disaster.

Threatened workers responded with enmity, not so much toward the changes themselves, but toward their bearers. In defensive actions, workers often looked beyond their trade boundaries, framing their struggles in more inclusive terms and forging class consciousness through such organizational alliances. We will see this particularly in the case of the cotton spinners and the National Association for the Protection of Labour and to a lesser extent with the silk weavers and the General Association.

At the dawn of the nineteenth century and through the 1820s, the collective consciousness of the English trades was focused as much upon Westminster as it was on their employers. In its reach into many aspects of production and labor relations—from the determination of wages and apprenticeship to the prohibitions on unions—the law was part of the social relations of production and circumscribed labor relations. Workers did not always turn to the courts to resolve disputes, but many trades had a keen sense that some parts of the law gave legal authority to their grievances or acted as fetters upon the exercise of perceived collective rights (Dobson 1980, pp. 139–150; see also Aspinall 1949; Bythell 1969; George 1927; Hedges and Winterbottom 1930; Henson and White 1823; Moher 1988; Orth 1980; Randall 1991; Simon 1956; Somers 1986, 1993, 1994). Certainly the former was the case for the silk weavers for whom the Spitalfields Acts quintessentially defined their productive relations.

With the rise of political economy and the pragmatic orientation to governance of many state leaders, the legal foundations of labor's claims perhaps were besieged more rapidly than the sanctity of the workplace. The first major blow was the repeal of the Statute of Apprenticeship in 1813, a violation, some artisans believed, of their very birthright (Thompson 1966, p. 546). For many artisans, the period from 1812 to 1814 was the turning point when labor was legally excised as property of the trade community and thrust into the turbulence of the market. In its broad sweep, this development was framed as a matter of class. This was to be a theme echoed among the silk weavers during the repeal of their own protective legislation, the Spitalfields Acts.

The second major legal transformation, the repeal of the Combination Laws in 1824, was liberating. The acts, passed initially in 1799, had banned unionization. Supporters of political economy found reason for repeal in the benign power of the market to control workers' demands (Aspinall 1949, p. xxv). Others, including members of the government, found repeal a convenient excuse to side step the thorny problem of capital-labor relations (Orth 1980, pp. 198–199; Prothero 1979, pp. 173–181; George 1927).

Yet the most significant effect of these parliamentary actions was to edge the larger question of the rights and privileges of labor out of the discursive (and legal) realm of the *social* contract and more squarely into that of the *economic* contract. Since law was part of the social relations of production, its transformation could substantively change relations between workers and capitalists. In this process, the moral foundations of labor, used by trade groups in seeking redress, faced new trials, and, as I will demonstrate, fighting words were central to these actions. Increasingly, bourgeois discourses emphasizing political economy called for a working-class response.

The silk weavers were caught in the throes of such conflict during the 1820s. Their struggle against the repeal of the Spitalfields Acts and subsequent efforts to revive some form of protection represent significant battles at the intersection of the law and productive relations, and reflect the manner in which these conflicts centered on discourse. The cotton spinners too, facing mill owners who constructed a social world through the discourse of political economy, engaged in such a vituperative dialogue.

English workers faced threats at the work bench and the legal bench. During these decades, the struggles they engaged in, were slowly transformed, and so too were their repertoire of collective actions. As Tilly has noted, in the realm of popular politics these decades saw a shift from "parochial and patronized" forms of collective activity toward more "national and autonomous" forms (1995, pp. 45–46; see also 1982). In the political sphere, nonviolent public demonstrations largely supplanted the riot as the vehicles for vocalizing dissatisfaction and publicly signaled the attenuation of claims-making through the old ties of parochial power (Belchem 1978, 1981; Parssinen 1972). Labor actions charted a similar course. At the beginning of the century, most such repertoires involved a combination of legal redress, work stoppages, and collective violence. By the 1830s, the lineaments of the repertoire in many trades increasingly emphasized union activity and the often more peaceful strike.

Collective legal claims-making was part of the rudimentary repertoire of most trade groups through the first two decades. Journeymen engaged in large-scale petition campaigns to defend protective statutes (such as the Statutes of Apprentices and Artificers), to repeal laws they saw as odious (such as the Combination Laws), or to press for new legislation to strengthen their collective power vis-à-vis their masters (Bohstedt 1983, pp. 93, 147–149, 214; Bythell 1969, pp. 149–152; Glenn 1984, pp. 148, 153–154; Hammonds 1967, pp. 61, 69, 73, 83, 87; Prothero 1979, pp. 222–224; Rule 1986, p. 273; Stevenson 1979, p. 154; Thompson 1966, p. 542; Turner 1962, pp. 64–65). Such collective action had a venerable lineage in eighteenth-century ideas of a moral economy of productive activity, which conceived of law as a means of maintaining the inviolable right to a livelihood and a necessary balance of trade relations (Prothero 1979, p. 39; see also Somers 1986, 1994). The actions of the Spitalfields weavers to revive some form of trade protection through petitioning Parliament had a venerable history behind them.

Petitioning Parliament was the most visible means of seeking redress through legal channels, but far from the most common. Even after 1814, a thicket of laws regarding conditions of employment, wages, and the contractual status of workers still bounded labor relations (A. S. Diamond

1932; Simon 1954; C. M. Smith 1852). Skirmishes on these issues were fought at the site of local justice, before magistrates or justices of the peace (Thompson 1966, p. 544; Somers 1986).[3] Local authorities often found themselves awkwardly situated between the letter of the law and the expectations of their peers, especially as large manufacturers took their place on the local bench. The recalcitrance of magistrates and Parliament made prosecution and petitioning uncertain channels for the validation of artisanal claims. As we shall see, in both cases the courts and Parliament could function as means of growing capitalist control. In Spitalfields, this form of legal control facilitated the transformations of outwork relations; in Ashton mill owners became local magistrates and cemented their class control in and beyond the point of production.

In these early years, one common alternative was the work stoppage, which depended on the informal networks of the workshop or work group (Thompson 1966, p. 514). We can only speculate, however, about the frequency of work stoppages during this period. As part of the workaday rhythms of ordinary labor, they certainly punctuated a workshop's history. Beyond the small-scale suspensions of the workshop were larger temporary fissures, often occurring around regularized bonding or hiring periods for workers (see, for example, Hair 1965 and Warburton 1930).

When all else failed, the last recourse was organized violence, carried out within the relatively delimited moral boundaries of the working community (Behagg 1982, pp. 165, 171; Thompson 1966, p. 515; Harrison 1988). Collective violence was an act of rough justice and a means of gaining specific goals; like all class action, it had both a moral and an instrumental dimension (Behagg 1984, p. 15; Bohstedt 1983).

At least three types of violence were common features of the artisanal repertoire. The first form, intimidation or assault, was most usually directed against recalcitrant compatriots and "knobsticks" (strikebreakers), and occasionally against masters or employers. It was often ritualized, in such forms as donkeying, which was designed to denigrate the transgressor and publicly reaffirm artisanal norms (Rule 1986, pp. 263-2644). The second type, machine breaking, was carried out in two distinct forms. The first was the destruction of machinery or other property, which served as a pressure tactic against employers and as a means of reinforcing group solidarity. This was a strategy employed in the heat of the silk weavers' 1829 strike, which I will investigate in detail. The second form was the destruction of technology that posed a direct threat to the established tech-

---

[3] In local courts, justice was more decidedly a matter of the disposition of the authorities. Many hardly claimed expertise, and often sentiment prevailed over legal knowledge. For some, non-interference was the abiding rule for pragmatic or ideological reasons. Many magistrates, however, were openly derisive of organized labor (Fox 1985, p. 79; Atiyah 1979, p. 275). Exactly how justice was played out was thus very much a matter of local elite relations and the composition of the local polity, as I detail in the case studies that follow.

nical and social relations of production, most well-known in the case of the Luddites in 1811–1816 (Dinwiddy 1979; Hobsbawm 1952; Stevenson 1979, pp. 155–162; Thomis 1970, 1972; Thompson 1966; see also Randall 1982, 1986, 1991).

The final piece of the typical repertoire was the riot. "Collective bargaining" by riot depended on stable networks of workers who could mobilize between workshops; a population that was sympathetic to the artisans' claims; and local authorities who for lack of resources, penchants for non-involvement, or sympathy for the workers did not wield a heavy hand of repression. Community politics was thus central in shaping this part of the workers' repertoire (Bohstedt 1983, pp. 26, 215). In this sense, rioting can be seen as a type of "irregular democracy" in the balance of labor relations, sanctioned implicitly or otherwise by non-trade actors. To the extent that violence succeeded, it did so because it was used sparingly.

From the middle of the second decade onward, a gradual metamorphosis of this instrumental repertoire occurred. In part, this shift was due to the changing threats workers faced in the social relations of production. In part, it was a product of the broader transformation of collective action noted above. A few trades, such as most of the hand loom cotton-weaving branches, were rapidly consumed by the onslaught of degradation and could not sustain organized opposition.[4] Many trade groups, however, responded through a protracted and contentious process of repertoire change roughly between 1815 and 1830. As they both engaged in these struggles and watched others in similar processes, class happened in their experiences.

The most basic transformation was in the frequency of collective action. The press of degradation imposed insuperable costs on some workers, who were coping with an increasingly threadbare existence. The pendulum of activity, however, swung the other way as well. The proliferation of work (especially processes for textile production) created potential for higher levels of contention, as in the coal and cotton industries and in the case of the cotton spinners particularly (Sykes 1982, v. 1, pp. 190–209; Cole 1953; Jaffe 1991; Kirby and Musson 1975; Challinor 1972). Other trades swept up in the process of urban expansion—such as many building trades—likewise arose as large and contentious blocs of organized labor (Price 1980).

For some trade groups, instrumental repertoire changes also brought about alterations in the rhythms of their collective actions. The strike, a more resource-intensive mode of contention than petitioning or bargaining by riot, was carried out during years of prosperity or at critical seasons of high production (Rule 1986, p. 261). Collective opposition to wage reductions and the reorganization of production was best reserved for times

---

[4] See, however, R. Hall 1989 for an analysis of the Lancashire weavers' strike of 1818.

of higher employment, while action on concerns such as wage fixing, half-work or short-time, and the price of provisions was pursued in times of economic downturn (Prothero 1979, p. 268).

In the panorama of contention in these years, such growth spelled regional shifts in frequency and intensity. More was heard from the North (especially the Northwest, where Ashton and Stalybridge are located) and less from the Southwest and East Anglia. London, with its myriad of artisans, remained a constant player in this history.

For all trade groups, legal changes transformed the terrain of contention. In razing old labor law with the growing fire of political economy, Parliament had transformed itself as a source of redress. Battles within Westminster were increasingly fought on more general issues of workers' claims to security and protection.[5] Conflict through local legal channels continued, although recourse to the bench was more often the effect of insufficient resources or tough times for other forms of contention (Prothero 1979, p. 217). In this sense, the silk weavers' struggles surrounding the repeal of their protective legislation signaled the end of an era. Many trade leaders, however, still wore caps of liberty, and their experiences as political radicals certainly informed their actions as champions of the workplace. We will witness such fertile mixing of political and union radicalism in the case of the cotton spinners.

Another gradual and uneven transformation in instrumental repertoires was that violence was less frequently the central lever of redress (Stevenson 1979, p. 229). Intermittent ruptures, such as the powerloom riots in Lancashire in 1826, kept the threat of violence firmly in the minds of many capitalists and authorities. Yet the repression following the Luddite campaigns, including statutes making machine breaking a capital offense, exposed the possible limitations of its use. Blacklegs and other interlopers continued to feel the sting of its retributive justice, particularly during strikes, but large-scale assaults on the workplace, machinery, or the employer's property diminished. By the mid 1820s, riots ignited alarm as much because of their increased rarity as the actual display of violence itself (Bohstedt 1983, p. 210; Berg 1980, p. 230). In my analyses, I will detail how both groups used violence strategically, albeit sparingly.

In politics, the rise of the mass meeting signaled a new era; in trade relations, the strike (or "turn-out" in contemporary parlance) was a bellwether of change (Pelling 1963, p. 9; Stevenson 1979, chap. 10). It blossomed from the mid-teens onward in tandem with more permanent forms of union organization, both among the nascent industrial trades, such as

---

[5] Parliament was still the object of attention, particularly as it related to calls by some outworkers' groups for wage protection legislation and among the rising group of male factory workers for short-time legislation (Prothero 1979; Gray 1988, 1993; Kirby and Musson 1975; Weaver 1988). These campaigns, however, tended to stand apart from other forms of workers' contention.

the cotton spinners and cotton dressers, as well as in more established sectors, such as the construction workers, coachmakers, keelmen, framework knitters, cotton weavers, and the hatters (Batt 1986, p. 193; Glenn 1984, pp. 71, 103; Rule 1986, pp. 274–275; Wearmouth 1948, p. 252; Webbs 1920, p. 80). This increase presaged an unprecedented strike wave with the repeal of the Combination Laws. In the minds of authorities and capitalists alike, the repeal unleashed a whirlwind of trade union agitation, creating organizations in which the cotton spinners were among the most active participants (Prothero 1979, pp. 160–161; Cole 1953; Kirby and Musson 1975; Turner 1962). As this heavy weather moved across the terrain, it reorganized the landscape's features, revealing to many workers more general divisions of interests between themselves and capitalists.

The dismantling of the old protectionist legislation damaged the paternalistic status of many employers. Particularly in the case of the new tide of large capitalist entrepreneurs, the employer appeared to be shorn of worth and purpose, and was often seen as a parasitic nonproducer. This transformation was fundamental to the silk weavers' tribulations of the 1820s. In parallel, the removal of legal protection necessitated organized action among artisans to preserve their control in the workplace and their male exclusivity (Rule 1988, p. 101). Newer factory-based trades such as that of the cotton spinners, often facing a more organized industrial bourgeoisie, also sought defense through more formal unification (Cuca 1977, p. 249). "The larger the industrial unit or the greater the specialization of skills involved, the sharper were the animosities between capital and labour, and the greater the understanding among the employers" (Thompson 1966, p. 506). The establishment of more permanent trade organizations, emerging from the subterranean obscurity of informal networks that had protected them, most frequently led to the ossification of long-time linkages (Musson 1972, p. 29). Although many were ephemeral experiments, they nonetheless marked a pathbreaking step toward enduring trade organizations (Cole 1953, pp. 180–186). The process of class became crystallized in networks and organizations on both sides of the divide, as the case of the spinners will show.

Local union growth spurred regional and national communication. Whereas in 1800 seventeen trades maintained inter-town contacts, by the mid-twenties at least twenty-eight had established some form of extralocal organization (Rule 1986, p. 267). By 1830, the cotton spinners and smiths had established the rudiments of national organizations, and they were to be followed in the early 1830s by the building trades (Cole 1953; Kirby and Musson 1975; Price 1980).

These public and more enduring organizations at once held promise and imposed constraints. The promise was in the increased coordination in the marshaling of resources for more protracted conflict. Constraints were found, however, in the public nature of contention and in more complex problems of organization. An open venue placed conflict in the light of public opinion, an often vital ally in the fight against more powerful adversaries (Stevenson 1979, p. 235; Behagg 1982, pp. 80–81). The silk weavers, for one, brought their grievances foursquare into the court of public opinion in many of their campaigns. The cotton spinners marched into the mire of complex coordination in their great strike of 1830–1831. Additionally, the novelty of their newfound legal status led many trades to cast a cautious eye on local and supra-local authorities.

A final fledgling piece of the reordered repertoire, the cooperative, was novel. From cooperative socialist thinkers, ideas proliferated, providing the intellectual underpinnings for a noncapitalist alternative to both consumption and production. At the same time, the increasing intrusiveness of large capitalists in the workplace forced, in the name of survival, a search for a productive system that would bypass them altogether (Claeys 1982, 1987; Harrison 1969; Musson 1958; Oliver 1958a, 1958b; Prothero 1979; Saville 1971; Thompson 1966; Yeo 1971). By the late 1820s, cooperation, mostly in the form of cooperative stores, was spreading in London, the Midlands, and the Northwest (Harrison 1969, p. 199; Prothero 1979, chap. 13). Such schemes were still largely curiosities of the period, but this nascent movement is indicative of the dynamism of the labor repertoire by 1830. Neither the silk weavers nor the cotton spinners were central actors in the push for cooperation, although the spinners were certainly informed by its ideas.

In sum, we can say that repertoire changes in the 1800–1830 period were on the whole toward more autonomous and public actions. Responding to changing circumstances and drawing on their experiential understandings of their positions, many trade groups adapted older patterns of collective action to new threats. Whereas in 1800 the riot and parliamentary recourse were major facets of this repertoire, by 1830 they were secondary. Both artisans with lineages of workplace control and newer industrial workers seeking to secure their own place in the world of labor faced challenges from above. Both the old and the new faced challenges of class exploitation through degradation and the reorganization of productive relations. The altered legal status of labor, both in the dismantling of old protectionist legislation and in the legitimization of unions, diminished the stature of Parliament in the eyes of most workers and made it less of a target for workers' claims. As a result, the strike became a more dominant form of action for many trade groups seeking redress. In this sense, the case of the silk weavers represents a waning and that of the cotton spinners a blossoming.

The lineaments of contention moved in reaction to the distinctive problems posed by the uneven pace of change within each trade. Nonetheless, most trades groups could sense that changes in their world of labor were afoot. Certainly the silk weavers viewed them with alarm, and the cotton spinners eyed their potential with great trepidation. Transformations in the repertoires of labor reflected a changing and more enveloping class consciousness through which workers made sense of these new challenges. The increased intertrade cohesiveness of these later years is indicative of this development and is a palpable representation of the making of English working class.

The silk weavers and cotton spinners were in the thick of these fundamental alterations. In the following case studies, I closely examine their instrumental and discursive repertoires as exemplars of these class processes and of changes in repertoires of collective action. Each group fashioned a distinct repertoire in response to the exigencies of their situations. Material, social, and political circumstances conjoined with the baggage of experience to shape the class consciousness and collective actions of both trade groups. For the silk weavers, the legal definitions of their position loomed large; for the cotton spinners, it was the increasingly unmediated power of industrial capitalists. In each case, responses to threats were a product of a consciousness fostered by experience and animated by discourse. My analysis is anchored in an understanding of their own standards of labor, justice, and moral worth, and in conceptions of trade gendering, for ultimately such standards were the primary guides in the quest for redress. The analysis of their fighting words will provide an important window on how these concepts were constructed, how they represented forms of class consciousness, and how they mediated collective decisions for action. We should appreciate, however, that their standards, although born of particular struggles, were hardly myopic. As world-weary warriors of labor, both groups cast their travails in larger terms and in doing so were caught up in the processes of class.

CHAPTER TWO

A Tale of Two Areas

*I*n this book I focus on two trade groups—the silk weavers of Spitalfields and the cotton spinners of Ashton and Stalybridge—and the regions in which they lived. My analysis centers on how the integument of social, political, and community life bounded these groups' existence and shaped their class experiences. I also focus on how those class experiences were articulated and mediated through the fighting words of the landmark struggles in their collective histories. As Thompson and many others have maintained, however, to understand class we must start in the actual locales of lived experience. This chapter introduces the two regions in which these experiences took form, in which weavers and spinners struggled to maintain their economic security and created their collective identities. I show the similarities and contrasts of these surroundings; how patterns of community development, social geography, social life, and senses of community created at once distinctive yet conjoined foundations for class experiences. After providing this introduction to the two terrains, the discussion moves to the more specific world of silk production.

In some senses, Spitalfields, on the one hand, and Ashton and Stalybridge, on the other, were worlds apart. Spitalfields lay within the eastern confines of the great city that dwarfed all others—London—in the rough and bawdy world of common labor that serviced the land of high society, highmindedness, and high finance to the west. Spanning five parishes,

Spitalfields comprised a significant piece of the eastern region, both in terms of territory and culture. Its border lay near the shadows of the Tower of London, and directly across the main thoroughfare of Bishopsgate on this western boundary stood the City of London proper. The recognized boundaries of Spitalfields were not clearly drawn and were as much defined by the poverty of its dwellers as by actual physical or administrative demarcations. "Here," observed William Hale, a master manufacturer, champion of the silk weavers, and long-time resident, "the mechanics of every trade reside, who work for their employers in the City: — Here dwell the carters, porters, and labourers, with the thousands who are engaged in the most servile employments, down to the mendicants, the lame, and the blind" (Hale 1806, p. 7). By his estimate, fully four-fifths of the district's laboring poor had masters across the divide of Bishopsgate.[1]

By contrast, the towns of Ashton-under-Lyne and Stalybridge were largely northern children of the Industrial Revolution, at least in the form in which we shall enter them. Clustered beyond the ever-widening shadows of Manchester, these towns stretched slightly across the northern Cheshire border. Ashton and Stalybridge, which lay six and seven miles east of the great grey metropolis, served as anchors for a series of smaller industrial villages, which formed an underbelly a couple of miles to their south, nestled in the river valleys.

The two regions had historical patterns of distinctive development. The parish of Christ Church, Spitalfields, dated back to the thirteenth century, but it was in the late seventeenth century that it became associated with London's laborers. Among the most celebrated settlers of this period were hundreds of Huguenot silk weavers from Lyons and Tours, prized by both the Crown and Parliament, who had previously attempted, unsuccessfully, to cultivate an indigenous silk industry. With the settlement of these weavers, Spital Square rose in prominence as the center of activity for the city's ascendant silk merchants. The larger parish area crystallized into a cultural enclave for the immigrants, with Huguenot chapels and benevolent societies rising to meet their needs. A small artisanal enclave begat a larger plebeian preserve, as other artisans and laborers sought cheaper housing in the eastern environs (Nightingale 1815, v. 3, pp. 170–171; Smiles 1881, pp. 263–264; *Survey of London* 1957, v. 27, p. 6).

Although Spitalfields' history was a rather small chapter in London's past, Ashton town had once defined its district. It was the commercial center of the four divisions of Ashton Parish, which before the Industrial Revolution was dominated by pasture land. Lying on the northern bank of the river Tame, Ashton had long been the market center for the hinterlands.

---

[1] Similarly, Schwarz in his study of the East End estimates that in 1813, 67 percent of the population was manual workers, of whom 10 percent were skilled (McCann 1977, p. 2).

Although a small, compact community (having perhaps only 2,900 inhabitants as late as 1775), Ashton was substantially larger than the tiny hamlets that it serviced. Ever since the sixteenth century, it had also been the center for the local production of woolen cloth. During the seventeenth century, it began to nurture a cotton fustian trade and by the 1730s was developing the domestic production of cotton wefts for the local weavers (E. Butterworth 1842, pp. 115–116; Harrop 1974, p. 29; Cotton 1977, p. 14).

A number of lesser communities, nestled in the valleys about Ashton, were equally integral to the cotton empire of southeast Lancashire. These towns developed much like Ashton, although they experienced more meteoric rises. Chief among these was Stalybridge, not only the largest of these communities, but also the most distinctive in its political geography. Officially, it was situated directly on the Lancashire and Cheshire border, and jurisdictionally its property was distributed among three parishes. Much like Ashton, the town was dominated by wool cloth production throughout most of the eighteenth century. By 1794, however, cotton manufacturers had outdistanced those of wool twenty-one to nine (Butterworth 1842, pp. 138, 141; Cotton 1977, pp. 14–15).

To the outside eye, each of these two regions was indelibly colored by key characteristics. To negotiate the silk weavers' community and their status within it was to understand the poverty that enveloped the district. Spitalfields Parish's economic vitality was bought at the cost of increasing urban squalor writ large, on a scale that was possible only in London. By the beginning of the nineteenth century, its population of a little more than fifteen thousand inhabitants was pressed into subdivided and ill-kept houses. Sections of the parish became sanctuaries for the itinerant and unemployed (P.P. 1840, XXIII, pt. 2, p. 214; *Survey of London*, 1957, v. 27, p. 248). To the outside observer, Spitalfields was an expanse of destitution and profligacy. The local Benevolent Society report of 1812 bleakly commented, "Spitalfields and its neighborhood, contain a vast number of manufacturing poor. Many of these persons are at once ignorant, industrious and wretched. . . . The population of this district has a far greater proportion of poor than any other, perhaps, of equal number in any part of the Empire" (*Spitalfields Benevolent Society Report* 1812, pp. 5–6).

By contrast, Ashton's image by the 1820s, beautified by distance, was of a compact commercial and industrial center bustling with activity. By the end of the decade, Ashton-Manchester traffic had swelled to thirty daily coaches (*MT,* Jan. 16, 1830). The small town gained a reputation for bigness, in the size of its mills, in its commercial volume, and in the expectations of those who controlled it. One enthusiast unabashedly referred to it as "the most important commercial area in the world" (*MG*, April 3, 1827). Stalybridge did not quite share the praises sung of its neighbor. The swift erection of mills and dwellings left the scars of hasty development (Harrop 1974, p. 29). Although developed in a relatively compact area, limited size did not dampen its chaotic growth.

The Spitalfields and the Ashton-Stalybridge regions arrived at their respective states through a combination of rapid economic growth and heady commercial speculation. In Spitalfields Parish, increasing numbers and deteriorating housing stock gradually built up pressure to move eastward into the adjoining parish of St. Matthew's, Bethnal Green. Given this mounting pressure and the temptation of speculative real estate profiteering, Bethnal Green witnessed a housing boom in the 1810s that intensified in 1816–1826. Between 1801 and 1831, the parish swelled from 22,310 to 62,018 residents (Lysons 1811, p. 17; Plummer 1972, p. 365; P.P. 1834, X, p. 324). Weavers moved en masse into the parish in search of better and cheaper housing. Areas such as Twigg Folly—a neighborhood of six streets and five to six thousand people, approximately fifteen hundred of whom were weavers—became synonymous with weaving. Much of this development was manipulated by the cronies of a corrupt parish officer named Joseph Merceron, whose power was unmatched during these decades (L.S.P. 1826, CLVI, p. 23; P.P. 1835, VII, p. 11: P.P. 1834, XXIX, app. A, pt. III, p. 115A; P. Clark 1983, p. 264; Webbs 1906, pp. 79–90). In response to this additional pressure, some weavers moved farther northeast into the village of Mile End New Town or to the adjacent southwest parish of Whitechapel, but these remained marginal in their identification with silk.

The reconstitution of the weavers' communities within these new surroundings was not, however, a simple replication of their old neighborhoods. The speculative motor behind the housing boom produced housing of a "meaner description" than that in Spitalfields. Blocks of small, poorly constructed row houses were packed into roughly hewn side streets that scarred the formerly pastoral landscape (P.P. 1834, XXXV, app. B.2, pt. IV, p. 83i; P.P. 1840, XXIII, pt. II, p. 239). In both Christ Church and St. Matthew's, the swelling of the ranks during the first decades of the nineteenth century was given impetus by the influx of casual laborers in search of employment and cheap housing. Whereas in 1770 55 percent of the adult laboring population of Spitalfields consisted of weavers, this proportion had dropped to 26 percent by 1813 (McCann 1977, p. 3; P.P. 1834, XXXV, app. B.2, pt. IV, pp. 83i, 87i).

Whereas in Spitalfields growth was underwritten by an uneasy and often chaotic cronyism, in Ashton, Stalybridge, and the surrounding mill villages the shape of town and village life arose more directly from the shrewd deliberations of aristocrats and industrialists. An emerging cotton merchant class, taking the reins from the old wool families, sought to refashion the town into a commercial and manufacturing mecca (Harrop 1980, p. 4). They were not left to their own devices, however. Behind them stood the Earl of Stamford and Warrington, the region's principal landowner. It was in fact the earl, with his substantial resources and business acumen, who put Ashton squarely on the modern map.[2] His farmland was an uncertain source of wealth, and by the 1790s the earl was searching for additional revenues, particularly in Ashton town, where he owned the bulk of all property. With the construction of the three canals between 1792 and 1794, Ashton was soon linked with virtually every major manufacturing area in the Northwest. To complement this commercial expansion, the earl mapped out a plan for growth, with the new town area laid out on a modern grid system and all of the proposed streets named for family members. Physical expansion lagged until 1824, when the nucleus of the new town area, Stamford Street, was almost fully occupied. Old farming villages such as Hurst Brook, Charlestown, Mossley, and Lees, began to emerge as working-class centers. The value of the parish's rated property doubled with expansion (Baines 1825, p. 490; Bowman 1960, pp. 365, 374–376, 410; Cotton 1977, pp. 23–24; Harrop 1974, p. 30; *Parliamentary Gazetteer*, 1844, pt. I, p. 67; Rose 1969, p. 5).

Stalybridge, not developed under the earl's pecuniary eye, grew more haphazardly. The swift erection of mills and dwellings during the building boom of the early 1820s left scars of hasty development: "pit coal and steam-engines, have diminished the natural beauties, and substituted in their place the employment of the poor and the increased opulence of the wealthy" (Baines 1825, v. 2, p. 555; Harrop 1974, p. 29). The local historian Edwin Butterworth characterized the community as a rag-tag collection of structures, with far too many crowded dwellings of poor construction (1842, p. 145). The construction of working-class housing was the sphere of the mill owner and the speculator. Mill owners such as John Leech constructed whole blocks of housing to accommodate their factory hands (Butterworth 1842, p. 146; Baines 1825, v. 2, p. 556).

To proper Londoners, the parishes of Christ Church, Spitalfields, and Saint Matthew's, Bethnal Green, were not only synonymous with the weavers, they were also seen as the underbelly of plebeian life. Urban development had created a distinct social geography. Enclaves of stratified social activity bustled in small niches of class-demarcated space. The main thoroughfares that bordered or crosscut the district—roads such as Bishopsgate, Hackney, Shoreditch, and Mile End—were swathes of petty-bourgeois respectability. Some smaller established streets, such as Brick Lane, also laid claim to this air of higher status. Retailers in provisions, fashionable clothing, and domestic goods lined these avenues, as well as some of the more exclusive drapers and silk merchants (Warner 1921,

---

[2] The Stamford and Warringtons were great landowners whose principal holdings were divided between the counties of Leicestershire, Cheshire, Staffordshire, and Lancashire. Of their 30,000 total acres, approximately half was located in Cheshire and Lancashire (about 8,600 and 5,200 acres respectively) (Bateman 1879, p. 412).

p. 63). A few pockets of bourgeois comfort and Georgian grandeur were found adjacent to these thoroughfares in sites such as Spital Square. Nearby, down the comfortable corridor of Church Street, Christ's Church towered over the immediate district. The church was a majestic monument that cast a long shadow on the surrounding square, but its social and culture presence rarely extended beyond the confines of its grounds.

Behind the thoroughfares and squares lay a grid of working-class life. On these rough streets and lanes, itinerant merchants could be found hawking basic provisions. The lines of small row houses punctuated by occasional shops marked out the social space of the laboring poor. Passing through the district, even a casual observer could easily spot a neighborhood of silk-weaving families. The technical demands of the trade and the commercial nature of housing development joined to create neighborhoods for the weavers without their forethought or active participation. To maximize the use of sunlight, weavers' houses were constructed with large windows running across much of the breadth of the top floor where the workshop was located. Since many houses in Spitalfields had been built in large tracts, often with the weavers in mind, weaving-family streets could be noted at a glance.[3] Despite internal migration within the district, the overall continuity of weaving neighborhoods was maintained by a forced geographical integrity. The rhythmic click-clack of the looms also demarcated weaving territory (Bayley 1829, v. 4, pp. 139–140; Armitage n.d., p. 268; Dodd 1851, pp. 399–400).

The towns and mill villages of Ashton Parish had features of class sharply etched into their social geography as well. In Ashton, industrial capitalism left indelible marks of class bifurcation with its rapid growth. By the mid-1830s, the Manchester Statistical Society was reporting that 81.5 percent of the town population was working class, compared to 64 percent in Manchester (Sykes 1982, v. 1, p. 17). John Joseph Betts, the secretary of the local spinners' union, was quick to note the chasm between the haves and the have-nots: "There seems to my eye's judgement, hardly any proportion of the middle class of society in this community. The grinders and the ground make up the bulk of its inhabitants" (*UTCJ*, May 8, 1830, p. 78).

This social structure crystallized into concentric rings of poverty and affluence that made up the town area. John R. Coulthart, in an investigation conducted for the Sanitary Commissioners in the early 1840s, identified five principal classes of housing that marked Ashton's terrain. In the old Charlestown district lived the poorest inhabitants (and often the most recent), about one-eighth of the population in ramshackle dwellings, housing from six to eight people. Above these were four grades of houses

---

[3] Interestingly, in his description of the row houses, Dodd characterized these blocks as looking similar to factories, because of these long stretches of oversized windows (Dodd 1851, p. 386).

totaling 3,700 units, each with successively superior construction and amenities, which mirrored the status and wages of the workers (Coulthart 1844, pp. 32–34, 36–37). Unlike Manchester, Ashton escaped the large-scale infestation of industrial squalor. Much of the housing, however, was owned and leased by the mill owners, and this power over tenancy cast a foreboding shadow over the hands.

In the outer ring, the class divide was clearly manifest in the fashionable estates erected by Ashton's nouveau bourgeoisie (Baines 1825, v. 1, p. 490; Harrop 1974, p. 40). In the 1820s and 1830s, mill owners increased the visible division by building even more lavish structures outside the town. To Edwin Butterworth's eye, "the environs of Ashton and Stalybridge are decorated by the elegant mansions of the wealthy manufacturers, which are mostly belted by tastefully disposed pleasure-grounds" (Butterworth 1842, p. 93). By the 1830s, a veritable ring of mansions, each named with aristocratic pretension, demarcated the "pleasure-grounds" of the rich from the toiling grounds of the poor.

Stalybridge mirrored this concentric pattern. Its extremes, however, were even more apparent, given that 90 percent of its population was working class and among them was a higher proportion of poor Irish laborers (Cotton 1977, pp. 33, 60, n. 37; Hill 1902, pp. 65–66, 68–69, 246; Kirk 1985, p. 43; Sykes 1982, v. 1, p. 17; M.C.L., Romilly MSS. 1836, f. 6; P.P. 1836, XXXIV, app. G., pp. 84–85).

Whereas Spitalfields built inward on itself, the impulses of industry in Ashton and Stalybridge reached outward. Like the bog plants of the hinterlands, Ashton and Stalybridge sent out roots that sprouted new shoots in their own image. These pockets of industry—such as Dukinfield, Hyde, Glossup, Hurst, Lees, Mossley, Audenshaw—were almost wholly the creation of the mill owners. Although physically small and rarely containing more than a few thousand people, the villages played an integral role in the region's production. Thomas Ashton's monstrous complex in Hyde was, in 1824, spinning 25,000 pounds of cotton per week. Hyde and a few other large combined mills accounted for fully one-half of the combined cotton consumption of Ashton and Stalybridge, and approximately one-eighth of all English export production (P.P. 1824, V, First Report, pp. 301, 303). The physical and social landscapes of each village were immutably stamped with their mill owners' visions.

Most of these towns paralleled the pace and timing of Stalybridge's rapid growth. Dukinfield, which had two modest structures at the turn of the century had seven mills by 1825. Cotton-devouring Hyde, a town essentially non-existent before the cotton boom, had fifteen mills by the early 1830s. Factory growth attracted a flock of short-distance migrants, many of them unemployed hand-loom weavers. Dukinfield grew from a community of 1,737 in 1801 to 5,096 by 1821. Hyde likewise expanded from 803 to 3,335, and doubled its population again in the following decade (Ashmore 1974, p. 96; Baines 1966, p. 387; Butterworth 1842, p. 99; Daniels 1930, p.109; Harrop 1980, p. 3). These communities were starkly working-class. Dukinfield was 94.7 percent proletarian, and the smaller towns probably had an even higher percentage. It is also likely that they contained a relatively smaller proportion of Irish. Class structure and the concentration of power were uncomplicated and transparent (Kirk 1985, p. 49; Sykes 1982, v. 1, p. 17; M.C.L., Romilly MSS. 1836, fo. 6).

The social terrain was a reflection of the mill owners' paternalism. Some, in constructing their empires, made a point of erecting simple but commodious dwellings for their workers. Thomas Ashton, in Hyde, for example, built several hundred sturdy stone structures, and others in Dukinfield mirrored him (Collier 1964, p. 51; Greg 1837, p. 34; Taylor 1842, p. 231; *Parliamentary Gazetteer*, 1844, pt. VI, p. 463). Increased comfort, however, was gained at the cost of diminished prerogatives. Mill owners also expected and exercised almost unquestioned control. One such mill owner in Hyde wrote with considerable braggadocio to a local paper that "we have them more under control than is possible in a large town; most of them are tenants and are bound by ties unnecessary for me to name" (*SA*, Feb. 20, 1829). For the factory hands, it was a nefarious fait accompli, and their resentment of their situation was undisguised. The *United Trades' Co-operative Journal* unabashedly described Hyde as "that base and miserable place, where everything mean, oppressive, and audacious have [sic] originated" (*UTCJ*, May, 22, 1830, p. 91).

The distinctive social geographies of each area sorted and circumscribed working people, carefully demarcating their territory, their neighbors, and their ways of life as being distinctive, other, and generally inferior in the minds of those who exercised control. This geography was to have a powerful influence on the potentials for class struggle in each case by providing multiplex networks for mobilization. The social geography, however, also corralled working people, who then produced insular and supportive class cultures, worldviews, and ways of life that at once were fused with gendered understandings and access, and were opposed to the cultures of their employers. Although the details of each culture were of distinctly regional hues, the processes of development had many parallels.

In both areas, the pub served as the anchor for the construction of masculine social life. Portions of Spitalfields were planted thick with these mainstays of male conviviality, although Spitalfields parish claimed a modest 55 by 1817 (P.P. 1817, VII, p. 111). In Bethnal Green, by contrast, public houses and beer shops appeared to the authorities to be spreading like weeds. By the end of the parish's spurt of growth in the early 1830s, it harbored 117 pubs and a further 100 beer shops (Gurney 1819, v. 2, pp. 41, 95; P.P. 1834, XXIX, app. A, pt. III, p. 111A). For parish officers, these were dens of debauchery, and in Bethnal Green publicans were periodically pitted against the law to curb perceived excesses (P.P. 1817, app. X, p. 302).

Those under the control of Merceron, the parish lord, catered to young weavers of both sexes and were popularly known as "cock and hen" clubs (Webbs 1906, pp. 85–86).

Pubs were perhaps even more important male preserves in the Ashton-Stalybridge district. As the region's market town, Ashton was the predominant home of public houses and inns. Beer shops proliferated with town expansion, and the Statistical Society counted one beer shop for every 113 people. The smaller towns provided less hospitable ground. Mill owners objected to such dens of iniquity and checked their expansion (Manchester Statistical Society 1838, pp. 7–8; Cooke-Taylor 1842, p. 231). Pubs were part of the foundation for male working-class sociability. A place where free discussion could thrive beyond the grasp of the mill owners, they were the critical spaces for the development of community organization. They were also hosts for a vibrant group of fraternal and burial societies, which fostered a cohesive male working-class culture that cut across trades. Ashton and Stalybridge abounded with fraternal lodges by the 1820s, many having multiple chapters and village branches (Bowman 1960, p. 556; Butterworth 1842, p. 153; *MT*, June 11, 1829, Nov. 13, 1831; Baines 1824, v. 2, p. 557). For the local authorities, however, the pubs represented hothouses of discontent and vice, and their vigilance over then had a missionary tinge (Cotton 1977, p. 91). In the words of Charles Hindley, a mill owner and future M.P., pub-goers "sacrifice all that is noble in man . . ." (Hindley 1825, p. 5).

Whereas adult men anchored their world in the pub, social life for both sexes was played out in the streets and alleys. Popular recreation among the denizens of the London's East End included skittles and bull baiting (which was not suppressed until the mid 1820s) (P.P. 1828, VI, p. 92; Gurney 1819, v. 1, p. xiv; McCann 1977, p. 3). The amiable chat on the front step, comfortably positioned with a pot of ale, was a Sunday staple for tradesmen, defining their authority over domestic and neighborhood space, but inviting the participation of family members as well (P.P. 1840, XXIII, pt III., p. 245). Within this working-class culture, the weavers had refined their own distinct set of leisure activities and patterns of social life. Throughout the eighteenth and into the nineteenth century, the weavers were viewed as aristocrats of the East End artisans. One of the most noted features of the weavers' way of life was their engagement in the more civilized activities of leisure and amusement, including botany, bird fancying, and pigeon breeding (P.P. 1840, XXIII, pt. III, p. 218; Armitage n.d., p. 267; Manchee 1913, p. 331; George 1925, p. 190; Partington 1825, p. 38).

The gentility of leisure was seen as typifying the high moral caliber of the weavers' lives. The weaving family's home life was often characterized as one of tranquillity and affection, sometimes to a fault (P.P. 1835, VII, p. 10). This civility was also taken to be emblematic of the weavers' general demeanor. Respectability, the byword of the superior artisan, was a term often used in describing their character. Many masters effusively praised the weavers, like one who noted, "There does not exist in these realms, or in any part of the world, a class of people more industrious, more moral, and in every sense more deserving the hand of the government, than the Spitalfields weavers" (P.P. 1832, XIX, p. 714; see also the testimony of Richard p. 230; P.P. 1818, IX, p. 160).

The weavers' moral fabric was viewed as the foundation for their civic independence, another mark of community respectability. William Hale noted a proud streak in the weavers' character; "The weavers in Spitalfields have never been accustomed to apply for parochial relief being well paid; but they would submit to the greatest privations, and go without the necessaries of life, and even bread itself, sooner than apply for relief" (P.P. 1834, X, p. 323).

Beyond these traits, perhaps the idealized weavers' most distinguishing characteristic was their intellectual penchant. Weavers were noted for reading aloud books on philosophical subjects while their fellows worked (Manchee, p. 332). Over the decades, many intellectuals and scientists had risen from the confines of Spitalfields to make their names in society, including John Thelwall, a key figure in the London Corresponding Society (Scott 1894, p. 19). The weavers were active propagators of intellectual societies, including the Mathematical, Historical, Floricultural, Entomological, Musical, and Columbarian Societies (several with substantial libraries) and a Recitation Society for Shakespearean readings (Hammonds 1919, pp. 212–213; Manchee 1913, p. 333; Nightingale 1815, v. 3, p. 177; Scott 1894, p. 18). Although many of these institutions in fact had dissolved by the 1820s, the impression they left on the outside world was enduring.

The intellectual perspicacity of the silk weavers was not lost on those who peered into the Spitalfields community from beyond Bishopsgate. The French social observer Gustave d'Eichtal (during his tour of England in 1828) was also quick to note their shrewd minds (P.P. 1835, VII, p. 10). After an excursion through the East End, he recorded in his journal, "It seems that these workers understand the questions they discuss as well as anyone and that nobody knows how to secure a reply from the government better than they" (Ratcliffe and Chaloner, p. 25).[4]

Certainly not all weavers were amateur scholars, but collectively they exhibited a relatively high rate of literacy through the first several decades of the 1800s. A remarkable survey of the Spitalfields district, compiled by the

---

[4] Even after years of degradation Henry Mayhew marked them as "possessing tastes and following pursuits the refinement and intelligence of which would be an honor and a grace to the artisan of even the present day" (Yeo and Thompson 1971, p. 106). The inimitable pontificator Francis Place also observed that the silk weavers were better informed than the common worker (P.P. 1835, VII, p. 87).

Soup Society in 1812, provides insight on the extent of their literacy.[5] During their investigation Society members surveyed 1,504 families (2,672 adults and 4,514 children) across 6 parishes and 79 separate streets. Forty-eight percent of the families surveyed were in silk-weaving, suggesting that the territory surveyed had an overrepresentation of the weaving population. Sixty percent of the adult population was judged literate by the surveyors. Although the rate was lower for children, it was positively correlated with the percentage of weaving families within a neighborhood.

The weavers thus stood apart from the bawdy plebeian culture of the East End and were routinely held up as examples of respectability. Their leisure and daily rounds of social life marked them as exemplary artisans in the eyes of their betters. This distinction laid the basis for possible paternalistic ties between the masters of the West End and their artisans, as I will show in Chapter 4. Where cultural interests could construct bridges, however, politics and economics could raise imposing walls. Because the silk trade was a last vestige of parliamentary protection, political and economic issues were sources of either firm alliances or of dangerous fissures. For these reasons, after exploring the organization and history of the trade, we will return to the political realm to investigate class conflict.

---

[5] For details of the Soup Society, see Chapter 4. For summary statistics of the four districts surveyed, see Steinberg 1989, v. 1, p. 170. The street-by-street tables of the survey can be found in "An Account of the Soup Society in Spitalfields" (*The Philanthropist*, v. 2, no. 6, 1812, pp. 186–189).

SPITALFIELDS

CHAPTER THREE

The Silk Trade: Memory, Market, and Means of Production

*I*n the previous chapters, I argued that class analysis extends far beyond the immediate social relations of production. Yet the world of work is critically important, and in *The Making of the English Working Class* Thompson highlighted experiences of trade degradation and exploitation: "For most working people the crucial experience of the Industrial Revolution was felt in terms of changes in the nature and intensity of exploitation" (1966, p. 199). His carefully itemized list of forms of degradation is worth rehearsing, for they mirror many of the silk weavers' and cotton spinners' grievances that we will be analyzing. "The rise of a master-class without traditional authority or obligations: the growing distance between master and man: the transparency of exploitation at the course of their new wealth and power: the loss of status and above all of independence for the worker, his reduction to total dependence on the master's instruments of production: the partiality of the law: the disruption of the traditional family economy: the discipline, monotony, hours and conditions of work: loss of leisure and amenities: the reduction of the man to the status of an 'instrument'" (p. 203).[1]

---

[1] Thompson also cautions, "The exploitive relationship is more than the sum of grievances and mutual antagonisms. It is a relationship which can be seen to take distinct forms in different historical contexts, forms which are related to corresponding forms of ownership and State power" (ibid., p. 203).

Frequently, these battles divided men and women within the working class, for they were not always a well-spring for collective resistance.[2] A growing amount of collective action in the 1820s, however, germinated in conflicts over the control of the labor process, entrance to trades, wages, and even of the existence of work itself. The impetus for these actions, their timing, and their moral justifications were forged in historical conflicts.

Recent critiques of class-struggle historiography argue that its centrality in the sphere of labor has been over-accentuated. Patrick Joyce, for example, maintains that too little attention has been paid to the natural cooperation between workers and employers (1990, pp. 163–164; 1992, p. 204). This materialist analysis defends class-struggle accounts by focusing attention on how work was both a focal point in and part of the integument of the class process.

The Spitalfields silk weavers lived with an accretion of such history that partly shaped their collective resistance in the 1820s. The particular history of the trade not only carved out a resilient structure and consciousness of work, it also colored the weavers' consciousness of domesticity, community, and citizenship. It was a politically charged and usable past, preserved and sculpted to battle current problems. Analyzing the weavers' collective actions and fighting words in the turbulent 1820s requires an understanding of this past. In summarizing it below, I emphasize the landmark struggles that became living memories and the dynamic features of the trade itself that made these memories so poignant.

I have subdivided the history of the trade into four parts. Part One reviews the rise of the trade in the eighteenth century and the events that led to the passing of the protective trade legislation known as the Spitalfields Acts, which became the moral foundation for the weavers' subsequent understanding of power in their trade. Parts Two and Three discuss changes in trade organization and production respectively, focusing on the overlooked dynamism of an industry often portrayed as stagnant. The changing face of the trade, although assuming age with a quiet dignity, had critical consequences that bore on the weavers in the 1820s and 1830s. This is particularly true in terms of control over outwork and the threats to the patriarchal authority of male weavers. Finally, in Part Four, I examine the history of unionism among the weavers and their strong, shop-based cohesion. Within this trade collectivism, the weavers nurtured a growing understanding of their class struggles.

---

[2] For work especially germane to these case studies, see Clark 1995; Morgan 1992; Rose 1992, 1993b; Valenze 1995; and Valverde 1988.

The Foundations of the Trade and the Spitalfields Acts — Conflict and Protection

The silk trade, averred a contemporary observer, was "a manufacture fostered by taste and fashion. The atmosphere it most delights in, is a crowded, opulent metropolis" (*Remarks* . . . , 1822, p. 19). Born of the immigration of the French Huguenot silk weavers at the end of the seventeenth century and protected by protectionist legislation, which one historian termed "mercantilism at its best," it picqued the attention of the higher ranks and merchant classes (Hertz 1898, p. 727). By 1713, the silk industry had grown to twenty times the size of what had existed some fifty years previously (p. 711). During the early part of the century, it experienced fluctuations that were broadly characteristic of the industry's later up and down trade cycles.

By mid-century, the expansion of an urban bourgeoisie allowed the trade to grow fat on the fancies of the well-to-do (Coleman 1969, p. 14). The Seven Years War also boosted production by cutting French imports, but by the mid-1760s peace returned to the Continent. The end of hostilities brought a renewed flow of French goods and depression in Spitalfields. By 1766, seven thousand looms stood idle (McCulloch 1834, p. 1030). Weavers became restive; grumbling turned to mobilization; and grim times without relief prompted a turn to action.

The Spitalfields Acts, the cornerstone of the weavers' existence, were born of collective violence of the 1760s and 1770s. Faced with inexorably deepening distress, weavers in tightly-knit pub-based organizations used demonstrations and destruction of looms and cloth to press their demands for trade protection in 1763, 1765, 1768, 1769, and 1771.[3] From the perspective of their moral economy of trade, the weavers viewed protection as the right of productive male labor to earn a secure livelihood for their families and to maintain independence and their honorable status in the trade and community. Depression and the piece-rate cuts it spawned threatened these foundations.

The rough justice of "cutting," the destruction of work still in the loom of masters resistant to piece-rate demands, marked the weavers as dangerous and fearsome combatants, as did their sometimes bloody confrontations with the authorities. As George Rudé observes, "Of all the groups of workers who used such devices to coerce their employers, none had so long a history of struggle, none were so remarkably persistent, and, maybe, none so violent as the silk weavers of Spitalfields" (1981, p. 72; see also see Linebaugh 1992, chap. 8).

---

[3] For accounts of these events, see Steinberg 1989, v. 1, pp. 132–141; and also Shelton 1972; Plummer 1972; and Hammonds 1967.

Tempestuous events, especially in 1769 and 1771, laid a foundation of both practical motivation and sympathetic understanding among the local authorities, who pressed for a political solution (Plummer 1972, p. 327; Hammonds 1967, p. 209). Politicking climaxed in the first of the famous Acts, 13 Geo. III c. 68, which on July 1, 1773, formally codified many of the weavers' paramount demands. The statute empowered city officers and local justices of the peace "to settle, regulate order and declare the wages and prices of work of the journeymen weavers' employed and working 'in the Silk Manufacture within their respective jurisdictions'" (Plummer 1972, p. 328; Bland, Brown, and Tawney 1919, pp. 547–551). In practical terms, it mandated a form of binding arbitration. Committees of masters and men first negotiated price lists for each of the articles manufactured in the district. Upon reaching an amicable accord, they then informed the local authorities, who validated the agreement. These negotiations were usually carried out successfully; however, in rare impasses the magistrates would adjudicate, usually basing their decisions on the price of provisions, to establish an equitable wage standard. Piece rates thus became in a substantive sense a "living wage," which in theory would support a male weaver and his family. Once prices were publicly fixed, they became inviolable, and both masters and men could be fined for deviating from the lists in either direction (Clapham 1916, pp. 460–461; Plummer 1972, pp. 328–329; L.S.P. CLVI, 1823, p. 157).

Several other important restrictions on trade practices were also enacted. Masters could supervise no more two apprentices at any one time. Another clause prohibited masters who employed weavers within the district from evading the law's provisions by hiring weavers beyond the confines of the Act's jurisdiction (Plummer 1972, p. 329; Clapham 1916, pp. 461–462).[4]

The passage of the 1773 Act was the triumphant culmination of a decade of bloody struggle. It elevated the weavers' moral economy to a *de jure* status, integrating the spheres of work and politics in their everyday lives. As a weavers' committee later argued, the Acts legitimized the belief that "when men forget the moral obligations due between man and man, and as often as they can take poor men's labor without fair compensation, it is high time to call in the strong arm of the law, and convince them that they must not oppress with impunity" (*Letters* . . . 1818, p. 43). The Acts legally sanctioned locally derived standards of the value of their labor, eschewing market-based constructions of wages. They also legitimized the notion that workers were entitled to a secure existence as productive members of the community. Moreover, at the time they seemed to secure the patriar-

---

[4] These provisions, particularly the clause on apprenticeship, were rarely enforced by the magistrates and were frequently evaded by the weavers themselves.

chal role of the male weaver in the domestic workshop and household as the family provider.[5]

Institutionalizing a social standard of remuneration had two other effects that chilled the maturation of a free labor market. First, the elasticity of the labor market was constricted. Weavers could be employed or not, but wages could not be reduced by increasing the labor pool. Similarly, masters could not permanently lower average wages through successive reductions in response to depressions or claims of increased competition.[6]

Second, the fixing of wages restricted the master's ability to extract fines and abrogate agreements, two basic mechanisms of labor control. Any reduction or non-payment of piece rates for claimed poor workmanship had to be adjudicated by a magistrate (P.P. 1818, IX, p. 190). As one commentator later maintained the Act "operates as a check of tyranny, as a bridle to rapaciousness. It prevents an avaricious master . . . from imposing on his men; it makes *him* just, and *them* industrious" (*Letters* . . . , 1818, p. 13, italicized in the original). This reinforced the weavers' notion of their right to a voice in trade governance, since manufacturers were legally bound to approach weavers' committees to negotiate piece rates.

The demarcation of trade activity within Spitalfields as an industrial vessel unto itself, charting a distinct and exclusive course from the industry's flotilla, reinforced these conceptions. Participation in the Spitalfields trade was privileged access to an economic sphere partially harbored from market capriciousness. These sentiments were shared by many of the lesser masters as well as by the weavers (Hammonds 1967, p. 211). More than just an idiosyncratic affirmation of the weavers' status, the Acts legally recapitulated a moral economy of labor and petty production whose tenets were the foundations of many artisanal ideologies. This moral economy contained a protean class consciousness, in that it recognized opposing interests between the world of the workshop and the magnates who controlled the trade.

In this context, the Acts stood out as a shining light of artisanal rights and for many, a wishful vision of an alternative normalcy. Their passage emboldened other groups, such as the silk weavers of Manchester and the masons of London, to assert their intention to prosecute masters violating apprenticeship clauses (Rule 1981, p. 111). Others, such as the Coventry ribbon weavers, were inspired to petition Parliament for similar provisions to regulate their own trade (Clapham 1916, pp. 463–464).

---

[5] In 1792, 32 Geo. III c. 44, extended the jurisdiction of the statutes to cover mixed goods, such as bombazines and poplins. In 1811, the laws were extended to cover journeywomen, under 51 Geo. III c. 7, an indication of the degree to which they had become fixtures at the loom (Clapham 1916, p. 462; Hammonds 1967, p. 209; Pinchbeck 1969, p. 176).

[6] Indeed, in testimony before the Lords' Committee on repeal of the Acts in 1823, Ambrose Moore, a champion of repeal, admitted that manufacturers had never approached the weavers' committee to negotiate reductions (L.S.P. CLVI, 1823, p. 155).

The weavers, in winning the bloody battle of trade protection, established themselves as emblematic guardians of trade rights for a vast number of the industrious poor. The Spitalfields Acts represented the bulwark of artisanal rights against the crass incursions of free trade during the succeeding decades. Of enormous significance, they deeply colored the silk weavers' consciousness of their rights and status. Moreover, the weavers' history of protracted and often violent contention was the stuff of a usable past, a memory of battles for rights that left a trail of cut silk and blood. This collective memory was to be pressed into service as the weavers' world came under siege.

The Organization of Production

Founded on the caprice of fashion and dependent on international supplies, security in the silk trade was a very slippery perch. Yet from the turn of the century through the next two decades Spitalfields witnessed a comparatively steady period of modest prosperity. Apart from the serious depression of 1816, these were halcyon days that set the context for later events.

The Spitalfields trade had always been subdivided between a variety of plain and fancy and figured goods. In the early nineteenth century, between a third and a half of the trade was devoted to the latter. The fancy trade especially was subdivided into a host of specialized branches, with fabrics such as velvets, lustres, and satins (P.P. 1832, XIX, pp. 39, 488, 716, 725, 735).

Each niche in the first decade and a half remained the preserve of a small group of independent master manufacturers who generally employed between 10 and 40 looms (Rothstein 1977, p. 286; Jordan 1931, p. 3; L.S.P. 1823, CLVI, p. 22). Much like the cloth that they wove and bartered, the merchants and weavers formed a dense web of petit-bourgeois tradespeople. In the interstices of the web of exchanges, some weavers elevated themselves into the ranks of the middling classes, while other endured on the margins, watching their meager existences fluctuate with the vagaries of demand.

The warp of this fabric was the weavers. Throughout most of the eighteenth century and into the nineteenth, many male weavers enjoyed the status of small masters, who after a traditional apprenticeship and stints as journeymen, tried to establish their market niche. This was particularly true in fancy goods such as brocades and velvets. With capital of between 50 and 100 pounds, such artisans could set up shop, employing two or three weavers on a yearly basis, and maintaining a respectable living (Jordan 1931, p. 2; L.S.P. 1823, CLVI, p. 20).

Circulation of marginal masters in and out of the trade made the accounting of their number difficult. In 1823, William Hale observed, "I do not apprehend that any individual Manufacturer knows half the Manufacturers in Spitalfields" (ibid., p. 22). John Poyton, a journeyman active in the weavers' trade committee, estimated the number of master manufacturers in 1823 at nearly 150 (B.L., Add. MSS. 27805, *An Account . . .* , 1823, p. 59; L.S.P. 1823, CLVI, p. 207). A listing of silk manufacturers in *Pigot and Co.'s London . . . Commercial Directory For 1822-3* shows a total of 205 manufacturers, close to half of whom had city addresses.[7] A little over one-third of this group had Spitalfields addresses, the traditional residence of the small master. This was the area where many had labored as journeymen and where their dreams of petty-bourgeois independence had been realized.

Appended to each master manufacturer was a stable of between 10 and 40 weavers, and masters preferred to retain the services of reliable workers. New hires were frequently done on the recommendation of their long-time employees (P.P. 1832, XIX, p. 715; P.P. 1834, X, p. 590; L.S.P. 1823, CLVI, p. 22). Since piece rates were fixed under the Acts, a major inducement to retain preferred hands was the meting out of work for the male weaver's wife and children, a practice that likely reinforced domestic patriarchy (ibid., p. 62).

Masters acquired necessary materials from a silkman or warehouser as in decades past. They passed on the organzine (warp thread) and tram (weft thread) to their weavers along with patterns and instructions and a cash advance to maintain the household. Credit was advanced by the wholesaler to the manufacturer on arrangements often spanning six to twelve months (P.P. 1832, XIX, p. 296). During pre-repeal prosperity, silk production serenely floated on this sea of long-term credit, sustaining the master manufacturer and his weavers until accounts were settled.

Throughout the early part of the pre-repeal period, the integrity of the status hierarchy of master, journeyman, and apprentice was largely maintained, and the gulf between the former two generally was not great (Jordan 1931, p. 156). Access to the more specialized branches particularly required formal apprenticeship. The apprenticeship system provided hereditary replacement, with children generally being brought up in their parents' trade. By the nineteenth century, the apprenticing of females was common, despite earlier attempts at restriction (P.P 1818, IX, p. 44).[8]

---

[7] Of the 199 identifiable addresses, fully 81 percent fell within the West End or Spitalfields (with 22 percent in Cheapside, 22 percent with other West End addresses, and 37 percent in Spitalfields). An additional 12 percent were located in the ward of Bishopsgate, the Old Artillery Ground, and the liberty of Norton Folgate, areas straddling these other locations. Only a handful of masters were listed in areas of more recent significant weaver concentration, such as Bethnal Green and Mile End New Town. To determine area location when it was not specifically listed in *Pigot's Directory*, I consulted James Elmes, *A Topographical Dictionary of London and Its Environs, London, 1831.*

[8] The apprenticing of females could have been viewed as a mark of degradation by male weavers. As Sally Alexander (1976) notes, the entrance of women into London trades was

During these years, the London silk industry increasingly differentiated into two worlds, those of the city and of the Spitalfields trades. Small masters composed the bulk of the latter, and they dealt with a variety of merchants at both ends of the production process. On one end was the mercer who brokered thrown silk, often with a standardized advance, and received manufactured orders to his specifications generally within four to six weeks. On the other end of petty exchange and production were the mackler and piece broker who would buy small lots of goods and ply them at local shops (George 1925, pp. 177–178; Lown 1990, p. 16).

Beyond this parochial world of petty production stood the city realm of the large brokerage, speculative capital, and international trade. All processes prior to the domestic production were within the purview of these merchants and manufacturers. Once silk moved through customs, it frequently passed into the hands of a silkman, typically a warehouser, whose stocks supplied the domestic thrower, the dyer, and the mercer.

Within this realm, a new breed of master manufacturers was on the rise. They came from both without and within the Spitalfields trade, but regardless of origins they willfully disregarded its customs. Merchant interlopers established warehouses in the west side of town, bypassing the mercers and membership in the largely moribund Weavers' Company (the old guild). Internally, silkmen and mercers who had managed to amass sizable stocks of capital (usually from 500 to 5,000 pounds) similarly founded such trading houses (Plummer 1972, p. 319; George 1925, pp. 177, 371 n. 64). In either case, many of these warehousemen were relative outsiders to the trade traditions, and few were steeped in the experience of apprenticeship. From this time onward, large capitalists and petty traders co-existed uneasily in an increasingly competitive market. The growing dominance of the former group represented the stirrings of a formidable threat for the weavers.

As we have seen, the ideal of the small master was integral to the weavers' conception of the trade. It offered hope for social mobility as well as assuaging fears of tyrannical control by entrepreneurs devoid of trade ethics. It also marked the weaver as an independent journeyman, a critical component of the identity of an honorable trade. By the 1800–1825 period, however, a steady turn to greater economies of scale and the rise of warehousers imperiled this organization. City wholesalers such as Lea & Wilson and Wilson and Moore controlled several hundred looms apiece through their warehouses (P.P. 1818, IX, pp. 59, 157; "Verax" 1822, p. 22).

---

taken as a clear sign of dishonorability. Certainly male weavers had resisted the entrance of women in the eighteenth century. The extension of the Acts to women in 1811, however, would suggest male resignation. By the 1810s, many households required the employment of all members, as inflation ate away at piece rates. As we shall see in a later section, by the post-repeal 1820s weavers were accepting unrelated females as apprentices in order to make ends meet.

By the dawn of the post-repeal era, one "friend to the trade" observed with alarm "that the silk trade is very much under the influence of a few leading houses, who are extremely active, and distinguished for their zeal and perseverance with which they endeavour (conscientiously, no doubt) to sustain their opinions" (P.C., set 16, v. 2, f. 32).

These warehouses or "slaughter houses" (a moniker coined with their growing infamy) developed several distinct advantages over their humbler counterparts. Given larger capital stocks, these large manufacturers could often respond to an upturn or change in fashion more readily. Further, by buying large lots they could afford to jettison goods onto a fickle market at less cost (Prothero 1979, p. 63). As with many other trades, nothing nurtured the fragile seedlings of success so well as money.

Warehousers also found an edge in their rationalization of the production, cutting both time and labor costs through consolidation. They assumed control over design and pattern instructions, eliminating some of the artistry from the ken of the highly-skilled weaver or small master (Manchee 1913, p. 336). Ancillary processes such as winding, warping, and finishing were subsumed within the warehouse by around 1810 (P.P. 1840, XXIII, pt. II, p. 236). For these secondary jobs, the benevolent Spitalfields Acts stood helplessly mute; wages and conditions were at the employer's discretion.

The rise of the warehousers divided the trade into two antagonistic camps. On the city side stood the warehousers, nascent market magnates not born of the trade. Two of the large masters more vocally hostile to the Spitalfields Acts, Thomas Gibson and Ambrose Moore, had virtually no weaving experience between them (P.P. 1818, IX, pp. 143, 161). On the other side were the small masters, who sported their journeyman's background as an honorific badge of their trade roots. To them, the warehousers' growing dominance signaled intensified competition and even the specter of annihilation. One such prescient master, forecasting a silk trade without protection of the Acts, predicted "there will be but Two Classes, the great Capitalists and the Labourers" (L.S.P. 1823, CLVL, p. 101).

By the 1810s, skirmishes between the two groups defined the market. Beyond these battles, however, was the even more public struggle over trade leadership. Debates over the utility of the Spitalfields Acts and other trade matters brought a contentious air to the quiet of normal trade practice (P.P. 1818, IX, pp. 185, 197). Increasing friction crystallized into a structure of trade antagonism. The weavers and small masters found strength in allying against the large capitalist interlopers. This bifurcation strongly influenced the weavers' conception of master-servant relations. While a nascent anticapitalist critique of industrial relations was developing among certain radicals and trade groups, weavers were often wont to distinguish between honorable and dishonorable masters. The former group shared their origins, sense of trade order, and dreams. Small masters were even elected to weavers' committees, whose task it was to uphold the Acts and the piece-rate lists (Bretano 1870, p. 127). This proclivity to support their trade brethren, and the reciprocal activities of the small masters, reinforced the weavers' moral economy of labor. Nonetheless, we should not misread this alliance as a sign of the absence of class consciousness among the weavers; rather we should perhaps see it as its incipient manifestation. Weavers were allying with small masters who were of the world of working people against a largely alien and threatening group. As Behagg argues in the case of the metal trades, "the class proximity between artisans and the small masters, in terms of nature, function, and self-image was precisely the cutting edge of working-class consciousness in this period" (1990, p. 78).

Apart from this growing rift, other forces impinged on the trade, forces that stretched beyond local confines and parochial concerns. For both master and weaver, two principal concerns were the rise of the "country" trade competitors and the smuggling of foreign goods, the former being the greatest worry. Portions of both the plain and fancy trades slowly had been leaving Spitalfields for many decades, as manufacturers had immigrated in search of lower wages and other cloth manufacturers, outside the trade, sought entrance. Much of this migration occurred in the lower end of the main branches, although Spitalfields did lose some of the production of prized figured goods (*Observations* ... 1822, pp. 26–27; *Remarks* ... 1822, p. 19; Porter 1831, p. 299; L.S.P. 1823, CLVI, pp. 13, 109, 126, 132, 150). Although much of this productive capacity grew in London's hinterlands, the rise of southeastern Lancashire as a weaving area was an ominous threat.

Production in the North was concentrated in Manchester, where 50 manufacturers had established houses by the 1820s, and across the border to the south in the Cheshire town of Macclesfield where there were 5,000 looms. As the fancy trade diminished in Spitalfields, the two regions grew more closely competitive, given the lower Northern wages. Manchester particularly threatened the integrity of the Spitalfields trade because, unlike Macclesfield, it arose outside of the silk industry proper and the structure of the Spitalfields piece-rate system (Davies 1961, p. 123; L.S.P. 1823, CLVI, pp. 55, 123; P.P. 1832, XIX, pp. 340, 741; P.P. 1833, VI, pp. 295–296, 306).

The shadowy world of French goods smuggling was a more immediate threat and a source of unending anxiety to local fancy goods producers. The damage caused by smuggling was one of the few points of agreement between trade defenders, warehousers, and political economists (Jordan 1931, p. 152; P.P. 1832, XIX, p. 502; *Hans.*, n.s., v. 14, 1826, c. 799; P.C., set 16, v. 2, ff. 10, 18). This illicit trade was so profitable that some Spitalfields manufacturers went through the elaborate ruse of having their goods shipped offshore and returned under the cover of darkness to give them the appearance of illegal French items. Although no accurate account of smuggling was possible, many claimed increased pressure from it as the years passed.

Perhaps to the idle observer who strolled down a weavers' lane in the 1820s the trade remained in an enduring, even complacent, stasis. The clack of the looms filled the air; weavers moved to and fro transporting materials and finished products; and the domestic workshop anchored the daily round of life. Yet behind this facade great changes had been wrought. All of these pressures were to converge on the domestic workshop, the foundation of the weavers' honorable status.

The World of the Workshop

Mr. Culver was rather surprised by the first view of Cooper's apartment this night. Its atmosphere was apparently made up of the remains of the orange fog of the morning . . . candles seemed to yield one-tenth part light, and the rest to be made up of yellow tallow, wick growing into perpetual cauliflowers, and smoke. The loom was going, with its eternal smack and tick, serving, in co-operation with the gap under the door, for as an admirable ventilator as could be wished for on the hottest day in August. Mrs. Cooper was discharging many offices in her person; being engaged now in snuffing the rapidly-wasting candles, now in giving a fresh impulse to the rocking cradle, but chiefly tying the threads of her husband's work, while he was intent, with foot, hands, and eye, on the complicated operations of his craft. (Martineau 1833, pp. 17–18)

Martineau provides her readers with an idyllic view of the weaving family at home. In almost diametric opposition stands another contemporary characterization:

The Spitalfields Weaver occupies a small tenement which, though newly-built, has, like himself, all the appearances of premature decay. His workshop is a long room, lighted front and back with a frame of small leaded windows, several of which are wanting, and their places supplied by old rags or paper, as may be most convenient. There are two looms in the apartment, at one of which is seated the father, a jaded man in a worsted nightcap, and a pair of gray stocking sleeves. At the other loom is employed a sickly boy of ten years of age, clad in a calico night shirt and a pair of corduroy trousers, suspended by a piece of list running traversely over his shoulder. . .

Full sixteen hours the Weaver keeps the treadles in motion with his feet, and the shuttle with his hands. He sees no such amazing hardship in this; a certain quantity of silk must be wove *per diem* to procure a certain quantity of food, . . . On extraordinary occasions, however, when the doctor is attending his wife for instance, he labors for an additional hour or two. If death be in his house, the Sunday is no day of rest for him. (Armitage, n.d., pp. 264–265)

In reality, of course, Armitage's depiction is far closer to the mark, especially after the mid-1820s. By this period, much as the weavers' tattered effects, years of wear in poor conditions had left many physically and spiritually maimed. Yet despite this, a kernel of truth lay in Martineau's depiction, an ideal for which the weavers struggled mightily. Male weavers especially wove a collective identity of respectability from their conceptions of the artistry, skill, and independence. Regardless of the political turbulence that swirled outside the protected district, this collective identity was anchored in the domestic quarters, and it all started at the loom seat.

The workshop was gendered through what Anna Clark (1995) has termed a system of patriarchal cooperation. Although male weavers clearly exercised authority, they also realized the necessity of women's contributions. In the 1780s and 1790s, male journeymen fought unsuccessfully to keep their male preserve; by the early nineteenth century, the exigencies of the household economy overawed male exclusivity.[9] Male weavers lobbied to have the Spitalfields Acts extended to women, and a clause was passed by Parliament in 1811 mandating equal application of the book rates. Women, however, still often made less then men, both because domestic responsibilities interfered with productivity and because men were the intermediaries between the warehouse and the household. Male journeymen thus recognized the importance of women and children to the workshop economy, while maintaining control both over its operations and its voice in the trade and community. The recognition that domestic solidarity was a foundation for economic security partially mitigated the misogynist cultures found in other metropolitan trades such as tailoring (P.P. 1835, VII, pp. 10–11; P.P. 1818, IX, pp. 44, 148; L.S.P. CLVI, 1823, pp. 5, 56, 62, 102, 126–128; Clark 1995, pp. 126–127; George 1925, pp. 181–182; Jordan 1931, p. 12; Pinchbeck 1969, pp. 168, 176–177; Sholl 1812, p. 34; *TN*, Feb. 23, 1828).

The average domestic workshop contained two to three looms. The standard silk loom was a more delicate version of looms used for weaving heavier cloths, although from its stark wooden figure could emerge a bewildering array of fabrics. The price book for 1821 contains 91 pages covering 27 basic fabrics and 2,150 further distinct sub-articles.

The weaving of plain broadcloth was the task of the apprentice, the less-

---

[9] There are bits of evidence to suggest that by the 1820s male weavers were even accepting girls with no kin ties as apprentices. It is possible that the apprenticeship premium became an important source of additional income, particularly after the repeal of the Spitalfields Acts (which I discuss below) (*TN*, Sept. 18, Oct. 9, 1825; Jan. 22, 1826).

skilled males, and women. It was universally recognized as a process that required little ingenuity and was viewed as a stepping stone to more complex work. The basic operation was readily learned, although dexterity, uniformity, and speed took cultivation. The simple repetitive task was performed by raising and lowering warp threads with foot treadles while passing the shuttle containing the tram (or shoot) back and forth in its trough. A hand batten aligned the completed throw. In addition, the warp required "picking the porry," the occasional combing to remove knots and waste dust that could mar the finish of the cloth (Porter 1831, pp. 222–223, 274).

The productivity of the weaver depended on the facility and speed with which he or she could operate the shuttle and treadles. An average weaver generally produced from 3.5 to 4.5 yards of broad cloth per diem, with an average work day of 12 hours (P.P. 1832, XIX, pp. 213, 350). Some appreciation of the tedium of the process can be gained by realizing that each inch of woven silk contained hundreds of tram threads.

Plain weaving thus was viewed as largely inglorious and monotonous. Even this relatively simple process, however, was subject to degradation. Processes preparatory to weaving, especially the setting up of the loom and warp, were part of the standard repertoire of knowledge that many a tyro had learned in a traditional apprenticeship. The warping process was a delicate operation, since as many as 8,000 warp threads had to be manipulated in a 20-inch breadth of warp, and preparation took several weeks on complicated fabrics (P.P. 1832, XIX, p. 218; L.S.P. 1823, CLVI, p. 140). Although plain weavers could not define themselves as skilled, the warping process helped them maintain at least an aura of expertise. Capitalist rationalization of the production system withdrew this function from many workshops and signaled degradation. For the male household head, it wrested away the supervision and control he had over his wife and children, who usually aided him in this process. Many apprentices brought into service for city masters never learned the preparatory arts. By the mid-1820s, a sector of degraded weavers emerged within the trade who were little more than shuttlecock throwers (George 1925, p. 189; P.P. 1840, XXIII, pt. 2, p. 235).

For those involved in the production of fancy goods, the substance of skill remained mostly intact. The aristocratic air of satins, velvets, and other rich goods lent status to their producers. Weavers in these branches were schooled in the complex mechanics of setting the loom up for detailed work and intricate designs. The labor process itself, which involved far more exacting loom craft, ensured respectable standing (Rothstein, p. 281; Tomlinson, v. 3, p. 958; P.P. 1832, XIX, p. 213).

The skill hierarchy was reinforced by a finely graded piece-rate hierarchy of significant breadth. "There can be no doubt," wrote one observer, "that between different branches of silk weaving, a great inequality of remuneration exists" (*Remarks* . . . 1822, p. 38). General books or lists of piece rates had been produced for the trade seven times from 1784 to 1806, with each rate book containing a full range of prices. Partial lists were also published in later years. Throughout much of the decade and a half before the repeal many of the prices of new variations of fabrics (perhaps as much as 25 percent of all articles) were mutually agreed upon and never formally printed as specified by the Acts (P.P. 1818, IX, p. 188; Clapham 1916, pp. 463, 470).

The average rate for variations of a standard broadcloth was from 9 to 11d. per yard. For most weavers, net of deductions and including short periods of idleness for loom changes, this came to an average weekly wage of between 12 and 15 shillings per week. This was not a lucrative sum; by one estimate, plain weavers earned about half that of an industrious carpenter. The actual average weekly intake was often less. Weavers not only suffered from periodic bouts of unemployment due to fashion demands, but also had to contend with periods of idleness between pieces, a period termed "play" in the trade. In the fancy trades, wages could be significantly higher, with the range varying from a little over 1 shilling to as much as 4–5 shillings per yard. The spectrum of weekly earnings hung in the range of between 15–20 shillings to 20–24 shillings per week (L.S.P., 1823, CLVI, pp. 86, 125; P.P. 1818, IX, pp. 40, 46, 141, 188; *Letters* . . . , 1818, pp. 11, 40–41; P.P. 1832, XIX, pp. 209, 213, 285, 299).

Although the price books served as a comparative guide of a trade's worth vis-à-vis other industries, they had equally important internal implications. The vast majority of weavers probably earned no more than 14–16 shillings per week, but the price books offered a potentiality of much more. With between one-third to as much as one-half of the trade engaged in the production of fancy goods, the prospects of diligence, experience, and sweat yielding long-term benefits were more than just chimerical visions. The hierarchy of wages represented the possibility of mobility, the mark of any respectable trade. Conversely, one of the sure marks of degraded or dishonorable trades was the beating down of piece rates and the sweating of labor (Thompson 1966, p. 258). The immutability of the piece rates represented collective privilege and rights—vital features of the trade's continuing integrity.

The piece rates, as well as providing a "fair and equitable" remuneration, buttressed the weavers' status in the community as artisans and heads of households. Through their provision of a moderate but stable income, the weavers argued: "We have been kept from general pauperism, and the public by reason of our industry have been able to carry on their business in supplying our numerous body with necessaries of life; and we, as useful members of society, have been able to provide for our families, and support the parishes, instead of being paupers on the same" (*An Account . . .* , 1823, p. 20).

The line between community respectability and pauperism was drawn precariously thin for many of the industrious poor. In a world populated by the petty-bourgeois and the respectable artisanate, pauperism was the scourge of community standing. The legitimacy of workers' claims to the privileges of a communal voice were based on their capacity to meet socially construed standards of communal obligation. Independence from the poor rates (and, indeed, adding to the coffers of the same) and socially productive labor (i.e., market-salable trade labor from which others benefited directly and otherwise) were the cornerstones of these obligations in Spitalfields.

The silk weavers' wages permitted them a buffer of security between this legitimate standing in the polity and the outcast status of pauperism. In addition, they allowed the cultivation of a literate and multifarious working-class culture, by at least a part of the weavers. This cultural life embellished and solidified the foundations of their standing.

In sum, the silk weavers, in terms of skill, privilege, or wages, were unlikely candidates for the title of labor aristocrats. Equally, they were somewhat safeguarded from being piled on the refuse heap of casual and sweated labor. In a world increasingly reduced to stark divisions between privileged crafts and the mass of the laboring poor, the weavers managed, almost defiantly, to hold their middle ground. Knowledge, experience, and technical facility in the fancy branches signaled silk weaving as a learned body of productive practice. Minimum levels of wage security, and the possibility of higher levels of comfort, differentiated the weavers from the dross below. This income also served as a ticket of legitimacy within the local polity. All rested on a set of trade rights, wrapped in the legal protection of the Spitalfields Acts, that the weavers implicitly understood to be meritoriously theirs by right of their production. These were clarion interests as the clashes of the late 1760s and early 1770s illustrated, and woe to anyone who would threaten them. When those threats materialized, they sharply impinged on the weavers' consciousness and begged for a response.

Combinations and Unions—The Continuity of Organization

Although the silk weavers relished their respectable standing, they were not content to rest on it as the sole assurance of their security. Their saga reveals an almost continuous history of branch or community organization, punctuated by intermittent loose confederations to meet particular exigencies. Such confederations served as venues in which the weavers could act out their roles as members of an honorable trade and maintain solidary networks for rapid mobilization. They were critical in the development of collective action repertoires, a discourse of struggle, and an emergent class consciousness.

The weavers operated within benefit societies almost from their inception, which in the turbulence prior to the Acts were transformed into militant units to press for rights. In the public houses, where city masters were never found and women perhaps often unwelcome, trade solidarity was regularly primed with conviviality. Several efforts were made in the 1770s, 1790s, and early 1800s to create "unions" of all benefit societies, but these were largely chimeras of ambitious organizing (Goodway 1984, p. 188; Manchee 1913, p. 322; Sholl 1812, pp. 4–6, 9–11; Warner 1921, pp. 505–508; Webbs 1920, p. 55). From the turn of the century, the weavers' organizations remained hidden in the shadows of history and the public house.

These corners of plebeian life are now so obscure that it is unclear whether the weavers maintained a standing general union during these decades. Many manufacturers, aggrieved by the weavers' prosecution of list-price violations, clearly believed that the weavers were in a constant state of conspiracy (*Letters* . . . 1818, p. 27). Less shrill claims concerning the weavers' organization and actions were added by other manufacturers during parliamentary hearings. A critical mass of frustrated manufacturers even formed their own organization in 1805 and offered ten guineas for information leading to the convictions of involved weavers, but they found no takers (P.P. 1818, IX, pp. 55, 158; L.S.P. 1823, CLVI, pp. 72, 155). Undoubtedly, almost all weavers would have considered such a sum a fool's reward.

The weavers vigorously claimed that the standing committee was the masters' illusory bogey and denied that they maintained any regular fund. They staunchly argued that ad hoc committees of two or three persons were formed in response to specific complaints and that their levies were purely voluntary (*Letters* . . . 1818, p. 42; P.P. 1818, IX, pp. 188, 194–196). The truth probably lies in an uncertain middle ground. In a September 1817 circular following a general trade meeting, "the Committee" lamented that subscriptions had at times dropped to as low as a third of the trade. They proudly noted 50 successful prosecutions over the preceding nine months, a figure, which if true, would certainly have been sufficient to gore the ox of many manufacturers. Moreover, manufacturers testified in other hearings of routine negotiations with weavers' representatives (L.S.P. 1823, CLVI, pp. 143, 147; P.P. 1818, IX, p. 55).

In 1823, with the manufacturers rattling their political sabers to repeal the Acts, the male weavers again solidified their societies' networks. A committee consisting of members proportionate from all branches was elected to conduct lobbying and publicity efforts. Two were also appointed for fund raising and accounting, while a solicitor, Robert Brutton, was appointed legal counsel (*An Account* . . . , pp. 11–12).[10]

The activities of these committees demonstrate a sophisticated organizational dynamics and suggest that this ground was as well-trodden as the sawdust on the pub floor. Two public houses served as dissemination points for information. Nightly briefings by committee members kept weavers abreast of the high-stakes politics that would determine the balance of their lives. A steady stream of memorials ran from Spitalfields to Westminster. So well organized were the weavers, that in a space of several days they garnered 21,000 signatures on a petition presented to the House of Lords on the first reading of the Repeal Bill. Several thousand weavers, male and female, were routinely mobilized to assemble in front of Parliament to reinforce their position with the silent but implicitly foreboding force of their numbers (Ibid., pp. 27, 29, 32, 47). The alliance of organizations provided the foundation for the mobilization through established repertoires as well as their transformation.

Both the success of the weavers in halting the passage of repeal and the continued peril of its pursuit by manufacturers gave rise to a renewed desire for a general silk weavers' union. From December 1823, the central committee rapidly progressed toward that goal. On February 24, 1824, the weavers inaugurated a "General Trade Union." Societies and ten public houses each selected two or three delegates (B.L., Add. MSS. 27799, *An Appeal* . . . ; B.L., Add. MSS. 27799, *Rules and Orders* . . .).

A perusal of the committee members' names from each campaign suggests a breadth of participation among male weavers, a penchant for democratic representation, and the temporary nature of centralized organization. There was a small number of carryovers from the last torch bearers, but the movement of men through positions of authority is indicative of the voice in trade affairs for which they argued in their campaigns. This was small "d" democracy, an organizational form resistant to the tyranny of centralized control and indicative of the moral economy of self-proclaimed honorable artisans. It was an enactment of a world in which the male vox populi of the trade was put on equal standing to the authoritative speech of large capital.

Three aspects of the weavers' lives ensured a relatively dense network of bridging ties to sustain mobilization. First, the congregation of weavers in neighborhoods within the district, because of the patterning of the housing stock, created ample opportunities for interaction. Second, many weavers crossed parish borders in search of livelihood and affordable

---

[10] Brutton illustrates the complex weave of district relations in which the weavers operated. He reappears in the post-repeal period as a champion of the increasingly destitute weavers, although this time in his role as the vestry clerk for St. Matthew's, Bethnal Green (*TN*, Jan. 25, 1826; *TFP*, Sept. 24, 1826, June 3, 1827).

housing, and at each juncture new neighborhood ties were crystallized. Finally, the mobility of the weavers themselves between branches also created bridging ties.

The weavers were thus highly facile actors in the business of mobilization. Their branch societies, nurtured in the insulated world of the public house, upheld trade law, custom, and male honor for decades after the passage of the Acts. When the weavers peered out from the public house in the ensuing years to measure the hostile forces in the city, they realized the importance of employing every bit of this organizational savvy. Moreover, this history of organization provided the strong foundations for a consciousness of struggle against forces they deemed fundamentally hostile to their honorable world of work.

These weavers' societies became increasingly critical as the 1820s progressed. The stable patterns of production that had ensured honorability came increasingly under threat from the rise of the large manufacturers. Their rising tide was eroding the foundations of the small masters and journeymen, creating the conditions for the increased conflict which motivated a developing class consciousness.

CHAPTER FOUR

Local Political Culture: From Reciprocity to Hegemony

The process of class was energized in the sphere of labor, but it percolated in diverse areas of social and political life. Within the larger community, political ties—mutually recognized rights and obligations—were equally the stuff of class. Within these relations, weavers and other working people mastered languages of political obligations that could be appropriated as fighting words. Also within this local political culture, lines of power and culpability were publicly drawn. As Theodore Koditschek reminds us of Thompson's vision of class formation, it "is a concrete historical process that evolves within the life of the actual human community, generating its wider social solidarities out of common experiences that can be felt on a more immediate and comprehensible plane" (1990, p. 22). That plane was often the common ground of the civil parish and its community.

Thompson's critics have widely questioned the link between class and community. Craig Calhoun (1982, 1983) argues that in the transformation to modernity the development of class and an urban industrial order, and the maintenance of community stood in fairly clear tension. Patrick Joyce, in his analysis of class conflict and deference in Victorian Lancashire textile towns, questions the link between urbanization and the class divide. He maintains that the propinquity of working peoples' social lives to those of their employers fostered a consciousness of deference rather than division (1975, pp. 116–119). In a different light, James Vernon suggests that town politics was a set of symbolic practices through which parish and community "talked to itself" and constituted a civic identity, often in ceremonial harmony rather than divisiveness, and frequently through an idiosyncratic local political dialectic rather than the language of class (1993, Chap. 2).

In one sense, these critiques of a link between working-class formation and urban development rightly question a mechanistic understanding of such ties. Critics, however, have often reified the process of working-class formation by seeking to find either the ganglia of the body politic laid bare in open conflict, or the unquestioned domination of capitalist authority oppressing a discontented mass. In fact, our second case does have some affinities with the latter image, but this should not confuse what class processes in the community were about.

As Ira Katznelson argues, the connections between class and community are contingent and historical, dependent on the interactions between developments in the processes of capital accumulation and the transformation of state power (1992, see esp. pp. 239–252). In the nineteenth-century English case, he finds that the forced retrenchment and suppression of trade unionism, coupled with the formal exclusion of working people from the polity, inlaid forms of working-class organization and consciousness in community life. Class and community ties thus became mutually nurturing. This conjuncture can be found both in Spitalfields and (as we shall see later) Ashton and Stalybridge in the micro-social and political structures of working peoples' lives. For the silk weavers, this conjoining foremost created and sustained alliances within circuits of local power. These alliances were cemented by a dense web of economic ties, both public and private, the accumulation and expenditure of status as a currency for civic privilege, and the administration of justice to legally sanctify these circuits. Working people most often first sought solidarity amongst their ranks and also with the petty-bourgeoisie with whom they worked and lived in daily life. But these alliances were often effected against bourgeois incursions into this plebeian world to control their lives through both civic and economic means.[1] The attempted transformations in the spatial relations of power in weavers' communities illustrates this process of class formation in the great working-class swath of East End life. It also provided the context within which struggles unfolded.

The silk weavers had a legitimate public presence and voice in the parishes of Spitalfields, particularly Bethnal Green, and this in part was a reflection of trade respectability. Their status as honorable artisans was their public garb of community life and a license of recognition. Within the parishes, it was equated with civic worthiness, including the right of protec-

---

[1] See Richard Whipp's refutation of Calhoun and his analysis of mutually reinforcing workplace-community links (1985, p. 775).

tion and maintenance that was the lot of the parish to provide. Civic duty and right were played out in a public political theater that had been well scripted over decades. In each parish, a web of reciprocal ties, founded on face-to-face relations and knotted by petty patronage, served as the mechanism of governance. In addition, weavers waited upon, and at times suffered through, the graces of local magistrates for the dispensing of justice. Since the trades relied on magistrates for the authoritative definition of a just price, the bench cast a long and definitive shadow across the trade landscape.

The silk weavers, however, increasingly found themselves in between the web of reciprocity and the net of hegemony. In the latter case, bourgeois charities sought a foothold as agents of social control in the local order, an alien presence toward whom working people often cast an equivocal eye. These legions of bourgeois morality marched into Spitalfields to impress the virtues of the Christian path, seeking a hegemonic foothold in a world that was both foreign and formidable to their sensibilities. In these actions, two class cultures crossed paths.

Despite bourgeois evangelism, the Spitalfields district was a fertile field for working-class political radicalism. The East End was a breeding ground for all manner of critique, including the blasphemous and the revolutionary. The silk weavers surely were cognizant of this political underbelly, but, as we shall see, for most of the period many of them seem to have been reluctant radicals.

The Parish and the People: Ties of Reciprocity

Local governance was largely the responsibility of the parish vestry, the collectivity of rate (tax) payers, who met certain property qualifications.[2] Vestry meetings were held quarterly, and open vestry meetings could be raucous political affairs. Through entrenched corruption, as in Bethnal Green, they often became rubber stamps of the existing order (Webbs 1906, pp. 79–90; Gurney 1819, *passim*). Each parish was chartered under authority of Parliament through local Acts, although the mechanics of governance were substantively similar (P.P. 1834, xxxv, app. B. 2, pt. 1, pp. 83f, 87f).

In Christ Church, Spitalfields, a board of thirty governors and five overseers were annually appointed by the vestry. The latter group collected rates, investigated claims upon the parish, and disbursed relief. Overseers never held successive terms, and their appointments were staggered by

---

[2] In Bethnal Green, this qualification was every adult male inhabitant who occupied premises rated at least 15 pounds per year, or 10 pounds per year for a former Overseer, which by the late 1810s was about 1,100 men (Webbs 1906, p. 80; Gurney 1819, v. 1, pp. 32, 77, 153). This was significantly more encompassing of the population than what we shall see in Ashton and Stalybridge.

pairs, ensuring some sitting experience. Along with a clerk, treasurer, independent auditors, workhouse administrator, and an array of minor vestry functionaries, some one hundred individuals in each parish were entangled in the administration of poor relief. The parish of St. Matthew, Bethnal Green, had thirty two governors and directors of the parish, although under his long rule parish boss and treasurer Joseph Merceron effectively controlled the vestry finances (ibid.; Gurney 1819, v. 1, p. 23).

The other side of vestry administrative responsibility was the watch and lamp. The watch and the local police were supervised by the parish treasurer. In Christ Church, the watch was usually composed of between twenty and thirty watchmen, two inspectors, a beadle and a constable. Special constables could also be sworn in, swelling the number of peace officers by over one hundred in special instances. The watchmen and inspectors who made regular patrols received daily wages for each watch (P.P. 1817, VII, p. 110; P.P. 1828, VI, pp. 90–93).

The mechanics of parish justice and relief were thus put in motion by about one hundred and fifty community members selected by the vestry membership or its authorities. The overwhelming majority of the latter hailed from the ranks of the petty bourgeoisie, usually tradesmen or small merchants. Tradesmen also predominated among the watchmen, although a few artisans were sprinkled in as well. The watch took as its primary responsibility the maintenance of their community's moral integrity (P.P. 1817, VII, p. 110; P.P. 1828, VI, pp. 92–94). So long as the peace was kept, and moral standards were not openly flouted, the watch functioned unobtrusively in plebeian life. They did not, in particular, serve as surrogate eyes and ears of local employers or the magistracy to expose the partially shrouded world of working-class radicalism.

The administrative apparatus for the poor relief was more active and paternalistic. The boards and related offices were populated with tradesmen and merchants, especially purveyors of foodstuffs and basic provisions (P.P. 1834, XXXV, app. B.2, pt. 1., p. 83f). In the exemplary years of 1828–1831, such merchants accounted for one-third of those elected to vestry offices. The remaining members of the board were almost entirely from the ranks of the respectable artisanate or other merchants, the familiar world of the weavers' web of daily life. Conspicuous in their scarcity are silk manufacturers, with only four serving on the board over these years. The weavers themselves had equal representation during the period (Christ Church Spitalfields Vestry Minute Books, 1828–1831).[3]

Patronage, cronyism, and laxity for fiscal detail seem to have been some

---

[3] The analysis covers eighty-two office appointments with listed occupations for each officer and tallies occupational listings, not individuals. Members of the parish were allowed to serve two terms on the board, although not in successive years. For the purposes of this analysis, I deemed it more important to dissect the occupational composition of the vestry board rather than the continuity in membership.

of the more outstanding features of parish administration in the early nineteenth century. With the vestry authorities determining the rates and exemptions, friends in the vestry were valuable assets. During the first decade and a half, landlords heavily greased the wheels of local administration (P.P. 1834, XXIX, app. A, pt. III, pp. 111–112a).

Tenants could benefit through lower rates and exclusions, but the nexus of benevolence was in the provision of outdoor relief. Generally, outdoor relief was provided to parishioners who lacked employment. Temporary relief could be distributed by an overseer on request (with proof of residence), but more permanent relief (in theory) required a site visit.[4] Applicants deemed able-bodied by a board review could be sent to the workhouse. In Bethnal Green, this board met weekly, dispensing aid for which they were later reimbursed. Maximum weekly allowances were generally no more than a meager 5 shillings in Spitalfields, although those for a family might reach ten to fourteen shillings per week. Although the support of the working poor was proscribed by the Poor Laws, overseers distributed wage supplements in times of exceptional distress. In these circumstances, community standing and artisanal respectability became an essential currency. Most importantly, overseers were given virtually complete discretion in aid disbursement (P.P. 1814–1815, III, p. 77; P.P. 1817, VI, pp. 32–33, 45; P.P. 1834, XXIX, app. A, pt. III, pp. 107–108a; P.P 1834, XXXV, app. B. 2, pp. 83h, 87h).

In this discretion lay the essence of a reciprocity between the merchant or tradesman and the weaver, couched in a moral economy of community maintenance. The male silk weaver, as a member of the industrious poor, a household head, and a usual rate payer, claimed relief by virtue of his independent and productive status. For the merchant or tradesman, this moral economy contained both ethical and pragmatic logic. Weavers were among their staple trade, and the well-being of the merchant was inextricably tied to them. Failure of a merchant to dole out relief when requests were made in front of customers could "raise mischievous tumults, and injure his business by their clamours and obstructions" (P.P. 1834, XXXV, app. A., pt. III, p. 117a). Moreover, under the moral economy of community, maintenance of the industrious poor was a recognition of their contributions to the larger well-being.

While the weavers abhorred parish relief and its connotations of dependency, it was an accepted communal right in times of dearth. During three such periods, 1800–1801, 1811–1812, and 1816–1817, the weavers extended their hands toward the parish. In the latter two cases, estimates were that as many as two thirds of Spitalfields looms stood idle for

---

[4] Residency requirements for the parish of Christ Church were a 4 shilling per week rent payment, paid over a continuous forty-day period. As with almost all parishes, Christ Church had "friendly order" arrangements with neighboring parishes to return nonresident paupers to their parish of official settlement (P.P. 1817, VI, p. 42).

stretches of time (*Philanthropist*, 1814, p. 185). During the 1816 crisis, Christ Church was aiding 360 people per week through outdoor relief, immensely straining the parish coffers (McCann 1977, p. 3; P.P. 1817, VI, p. 31; P.P. 1818, IX, p. 42).

Occasional parish assistance thus served to legitimate the weavers' status as honorable tradesmen, demarcating them from the idleness and parasitism of debased and casual toil. Weavers and tradespeople structured a worldview on which their daily lives were reciprocally enabled and ennobled. Moreover, this affirmation of the weavers' status validated the Spitalfields Acts, upon which their security depended. It was a circuit of moral logic that ensured social standing and modest economic security.

Additional affirmation of the weavers' status was provided by the local magistracy. The Spitalfields area fell under the jurisdiction of the Worship Street office in Bethnal Green. Individuals rejected by the board for outdoor relief could request that the bench overturn the judgment. Parish officers complained about the magistrates' liberality and sympathy. "If we were not to relieve [the casual poor]," lamented R. Brutton of Christ Church, "the alternative (which the weavers know) [would be] an application to the magistrates, who are sure to give an order against the parish" (P.P. 1834, XXXV, app. B.2, pt. 4, p. 83h, app. A., pt. 3, pp. 116a, 122a).

Such interventions were but one example of the defining qualities of the bench in weavers' lives. The law, as E. P. Thompson has reproved, "did not keep politely to a 'level' but was at *every* bloody level; it was imbricated within the mode of production and productive relations themselves . . . above all it was an arena for class struggle, within which alternative notions of law were fought out" (1978, p. 96). Indeed, for the weavers the law was bloody well about. Magistrates interceded in the whole tissue of labor relations. Sometimes, this was through mere presence, a potential inscribed in the Spitalfields Acts or other master and servant laws. At other times, it was through animated intervention in protracted conflict. In the matter of piece rates, as specified by the Acts, many large manufacturers believed that "the very touch of the Magistrate is paralyzing to the trade" (L.S.P. 1823, CLVI, p. 163).

The law inscribed these class relations with meaning, both through its administration of and discourses on justice. The magistrates played an essential role in defining and legitimizing the field of force of the weavers' moral economy. If the maintenance of a just price of labor was a positive manifestation of this defining power, prosecution for a series of offenses, particularly those of embezzlement, was the underbelly.

"To study embezzlement and associated frauds," observes John Styles, is "to study a major arena of conflict between capital and labour over the control of the labour process under the putting-out system" (1988, p. 174). The rights and status of the honorable artisan were partly realized through customary gleanings (Randall 1990; Rule 1980, chap. 5; Styles

1985, pp. 209–210). Linebaugh (1985) has argued for the eighteenth-century case that the laws of larceny represented the bellwether of change in the English legal system. Theft stood foursquare in the conceptualization of property, and property cum commodity-form was the lifeblood of capitalism. The transformation was from a definition of larceny as a betrayal of a hierarchical personal relationship to the transgression of a reified private domain (p. 222). As it was for larceny in the general case, so it was for embezzlement.

For the Spitalfields weavers, the essence of the triadic relationship of master, servant, and property was played out in the prosecution of embezzlement, which was a means of embellishing a modest income, and the weavers were old practitioners (Linebaugh 1992, pp. 264–268). They embezzled by dampening or adding soap or starch during the weaving process, thus adding weight to the material. Embezzled goods were then sold at "flash houses," low public houses that specialized in such trafficking (P.P. 1828, VI, p. 94).

Most masters agreed that embezzlement had not been endemic in the pre-repeal era. A committee was constituted in 1815 for its prevention, but was disbanded with the repeal (Rule 1980, p. 130; Jordan 1931, pp. 152–153). Nonetheless, after repeal many employers complained of a horrific proliferation of the practice, as well as the outright theft of materials (P.P. 1832, XIX, pp. 676–677, 770; P.P. 1840, XXIII, pt. 2, p. 259). By 1827, one magistrate grumbled, the volume of embezzlement cases was "every day increasing" (*TFP*, Dec. 16, 1827, p. 166). The practice became so widespread that some manufacturers required weavers to contribute to an insurance fund to buffer them from losses. In addition, by 1829 some weavers even formed societies to indemnify their members against losses to their respective employers, hoping to forestall further wage reductions (P.P. 1840, XXIII, pt. 2, pp. 259–260).

Embezzlement and related offenses were covered by a series of acts passed in the eighteenth and early nineteenth centuries intended to halt their spread in cloth industries. Under the provisions of the cornerstone law, 17 Gco. III c. 56, the crime of embezzlement was punishable by from two weeks to three months at hard labor and by the odious spectacle of a public whipping (Smith 1852, p. 298). Although some masters ardently sought to make a public display of miscreants, local magistrates were less zealous. On occasion, they took sympathy on the degraded weaver who struggled to maintain a decent home. One large master complained to Parliament that the bench was too inclined to put heart before law (P.P. 1832, XIX, p. 656).

Overall, however, a picture emerges of magistrates who sought to construct a theater of legal governance that assumed the air of impartiality. This theater became a contested and shifting terrain of class conflict. Through the bench, male weavers sought to maintain their status as hon-

Table 1. Adjudicated cases of silk embezzlement and theft in Spitalfields, 1828–1831

	1828	1829	1830	1831	Totals
Number of cases	33	35	19	23	110
Number of suspects	36	38	20	27	121
Male	33	32	17	21	103
Female	3	6	3	6	18
Convictions	20 (56)	13 (34)	5 (25)	10 (37)	48 (40)
Males	19 (58)	13 (41)	5 (29)	10 (48)	47 (46)
Females	1 (33)	—	—	—	1 (5.6)

Source: H.O. 62/1–7.
Note: Numbers in parentheses are percentages.

orable artisans and to affirm their moral economy of labor. With increasing ardor after repeal, warehousers sought to seize greater control of the production process, restructure the employment relationship, and affirm the principles of the free market.

The prosecution of embezzlement provides a more extensive picture of this. To explore this pattern of adjudication, I aggregated the daily reports of prosecution for the offense conducted at the Worship St. office, listed in the Metropolitan Police's daily reports for the period 1828–1831 (see Tables 1 and 2).

Of the 121 suspects upon whom sentence was passed, only 40 percent were convicted and punished. The rate of conviction rises to 46 percent with the exclusion of the eighteen females in the sample, only one of whom was successfully prosecuted. While the average male weaver had a flip-of-the-coin chance of conviction, it was woe for those lost the toss. Thirty-one percent of those males convicted received the maximum sentence of three months hard labor and a public whipping, while 42 percent of them received three months hard labor. Thus fully three-quarters of convicted males felt the heavy punitive force of the law.

Male weavers likely were singled out for scrutiny and punishment because they controlled the realm of the workshop. Through prosecution, manufacturers could extend the tentacles of labor control, relying on the relative servitude of the laborer as constructed by common law. Yet manufacturers could not themselves simply eviscerate the weavers' status as independent artisans, because this control was partly exercised through the bench. Magistrates could validate claims of malicious prosecution and overreaching control through acquittal.

Prosecution for embezzlement was only one of the tentacles of the manufacturers' legal reach. They sought to transform the employment relationship both by pursuing prosecutions for negligence and by refashioning the customary labor agreement. Negligence was defined as eight successive days of non-work, without permission or reasonable excuse.

Table 2: Punishments for adjudicated cases of silk embezzlement and theft in Spitalfields, 1828–1831

Type of Punishment	1828	1829	1830	1831	Totals
Incarceration with hard labor	19 (95)	12 (92)	3 (60)	8 (80)	42 (88)
One month or less	3 (15)	—	—	—	3 (7.5)
Between one and two months	—	1 (7.7)	—	2 (20)	3 (7.5)
Between two and three months	10 (50)	7 (54)	1 (20)	3 (30)	21 (48)
Three months and a public whipping	6 (30)	4 (31)	2 (40)	3 (30)	15 (31)
Incarceration without hard labor					
One month or less	—	—	—	—	—
Between two and three months	1 (5)	—	1 (20)	—	2 (4)
Between two and three months	—	1 (7.7)	—	2 (20)	3 (6)
Other punishment					
Fine	—	—	1 (20)	—	1 (2)

Source: H.O. 62/1–7.
Note: Numbers in parentheses are percentages.

Manufacturers, lacking direct supervisory control, were dependent on the diligence of weavers to complete work within a customary time period. Time lay at the heart of the struggle: the prize was the dictation of work pace, as well as trade practice and standards of productivity. Moreover, through such prosecution manufacturers sought to undermine the leverage weavers could exercise through work stoppages. In this legal arena, class tensions became increasingly evident.

Magistrates exercised summary jurisdiction over these cases, with a maximum punishment of three months hard labor (Smith 1852, p. 303). For manufacturers intent on refashioning labor relations, the negligence statute provided a potent disciplinary tool. In 1827, for example, the firm of Messrs. Remington, Wilson & Mills used the statute to force striking weavers back to work after they had sealed their looms over a wage dispute (*TFP*, Sept. 16, 1827).

In the case of negligence wily weavers, attuned to the civic largesse of the magistrates, could employ the bench's sympathy to their advantage, especially in the strike of 1829 (which I cover in Chapter 6). Weavers in many strikes would add an inch or two to their work on the seventh day, providing the magistrates with an excuse for dismissal. The tactic was so successful that Parliament in 1823 was prompted to extend 17 Geo. III c. 56, a more general neglect of work law, to cover the silk trade (Place Coll., set 16, v. 2, f. 129; Smith 1852, pp. 239–241).[5]

Finally, manufacturers tried to transform the standard terms of the employment relationship through the negligence statutes. Among the most distressing changes for the weavers was the spreading cessation of piece-rate advances, which had provided the weaving household with sustenance during the frequently long periods of finishing work. Manufacturers, however, increasingly saw such advances as fetters on productivity. In the bench they found an ally that affirmed the notion that piece rates were exchanged for expended labor power rather than its promise. In the post-repeal period, magistrates dismissed weavers' arguments that advances were a fixture of just trade relations. As a magistrate declared in a case in 1825, "as to the idea of getting money in advance, and receiving it as a matter of right, no idea could be more preposterous or absurd . . . although it may be customary with the masters to give such advances for the sake of accommodation as well as encouragement" (*TN*, Sept. 11, 1825).[6]

Through these battles at the bench, manufacturers thus sought to redefine the terms of employment. When manufacturers found often sympathetic allies in the magistrates, they could exercise unbridled legal power. Magistrates recognized the rights of labor as well, and in doing so burnished the increasingly tarnished image of the weaver as an honorable artisan. The right to plead their case before the law and the possibility of state protection lent some validation to their claims of trade and community citizenship. In a dialectic twist of the law, the bourgeois idea of the free labor contract provided a rationale for the weavers' defense of their claims of independence. This was particularly ironic because capitalist control over labor was juridically based on pre-industrial notions of the "relative liberty" of the laborer, which precisely denied such freedom (Orren 1991, p. 92).

Through this class struggle before the bench, the possible virtues of the law were reaffirmed in the continuing theater of adjudication. As a magistrate remarked in settling a dispute in a weaver's favor, "the Law" that provided him the authority to compel a weaver to obey a work contract, "surely . . . also enabled him to compel the masters to maintain their contract with the men" (*TFP*, Oct. 28, 1827, p. 107). Legal power could still

---

[5] My aggregation of prosecutions conducted at Worship Street, from the Metropolitan Police *Reports of the Proceedings at the Several Police Offices* of 1828–1831 (H.O. 62/1–7), shows very few prosecutions under the new extension.
[6] For additional cases, see *TN*, July 17, p. 7, Oct. 9, p. 207, Oct. 30, 1825, p. 252.

be seen as the Law with an even-handed capital L, even as capital slowly commandeered control through its reach by changing the contract itself. In these years, the language of political economy came to supplant a moral economy as the legal tongue.

The relationships between the weavers, parish authorities, and magistrates thus could reinforce elements of the weavers' moral economy. Respectability, social productivity, and deference were all features of the web of reciprocity that legitimated communal obligation. This web validated the weavers' understanding of a just standard of living, and gave credence to their claims for the preservation of their protected order. The actions of the vestry and bench could affirm their moral and civic claims. These actions were constructed through and themselves partly affirmed a rights discourse that was essential to the weavers' moral economy. The attempts of capitalists to assert greater control, however, extended well beyond Worship St.

Weaving a Net of Hegemony

Beside this seamed system of reciprocity and law a new webbing was being woven during the first decades of the nineteenth century—the net of hegemony. The specter of the French Revolution, the ultra-radical polemics that flowed from East End pens, and the branching out of democratic associations from the trunk of the Liberty Tree roused the ruling order to action. From the ranks of the Evangelical nouveau bourgeoisie came a cadre of philanthropists determined to instill piety and deference in those they feared were godless and republican. First haltingly, and then in more sustained forays, these philanthropic bodies made progressive incursions into the plebeian culture of the East End. Among their targets were the Spitalfields weavers.

In the late eighteenth and early nineteenth centuries, the East End working poor had enjoyed some generosity from the patrician order and Parliament in times of distress (*European Magazine*, June 1802, p. 428; Scott 1896, pp. 57–58; Hale 1806, pp. 10–11, 14–15). Silk wearers, however, rarely ventured into this other world to save the souls of silk weavers. The first sustained effort to salvage the working poor from the scourges of mendicancy, radicalism and atheism came with the depression of 1811 through the efforts of the Reverend Josiah Platt, a noted local missionary, the minister of Wheler Chapel. With Platt at the helm, a coalition of Evangelical Anglicans and Dissenters set sail on the largely uncharted sea of plebeian humanity. Their first organization was the Spitalfields Soup Society, run by a committee of approximately fifty well-heeled men. Members of the committee actively solicited contributions from the city's affluent and themselves did weekly service at the soup kitchen, supervising both the production and dispensing of food (*Report of . . . the Spitalfields Soup Society for 1811–1812; Philanthropist*, v. 2, no. 6, 1812, p. 184).

During the height of the distress, the society daily dispensed 3,200 quarts of soup for one penny each, feeding some 7,000 people (*Soup Society*, 1813, p. 9). Soup was doled out to those who had received a ticket from a society member, having passed the litmus test of poverty and piety. Subscribers were allowed six recommendations per week and were strongly encouraged to make personal visitations to the family before dispensing tickets (*Philanthropist*, v. 2, no. 6, 1812, pp. 178, 181). The measures of virtue and limitations on support were alien to the parish's web of reciprocity.

Concerned over the district's poverty and lack of religious sentiment, some of the committee's members founded the Spitalfields Association to investigate the spiritual and economic conditions of the poor. With the area divided into seventeen districts, the "gentlemen" of the Association surveyed over 1,500 families. The results spurred additional action. Almost half of the families visited were without Bibles and a fifth openly professed no religious beliefs (*First Report of the Spitalfields Benevolent Society*, 1812, p. 17; *Philanthropist*, v. 2, no. 6, 1812, p. 189; Ibid. v. 2, on. 7, p. 239).

This enthusiastic Evangelical vanguard was heavily populated by city Dissenters who owned large manufacturing and mercantile establishments. They rode the popular tide of political economy and were critical of the old regime for encouraging indolence and vice. They also championed nondenominational education as the best path to instilling virtue and obedience among the working class (McCann 1977, p. 17). Through their visitations and writings, these benefactors sought to instill the fear of God and an abhorrence of radicalism. Irving Brock, a member of the Benevolent Society, wrote to the inhabitants of the district, "At the same time that we administer to your temporal necessities, it also enters into our plan diligently to enquire into the state of your souls" (1817, p. 5). He went even further to provide a scripted catechism, a somewhat puerile mixture of utilitarianism and supine reverence:

> We are poor and industrious men, and cannot be expected to be conversant in politics, or the science of government. We are Christians, and are instructed to fear God, be subject to the higher powers, and not to meddle with them who are given to chance. It does not become us therefore to agitate a subject of which we are necessarily ignorant. . . .
>
> By one set of men we are invited to express disaffection to the government of our country, and even to infringe its laws; by another, we are exhorted to peace and contentment. Which of these two classes of persons demands our respect and attention? We must believe that it is the latter, inasmuch as they have afforded us substantial evidence that they really sympathize in our distresses, and are not inattentive to our wants. (Ibid., pp. 9–11)

Brock's arrogant advice was echoed in an increasing stream of cheap tracts and pamphlet literature. These bourgeois Evangelicals sought to mold a new working-class collective identity through such tracts, and the weavers were both exemplars and targets of a good deal of this. For Hannah More, an Evangelical Anglican and literary queen of this pap production, the weaver was a recurring character. In "The Delegate," James Dawson, a well-known weaver in his neighborhood, is portrayed as sober, industrious, and prudent because of his "sure foundation of genuine Christianity" (1819a, p. 1). In "The Contented Spital-Fields Weavers: Jeremiah Nott," Nott heartily inveighs his brother artificers against the radicals "running about the kingdom in coaches, making speeches and living like fighting cocks upon the pence of the poor whom they delude" (1819b, p. 2). And in "The True Rights of Man; or, The Contented Spital-Fields Weaver," the contented weaver lyrically recounts the discourse of the virtuous worker:

> That some *must* be poorer, this truth I will sing,
> Is a law of my maker and not of my King:
> And the true *Rights of Man*, and the life of his cause,
> Is not equal possessions, but equal just laws.
>
> (1819a, p. 151)

The efforts and numbers of the Evangelicals continued to expand in succeeding years. Amidst the onslaught of the 1816 depression, the societies made a concerted effort to enlarge their influence through increased relief. The Spitalfields Association made 8,460 visits to 3,336 families in eleven weeks; the Benevolent Society raised the princely sum of 43,369 pounds (1,300 of which came from silk manufacturers), while the East London Bible Association distributed 2,000 bibles. In its first twelve years, members of the Benevolent Society made 158,140 visits, conducted 116,400 interviews, and distributed 23,437 pounds (and undoubtedly all of the simple solace of Christianity that the poor could suffer) (P.P. 1814–1815, III, p. 71; P.P. 1818, IX, p. 192; Scott 1896, p. 18; McCann 1977, p. 26).

These Evangelicals simultaneously sought to mold the minds of the young. By 1817, about one thousand children were enrolled in infant or parochial schools. Over four times that number were registered in the eighteen Sunday schools in the two parishes (with Dissenters running all but one of them). By 1821, six monitorial schools had enough room (at least hypothetically) to accommodate 60 percent of the children between the ages of six to fourteen. These schools operated under similar principles as the relief societies, providing access through committee review and patronage and proffering a heavy dose of piety (P.P. 1817, VI, p. 49; McCann 1977, pp. 9, 26).[7]

---

[7] McCann's (1977) superb study of the social control functions of the charity schools in Spitalfields for the period 1812–1824 makes an analysis of the system superfluous.

The final strands of the hegemonic net were woven in the early post-repeal years of 1825 to 1826. In 1825, amidst much fanfare, the Spitalfields Mechanics' Institution was opened on 10 March. Like its cousins, the Institution was to teach local artisans the rudiments of mechanics and science, and enlighten them on the simple truths of political economy. Patronized by city notables, the Institution was especially targeted at the weavers. Its president, Thomas Gibson, was a leading city manufacturer. Three of the four vice-presidents, two of the three trustees, and all three auditors were also large manufacturers (Partington 1825, p. 48; P.P. 1840, XXIII, pt. 2, p. 249).

The Mechanics' Institution was, in part, an attempt to prepare the weavers for the coming changes of the post-repeal era. Doctor Birkbeck (founder of mechanics institutions), in his inaugural lecture, admonished the weavers to rouse their mechanical ingenuity and spirit of competition, which had been dormant under protection. With visionary optimism, he concluded that "with fair opportunities aided by British capital, British industry, and British ingenuity, I am firmly persuaded that you will successfully contend with your rivals, and that, ere long, even in their own markets" (Partington 1825, p. 39). He also noted that the useful knowledge offered would put the weavers "upon a more equal footing, thus creating a reciprocity of interest between masters and workmen, to the manifest increase of your comfort and happiness" (ibid. p. 40). Thomas Gibson, in a succeeding lecture, chimed in on this new relationship: "In this particular district its establishment promises one obvious and striking advantage; as it will have the effect of uniting two classes hitherto separated, viz. the *employers* and the *employed*; and by affording them opportunities of understanding one another better, it cannot fail to conduce to their mutual benefit. These remarks apply particularly to the Silk Trade" (ibid., p. 44). This sense of reciprocity, as we shall see, was far different from that proffered in the weavers' moral economy.

The halcyon days of prosperity did not come to pass, however, and in 1826 the trade slipped into a disastrous depression. With the parishes overburdened, charity organizations once again mobilized to fill the gap. In addition, a new charity, the Committee for the Distressed Weavers of Spitalfields, was born under the auspices of the Bishop of Chester, London authorities, and approximately twenty silk manufacturers. The Committee amassed funds at a fairly rapid pace, and at the close of their last meeting in mid-September they had received contributions totaling 27,478 pounds (P.C., set 16, v. 2, ff. 32, 153–154).

In this relief organization, the gestation of a new order was coming to fruition. The Committee of Management, which distributed relief, met daily in the vestry room at Christ Church, a cogent symbol of its usurpation of parish authority. In contrast to the parish, the committee members were adamant in not dispersing funds to any who had work in the loom, and strict limitations were placed on the amount of relief allowed (ibid., f. 35). Relief tickets this time played an even more insidious role. Applicants had to present a ticket "signed by their last employer, giving an exposition of the applicant's circumstances, and any remarks the master may have to make" (ibid.). The Committee refused to relieve any weaver who had turned down work, regardless of the paucity of the piece rates. Tickets for soup kitchens were also dispensed to applicants with families at the discretion of the Committee (ibid., ff. 35, 62).

Manufacturers thus loomed over the weaver in relief as well as labor. In keen distinction to the parish practices, this new relief was dependent on the conduct of the weaver, not as citizen, but as worker. As the web of reciprocity slowly unraveled, it was replaced by the net of hegemony cast over the impoverished weavers. This net held a new collective identity for the weavers, structured through the discourses of political economy. These and related discourses contained senses of justice and legitimacy fundamentally at odds with the weavers' moral economy.

After countless home visits, thousands of Bibles, and tens of thousands of pounds of relief some of the bourgeois crusaders were warmed by their successes (McCann 1977, p. 27). Their elation, however, was more an exercise in self-aggrandizement than in sociological analysis. There was certainly no good evidence of an Evangelical revival, or even a burst of chiliastic despair, among the working poor of Spitalfields. Henry Dunn observed that in Twigg Folly, a neighborhood heavily populated by weavers, five sixths to nine tenths of the inhabitants never attended church. He remarked that the denizens "read greedily anything that tells them they are injured and ill-treated," but had little taste for Evangelical tracts (P.P. 1835, VII, p. 12).

In education, the evangelists fared little better. Although hundreds participated, the most auspicious attendance record was the half-capacity achieved by the much touted Spicer St. Lancasterian school. At some schools, groups of youth assembled and threw mud at teachers and pupils alike, requiring the frequent intervention of the constabulary (P.P. 1817, VII, p. 108; P.P. 1835, VII, p. 18). By the early 1830s, the secretary of the East London Auxiliary Sunday School Union could report no improvement (P.P. 1834, VII, p. 113). Phillip McCann has suggested that the principal cause for the low attendance was "the conviction, shared by many of the poor, that the schools has been provided *for* them, by the middle classes, and were thus in some way alien to the interests of the labouring population" (1977, p. 29). This argument may be extended to the Mechanics' Institution, which at its height had no more than two hundred attendees, and witnessed a rapid demise in its first year. The weavers did not warm to the control of the manufacturers on its committee (P.P. 1840, XXIII, pt. 2, p. 249).

The efforts of the philanthropists who descended on the district and the weavers do not seem to have widely instilled any heartfelt deference. The weavers defended their identity as respectable artisans and continued to counterpose a discourse of moral economy against that of political economy, which was articulated through the nascent regime of control. Perhaps the most acute assessment of the overall impact of these hegemonic encroachments was inadvertently provided by two large city silk manufacturers. Thomas Gibson and William Bell, president and vice-president of the Mechanics' Institution, speaking plainly with Francis Place, noted a year after their philanthropic fiasco that a vast cultural chasm separated the manufacturers and the weavers. "We are," they poignantly observed, "a very different people on the one side of Bishopsgate-street, and on the other there is the appearance of a different nation" (P.P. 1835, VII, p. 86). A youthful Disraeli might readily have concurred.

The Silk Weavers and Radical Politics

As I have noted, one significant way in which workers defined their collective identities and interests was through the realm of radical politics. Historians associated with the linguistic turn have frequently counterpoised the language of radical politics to one they have construed as class. Those sympathetic to Thompson have countered that these revisionist analyses involve both serious misreadings of working peoples' use of radical language and participation in this politics, and maintain that class often was widely insinuated in radical political languages. Virtually all historians see such public participation and the discourses of popular rights as ways of establishing a sense of citizenship and community. London, the great center of political life, had nurtured radical politics from the latter eighteenth century, particularly among its artisans (Belchem 1978, 1985; Brewer 1976; Goodwin 1979; Hone 1982; McCalman 1989; Prothero 1979; Thompson 1966).

The silk weavers' involvement in this realm has been debated by historians. Some have argued that the weavers were a relatively complacent group, uninspired by the blossoming of the liberty tree (Rowe 1967). Others have maintained that the weavers were active (if erratic) participants and could be found in the upswings of agitation (Goodway 1984). In the shadowy and often subterranean world of radical politics it is difficult to distinguish identities, much as many of its participants intended. What we can say is that the weavers may have been reluctant radicals for the years covered by the Spitalfields Acts, shedding their complacency thereafter.

There is little evidence to suggest that the silk weavers distinguished themselves in word or deed when radicalism emerged from its chrysalis in the 1760s and 1770s (Rudé 1962, p. 102; Rowe 1967, p. 491). With the rise in the 1790s of the first significant radical organization, the London Corresponding Society, however, the Spitalfields area in general gained stature. Fostered in the radical politics of a literate London artisanate, the society's penchant for critique of political exclusion was warmed to by Spitalfields tradespeople, including some weavers (Hone 1982, p. 97; Thompson 1966, p. 121; Plummer 1972, p. 330).

In the following decades of heightened radical verve, the weavers appeared on both sides of the fence. They certainly were at times beckoned by the sirens of political injustice, as their participation in the Spa Fields meetings in 1816 suggests (Belchem 1985, p. 56; Thompson 1966, p. 634; Prothero 1979, p. 70). They were often quiescent, however, their democratic zeal mitigated by their sense of reciprocal obligation to the government for the Acts.[8] The benevolence of "the law" legitimated state authority, as Francis Place discovered when he solicited the weavers' support to repeal the Combination Laws in 1824. Responding to Place's letter, a weavers' meeting resolved that "protected as we have been for years under the salutary laws and wisdom of the legislature . . . we cannot therefore take any notice of the invitation held out by Mr. Place." The resolution was followed by the exclamation of the crowd, "The law, cling to the law, it will protect us" (Webb Coll., sec. A, XL, f. 88). The weavers and their supporters were quick to remark upon their patriotism during periods of "revolutionary frenzy" (*An Account . . . 1823*, pp. 20–21; L.S.P. 1823, CLVII, p. 16; P.P. 1834, X, p. 320).[9]

Radicals frequently denounced the weavers for their support of the state they deemed so vile, and such actions burned in their political memories. Weavers were roundly chastised for supporting the aristocracy and the Corn Laws during their early attempts to reinstate some form of trade or wage protection. One writer to the *Trades' Free Press* excoriated them as "the slave kissing the feet of his oppressors, and thanking him for his chains and fetters" (Oct. 29, 1826, p. 122). The dean of radical politics, William Cobbett, bitingly characterized the weavers as "base dogs" for their fair-weather support of radical causes. When told of their extreme poverty in the late 1820s, he replied with stinging abuse: "If I am asked what the poor creatures were to do, being without bread as they are, I answer by asking, whether they could find no knives to cut their throats with" (1912, v. 2, pp. 200–202).

From the peaking of London's radical fervor with the Spa Fields demonstrations in 1816 to the demise of the Spitalfields Acts in 1825, the participation of the weavers may well have ebbed and flowed with the tides of

---

[8] In recounting an encounter he had with the journeymen's committee amidst a recruiting foray in Spitalfields for a Spa Fields meeting, William Hale observed, "The Committee of journeymen then came to me and laid before me their answer, 'We are fairly paid for our labour, we are protected by the government, and do not wish to mix in the turmoil of society of a political nature'" (P.P. 1834, X, p. 320).

[9] In testimony before the Lords' Select Committee, a member of the Bethnal Green watch and ward noted that most of the one to two hundred offers to serve as special constables during the sedition trial of Arthur Thistlewood in 1820 were weavers (L.S.P. 1823, CLVII, p. 115).

their economic security and of repression.[10] Certainly, their own collective struggle centered on the growing battle to maintain the protective shield of the Spitalfields Acts. Beyond this struggle for life blood, the silk weavers were occasional participants in popular causes. Over 4,000 signed petitions for the radical cause célèbre of Queen Caroline (Prothero 1979, p. 142).[11] By mid-July they joined in the fight against reinstating the Combination Laws, myopically noting "that the repeal of the laws against combination of workmen was a boon which was gratefully received from the legislature as a compensation for the repeal of . . . 'the Spital Fields Acts'" (B.L., Add. MSS. 27803, f. 271).

Ultimately, the sense of reciprocal political justice depicted in the above quote may have led many weavers into a firmer compact with radicals. Their chrysalis of deference was gradually shed during the repeal debates, as it became clear that the government was intent on violating their fundamental rights. By 1829, support for radical parliamentary reform had made major strides among the weavers. In November 1830, a part-time resident of Shoreditch wrote to the Home Office to warn of the weavers' sordid revolutionary politics: "If person [sic] was but to go into the coffee houses within a mile round me . . . or into the tap rooms or public houses especially *The Well and Bucket* in Bethnal Green Road, *The Turkish Bath in Brick Lane*, . . . I am assured that they will not sit ten minutes when they hear down right sedition and treason. . . . I am told from the newspapers that the weavers are loyal. I never knew ONE in my life and I have had dealings with hundreds of them" (H.O. 40/25, ff. 274–275, 14 Nov. 1830, McIntosh to Wellington).[12]

Two active sections of the radical National Union of the Working Classes were established in July 1831 in weavers' houses in Bethnal Green (Prothero 1979, p. 285). The Lords' first rejection of the Reform Bill that same year stirred many weavers to champion radical measures. In addition, two members of the more moderate National Political Union council were weavers (Wolf 1975, p. 17). While the leaders of the N.P.U. tended to eschew specifically class discourses, the mission of the Bethnal Green chapter was quite direct: "The National Political Union for the parish of St. Matthew, Bethnal Green . . . has for its objects . . . to watch over and pro-

---

[10] The veteran radical Thomas Preston was dismayed with the complacency of the weavers in his attempts to mobilize them for a demonstration in the autumn of 1817 when the silk trade had revived (Thompson 1966, p. 694).

[11] The political battle centered around George IV's attempt to divorce his decidedly independent queen, and the ensuing attention churned up the most scandalous political affray of its era (Prothero 1979, chap. 7; Laqueur 1982; Clark 1990).

[12] John Ballance, a senior master and weavers' supporter, testified to the Commission on the Silk Trade in 1832 that "they do attribute to the measures of the Government all their privations and miseries; and I do not exaggerate when I say, there is a feeling of deadly hatred working in many thousands of them to the Government, which presents a contrast as striking as it is painful to their former known loyalty and attachment" (P.P. 1832, XIX, p. 450).

mote the interests and to better the condition, generally, of the Working Classes, and more particularly of this parish" (P.C., set 63, v.1, f. 87). The objectives suggest a body politic with a class heart. The groundswell of agitation for radical reform was rising to great heights in 1831, and the silk weavers were in the thick. The East End branch of the N.U.W.C. was vivified by silk weavers who provided at least a fifth of its supporters. The great voice of the radical working-class politics, the *Poor Mans' Guardian* was "extensively circulated in the district" (P.P. 1835, VII, p. 86).

Yet for all of these indications of radical enthusiasm, slight caution concerning some of the weavers' commitment should remain. Their trade society ranks suffered some friction over an explicit radical political analysis of their plight (*TFP*, Feb. 23, 1828, pp. 246–247). In July 1832, a maverick body of some 230 members broke away to form the Political Union of the Working Classes of Tower Hamlets, dissatisfied with the lack of attention the central body had shown to their particular economic concerns (Hollis, pp. 264–265). Some of the weavers still were keenly focused on the resuscitation of trade protection.

The history of the weavers' commitment to radicalism was not the stuff of popular political heroics. Their activism was, at times, tempered by the bonds of political reciprocity forged in government trade protection. Sometimes this provided them with ignominious political bedfellows. As E. P. Thompson has so perceptively noted, working-class radical agitation ebbed and flowed with the tide of prosperity and the stultifying repression in the 1820s (1966, p. 711). If the weavers were perhaps more susceptible to this swing and the hesitations it engendered, it was only because, as one of the last remaining protected trades, they had in fact more to lose. As political economy forced its brusque reality into their lives, however, the weavers' moral economy shifted toward a radical analysis.

By the mid-1820s, the community and its politics had become a central part of the class process. Weavers saw the gradual erosion of a moral economy of political relations that had once validated their honorable status and provided a safety net of security. As local parishes became overtaxed by their responsibilities, bourgeois charitable institutions stepped in to fill the growing chasm. They developed a net of control in which status and relief were tied to a manufacturer's accounting of the weaver's worth. Simultaneously, through the local bench, manufacturers were drawing on the power of magistrates to redefine the employment relationship through more strictly market-driven standards. This instrument of class control directly challenged the weavers' former status in the community, degrading their honorability and heightening their dependence. Although the transformation of this local political culture cannot be reduced to class, the process of class was certainly deeply insinuated in the weavers' lives and may ultimately have prodded them to much greater participation in radical politics.

Class and community were thus mutually reinforcing formations in Spitalfields in the early nineteenth century. Weavers congregated in distinctive communities, were recognized and validated as valued citizens, and had their labor valorized as a mark of respectability. As large manufacturers transformed productive relations, so too did they impinge on the web of reciprocity within which the weavers found support. Growing divisions within the trade created transmutations of the circuits of power and authority in the weavers' political culture. In disrupting the weavers' respectability, in transforming the intercession of the law and the bench in employment arrangements, and in extending bourgeois power through the tentacles of charity, capitalist incursions intertwined community and class formation in a tightening twist. Weavers came to see their plight in their communities in more conscious class terms, and in doing so they began to both act on and articulate this consciousness in new ways.

CHAPTER FIVE

The Repeal of the Spitalfields Acts

By the mid-1820s, the silk weavers' way of life was under siege. Their economic security, their trade, and their community status faced incursions from new bourgeois interlopers. This expanding capitalist control was critical to class formation, but hegemony was not built solely on trade practices, legal strictures, and charity organizations. Discourse as well, I initially argued, provides the ideological dimension through which domination and resistance are conducted, mediating social organization and bounding the possibilities for collective action. Through a moral economy, the silk weavers had discursively constructed their collective identity as honorable artisans, a status that guaranteed state protection of their livelihood, entitlement to parish support as productive citizens, and a voice in trade matters. Moreover, they substantiated the patriarchal authority of male weavers in the household. These discourses also framed and legitimated a collective defense of these claimed rights. With the rise of the warehousers, however, came a new discourse through which the world was to be understood—that of political economy. As the economic and political bases of the weavers' world were being eroded by the capitalist undertow, the ideological frameworks of their collective worth and action were being displaced.

The weavers, in Thompson's terms, found themselves in an ever-closer engagement over the moral language that defined their collective identity and the normative conduct of trade and polity. Critical in the development of the weavers' class consciousness was the battle to expose the dominant formation articulated by warehousers and free traders as deeply class-interested. For male weavers, the dialogic process also heightened focus on the moral justifications of their authority as workshop masters and principal breadwinners.

As they developed a repertoire of collective action to contest domination, the weavers constructed the framing for it through this dialogic struggle. They also articulated a sense of collective identity in the process. Their construction of their fighting words evolved through resistance, by appropriating meaning and moral force from the dominant formation, particularly from the discourse of political economy.

The struggles of the weavers with warehousers and political economists, which we will investigate in the next chapter, were thus formatively shaped and mediated by their engagement within the dominant discursive formations. Claims of justice, visions of an equitable order, and the possibilities by which these might be achieved were products of dialogic conflict. Rather than dismissing the relevancy of class conflict because of the multivocality of discourse, we will explore how such conflict is in fact revealed by the frictional contradictions within this clash of words. The weavers' fighting words represent the process of class in motion at the intersection of discourse and experience.

The contention surrounding the repeal of the Spitalfields Acts provides an excellent vantage on how the weavers engaged in this process of counter-hegemony. The campaigns involving repeal created an intense dialogic dynamic between the weavers and their adversaries in which the weavers' sought to appropriate and transform the dominant formation of the large manufacturers and government power brokers. Through the ensuing struggles, the weavers and warehousers fashioned the ideological terrain upon which definitions of political and trade rights, citizenship, standards of justice, claims against the state and capitalists, and male authority were refined. The warehousers and their allies proffered concepts of polity and economy, which emphasized individuated actors, free markets and trade, and a non-interventionist state. These spelled out a notion of the common good strikingly at variance with that defined through the weavers' previous collective experiences.

In this chapter, I chart the formation of fighting words during the repeal debate. My aim is not to systematically assess the actions of all of the parties involved, but to map out the discursive field on which the weavers found themselves battling. In the following chapter, I will analyze how this ideological terrain, which was produced in dialogic struggle, mediated the weavers' class consciousness and collective actions.

During the early 1820s, the influence of the political economists in Parliament and the public sphere was reaching a new apex, and political economy was cementing its position as a hegemonic discourse (H. S. Gordon 1971; Hilton 1977, 1988). The years of 1824 and 1825 in particular were, according to one historian, "halcyon years for the cause of political economists in general and of the Ricardians in particular" (B. Gordon 1979, p. 13). Liberal Tory ministers attentively listened as the rhetoric of the political economists boomed from the back benches. The members of the ruling coalition were by no means dogmatic adherents of the new wisdom, but they were savvy ideological pragmatists. The cry of free trade as it related to industrial and internal matters was a doctrinal force coming of age.

For the ruling Tories, free trade in some areas, especially the protection of agricultural interests, was an anathema.[1] Nonetheless, the strictures of free trade provided compelling justifications for the removal of old trade legislation that was viewed as an encumbrance to British fortunes. The discourse of political economy increasingly animated the business of maintaining the security and order of the state (Berg 1980, p. 39; Hilton 1977, p. 312).

As I noted earlier, the landmark laws through which artisans defined their claims to the state were dismantled in the wake of political economy's ascendancy. This scything of protectionist legislation was a harbinger for the impending contest of the early 1820s. By 1822, the Spitalfields Acts remained one of the last relics of domestic industrial protection, "*the* test case for the further progress of the application of laissez faire" (B. Gordon 1979, p. 19; italics in the original). The contest over the Acts, which ended with their repeal in 1824, was a cardinal dialogic struggle. The discursive battle centered on the normative understandings of both polity and economy and their interrelations. For the weavers, the two were intimately coupled, while for the manufacturers they were constituted as detached spheres separated by a laissez-faire state. For the male weavers, this engagement also served as a lens to focus their citizenship claims as household rulers and defenders of the nation. This contest over hegemony was thus part and parcel of the process of class formation, determining the ideological boundaries of identity, masculine authority, political and economic relations, and legitimate action.

On May 9, 1823, Thomas Wilson, M.P. for London, stood before the Commons and presented a petition from a group of metropolitan silk manufacturers. They humbly requested that the ruinous yoke of the Spitalfields Acts be lifted once and for all. One of the leading manufacturers had not long before informed William Hale of their intentions, observing, "We think that the Disposition of the Government is with us, and that the Eyes of the Country are open to the better Principles of Political Economy" (L.S.P. 1823, CLVII, p. 28). True to this word, the manufac-

---

[1] The prime case was the Corn Laws, a series of acts that placed protective restrictions on the trading of grain. In the enactments of 1815, Parliament sought to stabilize the grain market and ensure a profit for landowners through a variable duty imposed on imported grain. Political economists believed that the Corn Laws represented pernicious and outmoded protectionism (Gash 1979; B. Gordon 1979).

turers employed the discourses of political economy in a broad assault on the Acts.

The Acts, warehousers, argued, caused serious interference in their relations with their workmen in several respects. They placed meddling and ignorant magistrates in a position to decide work rules, interfering "in a vexious manner" with what should be an unfettered market relationship between employer and worker (*Hans.* n.s., 1823, IX, c. 146). Adding insult to injury, the magistrates also arbitrarily fixed wages:

> That, by the operation of this law the rate of wages, instead of being left to the recognized principles of regulation, has been arbitrarily fixed by the award of persons, whose ignorance of the details of this very intricate manufacture, necessarily renders them incompetent to give a just decision; and the result of this mode of regulation has been to fix the labour of many sorts of goods so extravagantly high, as to drive the manufacture of them altogether from the districts. . . . That these acts, by not permitting the masters to reward such of their workmen as exhibit superior skill or ingenuity, but compelling them to pay an equal price for all work, whether well or ill performed, have materially retarded the progress of improvement, and repressed industry and emulation. (Ibid.)

Government interference was destructive to the dynamic equilibrium of the market for labor and goods and therefore to the weavers' well-being and even to the larger community (c. 147). By interceding in the determination of piece rates, the Acts also chained the natural dynamism of capital. The panacea of progress—machinery—could not be administered, since fixed wages negated the "advantage of this powerful auxiliary" (ibid.).

Perhaps most egregiously, the Acts prevented the manufacturers from being true capitalists and free Britons, that is, from exercising freedom over their capital:

> It is not so much their desire to seek relief from their operation in the particulars lastly stated, as to be exempted from the arbitrary, injurious, and impolitic enactment which prevents them, while they continue to reside within certain districts, from employing any portion of their capital in such other parts of the kingdom as may be deemed most beneficial; thereby depriving them not only of the fair exercise of their privileges as free subjects, and totally preventing public benefit that would arise from a competition between the London and the country manufacturers, but depriving them also of all hope of ever participating in the foreign trade of the Empire. (Ibid., cc. 148–149)

The petition was the first volley in the final battle over the Acts. The debate had crystallized in previous months when the Acts were the subject of a Lords Select Committee. Through pamphlets, newspaper editorials, and letters to the editor it gained fervor, and by 1823 the groundwork had been laid for the warehousers' assault.

The above petition contained a condensation of several key elements of this discursive attack. Four of these themes—the interference in labor relations, the "artificial" structuring of wages, the dampening of trade activity, and the strangulation of capitalism—were recurrent aspects of the critique. More generally, through the discourses of political economy the warehousers and their allies offered conceptions of freedom, citizen rights, and the functions of the state. They constructed freedom of action in both polity and economy as affairs of the individual, construed the defining basis of these freedoms as property, and identified the fate of workers as tied to abstract market forces. This discourse defined the equitable measure of the value of labor, the roles of manufacturer and worker in the trade, and larger purposes of industry. Equally important, it depicted a masculine world of action and authority. Through this discursive formation, warehousers and their allies pursued a hegemony that signaled a new phase of class struggle.

The Acts were roundly deplored for their arbitrary effects on wages. Ricardo pronounced that "they were not merely an interference with the freedom of trade, but they cramped the freedom of labour itself" (*Hans.* n.s., 1823, IX, c. 149). The author of *Observations on the Ruinous Effects of the Spitalfields Acts* . . . claimed that "under a free system the master cannot have the workman unless he *pays his price*. This is the workman's security" (1822, p. 34). Freedom was thus the unrestrained capacity of the worker to bargain for wages in an open labor market. "I have no hesitation in calling it barbarous, oppressive and unjust," this observer continued, "for the weaver has the same natural right to the value of his labour, as the Nobleman has to the rents of his estates, the fundholder to his dividends. . . . To deprive the labourer of the full value of his work, is under any circumstances, an act of *Oppression and Robbery*; but to do this by means of a measure which affects to protect him, is indeed to add hypocrisy to injustice" (ibid., p. 76).

According to another commentator, the Acts were really laws nefariously designed so that petty, self-interested masters could "KEEP DOWN the wages of the journeymen, and do that, with which they unjustly charge others, namely PLUNDER their workmen of their due" (*Remarks* . . . 1822, p. 42). The champions of political economy in Parliament, Ricardo and Hume, confidently assured the weavers of a significant rise in their incomes with the freedom brought by repeal (*Hans.*, n.s., IX, c. 831; X, c. 742). The value of the weavers' efforts were thus divorced from their expressed rights as Britons, family needs, and standards as a self-defined collectivity.

The warehousers and their allies also sought to refashion the understanding of relations between state and economy. Neither the trade in general, nor any of those in its ranks, could claim any special protection. All interests were fairly represented when none were politically privileged. Favoritism caused unwarranted disturbances in the economic order: "The merchant and the manufacturer, the landlords and the farmer, who are *all labourers*, might claim under such a state of things, that their *rents and profits* should receive a corresponding augmentation" (*Observations* . . . 1822, p. 49).

The author of this tract equated the positions and actions of all economic actors as similarly productive, legitimating their claims through participation in an open market. Neither the weavers, nor any other workers, were owed protection because of their role as producers. In fact, such protection only depressed trade and increased the weavers' shameful reliance upon the parish (pp. 32–33). Labor was thus defined as just another commodity to be disposed of in the open market. This was in fundamental opposition to the artisans' moral economy, which envisioned labor as a marker of community and collective identities and a guarantor of citizenship claims.

The Acts, in a similar fashion, impinged on the freedom between the manufacturer and his employees. As "Verax" observed the truth was that weavers "would joyfully accede to the prices the masters could afford to pay; but they cannot judge for themselves, and are not at liberty to make a separate agreement with the master who employs them, because the work does, perhaps, belong, or is considered by a small body of journeymen, called a Committee" (1822, p. 9). The decision on wages was defined ideally as an atomized process, whereby each weaver was free to establish her or his own best return. More insidiously, trade wisdom was defined in terms of the degree of participation in market activity.

Beyond the boundaries of the trade relations, lay the greater realm of commerce. For the political economists, the blessings of unencumbered trade had born fruit in the great growth of the cotton industry. The rising tides of industrial expansion promoted by free commerce would wash away the periodic distress characteristic of the trade. As William Huskisson, president of the Board of Trade, explained, the Acts had "produced what monopoly is always sure to produce, indifference with regard to improvement" (*Hans.*, n.s., IX, c. 807). Echoing Huskisson, the handmaiden of the political economists, the *Edinburgh Review*, asserted that "had the silk manufacture been treated by the Government in the same way as the cotton manufacture . . . we should not have made equally rapid advances in both these great departments of manufacturing industry" (1825, v. 43, no. 85, p. 81; see also *Observations* . . . 1823, p. 18, *Hans*, n.s., X, 1824, c. 739).[2]

---

[2] The issue of machinery illustrates how discourse can create truth in the service of the powerful. Although much was made of the stagnation of the means of production, this had little to do with trade protection. As Natalie Rothstein has noted, most of the technology discussed was completely irrelevant to the trade, never used with the advent of steam power, or had

Free trade parented prosperity, and ultimately—repeal advocates intoned—capital must be set free to secure the weavers' well-being. "The great objects of the manufacturer are or ought to be, to extend the market for his commodities and increase the amount and productiveness of his capital; and the real interests of the labourer are secured exactly in proportion as these objects are accomplished" (*Observations* . . . 1823, p. 23). In the long run, the economic security of the weaver depended on the ability of the manufacturer to accumulate sufficient capital to expand the wage fund: "It is only as the capital of the masters is augmented that an increasing demand for labour can be created; and when once this *increasing demand* exists throughout the country, nothing short of the absurdity and injustice of the Spitalfields Act can possibly prevent the workmen from enjoying a rapid rise in wages" (ibid., pp. 73–74). This discourse thus placed the capitalist at the apex of decision making, defining the hierarchies of capital accumulation and trade authority as homologous. In so doing, it shifted the legitimate control of trade affairs, and undermined the weavers' claims to a voice in them as state and community matters. Indeed, the well-being of the nation was foremost construed as dependent upon the superiority of its capital.

The supporters of repeal acknowledged that the metamorphosis to free trade would bring suffering. Huskisson granted its inevitability: "There will always be partial interests that must suffer for a time; and all that Parliament can do, and that is its duty to do, is to deal with them as tenderly as possible" (P.C., set 16, v. 2, f. 16). The "partial interests" of course were those of the workers, and by implication the general interest was the alliance of consumers, capitalists, and the state. The state's duty to the workers was to see them through their misery.

To provide the rationale for quiescence in the face of acknowledged misery, the repealers moved outside of the boundaries of political economy to the terrain of religion. As Hilton (1958) and others have argued, forms of Evangelicalism intertwined with political economy in the hegemonic discourses, providing moral resonance for arguments that often sounded hollowly utilitarian. As we have seen, bourgeois proselytizers by this point had traversed Spitalfields' streets for over a decade, emphasizing spiritual resignation in the face of poverty. God's law continued where Ricardo's could not reach. As a proponent observed, "All men who have not property, whatever be their rank, profession, or pretensions, are obliged in order to live to dispose of their commodity, be it what it may, at the market price, . . . The labourer is obliged to dispose of his labour 'instantly' not because he is a labourer, but because he is poor. . . . His helplessness, so far as it consists in the necessity of constantly bringing his

---

little impact on productivity (1977, pp. 282–283). Indeed, the Act's supporters noted that any machinery used for silk weaving located elsewhere in England could be found in Spitalfields (*An Account* . . . 1823, p. 16; Hale 1822, p. 13).

labour to the existing market, is not caused by them. It is part of that higher legislation which has decreed that 'the poor shall always be with us'" (*Observations* . . . 1822, pp. 54–55).

The weavers and their allies zealously responded to the onslaught on the Acts. The defending group was an amalgam of weavers, small masters, local tradesmen and parishioners, other artisans, and Tories fearful of the seamless logic of political economy. They dialogically emphasized workers' collective rights; a notion of the common good, which was focused on the contributions of producers; an interventionist concept of the state; and ideas of freedom, property, and markets that were markedly at variance with those of political economy. The weavers did not denounce capitalism nor champion socialism. Rather, their ideological struggles occurred within the discursive formation demarcated by their combatants. Their fighting words are a dialogic engagement with this hegemonic discourse, and this marks it as a process of class formation.

Proponents contested the core assumption of political economy, that unfettered commerce was the natural order. They countered that all economic systems were necessarily social constructions created for the benefit of the entire community. This artifice was held together by the laws that regulated the system. "The law," wrote John Poyton, an activist weaver, "was designed at the first formation of civil society, for the mutual protection of the community at large" (*An Account* . . . , 1823, pp. 60–61). John Powell, a radical sympathetic to the weavers, propounded further lines on this theme:

> What is the end of all legislation, and even all human labour? Is it not regulation? Can that which is so useful in all other things become worse than useless in its application to labour? What principle of regulation, so equitable, so efficacious, so conformable to the genius of British legislation, and so calculated to secure the first principles of a well-regulated society, as the Spitalfields Acts? . . . But competition sustained at the expenses of the working classes will derange all legitimate interest in society, which interest can only be secured by the principle of the Spitalfields Acts. The insatiable avarice of many of the rich, into whose hands the power of legislation has fallen, has in all ages led them to adopt artificial arrangements further to separate labour and profit; and every succeeding age has refined upon this former art. (B.L., Add. MSS. 27805, Powell 1824, pp. 4–5)

Repeal was portrayed as an insidious means of extending economic and political inequities, and reinforcing the government as the sphere of the rich and powerful. It marked the transmutation of the government from a balancer of collective interests for the common good to the preserver of privileged interests. Class legislation was supplanting commonwealth regulation. A "Coventry Freeman" pointedly observed that, "It is notorious, that our new measures of legislation, are for the benefit of the rich, at the expense of the working classes" (B.L., Add. MSS. 27805, "Coventry Freeman" 1824, p. 3).

A weaver took this logic a step further. He noted with perspicacity that political economists wholly agreed that government was obliged to protect property. In dialectic fashion he argued that labor, being the weaver's sole property, deserved equal treatment to that of the estate or the factory. Like many among the working class, he seized upon a type of labor theory of value as a discourse of working-class rights: "It has been stated to the committee of the lords, 'that no interference of the law in labour is just.' Not just, Sir, why not? is not all acquired property protected by law, and is not that just? Why then should it not be just to protect natural property which is labour. Labour is the only property a poor man has, which is the root and origin of all the riches of the great and mighty, who are able to protect themselves, while the poor have neither the means nor the power of self-defense without the assistance of the law" (*An Account* ... 1823, p. 60; see also Powell 1824, p. 6). The Coventry Freeman echoed this labor theory of value, using it to reason that the workers' interests were indeed the *general* economic interest: "Human labour is the real standard of value, and it is in the interest of the capitalist, the agriculturalist, the merchant, and the manufacturer, that it should never be exchanged for less than its real worth" (p. 4).

This focus on labor was not merely a property of skill argument, as so aptly detailed by John Rule (1988). Rather, it was a more encompassing construction that those who controlled productive labor had legitimate collective claims on their trade and polity for their economic well-being. The result was simultaneously to validate the claims of the weaving community for protection and to valorize the masculine voice as authoritative. As we have noted, patriarchal cooperation in weaving households functionally acknowledged the importance of wives and daughters to the maintenance of the household economy. The bourgeois language of property rights, however, as a number of feminist scholars note, was specifically masculine in its definition of power and control.[3] In similar fashion, as Deborah Valenze argues, the discourse of political economy marked a radical transformation in the depiction of working women, solidifying a new conceptualization of poor women as morally deficient and incapable of independent action in the public sphere of the market (1995 pp. 129–130, 138–39). Women's claims thus were voiced by the independent men whose control of labor and household demarcated them as defenders of collective rights.

---

[3] Carole Pateman (1988), Ursula Vogel (1994), and Nancy Fraser and Linda Gordon (1994) all delineate how the possessive individualism of liberal social contract theory defined masculine prerogative.

Far from belying the natural order of society, the Acts perfectly mirrored the principles of accommodation that were the hallmarks of the British polity. Society did not cohere through free competition, but through the active accord of its members. "And what is the principle of the Spitalfields Acts?—Why an arbitration perfectly agreeing with the Constitution. It is not, as many may think, the magistrate who fixes the prices, any more than it is the King who makes the laws. But like the King, whose representative he is, the magistrate confirms the agreement made by the masters, who are the Lords—and the work people, who are the Commons; which confirmation makes the agreement general. . . . For what were those Acts given? To restrain the cunning, the fraud, the avarice and the tyranny of the Lords of the trade" (Powell 1824, pp. 2–3; see also Hale 1822, p. 6). This reliance on popular Constitutionalism should not be seen as precluding class interest. Rather, as James Epstein (1994) cogently demonstrates, workers expressed class-based citizenship claims through this radical discourse. The weavers engaged liberal social contract theory with the available discursive materials. Class resistance was and is often the fine art of making do.

Supporters also met the question of freedom of trade head on. Equating open markets to freedom was nothing more than a ruse for enslavement of workers (*An Account* . . . 1823, p. 13). "They with all the enmity to a free representation in Parliament, are clamorous advocates for a free trade as they call it. But what sort of freedom is it that they advocate? Why a freedom the very reverse of the thing they pretend; it is nothing more nor less, in application to the productive classes, *than freedom for the powerful to oppress and defraud the weak*" (Coventry Freeman 1824, p. 5). The definition of freedom was defined not by control of markets or capital but by productive contributions to society. And it is at least plausible to read in these lines a manifest tension between free traders and producers.

Again appropriating a labor theory of value, Powell argued that the state and employers had a responsibility to workers. The weavers were part of the productive classes whose sweat secured the resources of the state and produced the employers' profits. The productive supported the nonproductive: moral and civic reciprocity demanded protection in return. "Do not producers pay all the taxes? Is not profit a tax? And why should not that be restrained within due limits? But what tax is so oppressive as that tax imposed by the avaricious employer upon his work people? If the work people are compelled to produce beyond what is necessary for themselves, all that excess which sustains the national taxes, the result of an artificial state of society, ought they not to enjoy some artificial production that will secure them sufficient for subsistence?" (1824, p. 3).

Within the weavers' response, full employment and fair remuneration were at parity with the manufacturers' profits. This was skillfully articulated through counter-hegemonic appropriation. Hale invoked Father Smith as a foil to the repealers, observing that "the very principles of sound political economy have been violated. Dr. Adam Smith says 'a man must always live by his work; and his wages must, at least, be sufficient to maintain him'" (1822, p. 41). And Powell sardonically cited Smith on prosperity: "Adam Smith, an authority our great pretenders are fond of quoting, says, 'the prosperity of a country consists in the comforts and enjoyments that the people, both rich and poor, possess beyond the common necessaries of life'" (1824, p. 5). By drawing upon Smith and other luminaries to fashion their dialogic response, the weavers attempted to build legitimacy for their claims through the dominant formation. These were small acts of subversion through selective appropriation.

The weavers and their supporters counterposed a "practical" knowledge of trade to the theoretical nostrums of political economy. In so doing, they sought to expose those discourses as ungrounded in its very objects, biased and dangerous to the larger good. "I find that the doctrine of *unrestrained Freedom of Trade* is at variance with all that I know of in nature or society, and evinces a superficial knowledge of human labour," wrote the Coventry Freeman (1824, p. 13). The weavers petitioned the Lords not to allow them "to be sacrificed under the principles of what is called 'political economy,' which at most can be considered a speculative measure" (*An Account . . .* 1823, p. 47).

The weavers and their allies also sought to re-link matters of economy and polity where they had been uncoupled through political economy discourses. Because they were productive workers, weavers were also able to maintain their roles as loyal, independent, and responsible citizens. Political and economic rights were the warp and weft of common good and societal stability. Protection, prosperity, and order were thus part of the whole cloth of society. "Through this salutary Act we have been kept from general pauperism, and the public by our reason and industry have been able to carry on their business in supplying our numerous body with the necessaries of life; and we, as useful members of society, have been able to provide for our families, and support the parishes, instead of being paupers on the same. . . . At a time when in almost every part of the kingdom minds of the lower classes of society were seized with a revolutionary frenzy, the weavers of Spitalfields remained well affected towards the government" (*An Account* 1823, p. 20; see also Hale 1822, p. 16, Coventry Freeman, 1824, p. 19).[4] Through such statements, the weavers attempted to shift the bases of their claims as citizens away from the sphere of the economy to that of the nation. Patriotism was a currency of citizenship for

---

[4] As I argue elsewhere (1995b), the weavers dialogically developed citizenship claims through intersecting discourses of popular political economy and Constitutionalism, nationalism and patriotism, and masculine responsibility and prerogative. The free Briton, a male householder who had served his country and whose labor was the backbone of national prosperity, was a legitimate collective identity with which to assert claims on the state. The emphases on property ownership and military service in particular structured women's claims as dependents, since they were largely *de jure* excluded from these categories.

the disenfranchised. Male workers long had been able to assert rights as defenders of the nation, with military service validating their both their masculinity and status as free Britons (see Colley 1992, Steinberg 1995b). Many weavers were veterans of the Napoleonic wars, and as we have seen a number held tepid enthusiasm for radical agitation.

Most profoundly, the weavers argued that repeal was not just an issue of economic policy, but of the destruction of a cultivated way of life. In this sense it politically abnegated basic civic rights. It was, as one weaver termed it, "the worst species of assassination" (*An Account* . . . 1823, p. 60). It also was a direct threat to the male weaver's status as workshop and household head. Repeal would undermine the male weaver's capacity to provide for his family. Under the Acts he was able to argue that he could "maintain his family in a certain degree of comfort and peace" (*An Account* . . . 1823, p. 3). The control of production that provided for the household needs validated patriarchal authority. By threatening the economic independence of the household, repeal would subvert this authority.

The weavers countered the religious messages contained in the dominant formation with their own partly subversive reading of the Bible. "There is no law" observed the Coventry Freeman, "that any man should labour for another; for nature has bestowed all her gifts in common, and the appropriation can only be maintained by a compact or mutual agreement" (1824, p. 8). Providence in no way mandated poverty.

Instead, they found in the gospel an affirmation that the earth's bounty was common property. In a circular delivered to members of Parliament during the debates, they observed that "It may be said of the weaving business, what Solomon said of husbandry—the profits of the earth are for all" (*Account* . . . 1823, p. 25). John Poyton, a union leader, pointedly reminded warehousers of the Lord's wrath should they become blind to this principle:

> The Lord will pour out his vengeance on the oppressors of the poor and needy, that keep back the hire of the labourer by fraud and violence, which (by the by) is entered into the ears of the Lord of the Saboath, whose voice is, "go to now, ye rich men, howl and weep, for the miseries that shall come upon you. Your riches are corrupted; your gold and silver is cankered; and the rust of them shall be a witness against you, and shall eat your flesh like fire, and be as burning metal in your bowels." James v. 3, 4
>
> Thus, Sir, humanity and Christianity both entreat, that you should use all means in your power, to save the rich from perdition, and the poor from being destroyed by oppression. (Ibid., p. 62)

The struggle over the Acts continued at a pitched level for over two years. The weavers, using sophisticated lobbying techniques and public demonstrations, halted repeal in the House of Lords in 1823. As one weaver lyrically recorded of this victorious skirmish:

> Against our lawful rights with vengeance fired,
> Obdurate fiends and treacherous friends conspired;
> In secret ambush long the ambiguous foe,
> Aimed at our commonwealth the deadly blow;
> Impending ruin stormed each vital pore,
> *Still Hope's* indulging influence watched the door.
> Wrongs unprovoked the British Lion roused,
> And freedom's sons her native cause espoused.
> (*An Account* . . . 1823, p. 67)

But in 1824 the lion grew listless, and Hope no longer stood vigilant. In early February, Francis Place, writing to Joseph Hume on the upcoming parliamentary agenda, took particular note of the repeal debate. He commented that the weavers' campaigns reflected what "poverty and dependence does to mankind." "People such as these miserable weavers," he smugly observed, "must be saved against their own inclinations" (B.L., Add. MSS. 27804, Place Papers; Place to Hume, Feb. 9, 1824).

The repeal bill introduced by William Huskisson speedily swept through both Houses in May and was given royal consent in June. A few concessions were made, largely in the interests of merchants and warehousers.[5] The weavers turned their sights toward their impending degradation, and prepared for a largely new terrain of struggle.

The battles fought over repeal had forced the silk weavers to confront political economy, what they themselves admitted was "the ruling order of the day in both Houses of Parliament" (*An Account* . . . 1823, pp. 3–4). Through their collective actions, the weavers constructed counterhegemonic discourses to denaturalize and expose this discursive formation. The response was dialogically attuned to the dominant formation structured by capitalists and the state. The Acts' half century of labor peace precipitated few confrontations mandating fighting words. The repeal threat, however, demanded framing; the voices of power required the chorus of a collective response.

That response met head on the discourses of political economy, with fighting words whose constructions of the world were often contrapuntal in meanings. Where the repealers offered private contracts of the marketplace, the weavers argued for a social contract between themselves, their employers, and the state. Where capitalists found freedom in unregulated

---

[5] The prohibition against foreign goods was extended into 1826 to ensure that the trade had adequate time to prepare for the invasion of imports. Size restrictions were placed on imported wrought cloth in an effort to forestall the onslaught, since the French customarily made fabrics in a different standard size. Duties on wrought silk were set at 30% ad valorem.

markets, the weavers found it in trade protection. Where political economists constructed the unfettered control of capital as an absolute right, weavers found the control of their only property, their labor, and its reasonable remuneration as a foundation of a just society. In this dialogic interplay, fundamental notions of polity and economy, citizenship and artisanship, justice and property were both products of and further guides for struggle into the 1830s.

This was a part of a process of class formation much as Thompson has argued, an ever-closer engagement with the moral language of the ruling order as the struggle intensified. It is also precisely what some post-materialists misconstrue as populist political discourse when they errantly search for a specific class vocabulary. As we have seen, however, class interests are dialogic constructions; their articulation is from within and frequently is constructed through battles at the margins of dominant meanings, not from beyond them.

Moreover, the construction of rights within a discourse focused on the moral claims of property and civic liberties reinforced a specifically masculine basis to the weavers' claims. Since wives were legally dependents, and thus precluded from the public spheres of economy and polity, their claims had to be asserted through their husbands. Their silence throughout the years of this conflict represents not only the general exclusion of women's voices from the public sphere but their occlusion as legitimate claimants within the dialogue of struggle. Thus, the dialogic battle within political economy simultaneously affirmed the male weavers' rights as producers, citizens, and household heads at the same time that it marginalized women. Claims made on their behalf as members of productive households presage the discourse of militant domesticity that Anna Clark (1992, 1995) documents in the rhetoric of Chartism.

Through these fighting words, the male silk weavers also articulated a powerful sense of collective identity that generalized to a wider understanding of class. Their productive labor affirmed their status as valued members of the community and the society, citizens deserving protection. As the controllers of this labor, male weavers also validated their identities as heads of the household and workshop, a masculinity requisite for their status as honorable tradesmen. Their loyalty to nation and military service marked them as patriots. In combination, *and* posed in contrast to those whom they saw as their oppressors, these facets melded into a nascent identity of class.

The silk weavers' moral economy legitimated redress from both the state and capital. The history of post-repeal collective actions illustrates how this understanding led the weavers to defend their lawful rights against obdurate fiends and treacherous friends on both fronts of power.

CHAPTER SIX

Post-Repeal Collective Actions: Battling the Hydra of Degradation

*T*he emergence of class consciousness, Thompson insisted, was always the last part of the process of class formation, not the first. Class struggle was its necessary precursor. The collective actions that compose this struggle, argue social scientists, are learned collective repertoires that develop over time and are, dependent on patterns of interaction and social networks, sustainable resources, and structures of opportunity that make the risks intelligible and bearable to the participants. In this book, I maintain that we should see these perspectives as profitable but incomplete and that an analysis of fighting words shows both the discursive foundations of class consciousness and the standards of justice that underpin the decision to act collectively. In the preceding chapter, I analyzed the ways in which the fighting words of the Spitalfields silk weavers were a product of a particular dialogic process.

To wholly understand how the weavers articulated a class consciousness and to identity through these fighting words the ways they made their collective actions intelligible, we need to take careful account of the fights as well. In this chapter, I conjoin the analysis of discursive and instrumental repertoires of collective action to provide this dynamic. As I suggested in the introduction, repertoires of fighting words and collective actions are recursively tied to each other. Discourse bounds and shapes the collective intelligibility of action and in doing so illuminates oppressors and the appropriate channels for redress. To the extent that the two repertoires are not mutually reinforcing, groups can be pressed to examine the assumptions and understandings that underlie their actions. As we shall see, however, in the case of the silk weavers, the performatives of collective action can in and of themselves validate collective identities, even if actors do not realize collective goals. Moreover, the constrictions of the dialogic process and the inertia of learned instrumental repertoires, make change a very protracted process.

In this chapter, I analyze the dynamic between instrumental and discursive repertoires in the context of post-repeal conditions. Repeal started a new chapter in the silk weavers' collective life and struggles. The once honorable artisans found their collective identity, economic security, and community status under siege by free trade. In both words and deeds, the weavers fought back. The silk weavers pressed both the state and the warehousers through the end of the decade. In the half-dozen years after repeal, the weavers believed that some form of renewed government protection was possible, or at least legitimately mandated by their conditions. At the same time, they also turned to the strike to shore up sagging piece rates. This interplay of action on two fronts was a distinctive feature of their repertoire.

The weavers framed redress through a revamped moral economy that had been conditioned by the repeal fight, one that in the weavers' terms called for "equal justice." Through their fighting words, the weavers elaborated their collective interests as aggrieved artisans and citizens. This framing of their plight created multiple possibilities for action and suggested the reasonableness of making the state and capitalists their targets. Although these fighting words framed paths for redress, they could not ensure their success. A critical piece of the post-repeal story is how the senses of collective identity, rights, and redress made intelligible a set of actions that yielded little lasting success. An equally important piece of this tale is how fleeting triumphs and more enduring losses deepened a collective consciousness of class.

This chapter is divided into three parts. In the first two, I survey the post-repeal changes in the silk industry and the local political culture respectively. I then analyze the discursive and instrumental repertoires of the weavers, concentrating on the period from 1826 to 1831.

The Silk Trade in the Post-Repeal Period: The Backward March of Progress

Despite the cheery prognostications of the political economists, repeal led the silk trade into progressively worsening cycles of depression. Between each slump, there were brief plateaus of respite. Ultimately, the silk trade succumbed to these successive blows, throwing thousands of weavers into destitution and reducing the once honorable trade to sweated outwork.

With foreign silks destined to reach London docks in July, the start of 1826 saw the trade plunge into what one merchant termed a "calamitous depression" (P.P. 1832, XIX, p. 232). The following year brought a partial relief from the ravages of 1826. Although French imports increased modestly, a marked rise in thrown silk imported for domestic production brought Huskisson to crowing, "I am enabled to add that the result of free competition has been this—that more real improvement has been made in the silk manufacture of this country within the last twelve months than had been made for half a century before" (Smart 1964, v. 2, p. 373).

While both sides continued to debate the increasing encroachment of legal French imports (a meteoric 75 percent over 1826) more troubling to many in the trade was the seemingly endless flood of illegal goods. Virtually all manufacturers, including members of the repeal vanguard, complained of a large increase in smuggling (P.P. 1832, XIX, pp. 13, 34, 258, 294, 479, 495, 752; Badnall 1828, p. 92). Even Huskisson conceded the practice to be widespread, and its extent convinced a few ardent free traders in Parliament that repeal had been an unfortunate experiment (*Hans.*, n.s, v. 21, 1829, cc. 758, 761).

As the depression stretched into 1829, at least one-third of the looms in the trade stood silent. Parliament debated the issue of smuggling as Spitalfields languished. Thomas Fyler, M.P. for Coventry, queried in a motion for a select committee investigation: "Were vested rights to be obliged to yield to the influence of political or experimental opinions?" (*Hans.*, n.s., v. 21, 1829, c. 745; Smart 1964, v. 2, p. 479). Firm free traders, however, were unmoved by these emotional pleas. Several, such as Poulett-Thomson, found affirmation of their ideology in the smuggling issue.

> There is, in economical as well as political affairs, a point beyond which it is not possible to go—a point [at] which legislation becomes ineffectual, and power powerless. Governments may enact laws, but mankind will successfully resist them. Thus it is with these attempts. The smuggler becomes, in such a case, the corrector of faulty legislation, and the friend and defender of mankind. . . . The very essence of manufacturing and commercial industry is freedom from legislative interference. (1829, cc. 840, 843)

The dominant discursive formation could explain policy successes and failures equally well.

In the weavers' eyes, such statements rubbed salt in a festering wound, even though duties were relaxed to discourage the covert trade (B. Gordon 1979, p. 111). Ideologically and politically, however, the lines and balance of power between free trade and protection held fast. The trade maintained a tenuous viability into the 1831 season, but soon fell into what Ambrose Moore described as the worst distress he had ever seen. Once again, at least a third of the looms in Spitalfields were idled for nine months (P.P. 1832, XIX, pp. 654, 759, 918; P.P. 1834, X, p. 9).

The short spates of slight relief that the trade experienced partially obscured more underlying and cumulative processes. Throughout the period, profits for the manufacturer and wholesaler were increasingly depressed. By 1829, a veteran manufacturer was claiming that the total capital involved in the trade had been slashed by half (P.P. 1833, VI, p. 86). As capital shrank, it also coagulated in the centers of market power. A Coventry ribbon merchant who had a London office decried the power of this oligopoly: "Two or three individuals exercise more power over the silk trade than the government have the power to entirely counteract. . . . The trade requires more protection against the power of these men than against foreign competition" (H.O. 44/18; W. Merry to Wellington; 8 May 1829).

Commanding the largest amount of capital, warehousers escalated their control by buying large stocks at discounted cash prices. Although formerly credit had been advanced six to twelve months ahead of delivery of an order, warehousers were now demanding ready goods for ready money. Many smaller manufacturers were unable to survive without credit; this competition sounded their death knell. In the six years after repeal, between one-third and a half of all firms in the Spitalfields trade went bankrupt, most from 1828 on. Upheaval victimized only two or three of the substantial houses. Although larger amounts of capital were controlled by fewer hands, the expected triumph of machinery was, as the weavers had predicted, a chimera. In fact, the use of the more sophisticated and newer looms actually decreased (P.P. 1832, XIX, pp. 296, 338, 436, 488, 685; P.P. 1833, VI, p. 86; P.P. 1834, X, p. 340; P.C., set 16, v. 2., f. 59; Badnall 1828, p. 93; Rothstein 1977, p. 284; Warner 1921, p. 458).

For the weavers, this reality was an almost continuous nightmare. Post-repeal depressions eroded the foundations of honorability and brought the scourge of degradation. There was a marked shrinkage of the privileged fancy branches. One veteran manufacturer estimated that by 1831 these branches, which had produced as much as half of all goods before repeal, constituted only one-tenth to one-eighth of the trade, perhaps a meager three hundred looms. By 1832, only seventy-nine firms had survived free trade, and only thirteen of them dealt in any fancy branches (P.P. 1832, XIX, pp. 212, 488, 701, 725, 739).

With the skilled portion of the trade whittled away, the weavers' artisanal status suffered irreversibly. Weavers were rapidly becoming little more than shuttlecock throwers; the honorability of the trade was dissolving with its artistry. Moreover, by excising an enormous portion of the highest-paid weaving positions, plain branches weavers could no longer aspire to greater heights. Finally, the crisis further aggravated a bad situation by exiling the skilled weavers into the lower end of an already glutted labor market.

All these events pushed piece rates through the floor. The Spitalfields district suffered an estimated aggregate loss of over 300,000 pounds in wages each year due to the competition. Piece rates in what remained of the fancy branches dropped by at least 25 to 30 percent and at least 20 to 25 percent in the plain branches in the first few years. For the entire six years, estimates of 40 to 50 percent were commonly stated (P.P. 1832, XIX, pp. 387–389, 476, 479; P.P. 1834, X, pp. 4, 324; Prout 1829, p. 23). By 1831, a plain branch weaver, working a sixty to seventy-four hour week, earned between seven and ten shillings. One manufacturer estimated that weavers' average wages were dropping at a rate five times faster than the price of provisions. Many weavers, however, were lucky even to receive this pittance: half-work became increasingly common, even in the lowest end of the trade. Additionally, as the weavers sank into degradation, many sold their looms to alleviate their misery. Loom brokering spread; added deductions for rentals further constricted net wages, especially hitting part-timers (P.P. 1832, XIX, pp. 211, 213–214, 476, 651, 770; P.P. 1834, X, p. 8).

As this process of progressive immiseration unfolded, the weavers received another stunning blow in 1829. Because of the tremendous rise in embezzlement of goods (analyzed previously) the number of manufacturers who withheld advances for work rose significantly. With about £160,000 worth of silk out to weavers at any one time, the manufacturers were understandably nervous. Increasingly, they paid only upon receiving the finished goods, a process that took, on average, from two to four weeks for a plain broadcloth. In the interim, the rumbling of stomachs became a familiar accompaniment to the clacking of the looms (P.P. 1834, XXIX, app. A, pt. III, p. 109a; P.P. 1832, XIX, p. 739; P.C., set 16, v. 2, f. 134).

The protracted depression reduced many weavers to utter destitution. A number took to hawking common provisions in the street. Pawn-brokers reaped a grim reward with heavy traffic. The extreme destitution caught the notice of many observers. An informant to the Home Office wrote in the spring of 1830 that some weavers were "literally starving with work" (H.O. 40/27, ff. 514–519; Whatton to Peel, March 20, 1830). The London radical William Lovett was repelled by the devastation of depression:

> In whole streets that we visited we found nothing worthy of the name of bed, bedding or furniture; a little straw, a few shavings, a few rags in the corner formed their beds—a broken chair, stool or butter-barrel their seats—and a saucepan or a cup or two, their only cooking utensils. Their unpaved yards, and filthy courts, and the want of drainage and cleansing, rendered their houses hotbeds of disease; so that fever combined with hunger was committing great ravages among them. (1967, v. 1, p. 57)

Even the contentious warehouser, Ambrose Moore, was moved to observe, "They, in fact, possess nothing, if I may so speak, really beyond the extent of their own skins" (P.P. 1832, XIX, p. 770).

The Post-Repeal Parish

The depression brought increasing strain upon parishes in Spitalfields. Many, especially the small tradesmen and merchants, who formed the backbone of the vestries, had voiced fears about repeal, since their prosperity was firmly tied to that of the weavers. Parish officials, led by Robert Brutton (who had served as a weavers' society solicitor), continued to lend their political and moral support to the weavers' cause with petitions for import prohibitions and trade regulation in 1826 and 1827 (P.C., set 16, v. 2, ff. 38–39, 78; *TFP,* Jan. 22, 29, 1826).

Initially after repeal, St. Matthew's Bethnal Green parish aided weavers with wage supplements. The explosion of half-work, however, coupled with rising unemployment, forced a sharp reduction in this practice by 1828. From 1824 to 1832, the workhouse population rose 183 percent, while outdoor relief rocketed 2,152 percent. Although the increases were most dramatic in Bethnal Green, other parishes also felt the full weight of distress (P.P. 1832, XIX, pp. 719, 732; P.P. 1834, XXIX, app. A, pt. III, pp. 107a, 109a; H.O. 40/24, ff. 110–111; Aug. 10, 1829, Whatton to Peel; Tower Hamlets Local History Coll., Old Artillery Ground Trustees' Minutes Book 1828–1831 [S.46]; Old Artillery Ground Treasurer's Account Book for Disbursements on Behalf of the Poor, 1826–1836 [S.73]; Old Artillery Ground Pauper Examination Books, 1826–1836 [(S.80]).

Need rapidly began to outstrip the parishes' capacity to provide relief. In Bethnal Green, poor rates more than doubled between 1821 and 1831, and the parish accumulated a debt of 13,000 pounds. Only about one-fifth of the parish's shopkeepers, caught between shrinking business and rising rates, could afford to pay parish rates. James Bunn, an overseer, observed grimly, "We must depend on providence, I do not see what is to save us from ruin, if Government doesn't do something for us." Overseers increasingly used the ultimate threat of artisanal degradation, the workhouse, to discourage requests for outdoor relief (P.P. 1832, XIX, p. 719; P.P. 1834, XXIX, app. A, pt. III, p. 108a; P.P. 1834, XXXV, app. B.2, pt. IV. pp. 83f, 83i; *TFP,* July 23, 1826).

Many weavers staggered into the net of hegemony to seek relief from the Evangelical bourgeoisie's charities. In March of 1829, the Soup Society was dispensing seven thousand quarts of soup a day, and by April it was reported that twenty thousand a day were receiving relief, many no doubt from benefit societies primed by city funds (P.P. 1834, XXIX, app. A, pt. III, p. 120a; *WFP,* March 14, April 25, 1829).

On the legal side, I have shown how the weavers' moral economy became increasingly subject to attacks by manufacturers. Magistrates such as Bennett and Twyford could be sympathetic. The tissue of trade practices, however, which had been the common stock of production, including wage advances and the expectations upon finishing dates, was not legally fortified. Compassion and empathy could neither negate nor exceed the law's dictates, which the bench dispensed through the legal theatrics of impartiality. Increasingly, the law chafed against some of the central tenets of the weavers' standards of trade propriety and equity. Moreover, the growing prosecution of embezzlement and neglect of work made the approach to the bench increasingly foreboding. For the most part, then, the local rule of law, intertwined with the discourse of political economy, became increasingly distant from the weavers' moral economy.

The parish world, which had once affirmed the weavers as honorable artisans, was collapsing under pressure. With adequate relief no longer a guaranteed community right, their collective identity under siege, and their standards of rights and justice increasingly betrayed and denied, the hardscrabble quest for security, respectability, and indemnity had to be conducted by other means.

The Post-Repeal Repertoire of Discursive and Instrumental Action

After repeal, old patterns of trade and community life were fading, and a new order was emerging. In their search for redress, the weavers drew on the fighting words that had matured in their struggles over repeal in order to inject their own moral standards and preferred solutions. Their collective actions were neither simply reactive nor guided by a supra-class political populism. The repeal of the Acts fostered increasing disaffection from their former allies in the state and the trade, which we can understand as embedded in a class perspective. As Hale informed the Home Office, "they think themselves altogether out of the Protection of Government and are consequently becoming disaffected, and as their minds become alienated from Government they become equally so from their Masters" (H.O. 40/19, ff. 3–4).

The pressing goal of the weavers' actions was to resurrect some form of protection for their labor. As we have seen, weavers argued that such protection was due their "only property" as productive contributors to the nation, and to male weavers particularly as maintainers of the household and defenders of the country.

Before turning to a selective narrative of the weavers' discursive and instrumental repertoires, I present an overview of the latter. A partial list of the weavers' collective actions is presented in tabular form in Appendix 1. Given that much of the male weavers' activities may have transpired in the obscurity of public-house branch organizations, the actual activity level is understated.

This list reveals several features of the weavers' collective action repertoire. First, there was a relatively high and continuing level of mobilization among some portion of the weavers from 1826 through 1830. Although there are fewer collective actions listed for 1828, a great deal of the activity in this year surrounding wage protection legislation likely transpired in branch organizations and through lobbying efforts.

The relative constancy of the mobilization among the weavers' community suggests that the weavers' actions were not just reflexive with trade cycles, or based on a simple economic calculus. Conversely, the list suggests that levels of collective action were not a simple function of mobilized resources nor of opportunity costs. Increasing levels of unemployment, and the major bouts of extreme distress, were in themselves insufficient to prevent mobilization, as shown by the two general strikes of 1827 and 1829. In addition, migration to a neighboring parish to claim relief, or to another weaving region in search of work, attenuated ties created by neighborhood, trade branch, common employer, and shared recreation (H.O. 40/23, f. 143; Whatton to Peel, April 7, 1829). Despite these growing disadvantages, weavers continued to mobilize and act.

Secondly, the list reveals a changing repertoire that spanned most of the spectrum of activities used by working-class groups reviewed in Chapter 2, as well as the contrapuntal character of the targets of collective action. Petitioning the government in particular was one form that predominated, as it did among many trade groups during these years. The periodic reconstitution of a general trade society was also a familiar action for their pub-based trade societies. Yet the weavers moved well beyond these two standard forms of their pre-repeal repertoire, and eclectically drew upon unfamiliar strategies, including most importantly the general strike. The manufacturers and the arms of the state oscillated as the weavers' principal targets in a fairly stable pattern. Although other trades directed their efforts in varying degrees at both employers and the states, few exhibited such shifting temporal rhythms.

The final feature revealed by the list is the weavers' overarching goal of labor protection. Although their actions varied, their mission was always the same and wholly intelligible within the moral calculus of their fighting words.

In a comparative perspective, the weavers' repertoire seems to be somewhat at variance with those of other London trades and with national patterns of labor contention. Few if any of the other London trades devoted as much effort to trade or wage protection. Additionally, the silk weavers were late comers to, or lesser participants in, other working-class actions of these years. This was perhaps true of radical politics through the mid-1820s, and certainly so for cooperation, despite some attention by pundits within the movement (*The Co-Operative Magazine and Monthly Herald*, v. 1, no. 11, Nov. 1826, pp. 333–337 and n.s., no. 5, May 1827, p. 227; *The Lancashire Co-Operator*, no. 6, Aug. 20, 1831, p. 5; P.C., set 16, v. 2, f. 70; *TFP*, Dec. 3, 1826; *WFP*, Aug. 22, 1829).

The content and pattern of the weavers' repertoire lies in their discourses of contention that mediated between experience and action. The notion of working peoples' just entitlement to a living wage provided a cogent logic for targeting both the state and capitalists for redress. Just as important, this was a class (and increasingly patriarchal) logic. Its inner logic can be understood only within the ways of struggle that the weavers created to oppose the exploitative and oppressive relationships that had arrived with the annunciation of Acquisitive Man.

To understand the persistence of the weavers in the face of repeated failure requires not only a careful contextual reading of their fighting words, but also of the ways in which their discursive and instrumental repertoires were mutually reinforcing. Even though the state remained intransigent in the face of repeated pleas for protection, the public theater of petitioning reinforced the actions directed at the state as a "peculiar privilege" of working people and free Britons. Authorities played their roles in the drama, giving the process credibility, and support from a few M.P.s further legitimized their efforts. The organs of government, through the processes of denying the weavers' claims, legitimated their rights and identities as claimants as inscribed by the discourses.

It is the relationship between the weavers' instrumental and discursive repertoire to which I devote the remainder of this analysis. In the exploration of selected actions below, I illustrate how through these fighting words silk weavers framed possibilities for action, provided collective efficacy, and legitimated claims and targets of redress. In these fighting words is a class vision of a just world for which pain should be endured and blood shed, even as the weavers slowly edged toward the precipice of extinction.

Post-Repeal Collective Actions

"PERISH POLITICAL ECONOMY," trumpeted an editorial in the *Trades' Free Press* on the weavers' plight, "BUT LET THE PEOPLE LIVE" (Jan. 22, 1826). In the post-repeal era, the weavers warmed to such pronouncements. The dawn of this brave new world witnessed continued appeals to the government to reverse or postpone the opening of ports to foreign silks. These lobbying efforts, however, were met with intransigence by the architects of the new trade policy. During a January 1826 audience with the Board of Trade, free traders lectured the weavers that they were "very much mistaken" in their analysis of their situation. The weavers' delegation listened with incredulity and dismay. A friend of the weavers, in lieu of this snub, described the government's relief efforts as a "sop for Cerberus—a mere bribe to quiet the loyalty of the Spitalfields weavers." "Having first broken the heads of these poor 'Operatives,'" he commented sarcastically, "this is the plaister" (P.C., set 16, v. 2, f. 29).

The weavers themselves deferentially framed the issues as ones of justice and societal needs, common themes of the discursive repertoire developed during the repeal struggles. In March, they again petitioned the Commons for some relief, maintaining their argument that the theory of free trade could not realize the reality of maintaining a productive and equitable economy. Their plea contained a hint of their growing underlying "alienation from the government."

> His Majesty's Ministers thought our fears were childish, and that our views were those of unlettered poor journeymen. . . . Your petitioners cannot for a moment see the prospect of free competition or foreign trade, at the approaching critical juncture as but a fatal derangement of the whole system of that artificial state (the Prohibition Laws) under which this nation has flourished and under which your petitioners have prospered in a state of happiness and tranquility for a long series of years. Your petitioners, therefore, with all humility, venture to call upon your honourable House still to exercise justice, and continue to observe that line of policy . . . as will enable them to live by their own industry in that branch of manufacture to which they have always been accustomed . . . England does not stand in need of foreign competition of any article whatever in the Silk Trade; for it can be clearly shown that our operatives are fully competent to supply to the utmost demand which could possibly be required. (*TFP*, March 16, 1826)

The recrudescent themes of guaranteeing equity for independent productive labor and the balancing of social interests were repertoire features echoed from the recent repeal debates.

As the weavers shed their suppliant position, a transformed collective determination began to emerge. Speakers depicted the weavers' interests as opposed to those of the manufacturers and Parliament, and themselves as the vanguard element in the struggle for protection and against degradation. Proactive collective and independent action became another element of the discursive repertoire. It was increasingly clear that they could not rely on the wisdom or fairness of either the manufacturers or Parliament. This new emphasis was voiced during a May 1826 meeting.

> Mr. Jones rose again, and said . . . It was right to tell them that they had nothing to expect from their masters or the Government,—they must rely upon themselves alone. They must be united. If they suffered themselves to be separated they would be easily broken, like the bundle of sticks in the fable; they would be degraded,—and in six month's time in a much worse state than at present: but if united, they might resist oppression. . . .
>
> Mr. Robert Noquet then rose to move the first resolution, to the effect that during the late distresses their employers had taken an unjust advantage of their workmen, in reducing the price of work nearly 30 per cent., while provisions had increased in price.
>
> Mr. Wallis wished to make a few observations on this. It was true, he said, that the masters were highly blamable [*sic*], and had carried the reductions to a grievous extent, but he must say that it was in part the men's fault. They

were not united and true to themselves. He highly eulogized the principles of Mr. Hale [i.e., protection], but he said that the men had it in their own power to fix a minimum without having it fixed by an Act of Parliament. The security which they had enjoyed for 50 years, under the Spitalfields Acts, had made them lax and supine, but they must now rally again, prosperity had passed away and adversity had come upon them. What he should propose was the raising of a fund to support each other against any unjust depreciation attempted by their employers. (P.C., set 16, v. 2, f. 59)

From this meeting emerged the General Protection Society, an umbrella organization for the local trade societies. In a solicitation to their brother tradesmen, the secretaries of the new society reminded them of their righteous status as household providers: "The often-asserted fact, that no Journeyman Mechanic (who is willing to work for his living) should be paid a less rate for labour than will enable him to provide for the wants of his family, is a truth which the enemies of fair remuneration for labour cannot successfully disprove; and, when innovations for labour are made by avaricious and unprincipled employers, it is a duty incumbent upon us, the working classes, to resist such innovations to the utmost of our power" (*TFP*, July 2, 1826). The responsibility of the household, which in Evangelical bourgeois discourses suggested supplication to trade forces and an aversion to radicalism, became a call for class action and the reassertion of patriarchal authority. As Anna Clark (1995) argues, patriarchal organization of the family became a pivot point by which male workers were able to turn such bourgeois discourse against itself.

Subscriptions were started, and a delegation visited masters to determine their willingness to return to 1824 prices. A large number of masters, many with some reluctance, agreed, contingent on acceptance by their peers. Several large firms, however, expressed unmitigated opposition, and negotiations continued into the late summer (*TFP*, July 30, 1826; P.C., set 16, v. 2, ff. 61–62).

The weavers received public support from their Macclesfield brethren, with whom they had been in contact. Issuing an address in support of trade protection, the Macclesfield weavers argued that free trade undermined the male weaver's role as guardian and provider, reinforcing this element of the repertoire: "His industry, which should promote the welfare of his family, ultimately hastens to its ruin; . . . he beholds his helpless family bereft of their natural protector, and compelled to apply to that miserable and degrading substitute, the parochial fund" (*TFP*, July 9, 1826). The weavers castigated the freedom touted by political economy as the liberty of manufacturers and the government to extract the fruits of the workers' toil, dialogically engaging both in the meaning of the term. Their formulation of freedom reflects a critical element of the Spitalfields weavers' discursive repertoire:

Is labour free?—Yes—for the rich capitalist to command it at his will and pleasure, and generally speaking, for what price he chooses. . . .

Is labour free?—Yes—to pay immense taxation, enormous pensions, and a standing army in time of peace, a great part of whose employment is to keep people in awe, which, if properly paid for their labour, would be loyal and obedient subjects.

Is labour free for the operative to fix the value of his labour? We answer, no; for though he is not compelled by the law of the land to work for what is not a living price, yet he is compelled by necessity—his poverty renders him dependent—his master's will is his law. (Ibid.)

The weavers were dismayed with the manufacturers' foot-dragging. William Thompson, a committee member, reflecting on their unsuccessful negotiations, observed, "No class of men . . . was more ill-used than the Journeymen Weavers; not so much by the Government as by many of the silk-manufacturers, who having exerted themselves to get the Spitalfields Act repealed, took advantage of the repeal to reduce the price so low, that with their utmost endeavours, the men could barely obtain sufficient to support a miserable existence" (P.C., set 16, v. 2, f. 66). The weight of recent experience with the large manufacturers echoed in the weavers' discourse. Because of the history of the small masters in the trade, the discourses of the repeal debate partly had constructed manufacturers as guardians and partners who shared a moral responsibility to ensure the health of the industry. Based on their experiences with warehousers and the district's small masters, weavers had made distinctions between rapacious masters and those with scruples. As the former warehousers ascended to dominance, however, the old appellations of "honourable" and "dishonourable" were disappearing from the weavers' discourse. In a narrative that increasingly pitted big capitalists against the weavers, divisions of class interest were being drawn and the critique of labor exploitation sharpened. This shift is one among many that demonstrates the recursive ties between instrumental and discursive repertoires: new actions could change old story lines, just as narratives informed collective action.

By late March 1826, the weavers struck to force their masters to return to the book prices of 1824, idling ten thousand hands. Initially, a number of city manufacturers renounced the demands. Within a week, however, a large manufacturer called for the weavers to finish all outstanding work at the previous prices; in return they would receive the 1824 prices on all subsequent work. The proposal caused great controversy at an April 2 weavers' meeting, prompting William Thompson to urge that they "not to be led away by the sophistry of any of the employers, but nobly continue the strike until all their tyrants were subdued" (P.C., set 16, v. 2, f. 70). The result, however, was that the proposition was accepted by a majority of 1,141 (ibid.). The considerable dissension nonetheless suggests the increasing fissure between weavers and manufacturers.

Many city manufacturers failed to consent to the accord and the promised raise proved chimerical. By mid-May, the weavers were again active on two fronts. On May 23, the weavers assembled and ratified a petition to Parliament for wage regulation. Abandoning deference, they bluntly stated that Parliament's past actions were, "indecent and monstrous inroads on their rights" (*TFP*, July 1, 1827). The weavers then offered a searing indictment of the Government:

> While the voracious system of excessive taxation, and its unjust and profligate expenditure, together with the ruinous paper currency, cruel and oppressive Corn Laws, and the unnatural and monstrous overgrown debt, called National, continue to exist, they devour, with unrelenting rapacity, the greatest portion of the produce of their petitioners paltry but hard-earned labour. . . . The petitioners are well aware that the misery of the times . . . is the result, the natural result of laws emanating from the House, such having arisen solely from the want of a fair and equal representation of the people in the House; and that, therefore, the petitioners earnestly and urgently implore the House, in its wisdom and clemency, to do something (and that promptly) to benefit their unhappy and wretched condition. . . . The petitioners most earnestly and respectfully entreat the House (for the protection and security of their trade, and to prevent in the future such alarming and shameful recurrence of repeated reduction of their wages), to grant them an Act, by which the misery of the petitioners will, in some degree, be alleviated. . . .

They closed with a radical critique of Old Corruption and the Corn Laws and called upon the House,

> to take into its early and serious consideration, to institute the best means to accomplish that most important and desirable of all requests,—viz. an effectual and real Reform in the House, the want of which has been the principal cause of the wretched and miserable state of the petitioners, whose rights and liberties have from time to time been bartered away, and sacrificed, like cattle in Smithfield. From the want of Reform has originated all their grievances. (Ibid.)

Although the discourse is suffused with the characteristic chords of popular political radicalism, we should not simply read this as a "political" rather than a "class" statement, for the weavers were demanding their rights as producers, industrious laborers who underwrote the state. That the weavers could in a short time span damn both manufacturers and government as the root cause of their condition is understandable within the context of their narrative of oppression. Each trammeled on the weavers' essential rights to a secure and comfortable livelihood for their families and to a dependable return on their labor. The resulting degradation and immiseration clearly stained the hands of each. The periodic use of such Old Corruption language in their discursive repertoire shows that multivocal discourse allowed a particular wedding of the "political" and the "economic." The Commons, as usual, ignored the pleadings.

Despite periods of unparalleled dearth and little success, portions of the weavers thus frequently mobilized after repeal. They continued to frame their identity through their discursive repertoire as part of the productive classes of the society who deserved protection. They articulated their interests as opposed to their employers and the corrupt governors, a class vision in Thompsonian terms. Their discursive repertoire propounded the sense of justice upon which they sought redress and provided legitimacy and a substantive narrative logic for their continued actions directed at both Parliament and the manufacturers.

The new year brought renewed lobbying for wage protection. In late February, a general meeting of the broad-silk weavers convened to approve a petition to Parliament.[1] The chair of the meeting opened with fighting words typical of working-class appropriation of political economy: "They found, generally, in all situations where capital was employed, the individuals so employing it sought the Legislature to protect that capital. If he understood the business which had called them together, it was for the protection of capital; that capital which was the most valued in all states—it was labour" (*TFP*, Feb. 23, 1828). The long meeting ranged over the weavers' trials and debates on the wisdom of injecting radical politics into their demands. The heart of the gathering, however, was a reading of the report, lasting over an hour.

The report, a veritable manifesto, listed a familiar litany of causes for their impoverishment and of the means of their rejuvenation.

> That from the long misrule, which has been pursued by legislators,—from the manifestly erroneous policy of our commercial transactions,—from the cruel, overreaching and tyrannical conduct of certain unprincipled, greedy, and speculative employers,—from the dangerous tendency of the pestilential dogmas of certain professors of political economy,—from the unjust and oppressive exactions of the lords of the soil and the loom,—from the cold and stoical indifference manifested in the great mass of public men as to the welfare of their fellow creatures,—from the hopeless degradation, the insufferable poverty, and the cheerless prospect of the industrious but much injured artisan and labourer; your Committee cannot but conclude, that there is no hope, no reasonable, well-grounded hope that the growing,

---

[1] The petition was presented with twenty thousand signatures as part of a larger campaign for a Wages Protection Bill. Petitions were also sent from the silk weaving towns of Coventry (ribbon weaving) Macclesfield, Manchester, and Norwich, as well as other industrial areas (*TFP*, April 5, 26, May 3, 1828).

enormous, and overwhelming evils which now afflict this country, will ever be arrested in their destructive progress—that the iron hand of oppression will be stayed by equal-handed justice,—that monopoly and avarice will give way to the benevolent sway of knowledge and equity,—or, that the industrious and wealth producing population of the United Kingdom will ever obtain a fair remunerative price for their labour, but by and through the united and devoted energies,—the temperate, yet firm, fearless, and uncompromising remonstrances,—and the dear bought, but increasing knowledge of the labouring producers themselves; aided by the benevolent, patriotic, and virtuous portion of the legislature, and of the community at large. (*Report . . . For a Wages Protection Bill*, 1828, p. 31)

The weavers highlighted the government's culpability in this critique, now a key feature of the discursive repertoire. "The great end of all government, and that alone which renders a government necessary, is to prevent one man from taking advantage of another, by withholding or abstracting from him the fruits of his industry, and is most fully accomplished when every man has secured to him the greatest amount of the products of his labour (ibid., pp. 12–14).

Drawing on a common repertoire theme, the weavers chastised the government for their partiality in protecting the unproductive. All persons whose incomes are derived from landed property, the funds, the tythes, law fees, and monopolies of every kind are subject to, protected by, legislative or conventional regulations; and that labour, and labourers alone, are subjected to the individual competition of unprincipled speculative contractors and employers" (ibid., p. 24). And in their petition they reiterated their basic rights to their protection of their property, just as the unproductive had their rights secured. "As the artisan's power of labour is his only property, it is irreconcilable with every sense of justice, and of common right, that the incomes and property of all other classes should be protected, whilst the artisans and labourers alone are left a prey to be plundered by needy, rapacious, and unprincipled employers" (*Report/Petition*, p. 7).[2]

In their analysis of the origins of the capitalists' power, the weavers maintained their focus on their employers as another principal cause of their distress. "The labouring classes [are] a ready prey to the capitalists, who have the means of acquiring authority over others, in proportion to the quantity of the objects of desire which they are able to possess, by whatever means these objects are attained" (pp. 25–26). In addition, they reaffirmed that manufacturers often exercised this power in an unbridled manner. "Unprincipled and rapacious capitalists and employers are al-

---

[2] Page numbering for the petition is done separately. From here on, extracts from the Petition will be cited as "*Report/Petition*."

lowed to take advantage of a state of weakness among the labouring classes, to pull down wages; and which they do with the utmost impunity" (ibid., p. 20).

Echoing past pronouncements they ridiculed the free traders' notion of "freedom," finding in it the chains of impoverishment:

> the present incongruous application of the principle of freedom, so far from tending to promote the prosperity of the country in the aggregate,—on the contrary tends to impoverish it . . . by increasing the riches of a portion of the wealthy, and the poverty of the industrious classes, in a greater proportion than the advantages which it gives to those who benefit by its operation. (Ibid., p. 21)

To counter the foil of political economy, the weavers drew their own rapier, "the indubitable laws of social economy,"

> that there can be no profitable commerce,—no national prosperity,—no security to property,—no stability to institutions,—and that machinery must accelerate their dissolution,—unless measures are speedily adopted, tending to reinstate artizans and labourers in their just sphere of influence and reward, by securing them such an amount of wages as will enable them, with a moderate portion of exertion, to command, not only necessaries, but even the comforts of life. Wages being the grand pivotal point round which all great interests of society turn, unless they are raised to the level of subsistence, and a declaratory law be adopted, recognizing the maxim, that MAN IS TO LIVE BY HIS LABOUR,—all other remedies will be of no avail,—tinkling cymbal, sounding brass. (Ibid., p. 22)

The substantive rationale of this social economy was laid out in a series of simple propositions predicated on a labor theory of value now central to their fighting words.

> An equitable reward for labour is best adapted, and is indeed indispensable to secure the greatest quantity of wealth in any country, and to promote the legitimate interests of all classes of society.
>
> 1st. Because it is labour which gives value to land and raw material for manufactures. "The labour of the country is the wealth of the country" (Adam Smith), and in proportion as the wages are high or low, the value of wealth of such country is increased or diminished.
>
> 2nd. Because the great majority of the people of every country is necessarily composed of those whose sole property is their labour, by securing therefore to labour an adequate reward, the positive comfort of the greatest possible number would be secured also; and, as Labourers form the base of society, all the other classes must be benefited in due proportion.

3d. Because the demand for the products of labour, in cases where it is equitably rewarded, would always be commensurate with the power to produce: under its influence there could be no appearance of redundant population, and the free circulation of wages would cause that healthful and vigorous state in the social system which the free circulation of the venal blood does to the animal economy. . . .

5th. Because adequate wages are necessary to the support of that self-esteem, that honest and manly pride, and that state of comfortable enjoyment and easy circumstances which constitute the greatness of a country; and that state of society, in which alone the mass of the people can be expected to be virtuous and orderly. . . .

6th. Because an inequitable remuneration for labour necessarily diminishes the means of purchasing the products of labour, in a greater degree than the reduced price of commodities tends to increase the means. (Ibid. pp. 14—15)

The Report clearly articulated a class identity upon which claims of entitlement and fissures of interest were laid out. Oppression was exercised by capitalists and the idle rich who robbed the weavers of the products of their labor. By creatively appropriating pieces of liberal political and economic discourses, including Smith and the vocabulary of political economy, the weavers dialogically constructed their vision of social economy. Simultaneously, the discourse of political economy was exposed as steeped in the interests of the wealthy and powerful, "the lords of the soil and loom," who drew on it to forge the ideological manacles of acquiescence.

That the weavers' discussed the resolution to their economic crisis in political action does not make this a popular political discourse as opposed to a class one. Nor are the *Report* and the collective actions that circumscribe it interpretable as a forms of reactionary radicalism. Rather, within the contexts of the struggle and the social memory of experience, government protection provided the only substantive possibility for a viable enduring solution.

The *Report* also reveals a dynamic side of the discursive repertoire pressed into change by the hard lessons of experience. Injudicious policy and distress were no longer seen as resulting from sincere mistaken intentions, but as the deliberate result of a manipulative, plundering, and nonproductive oligarchy. Among the chief culprits were the manufacturers, who took every advantage to squeeze the wealth out of the weavers' labor. The lesson was that the power to exploit and oppress had to be met with an equal and countervailing force.

Parliament again disclaimed responsibility, and the cry for "equal justice" began to resound at weavers' meetings. The year 1829 brought an intensified debate in Westminster and the newspapers as the weavers sought other avenues of relief. In mid-February, over ten thousand weavers marched en masse to Downing Street to memorialize Prime Minister Wellington for relief. The parade was a solemn spectacle, with a number of black banners declaring the evils of free trade and with looms draped in crepe. The weavers exhibited the traditional patrician mourning cloth that they produced to signal their own demise. In his curt response, the prime minister attributed distress not to free trade but to smuggling and offered to consider a more permanent form of relief (*WFP*, Feb. 28, 1829).

Rifts widened within the ranks of the master manufacturers as veteran Spitalfields masters argued that increased protection was vital to save the trade from utter ruin. City manufacturers, however, vehemently rebutted such suggestions. Ambrose Moore led the counter-attack, arguing that repeal had been beneficial rather than destructive. During an April debate, he sardonically reiterated the division between conscience and capital: "The gentleman opposite [Mr. Balance] had talked of the depreciation of wages, and the consequent immorality of the workmen. For his part, he did not know that it was always safe to introduce morality when they were discussing a return upon capital and commercial transactions (a laugh)" (P.C., set 16, v. 2, f. 118).

With the manufacturers at odds, weavers' delegates from Manchester, Macclesfield, and Spitalfields assembled in mid-April in London to discuss a united lobbying strategy. This was the first public action taken collectively by the silk weavers of all three major silk towns, and it signaled the national scope of the intense distress. The united delegation solicited an interview with the Board of Trade, but they were coolly rebuffed (P.C., set 16, v. 2, f. 126).

At a general meeting of the trade, the weavers responded to Parliament's indifference. The many resolutions they adopted again clearly mark the government as violators of the weavers' basic right to secure support for their families and as usurpers of control over their labor:

> V. Resolved.—That His Majesty's Government being determined to pursue their system of Free Trade in Foreign Wrought Silks, and thereby deprive many thousand industrious Mechanics of employment, and consequently the means of supporting their families, and that as the Government are receiving large sums as import duties therefrom, which if it was not for such importations we should receive wages, we therefore consider that we are in justice entitled to support from the above source until we can find employment in the Silk or in some other Trade....
>
> VII. Resolved,—That this Meeting views with unutterable astonishment and dismay the present proceedings of the Government respecting the system of "Free Trade," seeing it has not only reduced the price of labour below a subsisting point, but has actually taken that labour out of our hands.... It has changed the Poor Man's motto from WORK OR STARVE, to WORK AND STARVE, the former is the lot of nature, the latter is inflicted by man, and with it we

are not content, neither can it be expected while the earth continues to yield in abundance for all mankind. . . .

IX. Resolved,—That it is the opinion of this Meeting that the Legislature refusing to grant a Committee of Inquiry, they are responsible for the misery and degradation brought on this nation, in pursuing a system incompatible with the present political situation of the Country. . . .

XI. Resolved.—That in consequence of the deep distress now existing in the Silk Trade, without any hope of amelioration, it is the opinion of this Meeting, that we are totally incapable of paying any more Rent or Taxes of any description; and should any Brother Tradesmen be distrained on, we are determined to protect them to our utmost power. (H.O. 40/23, f. 167)

Through their discursive repertoire, it was clear to the weavers that the bonds of mutual obligation were being ripped asunder, that this had effectively robbed them of the value of their labor, and that in turn they were due the justice of support. The last resolution was particularly telling. Up to this juncture, their fighting words had not sanctioned collective violence. The weavers now hinted at its validity, however: might was right if rights were made refuse.

On the evening of May 3, the type of action ominously portended by resolution XI commenced. Groups of "cutters" stealthily moved about the district destroying the partially finished fabrics of several manufacturers as they lay in their weavers' looms. The practice continued unabated for the next two days, with the goods of at least twenty-five looms being destroyed in the process (P.C., set 16, v. 2, f. 127; *MC* May 4, 1829).

The manufacturers and the magistrates were alarmed. The district had not witnessed such violence since the protests of the 1760s. The Home Office sent twenty-one additional patrolmen to help restore order, and took the unusual step of authorizing a public reward of two hundred pounds leading to the arrest and conviction of the cutters (the manufacturers consenting to pay the reward should it be found necessary). A number of masters sent their foremen to the district to remove the remaining unharmed work (ibid.; H.O. 40/24, ff. 1–2; *Times* May 8, 1829).

On May 5, over ten thousand assembled at the front of the Crown and Anchor public house to hear the fervent call for a general strike. Isaac Hunter addressed the assemblage.

> It was said that they would not work—but his answer to that was, they could not live by working at the masters' prices. The Masters should come forward with some proposition offering them a living price. *If the Weavers were united they could force the Masters to do that which was just and equitable.* It was not foreign competition they had to fear, but from one workman's labouring at a lower rate of wages than another. Some of the employers allowed a living price; and if they could do so, why not all? A want of unity was the reason;

and if there was a fixed determination among the operatives not to work under a stipulated price, the Masters must, in self-defense, agree to it, and the oppression he complained of would be removed. (P.C., set 16, v. 2, f. 127)

The following day the magistrates were occupied interviewing those weavers whose looms were attacked, but all were dismissed for lack of evidence: might was pragmatically and morally ascendant.

That evening at a manufacturers' meeting, a weavers' deputation explained their demands. The masters were apprised by William Hunter that the weavers were determined to have the prices of 1824. Hunter then further counseled them on the essential reciprocity of trade relations:

> The Frenchman was in their own market, and it required a cordial cooperation of both to beat them out; and he well knew that, with the protecting duty afforded by the Government, the masters could, with safety to themselves, return to the book prices, and afterwards beat the foreigner. It was, no doubt, the duty of the masters to protect the property of their journeymen, as it was the bounden duty of the journeymen to protect the property of their masters. (*MC*, May 7, 1829)[3]

The masters recognized the barely veiled fighting words in this speech —lack of reciprocity could have cutting consequences—and took the warning to heart. Facing the terror of the knife, they appointed a committee of twelve for further negotiations. Later that night, despite the addition of another forty patrolmen, another forty-two looms were attacked (ibid.; *Times*, May 12, 1829).

The weavers' committee busied itself with negotiations and petitions over the course of the next day. That evening at a delegates' meeting, twelve to fourteen thousand thronged the Crown and Anchor. Being in the middle of delicate negotiations, a committee member tried to impress upon the meeting that it was important to halt destruction. While he counseled peace, the discourse in which he made his plea was couched in the metaphor of sovereign states at war:

> Now that the flag of truce was held out, they should cease all hostility; if in the armistice their wishes were not acceded to, they might again resume warfare, the weapons were in their hands; but when a treaty was entered on, they should not employ them. He implored of his fellow-workmen to abstain from acts of violence: . . . "I hope," said he, "hostilities will, at least for the present, be suspended" (Cries of "No, no."). (*Times*, May 8, 1829)

---

[3] As I argue elsewhere (1995b), the weavers defined their collective identities as free Britons through nationalist discourse and in opposition to the subjugation experienced by other peoples in foreign lands. The French silk weavers were exemplary cases in both regards.

Strike leaders were now adding an element of masculine class warfare to the discursive repertoire, legitimating violence as a path to redress.

The initial proposal of the masters' committee was roundly condemned since it fell short of the prices of 1824. One of the delegates observed that "if he were to propose to the 13,000 weavers assembled that they should accept the starvation prices which had been proposed by the masters, the consequence would be, that the feeling of weavers would be harrowed up to such a pitch of frenzy, as to endanger the 100,000 [pounds] worth of property which they had in their possession belonging to the masters" (*MC*, May 8, 1829). It was a threat with the thinnest of veils. The weavers readily concurred with the delegates and voted down the masters' proposal. Negotiations dragged on while that evening between eighty and ninety looms were assaulted, and some destroyed along with the silk contained in them.

The next day the committee returned with heartening news. Isaac Duce, addressing an immense and anxious crowd outside of the Crown and Anchor, read the manufacturers' resolution acceding to their demands for the present. Later, after direct talks, the committee reported their triumph to a jubilant crowd, and the news flashed to meetings about the district (*Times*, May 8, 1829).

In succeeding days, letters to the *Times* from the manufacturers' camp painted the strike as "an act of regularly organized warfare" and "a bloodless revolution" (May 10, 12, 1829). The descriptions may have been apt if we remember that behind such organized violence lay a declaration of a war of independence. The weavers' identity was clearly bound up in discursive constructions of patriotism and citizenship through dialogic struggle. Constructions of collective worth and belonging had become wed to their collective identity as part of the nation's wealth producers. In the weavers' own terms, collective violence was not only a tactically sound but a morally efficacious response to what within this discourse could be construed as tyranny. For at least six years, they had tried to parry the rapiers of political economists and city manufacturers. Their discourses of contention were ready foils, but they also framed their adversaries' continued thrusts as beyond the pale of fair play. By 1829, their fighting words framed collective violence as legitimate: one crippling lunge bloody well deserved another. Such was reciprocity of class warfare.

The agreement unraveled rapidly within two weeks. At a general trade meeting on May 20, it was agreed to have shop-based parties seal the looms of all masters who were not complying with the agreement. Shop-based groups met manufacturers to explain the conditions of the strike and were often met with resistance and outward hostility. The always hostile Ambrose Moore had five of his weavers brought up on charges of conspiracy and intimidation, and Messrs. Tarrant & Co. followed suit against three of their journeymen. By June 24, only twelve manufacturers had agreed to reinstitute the book rates (P.C., set 16, v. 2, f. 129).

With continued property destruction and sporadic attacks on manufacturers' agents, the previously reserved magistrates had seen enough. It was abundantly clear to them that the weavers were violating the community moral order that the weavers' own discourses seemed to laud. They solicited an additional armed patrol for a public whipping of an embezzler. The same day their request was granted, all of the defendants in the conspiracy cases brought by Moore and Tarrant & Co. were convicted, receiving three months imprisonment (H.O. 40/24, ff. 1–2; P.C., set 16, v. 2, ff. 129–131; *WFP*, June 13, 1829). The cycle of violence and repression continued, with sporadic loom attacks occurring well into June. The violence waned, however; the strike petered out; and the weavers were gradually starved into submission. By the third week of June, the extra patrol quietly left for reassignment (P.C., set 16, v. 2, f. 130; H.O. 40/24 ff. 31, 37, 43).

The masters had won the war, but had paid a heavy toll. In all, 175 looms and thousands of pounds worth of silk had been destroyed. These attacks, orchestrated by the branch societies, bore the marks of calculated retribution. A number of manufacturers had noted that those especially intransigent to the weavers' demands were singled out for punishment. Following the moral precepts constructed through the weavers' discourses of contention this should be of little surprise. Table 6.1 below summarizes forty-two incidents listed in the Police Reports, by firm for the May/June period.[4]

The list suggests a pattern of intent. A number of the firms that experienced multiple attacks were large city establishments, including Ames & Atkinson, Ambrose Moore, Thompson, and Daniel Walters. Additionally, several other larger Spitalfields firms, including Duff & Brooks, Eastman & Hill, Hunt, and Rugg, had been at best cool, and at times openly hostile to the weavers' previous requests for price rises (P.C., set 16, v. 2, f. 61). Because a number of firms accidentally had their looms destroyed in raids, due to the common post-repeal practice of accepting work from several different manufacturers simultaneously, the list seems well representative of the weavers' principal nemeses.

Those weavers who had silk destroyed in their looms were blacklisted by the masters, and they formed themselves into a separate society called the "Unfortunates" (P.C., set 16, v. 2, f. 130). A new level of antagonism had been reached between manufacturer and weaver. In post-strike reflections, a correspondent to Peel observed that the sores of conflict would continue their slow bleed for some time (H.O. 40/24, ff. 110–111; Whatton to Peel, 10 Aug. 1829).

With the war at an end and distress still plaguing their trade, the weavers reverted to appeals to the government. After the pitched battles of the

---

[4] For tabular accounts of cutting and destroying incidents for 1828 and the months of May, June, and July of 1829, see Steinberg 1989, v. 1, pp. 269–272.

Table 3. May/June 1829 cutting and destroying incidents, by firm

Firm	Number of incidents
Ames & Atkinson	2
Appeling & Sons	1
John Appeling	1
Mr. Brandon	1
Bridges & Campbell	1
J. J. Buttress	1
Duff & Brooks	3
Eastman & Hill	4
John Edmunds	1
Henry Farrant	1
F. & J. Giles	3
James Howard	1
Robert Hunt	3
Ambrose Moore	5
John Reed	1
Mr. Rugg	2
Mr. Sackerson	1
Stone & Brooks	1
Hugh Tate	1
John Tharpe	1
William Thompson	2
Daniel Walters	3
David Walters	1
Wilson & Co	1
Edward Wilson	1

Source: H.O. 62/1–4.

previous months, this may seem convoluted, but through the weavers' discursive repertoire, they still plainly perceived that the power-holders owed them some due. However, a petition to the government with four thousand signatures and various handbills calling upon the nobility and the public to underwrite emigration to Australia failed to generate enthusiasm (P.C., set 16, v. 2, ff. 129, 131; H.O. 40/24, ff. 94–99; Whatton to Peel, 2 Aug. 1829).

With emigration foreclosed, the weavers again focused on the manufacturers into the winter months, and by the start of 1830 the weavers were trying to rejuvenate their hobbled union. As winter shaded into spring, they turned their efforts back toward the government. The contrapuntal pleas for assistance between state authorities and manufacturers resumed their previous cadence as the months dragged on (H.O. 40/24, f. 267; H.O. 40/27, ff. 514–519, Whatton to Peel, March 20, 1830; P.C., set 16, v. 2, f. 134; *WFP*, March 13, May 22, Oct. 2, 22, 1830).

In late January, a meeting was held to discuss the formation of a general union and a campaign to lobby for a wages protection bill. The words had a familiar ring: "Robert Noquet said he thought the operative classes were entitled to protection. The aristocracy, the commons, the landed and funded interests, were all protected, and none but the weakest of all were left unprotected" (*VP*, Jan. 29, 1831).

A committee was formed, and the weavers lobbied Parliament. By mid-March, the weavers again assembled to ratify the committee's work. John Poyton, a veteran activist whose words had set the tone of many previous gatherings, decried their destitution and found its origins in the lack of trade protection.

> He deplored the present low rate of wages, and which had nearly reached the starving point in almost every branch of manufacture and the silk trade in particular. . . . He lamented that other trades were left as equally unprotected as they were, and every law that had been passed or repealed for the last 15 years, had the effect of leaving the working classes less protected, and more defenseless than they were. The alterations in the poor-laws, the game laws, and free trade, all, all had a tendency to operate against the working classes; and the whole of the evils under which they labour, are to be attributed to the want of legislative protection. (Ibid.)

The words of another seasoned fighter, William Wallis, also echoed those we have chronicled throughout these struggles, fighting words whose content was by now as familiar as a weaver's well-worn fustian coat.

> Mr. Wallis thought that the great end for which governments were first established, was to protect man from the injustice, oppression, and tyranny of his fellow man, and it was upon these principles governments ought to act. If they looked in the page of England's history, down through our Henry's and our Edward's, they would find nothing but anarchy and confusion, and the want of security, until we got to the reign of Elizabeth; then indeed, they would find property secure; and why? because labour she protected. (Ibid.)

The weavers presented an historical narrative that linked their concepts of justice to the grand march of a progressive national order. This narrative provided protection with a teleology of civic virtue, a foil to its Whiggish counterparts of the time. The weavers struggled to subvert the construction of a bourgeois national historical consciousness, a collective memory whose usable past validated all that to the weavers spelled destruction.

As the months passed, the trade sank into another bout of depression. Several pro-repeal masters, alarmed that free trade was pushing them to the precipice of collapse, pressed Parliament for a select committee inquiry into the state of the trade. The united chorus of weavers and manufacturers ultimately prodded the Commons into an investigation the following year. As in the past, however, it was to stimulate a great deal of bluster and debate, which produced nothing of substance. The triumph of the city manufacturers and political economy was indeed complete.

The Spitalfields weavers provide one example of the discursive processes of class formation and the ways in which discourses of contention inform the collective intelligibility of collective actions. Embedded in a dense web of community and trade relations, the male weavers had constructed a moral economy through which they defined themselves as respectable artisans, citizens of the community and nation, and masters of the workshop and household. This moral economy was challenged by the rise of large manufacturers and their alliances with parliamentary free traders. From the start of the repeal debates into the 1830s, the weavers fought to preserve their small island of modest security against the terrors they presumed would follow in the wake of unrestrained capitalism. History cruelly proves them prescient.

Throughout their struggles, the weavers constructed fighting words to battle the hegemonic discourse of political economy, which naturalized unrestrained competition, objectified market forces beyond the power of civic intervention, and justified the gross inequities of accumulation and exploitation. Through a dialogic engagement of this discourse, in their many battles the weavers skillfully appropriated many of its terms and icons, inflected new meanings in their use, and exposed the class interests that were glossed in the encomiums to the new order. As the contest endured, shades of a discourse of ennobled patriarchy, which were to be essential to the radicalism of the 1830s and 1840s, gradually emerged. Among the weavers, processes of class and gender conjoined to yield divergent outcomes; male weavers within the domestic order of patriarchal cooperation were valorised independent producers, while their female family members were successively marginalized as dependent, although worthy, ancillaries.

Their struggle was part of a process of class formation, for in Thompsonian terms it led to the formation of a collective consciousness of opposed interests against those of the rising tide of large manufactures. These interests were constructed through the weavers' fighting words in the process of dialogic appropriation and transformation. That this involved political language and was in reaction to the continuing development of a modern capitalist system does not make it necessarily "popular" or "reactionary" as opposed to class-based. Class formation always occurs in situ, and in the weavers' circumstances such politics pressingly defined their uncertain future as well as their collective memories of the past.

These discourses of contention also defined the intelligible boundaries of collective action, providing the conceptual tools for fashioning an instrumental repertoire, and legitimating both the targets of claims and the methods used. To make sense of the weavers' repeated claims against the government, actions that yielded only frustration and embitterment, we must explore the constructions of justice and entitlement, citizenship and polity in their discursive repertoire. These fighting words framed the government as a full partner in their destitution and a principal source of their desired restitution. Within the epic of their lived experience, it is hard to imagine an intelligible narrative that could cleanly write the state out of their tragic story.

Fighting words were thus central to both class formation and collective action, and in very particular ways. In the following case of the Ashton-Stalybridge cotton spinners, we shall investigate how substantively similar processes produced a distinctly different yarn.

ASHTON-STALYBRIDGE

CHAPTER SEVEN

King Cotton:
Markets, Mills, and Mechanics

*T*hrough the past several chapters, we have peered into a district of England's great metropolis, looking at both a trade group and its communities, whose histories and social memories stretched back over a century. In turning now to a district in the broad shoulders of the industrial North, we enter a region that poses great contrasts. As I have described in the introduction to the case studies, the social world of Ashton-under-Lyne and Stalybridge that we will investigate was in many respects born with the Industrial Revolution. The rise of the cotton mill fueled the local economy, gave form to the district's social geography and structure of political power, and contoured the social and cultural lives of those within the shadows of the mills. The district, in the form we will enter it, was barely a generation old, and its growing pains provided the stuff of class formation analyzed in this and succeeding chapters.

Much of the history of the district and the class formation within it will stand in marked contrast to the Spitalfields case. The structure of the labor process and indeed of the entire spinning industry, the gendering of factory work and its impact on family and community life, the concentration of community power in the hands of mill magnates, the palpable cleavages in the social and cultural lives of mill owners and workers, and the dynamics of class struggle—all will seem foreign to what we have viewed in Spitalfields. Part of the point of these contrasts, however, is to underscore similarities in process. The cotton spinners' discourses of contention differed from those of the silk weavers, reflecting the dialogic struggle in which the former were embroiled. Yet in a more general sense the process by which these discourses were imbricated in class formation and the ways in which they mediated the dynamics of collective action were substantively similar. The contrasts also demonstrate how class formation is, as Thompson argued, always local and contingent, a happening in particular ways, but a common happening nonetheless.

"The rapid and prodigious magnitude of the cotton manufacture of Great Britain," marveled the political economist J. R. McCulloch, "are beyond all question, the most extraordinary phenomena in the history of industry" (1827, p. 1). The rising tide of the cotton industry was extraordinary, not the least for the ways in which its wake washed over the fortunes of so many people in southeast Lancashire. In this chapter, I investigate three facets of the cotton industry and the spinners' place within it. First, I briefly explore the industry as a sector of a world capitalist economy. Second, I enter the mill itself, investigating its internal economy, its labor market (particularly the market for spinners), and its variations in size and productive scope. The organization of the mill as a profit machine defined the parameters of conflict. Third, I focus on the process of cotton spinning itself, examining the evolution of its social and technical relations of production, which created the flash points of struggle.

My object is to illuminate the forces that were determinative of class friction. As opposed to Calhoun's conception of factory worker reformism and Joyce's claims that workers shared much in common with mill owners, I explore how the industry's course in the 1820s produced increasing conflict. My argument is neither that factory labor per se yielded class consciousness, nor that it served as the substructure upon which all other determinative pressures were constructed. Rather, contingent dynamics led both mill owners and spinners to collective realizations that they were locked in substantial conflict.

The World's Warp and Weft: The Cotton Industry in a National and Global Economy

The renowned chronicler of cotton, Edward Baines, scanned the empire in the mid-1830s and proclaimed, "The civilization of England flies abroad on the wings of commerce" (1966, p. 531). To the spinner passing through the factory gates, the mill may have loomed as a Bastille of work, but it was also a node in a complex and vast commercial network. In 1832, British mills produced 249,046,875 pounds of yarn, roughly 5.9 billion miles of product. By this time, cotton products accounted for almost half of the value of all British exports. Industrial Lancashire sat at the nexus of this enormous commercial network (Baines 1966, p. 432; Farnie 1979, p. 82; Montgomery 1833, 2d ed., p. 289; McCulloch 1834, p. 441).

A complex network of cotton dealers and commission agents stationed in Manchester and Liverpool knit together the kinetics of industry, linking the manufacturers to their markets, and providing needed capital to smaller manufacturers. Mill owners thus had to secure their position in a system of volatile international markets over which they exercised precious little control (Edwards 1967, p. 134; S. J. Chapman 1904, p. 63; Shapiro 1967, pp. 103, 105).

The lure of fat profits of up to 30 percent from the early 1810s was a siren song for those with a modicum of capital and entrepreneurial spirit, particularly from 1818 into the early 1820s (Boyson 1970, p. 29; Daniels 1927, p. 81; Lee 1972, p. 139). With expansion, however, came increased competition that sharpened the struggle for survival (S. D. Chapman 1979, p. 55). Profit margins slumped 72 percent from 1815 to 1832, with the fall being especially precipitous from the mid-1820s. (Baines 1966, p. 359; S. D. Chapman 1979, p. 62; Howe 1984, p. 25; Lee 1972, p. 12; Montgomery 1833, 2d. ed., p. 286; Prentice 1829, passim; Smith 1953, p. 60; P.P. 1833, VI, p. 652). As a Stalybridge mill owner morosely commented, "The very system of carrying our manufactures to such an enormous extent has been the cause of annihilating the profits of the manufacturer and reducing the wages of the workman. . . . Trade is uncontrollable either by masters or men" (*SA*, Jan. 23, 1829).

From the late 1810s through the 1840s, industry cycles dragged mill owners through often fierce slumps and short rapid recoveries (Barr 1980). In 1826, the industry was rocked by depression, and again in 1828 markets collapsed, plunging spinning into a trade-wide depression that finally lifted in 1832 (Kirby and Musson 1975, p. 111; Prentice 1851, p. 344; Sykes 1982, v. 1, pp. 23, 123). In February of 1830, 100 mills in the cotton district stood idle. To combat the ravages of the slump, 114 mill owners set aside vaunted tenets of competition and agreed to work their 250 mills solely during the daylight (*SA*, Jan. 29, Feb. 5, 1830; *WMC*, Feb. 6, 1830). Inevitably, some mill owners fell prey to these onslaughts. Bankruptcies among all Manchester cotton manufacturers firms were about two dozen per year in the later 1820s and of epidemic proportions when sixty-nine failed in 1826 (*MG*, Feb. 2, 1830). Between 1827 and 1831 at least eight mill owners filed for bankruptcy in the Ashton-Stalybridge district (*MG*, July 7, 1827; Jan. 5, Aug 16, Dec. 20, 1828; Feb. 21, 1829; May 29, Dec. 18, 1830; Dec. 3, 1831).

Although such boom and bust cycles affected virtually all sectors of the industry, their impact varied. Coarse spinning, the foundation for the domestic trade, was less subject to wild swings, but more sensitive to price changes because of the heavy competition. Fine spinning, while more profitable, experienced considerable price fluctuations, because it depended on the luxury markets (Edwards 1967, pp. 126, 128; Lee 1972, p. 115). Thus, in the fine branches the key to survival was expansion and the intensification of production, while the coarse branches opted for vertical integration of spinning and weaving (Collier 1964, p. 12; Daniels 1927, p. 81; Jewkes 1930, pp. 92–93; Shapiro 1967, pp. 16–17; P.P. 1833, v. VI, p. 685).

The mill owners of the Ashton-Stalybridge district were wholly involved in this survival game. The majority produced coarser grades of yarn (although there was also a large production of finer grades), and the district was one of the least diversified in its range of production. Much of the yarn, particularly the medium counts, was destined for American markets. Although abundant local coal supplies gave the district mill owners an advantage, competitive pressures forced many to adopt vertical integration strategies. This was especially true in Hyde, Dukinfield, and Stalybridge, sites of some of the largest integrated mills in the country (Butterworth 1841, pp. 82, 144; Kirk 1985, p. 43; Rodgers 1960, p. 140; Sykes 1982, v. 1, pp. 18–19; *MM* Dec. 14, 1830).

By 1830, market swings had assumed a supernatural character, looming above like an alienated ruling force. The mill owners' attempts to stabilize return on capital in the face of these topsy-turvy markets put them at loggerheads with their labor force as they intensified production and reduced piece rates. As we shall see, these captains of industry sometimes drove their work force to mutiny as they sought to navigate the treacherous waves of the international economy.

Monuments to Mammon:
Economy and Production in the Mill

"The factory system, replete with prodigies in mechanics and political economy . . . promises, in its future growth, to become the great minister of civilization to the terraqueous globe, enabling this country, as its heart, to diffuse along with its commerce, the life-blood of science and religion to myriads of people still lying 'in the region of the shadow of death'" (Ure 1835). For Ure, the mill was a divine sign of a coming utopia; the world was to find deliverance on the arm of a steam engine. Those who labored within its confines had a far less sanguine assessment. John Doherty, secretary of the Manchester spinners' union, described the factory as "a system which, in point of cruel and classified refinement of tyranny, leaves far behind all that was ever known in the management of negro slaves" (*PMA*, "Introduction," p. viii).

By the late 1820s, cotton-spinning in the Ashton-Stalybridge area had moved from unassuming workshops to imposing six-story mills, buildings whose blank facades mirrored the deadening nature of the work inside them. This transformation brought profound change in the industry's economics, including market pressures that led to new friction in the relations of production.

Table 4. Assessed value of mill property for sixteen Stalybridge firms, 1830

Firm	Assessed value (in £)
Albert Hall	14,099[a]
John Cheetham	18,258
Thomas Harrison & Sons	32,470
Johnson & Brothers	23,882
Water Street Co.	6,516
David Thackery and Bros.	3,050
John Leech & Sons	43,941
William Bayley & Bros.	34,125[a]
Benson & Bros.	14,550
Wagstaff & Co.	10,470
Bayley & Dowse	3,314
Hall, Bates & Co.	11,488
Joseph Donnell	5,388
George Adshead	21,334
Robert Platt	15,407
Executor of James Wilkinson	14,739

Source: T.L.L.H., IC/STA/11, "Stalybridge Rate Book, 1830."
[a] Assessed value of property for two mill sites.

THE MILL ECONOMY

The modern mill consumed capital as voraciously as it did coal. By the mid-1830s, estimates of the total fixed capital in the industry ranged between 10,800,000 to 20,000,000 pounds. Of that total sum, 600,000 pounds had been sunk into the mills of Ashton Town, and 1,100,000 pounds in the parish industry as a whole (Baines 1966, p. 415; Butterworth 1842, pp. 82, 89; McCulloch 1834, p. 443). Modest mills could only be constructed and filled for a very immodest price of at least 8,000 to 9,000 pounds (S. D. Chapman 1972, p. 26; Fong 1930, p. 43). With production volume a close ally of profits, however, many cotton lords built far more expansive structures costing tens of thousands of pounds (Tufnell 1834, p. 98).

The amount of fixed capital invested by area firms is difficult to evaluate, given few existing records. An inkling can be gathered, however, from a partial mill census conducted by the Stalybridge assessor for parish rates. The ratings for sixteen firms remain, and extrapolating backwards from the assessments it is possible to get a rough value of their mill property (exclusive of the mill contents).[1] Table 4 presents the results of the extrapolation.

---

[1] The assessments seem to be for the buildings only and not their contents. The square-yardage of all sections of the mill is recorded in detail. Fireproof buildings were rated at 1s 7.5d./£ and buildings that were not fireproof were rated at 1s 4.5d./£.

King Cotton 133

Contemporaries estimated that expenditures for machinery in a moderately-sized or large integrated mill could amount to two-thirds or three-quarters of the total fixed capital (S. D. Chapman 1971, p. 78). At least matching the amount of fixed capital was the investment in variable capital needed to keep the mill in motion. Experts suggested that the ratio of fixed to working capital was at least 1:1 and could often be as much as 1:2, depending on the mill size and its market orientation (Blaug 1961, p. 359; Pollard 1964, p. 302; Shapiro 1967, p. 79; P.P. 1833, v. VI, p. 656). Using these ratios, and adding on appropriately for additional fixed and variable capital, we can see that mill owners had tens of thousands of pounds at stake.

For many mill owners, it became axiomatic "that in manufactures in which much capital is sunk in buildings and machinery proprietors have at all times a strong motive to push production, and consequently to prolong the hours of labour to the utmost possible extent" (P.P. 1833, v. XX, pt. D.2, p. 105). As opposed to many other capitalists, such as silk manufacturers, whose greatest outlays were in variable capital, mill owners placed a premium on continual production to receive some return on their investments. The mill owners were thus tethered to their progeny of brick and metal; and production, surplus extraction, and capital reinvestment were connected in a seamless circle of perpetual if erratic motion.

The Mill: Its Size and Scope

As Detroisier remarked, "The great object in a cotton-mill is to turn as much work off as possible, in order to compensate by quantity for smallness of profit. To that end everything is made subservient" (P.P. 1833, v. XX, pp. 13–14). By the 1820s, the typical mill was an immense five or six-story unadorned production box designed to fulfill this quest (Ashmore 1974, p. 90; Hill 1927, p. 57; Montgomery 1833, 2d ed., p. 18). All mills had roughly the same organization of space. Production was functionally arranged for continuous processing of materials, from baled cotton to (in some instances) broadcloth (Baines 1966, p. 243). Each part of the process had its own niche within the mill. Preparatory activities were generally lodged in the heart of the mill on the third and fourth stories, while spinning was carried out on adjacent floors. Power-loom weaving, a relative late-comer in the mechanization process, was usually carried out in weaving sheds that were appended to the mill (Montgomery 1833, 2d ed., p. 20; Ure 1836, v. 1, p. 298).

By the beginning of the 1830s, the district was planted thick with these technological titans. Ashton town had twenty-seven mills (with the parish encapsulating fifty-one), Stalybridge twenty-five, Dukinfield eleven, and Hyde fifteen (Baines 1966, pp. 386–387; Cotton 1977, p. 15). The district was also widely recognized for its high concentration of integrated mills,

Table 5. Distribution of mills, by height, for sixteen Stalybridge firms, 1830

Firm	2	3	4	5	6	7	Total	Number of weaving sheds
Albert Hall	1			1	2		4[a]	1
John Cheetham		5	1				6	
Thomas Harrison	1	1	3		3		8	2
Johnson & Bros.	1		1	2		1	5	2
Water Street Co.					1	1	2	1
David Thackery				1			1	
John Leech & Sons		3		1	1	1	6[a]	9
Wm. Bayley & Bros.	5			1			8	2
Benson & Bros.				2			3	2
Wagstaff & Co.							2	2
Bayley & Dowse		1		1			2	2
Hall, Bates & Co.					1		2	2
Joseph Donnell		1	1				2	2
George Adshead				1			2	2
Robert Platt	1						3	3
Exec. of J. Wilkinson			1	2			3	

Source: T.L.L.H. IC/STA/11.
[a]Totals for two mill sites.

especially in Hyde where some of the true behemoths of the age were to be found (Gadian 1986, p. 43; Rodgers 1960, p. 146; Taylor 1949, pp. 120–121). The Stalybridge assessor's survey reveals a pattern of development that is more complex than has been recognized in the past. The number of mills owned by each of these sixteen firms and their respective sizes are detailed in Table 5.

Plowing profits back into fixed capital was a business strategy adopted by many mill owners, especially those in the most competitive sectors of the industry (for a detailed example, see Clark 1978). The assessor's survey, showing multiple buildings that varied in size, suggests local mill owners heeded this accepted wisdom in their quest to maintain their market footholds. Much of this increase in capacity was likely added in the later 1820s when competition became particularly fierce.

The Organization of Authority

As productive capacity swelled with the mill walls, old patterns of authority came under growing strain, and personal relations between mill owners and operatives became increasingly attenuated (Carson 1974, p. 121). The face-to-face relationships of the early factory, even if predicated on arbitrariness, were nonetheless personal ties between mill owner and operative. Increasing magnitude and rationalization weakened such ties and increased frictions.

At the pinnacle of the hierarchy sat the general manager, who orchestrated all of the functions of the mill, and generally was staffed by a firm partner (not infrequently an offspring of the firm's namesake). Assisted by a mill manager, a salesman, and a secretary, the general manager's ultimate responsibility was to ensure that all of the organs of the behemoth were kept animated in unison (Catling 1970, p. 150; Montgomery 1833, 2d ed., p. 242).

Below the general and his lieutenants were the sergeants who directly supervised the industrial army—the overlookers. These supervisors at once served as organizers, facilitators, and disciplinarians for each department. Under their constant eye, cotton was unpacked and cleaned and processed (or "carded") into uniform masses, and then turned into roving, loosely wound strands of cotton (Catling 1970, p. 150). The roving then was transferred by hoist to the spinning floors. There the spinning-room overlooker or "gaffer," and his assistant the "under-gaffer," dispersed the materials to the spinner and coordinated production. The gaffer, sporting white trousers and jacket that clearly demarcated his authority, cast his imperious eyes upon the floor from a small room positioned at one end of the department. The under-gaffer supervised repair and conditioning of the spinning machinery that was the mill's lifeline (Catling 1970, pp. 153–154).

Although each department remained physically and socially isolated, their common and incessant master of flow and pace was the steam engine. Overlookers were frequently paid in proportion to the volume and quality of work of their departments; pace and pay were synchronized in a single modal logic.[2] Such systems became mechanisms of compulsion, as engine pace dictated the production speed to the overlooker, who in turn dictated it to his operatives. Doherty sardonically depicted the overlooker as "the cotton satrap" (*PMA*, Intro., p. vii), and Rowland Detroisier described the whole system of authority more generally as, "one continuous system of driving . . . the manager drives the overlookers, and the overlookers drive the men" (P.P. 1833, v. xx, p. 13). Such driving, as we will see, led to increasing class tensions as managers ratcheted up the pace of production to respond to market exigencies.

The Spinning Room: The Point and Pointedness of Production

The heart and soul of the mill was the spinning room, and the spinner the key actor. As the nexus of production, the spinning room was also the quintessential locus for conflict and a seedbed of technical and social transformation. A distinctly adult male bastion in a world otherwise

---

[2] For an account of how these calculations were culturally conditioned, see Richard Biernacki 1995.

populated by women and children, the spinning room was readily distinguished. Within its confines were the most skilled and privileged factory operatives. It was precisely this status, however, that made the spinners a magnet for conflict with the mill owners.

Over the first few decades, shop floor relations and techniques of production had crystallized into stable facets of the production system. Much like the male silk weavers in their domestic workshops, the spinners constructed their masculinity and respectability through their authority in the spinning room. Struggles over control and wages were thus central to their collective identities as an honorable trade and as family providers.

Each spinner was in charge of one syncopated pair of mules—"a self-contained, organic unit in which work was performed independently by the spinner and his helpers"—which themselves were nested in larger groups or "flats" (Cohen 1985, p. 61; Montgomery 1833, 2d ed., p. 18). This was the spinner's kingdom, founded on his skill, experience, and masculinity. Most gaffers normally knew better than to lord about over a spinner at his machines, for this was staked territory (Montgomery 1833, 2d. ed., pp. 255–256).

The fundamental reality of mill production bluntly impinged upon claims to freedom, however. Pace and intensity were largely dictated by the mill's engines. "You must go with the speed of the engine," observed a seasoned spinner, "and you must follow your work, let it be ten or twelve hours" (P.P. 1833, v.xx, p. 27). While the engine drove the spinner, the manager dictated to the engine: the line of succession did not escape the spinners.

The skill of the spinner was a panoply of technical knowledge, facility of technique, and mechanical ability—all accumulated experience. Knowledge of the fiber, the effects of varying temperature and humidity, and the quality of roving were essential to maintain efficient production. An understanding of machine repair and adjustment was equally indispensable. In fact, even if the manager tried to standardize the machinery, the spinner's habits could undo his intentions, tinkering with the mule to make its functioning slightly idiosyncratic (Bruland 1982, p. 99; Catling 1970, p. 149; Cohen 1985, p. 57; Freifeld 1986, p. 322; Huberman 1986, pp. 988–989).

The spinner's chief concern was with the carriage, the movable component of the mule connected to the frame or "creel," the stationery mechanism that held the bobbins of rovings for spinning. The number of spindles was variable according to power supply, the size of the yarn, and machine construction, though machines of four hundred to six hundred spindles were common by 1830. Rovings passed through rollers on beams mounted in front of the creel and were fastened to the spindles onto a carriage, which imparted the twist when it moved (Catling 1978, p. 42; Ure 1836, v. 2, p. 151). The mule was in fact a semi-automatic device: the first half of the process required no intervention by the spinner. As rollers and bobbin turned, the carriage receded from the frame, stretching and imparting a twist to the rovings, and creating a fully and evenly twisted stretch of yarn (Ure 1836, v. 2, pp. 149–150, 165; von Tunzelman 1978, p. 186).

The second half of the process required the spinner's singular skills. This was anchored in his ability to coordinate several simultaneous tasks that, though simple, required precision and delicacy, while at the same time using his considerable strength to push the carriage back into its original position for the next draw. The process required three simultaneous movements—guiding the yarn, rewinding the spindles, and pushing the carriage. At the end of this process, and while the re-engaged mule was drawing out yarn, the spinner would turn on his heel to his other mule and perform the same operation. The face-to-face positioning of the mules was ergonomically efficient, although it kept the mule spinner in constant rotation between the pair (Catling 1978, p. 41; Ure 1835, p. 309; Ure 1836, v. 2, pp. 153–154).

The arduousness of this operation is difficult to comprehend. A spinner working a pair of mules in the early 1830s was likely to perform between four to five thousand iterations of the process in a twelve-hour day (or about seven times a minute). The carriage, constructed of wood and metal, often weighed over a thousand pounds, and pushing it was performed synchronously with the delicate rewinding process (Cohen 1985, p. 63; Lazonick 1979, p. 235).

While the spinner was engrossed in his work, his two or three assistants—the "piecers"—were also busily engaged with the mule. The "big piecer" (generally a male between fifteen and twenty years of age) was a de facto apprentice who mended broken strands of yarn, kept input and output flowing on the mule, and filled in for the spinner at the carriage should he need relief. Little piecers were younger, performed the basic mending and gathering functions, and often cleaned off the cotton waste that could wreak havoc on machinery. Piecers were in almost incessant motion, and often traversing the equivalent of twenty to twenty-five miles in a twelve-hour day (Catling 1970, pp. 154–158, 161; Cohen 1985, p. 63). They normally were hired directly by the spinner, creating a subcontracting system unique to the mill, and adding to the social construction of the occupation as requiring masculine authority. For the mill manager, it was an efficient system, and it also relieved the gaffer from the responsibility of supervising the small battalion of assistants (Cohen 1985, pp. 59, 61; Freifeld 1986, p. 337; Lazonick 1979, p. 233; Lazonick 1981, p. 18; Sykes 1982, v. 2, p. 101; Ure 1835, p. 290).

The output of this daily routine varied, with the fineness of the yarn, mule size and type, and environmental factors all determining productivity. Contemporary authorities estimated that a normal spinner spinning

#40s (a medium fineness) could produce between 2.75 and 3.75 hanks in a twelve-hour day (Montgomery 1833, 2d ed., p. 196; Ure 1836, v. 2, p. 425). This was equivalent to 2310–3150 yards, all accomplished in 54-inch increments.

Piecers and spinners thus moved in a contrapuntal interplay as the carriages beat out a continuous cadence accompanied by the hum of the spindles. The incessant rhythm of production was broken only by meals and the occasional glitch. Validation of skill, technical knowledge, masculinity, and comparatively good pay could cut the sting of degradation inflicted by this process. Nonetheless, compensation and privilege could not entirely deaden the awareness that the spinner was tethered to a larger system that was beyond his immediate control.

Work Week and Work Life: Time in the Factory

The motion of the carriage was the fundamental rhythm imposed on the spinner by the factory, but it was not the only one. Mill owners had a keen eye for profits, particularly as rates of return shrank over the 1820s. Huge investments demanded regularized production. Days often began at 5:00 A.M., and the average work week was sixty-nine hours (Wood 1910a, p. 40).

The tenure of the spinner at any one firm was almost as variable as the fine workings of the mules. Some mills were, for many, little more than way stations. In the "steady shops," spinners could be found attached to the same pair of mules for several years, and Thomas Ashton of Hyde boasted that he had employed many of his for decades. Spinners were hired under oral agreements that rarely endured more than three months. Such agreements could be rolled over by both parties, although the workings of this practice are obscure (Huberman 1986, p. 992; Shapiro 1967, p. 137; P.P. 1831–1832, XV, p. 280). The standard hiring practices of the Ashton-Stalybridge mill owners have now been lost to time.

Although the spinner's stay in any particular firm was quite variable, his tenure in the trade was not. Most spinners entered the trade in their early twenties; by their early forties, managers were edging them out the factory gates toward the scrap heap of lesser employment (P.P. 1833, XX, D.2, p. 4). An 1830 survey of fifty-two mills in the Ashton-Stalybridge area shows 55 percent of all enumerated spinners to be between twenty and thirty (P.P. 1831–1832, XV, p. 452). Compared to other factory trades, and certainly many crafts, the spinner had a cropped occupational lifespan. Doherty observed that, "it is well known that Spinners at the age of forty are old men. The nature of their employment requires vigilance and activity, and when those are gone, they are cast off like useless lumber, and totally incapable of following any other occupation" (P.C., set 16, v. 2,

"Cotton," f. 66; Baines 1966, p. 457; Sykes 1982, v. 1, pp. 108–109; P.P. 1833, XX, D.2, p. 6). Spinners thus understood that the window of opportunity for high wages closed relatively early.

Wages

Most bourgeois observers were firmly of the opinion that the spinner was amply (if not handsomely) remunerated. Baines painted a picture of prosperity: "Where a spinner is assisted by his own children in the mill, as is very frequently the case, his income is so large that he can live more generously, and clothe himself and his family better, than many of the lower class tradesmen" (1966, p. 446). The spinners hardly fancied themselves working-class princes, however. Their union leader, Doherty, brought to bitter invective on the issue of earnings, measured their pay as "absolutely insufficient to support a dog" (P.C., set 16, v. 2, "Cotton," f. 72). In between these two extremities lay reality. Spinners did not receive wages that placed them among the craft elite. Within the mill, however, they were clearly among the best remunerated operatives and were only below the overlookers in weekly earnings in the Ashton mills (Wood 1910c, p. 292).

Earnings were not highly elastic. By most calculations, the average weekly wage inclusive of all classes of spinners hovered in the range of between twenty-six and thirty shillings in the late 1820s and early 1830s for the Manchester area (Huberman 1986, p. 988; Sykes 1982, v.1 ,p. 105; Wood 1910c, p. 129; P.P. 1837–1838, VIII, p. 276). The writer John Bowring and Major General Henry Bouverie estimated that the spinners in the Ashton district earned roughly from twenty-five to thirty-five shillings per week (L.C.R.O., DDX/880/2, Bowring to Lamb, Dec. 30, 1830; H.O. 40/26, ff. 153–154, Bouverie to H.O., Dec. 4, 1830). Local union head J. J. Betts stridently contended that the weekly average was closer to twenty-one shillings (*MG*, Jan. 8, 1831).

Weekly earnings were a function of piece rates, which had marked regional variations. Larger establishments generally provided superior pay. Such a spectrum of rates makes the determination of an average difficult if not impossible (Wood 1910c, p. 128; Sykes 1982, v. 1, p. 107; Ure 1835, p. 324; Ure 1836, v. 2, p. 444; *PMA* , Feb. 4, 1832, p. 17). In the Ashton/Stalybridge area, piece rates for #40s (a medium fineness and local industry standard) ranged from about three shillings to three shillings, five pence, in Stalybridge to a high in some Ashton mills of four shillings, tuppence (Cotton 1977, p. 212; Kirby and Musson 1975, p. 104). This was a fundamental point of contention between district spinners and mill owners, and we will see was one of the catalysts for the strike of 1830–1831.

Fines imposed for faulty work bit into wages and most quickly drew the spinners' ire. Fines covered a variety of defects in work, but according to spinners all standards were imperiously determined by managers to lower wages (*PMA*, Intro., p. vi; S. J. Chapman 1904, p. 219). Wages could be bled slowly, with fines amounting to at least 13 percent of the net wage. These deductions gnawed at the spinners' sense of economic justice, and Doherty roundly rebuked them as "a perfect mockery of justice" (*PMA*, no. 3, Feb. 4, 1832, pp. 18–19). Piece rates and fines formed part of the ongoing contest of control within the mill, contention that fueled serious discord.

Starting Points: The Foundations of the Spinners' Status

From its inception, the status of the factory-based spinners was determined by a fundamental tension between their needs and those of the mill owner. As Ure acutely observed, the whole modal logic of the factory was to peel away the trappings of occupations that allowed operatives a basis for independence (Ure 1835, pp. 20–21).

Of all mill occupations, spinning proved to be the most refractory in the face of this process. Until the late 1830s and 1840s, when the "self-actor" or automatic spinning mule was sufficiently ensconced in the mill system, spinning remained a half-breed occupation, neither distinctly artisanal nor proletarian in nature. The gendering of the trade remained fairly stable, but all sides recognized that it, and the spinner's status and authority, were mutable. They rested on the balance of power between the exclusive knowledge and abilities of the spinners and their control of trade entrance and the mill owner's capacity for domination, often based in the control and manipulation of technology (Lazonick 1981, p. 14). Lines of conflicting interest were thus clearly embedded in this balance.

THE PRESSURE POINTS OF PRIVILEGE: FOUR POTENTIALITIES FOR DEGRADATION

Although they were the elite of the factory, the spinners faced impingements in four areas: the growth of a reserve army that threatened their control over the labor market, the growing infiltration of women in the labor market, the intensification of the labor process, and the complete automation of the production process itself. Each menace had its own rhythm, although they often combined to create worrisome assaults. All were responsible for collective discussion and mobilization.

From the second generation of spinners, entrants were almost exclusively recruited from the ranks of the big piecers (Sykes 1982, v. 1, p. 101: Turner 1962, p. 95). The structure of production, however, created a fundamental, arithmetical dilemma: every spinner in effect trained two replacements, a pair of big piecers. Further, big piecers matured within six or seven years, while the occupational life-span of the spinner was fifteen to twenty years. Each spinner thus produced several more youthful pairs of potential replacements. Stasis in the labor market brought this problem to the surface and prompted words of concern within the spinners' union ([Doherty] 1829, pp. 17, 38).

The threat of substitution in the late 1820s was nascent but ominous. Firms in the Manchester area, to undermine the union, had already started employing piecers successfully, and whole factories were experiencing such supersession (H.O. 40/27, f. 342, Foster to Peel, Nov. 13, 1830; ff. 163–164, G. R. Chappell to Peel, Oct. 23, 1830). Additionally, periodic discharging due to both slumps and strikes added to these ranks of the reserve labor army. The district strike of 1825 and depression of 1826–1827 produced scores of unemployed spinners, and the slow recoveries meant that many remained idle for long stretches of time (Cotton 1977 p. 151; Kirby and Musson 1975, p. 79; Sykes 1982, v. 1, p. 116; [Tufnell] 1834, p. 27; P.P. 1837–1838, VIII, p. 276). The local labor market in the Ashton-Stalybridge area was not immediately hard-pressed by such a group in the late 1820s and early 1830s (Gatrell 1977, p. 115; L.C.R.O., DDX/880/2, Bowring to Lamb, Dec 30, 1830). Mill owners, however, could readily advertise for labor in nearby markets, and the district spinners were well aware of their brethren's experiences in Manchester. The threat of replacement was thus never far removed.

COMPETITION FROM WOMEN

Although the trade was dominated by males, it was not their exclusive club. A diminishing but important number of women continued to operate mules throughout the 1820s. A report to the Factory Commissioners in 1833 revealed that at that late date 23 percent of the spinning-room labor in the mills surveyed was female (Cohen 1985, p. 62). Women had never been entirely barred from the spinning room, although the increasing size of the mules, and the stiff objections of their male counterparts, limited their numbers. Women generally produced coarser yarns on smaller wheels, often leading to segregated departments, and even more usually entire mills (Freifeld 1986, p. 334; Kirby and Musson, p. 76; Morgan 1992, p. 27).

Male spinners worried about this enclave, and over the course of the first several decades developed two different tactics. The dominant tendency was to strike firms employing females to enforce exclusionary policies (Freifeld 1986, p. 334). By the 1820s, however, males sought to contain and isolate women in these enclaves while spurring them on to form their own unions.[3] Despite this small conciliatory gesture, male spinners

[3] Delegates to conference that established the spinners' union urged women to form their own union to advance their piece rates, resolving "that they receive all the aid of the whole

continued to maintain a strong enmity toward females (*UTJC*, April 3, 1830, p. 34).

The possibility of increasing female numbers portended a drop in wages, lost jobs, and the undermining of masculine work culture. The room was the only bastion of male dominance in a brick box of labor, and its distinctiveness as a skilled occupation was intertwined with the male presence (Valverde 1988, p. 622). To undermine male dominance would have degraded the male inside the factory and eliminated one of the few factory occupations through which he could be validated as a sole bread winner for the family. It is possible that the men constructed an image of these small-wheel mules as inferior machines, thus preserving their sense of male exclusivity in the trade. The positioning of women in any spinning room, however, was likely more than enough to call its masculine character into question.

As Anna Clark argues, outside of the spinning room a form of patriarchal cooperation developed between the male spinners and female factory workers (1995, pp. 132–133, 210). Savvy spinners understood that they needed the support of the majority of the factory hands for effective strike actions. The women were also more often than not kin, and bonds of community and family could mitigate the suspicion and enmity male spinners had for women who had the potential to encroach on their trade. The spinners' union went so far in 1829 as to encourage the establishment of a separate women's union, and in 1830 the male spinners of the great McConnel works in Manchester supported (and indeed pressured) women spinners in a strike for equal wages (Doherty 1829, p. 51; *MG*, Dec. 18, 1830; *MT*, Dec. 25, 1830). On the whole, however, the male spinners remained highly protective of their masculine enclave and increasingly worried that women and child piecers would be used as a wedge against them in wage disputes.

Intensification of the Labor Process

While threats loomed beyond the factory gates, the spinners faced the press of degradation from within. Through successive industrial slumps, mill owners had sought to maintain profit margins by embracing low-cost strategies for productivity gains. Low cost, however, meant high sweat. By the latter part of the 1820s, the push was endemic.

The most cost-effective means to boost productivity was to modify existing mules to hold more spindles. One mill worker testified, with some dis-

---

confederation, in supporting them to obtain men's prices, or such remuneration for their labour as may be deemed sufficient, under general or particular circumstances" ([Doherty] 1829, p. 51). In February 1831, a Manchester paper reported a tentative accord between the union and the mill owners barring women from the trade, but it is not clear whether the plan was effected (*MT*, Feb. 26, 1831).

tress, "They [the mill owners] are now daily increasing the size, and they will continue to increase the size so long as a man is able to stand under them" (P.P. 1833, XX, p. 13). Small mules were easily transformed into greater beasts of burden by engineering advances. In the early 1820s, mule sizes generally peaked at around 220 to 230 spindles. By the end of the 1820s, carriages containing well over 400 spindles were commonplace; those holding 600 were not unusual (Boyson 1970, p. 15; Catling 1978, p. 42; Gatrell 1979, p. 109; Lazonick 1981, p. 15; Ure 1835, p. 341; P.P. 1831–1832, XV, p. 432).

Contemporary estimates, and those of historians, vary on the actual increase in productivity. Thomas Ashton, the district mill magnate, believed that productivity had risen over the first three decades by 50 percent. From the vantage point of the spinners themselves, the work had fully doubled, and that difficulty was compounded by increases in machine speed. These productivity gains, according to one operative, swelled the reserve army by 20 percent (Baines 1966, p. 381; Catling 1970, p. 54; Cohen 1985, p. 58; Huberman 1986, p. 993; Lazonick 1981, pp. 15–16; Ure 1836, v.2, p. 446; P.P. 1831–1832, XV, p. 430; P.P. 1833, XX, pp. 14, 86; P.P. 1837–1838, VIII, pp. 271272; *MT*, Feb. 26, 1831).

By the late 1820s, industrial competition had created two fractious camps, the "small-wheel" and "large-wheel" owners. The large-wheel owners controlled sufficient capital to increase their productivity and increasingly distance themselves from their more diminutive rivals. To squeeze a further advantage from this situation, large-wheel mill owners discounted piece rates on larger mules, establishing a lower return per spindle for all machines above a base count.[4] The discount rate itself rose with the number of spindles, so that those who struggled with the largest mules received proportionately the lowest remuneration (Kirby and Musson 1975, pp. 28, 62; McCulloch 1837, p. 83; Senior 1865, v. 2, p. 160; Turner 1962, p. 73; P.P 1837–1838, VIII, p. 252; *MT*, Sept. 12, 1829).

Both the small-wheel masters and the spinners were incensed by these actions, and each doggedly pursued remedies with increasing frequency from the mid-1820s. The masters' solution, the reduction of piece rates to maintain competitiveness, was viewed by the spinners as an ineluctable spiral toward complete destitution. They also attempted negotiations with the large-wheel mill owners to equalize piece rates and even effected a temporary alliance with the spinners' union when talks sputtered (S. J. Chapman 1904, p. 80; *MG*, Dec. 11, 1830). In an age of unbridled competition, however, the call for restraint was a non sequitur, and the large-

---

[4] A commonly used formula was to discount the piece rate by 1.5 percent for every additional 12 spindles over 300. A spinner on a 600-spindle mule thus realized 21 percent less than if there were no discounting (Freifeld 1986, p. 335). Doherty claimed during the 1829 Manchester fine-spinners strike that the differential was 21 percent between mules of 300 and 468 spindles respectively (P.C., set 16, v. 2, "Cotton," f. 73).

wheel manufacturers ignored all such overtures. In a determined effort to halt this menace of destructive competition, 1,100 Manchester fine spinners mounted a 25-week unsuccessful strike against all of the firms engaging in the nefarious practice (Kirby and Musson 1975, pp. 73–78). Large capital was coming of age, and relishing its power.

THE PUSH FOR AUTOMATION

"It would be possible," Marx remarked, "to write quite a history of the inventions made since 1830, for the sole purpose of supplying capital with weapons against the revolts of the working class.... At the head of these in importance, stands the self-acting mule, because it opened up a new epoch in the automatic system" (quoted in Stedman Jones 1975, p. 51). The spinning mule was not the first automated machine within the factory system, but, as the nexus of the production process, it was the locus of the most pitched contests. The "self-acting" mule was a largely automated spinning machine that performed both the drawing and retraction processes. Its operator tuned and superintended the system rather than animated it. The quest for a self-acting mule was motivated by the cotton lords' drive for power in the mill. Contemporaries such as Baines prosaically noted that increased control was one its principal advantages: "One of the recommendations of this machine is that it renders them independent of the working spinners whose combinations and stoppages have often been extremely annoying to the masters" (1966, p. 208).

An earnest push for the self-actor began after an acrimonious strike by Hyde spinners in 1825. A delegation of mill owners, including Thomas Ashton, paid a public visit to a technological wizard of the region, Richard Roberts of the Sharp Brothers firm (Catling 1970, pp. 62, 170; Kirby and Musson 1975, p. 32; Lazonick 1979, p. 237; Mann 1958, p. 288). During the Stockport spinners' strike of 1828, Roberts himself circulated a flyer to the town's mill owners, announcing that the self-actor had reached perfection (Kirby and Musson 1975, p. 57). At the start of the great strike of 1830, the *Manchester Guardian* was patronizingly warning about the substitution of machine for man: "They know and we know too, that it is possible to spin mule yarn, just as well without their assistance as with it, and indeed even more economically; and it depends chiefly on their conduct, whether this important invention shall be introduced so gradually as to be of unmixed benefit, or whether, by their unruly conduct, they will compel many masters to have recourse to it at once, and thus plunge themselves and their families into deep and lasting distress" (Dec. 18, 1830, p. 3). The menace was made more disturbing by the switch to power looms, an abject lesson in improved machinery (Cotton 1977, p. 16).

Although the self-actor did not become a fixture of the production process until the mid-1830s, and did not fundamentally undermine the status of the male spinner, spinners in the late 1820s could not have the prescience to foresee this. The push for the self-actor demonstrated the mill owners' enmity towards them, and the unsteadiness of their status.

By the 1820s, spinning had matured as a skilled trade with a relatively stable labor process within the factory system. The spinners' authority within the mill, however, was not secure, precisely because their power was obstructed the mill owners' desire for full control. From within the factory and without, threats to their status were fixtures of the spinners' existence. The growth of the reserve army, the potential for women spinners, the intensification of the labor process, and their own looming obsolescence due to automation were palpable dangers. Solidarity and collective action had laid the foundations for both their high status and their acrimonious relations with the mill owners, and the spinners held fast to tried routines in the increasingly trying 1820s.

Ties against Tyranny: The Spinners and Unionism

A legacy of contention between spinners and mill owners had left the scars of experience, providing the collective memory for class consciousness on both sides. In unions, the spinners found strength to resist the attacks on their status and work control. "It is only by uniting with, and assisting each other, that the workmen can hope to be a match for their employers," proclaimed their union secretary, John Doherty (P.C., set 16, v. 2, "Cotton," f. 96). Trade observers recognized that "the most powerful, extensive, and best organized Union in the kingdom, appears to be that of the working cotton spinners" (Tufnell, 1834, p. 2). Some, such as Ure, viewed their combinations as a great cabal "proud of the power of malefaction" and reviled their modest triumphs (1835, p. 232). The spinners were hardly omnipotent, but they were among the most cohesive and active trade groups of their day. Mill owners recognized their combinations as an abrasive annoyance and a potentially serious menace. These ingredients combined into an unstable and sometimes flammable mixture of collective wills.

One universally recognized feature of the spinners' combinations was their strong internal organization at the local level, starting in the 1790s shop-based societies. For their first large-scale strike in 1810, the spinners organized a congress of forty to fifty delegates from local societies to coordinate activities. Such multitiered federations became a standard feature of the spinners' organizations (Daniels 1920, pp. 144–145, n. 3; Kirby and Musson 1975, p. 14; Sykes 1982, v. 1, p. 139; Tufnell 1834, p. 13; Turner 1962, pp. 54–55, 66–67).

A second distinctive feature, their collective action repertoire, was anchored in the mass strike. Brisk trade created opportune conditions for the spinners to seek an equalization in their piece rates between firms and regions. Throughout their history, many of their battles were to stem from precisely this issue (Kirby and Musson 1975, p. 100; Lazonick 1979, p. 234; Lazonick 1981, p. 15; Turner 1962, p. 72). The exemplary regional strikes of 1810 and 1818, involving ten-thousand and twenty thousand workers respectively, crystallized several features of the spinners' repertoire anchored in the mass strike. With the rolling strike (such as the one initiated in Stalybridge in 1810), spinners turned out several mills at a time to force progressive capitulation, while ensuring a steady intake of funds from working spinners. Messengers were assigned to each mill to keep the strike committee appraised. Striking spinners were paid a weekly stipend out of the federation's fund. They paraded daily through towns and past their mills in an effort to discourage blacklegs (scabs) and turn out recalcitrant mills. The spinners also developed coordinated picketing, posting sentries outside each mill to monitor activity and discourage blacklegs. Spinners alien to the mill and area were chosen to frustrate law enforcement. The picketing system was a stroke of organizational and legal artistry, and it proved to be a festering vexation for mill owner and magistrate alike (Aspinall 1949, p. 254; Cotton 1977, pp. 81–82; Cuca 1977, p. 245; Lee 1972, p. 122; Tufnell 1834, pp. 15, 118–119; Turner 1962, p. 68; P.P. 1824, v, pp. 573–574, 604; H.O. 40/27, f. 334–337, B. Gray to Peel, Nov. 6, 1830).

The spinners carried high the banner of general unionism throughout these turbulent decades (Kirk 1985, p. 61; Sykes 1982, v. 1, p. 156). During the turn-out of 1818, the spinners in Ashton and Stalybridge succeeded in temporarily drawing a variety of trades into the fold, including hatters, bricklayers, sawyers, machine makers, shoemakers, colliers, and a host of branches from the cloth trades from towns about the district (Aspinall 1949, p. 272; Cole 1953, pp. 8–9; Cotton 1977, p. 112; Hammonds 1967, p. 104; Kirby and Musson 1975, p. 25).

Although the attempts at general unionism were stillborn children of a fertile working-class vision, and the strikes ended in inglorious defeats, the spinners had been bested, but not cowed. These losses only temporarily dampened union activity, although they burned deep into the collective memory. These mass strikes consolidated a repertoire of tactics that the spinners were to employ routinely later on, and future acts of federation were given solid historical footing. Inter-trade cooperation was strengthened in their ranks and nurtured a greater vision of greater working-class power. This accrued experience set the stage for the battles in the mid and late 1820s, when the two sides squared off for protracted industrial warfare.

"The repeal of the combination laws in 1824 was quickly followed by the emergence of an extremely strong and closely knit operative-spinners' organization determined at all costs to sustain the tradesman status of the operative spinners" (Catling 1970, p. 148–149). From their base of solidarity, the spinners remained implacable in their opposition. In their steadfast defense, the spinners of the Ashton-Stalybridge district were central actors. The first important post-repeal action was in Hyde, a neighborhood notorious for its feeble piece rates in late 1824 and early 1825, but the local magnates were more than their match (Kirby and Musson, p. 31; Tufnell 1834, pp. 18–19; *London Quarterly Review*, v. 106, no. 212, Oct. 1859, p. 273.)

Ashton spinners soon followed with a turn-out of their own. The tenacious contest ended in frustration for the spinners, who saw three hundred of their comrades replaced by blacklegs. The mill owners of Stalybridge, emboldened by the success of their peers, sought to vanquish the union on the heels of the defeat. A town operative wrote with disgust of the attempt to have spinners sign a denunciation of the union, which, if violated, exacted the disabling sum of four-weeks' wages (Cotton 1977, p. 150; Kirby and Musson 1975, p. 43; *London Quarterly Review*, v. 106, 1859, p. 283).

As the strife of the depression began to lift in 1828, the spinners of Stockport took the lead in a series of fearsome contests to retake lost ground and prevent further erosion. By the second week of January, thirty mills stood silent and ten thousand operatives were idle (Kirby and Musson 1975, p. 57). Regular contributions for the Stockport spinners were funneled through other district unions, drawing a stark line between the area's spinners and the mill owners. Leaders such as Doherty urged the turn-outs "to resist, to the utmost, and not submit to be trodden upon by tyrannical cotton lords, and brought down to the starvation point" (Kirby and Musson 1975, p. 58).

This warfare fostered open belligerence among the mill owners. A Hyde manufacturer wrote with disgust, "Are the masters to be compelled to surrender to popular clamour all right to make their own contracts, and to submit to the lowest state of degradation, and to become victims of, and, dependents on, the capricious domination of their own work-people?" (*SA*, Feb. 27, 1829).

In mid-March, they assembled in Manchester to coordinate a counterassault. At this meeting, chaired by one of their captains of industry, Thomas Ashton, the mill owners forthrightly articulated their intentions to break the spirit and the organization of the spinners throughout the district: "That this organized and widely extended combination of operatives employed in cotton manufactures, has become so injurious to the interest of the trade of the country, and threatens the destruction of the property of their employers, and the comfort and respectability of the lower classes of Society, and also to endanger the peace and welfare of the state. That for the purpose of protecting the property and interest of the employers from the injurious effects of the dangerous combination of operatives, it is absolutely necessary to adopt all such measures as the law will permit, to prevent and counteract the pernicious proceedings and objects of the combination" (*MT*, April 11, 1829).

Responding to the call of the meeting, twenty-four firms in Hyde, Dukinfield, and Stalybridge associated to quash support for the Stockport turn-outs and to deal the union a death blow. They demanded that their operatives renounce any connection with the union. Those who refused to sign a repudiation were to have their wages reduced by 10 percent every fortnight. Operatives found to be violating the signed accord were to be fined a fortnight's wages as retribution (*MT*, April 4, 1829). The Hyde masters publicly declared their intent to drive the union to extinction: "The master-spinners and manufacturers of Hyde and the surrounding district feel it to be due to themselves to state, that they were driven to the measure of uniting together by the ruinous consequences of the combination of work-people, which threatened the country.... While, therefore the master-spinners and manufacturers declare it to be their intention to prevent, as far as possible, the system of raising combination among their hands for the support of organized turn-outs,—a system alike subversive to the comfort and good order of the working class, and ruinous to the trade and prosperity of the country" (*MT*, April 11, 1829).

The spinners in the district responded to this challenge of industrial Armageddon with rapid counter-mobilization. Within a week, however, the mill owners had beaten down their display of contemptuous unity. The rout of the spinners in Hyde was a jewel in the crown of the increasingly self-confident mill owners. By July, the Stockport leaders were arrested and violence quelled, and the strike languished until its quiet exhaustion in September (Kirby and Musson 1975, p. 59; *MT*, April 4, 1829; *MM*, April 28, May 5, 1829; *MG*, April 25, 1829).

The cotton lords, had cowed the Hyde spinners, leaving the Ashton spinners to carry the banner (Kirby and Musson 1975, p. 123; P.P. 1831–1832, xv, p. 430). The principal lesson of the 1829 defeats was the need for a more coordinated and solid resource base. Too often, spinners found themselves rich in ties but poor in the material resources necessary to sustain them at essential moments. As the spinners mused on how to increase their collective power, the powerful of Westminster searched for ways to undermine it. Peel wrote worriedly to a local magistrate that some plan must be effected to undermine their capacity for mobilization (M.C.L., MSS, Misc. 223, Peel to Foster, Sept. 11, 1829).

The fundamental and irreconcilable nature of the conflict had became more transparent with each successive contest. The war was not simply a matter of pounds and pence, but was deeply-rooted in the contest for control over the organization of production (Stedman Jones 1975, p. 54). Wages were the flash point, but not the fuel. Class and gender struggle thus impressed itself upon the spinners. Successive defeats, while temporarily dampening their activities, produced an entrenched determination to repel the encroachment. The times and their position seemed to dictate no alternative. By the winter of 1830, the spark of a wage dispute ignited an explosion that surpassed all others.

Large-scale struggles with mill owners who openly pronounced their intent to subordinate the workers created a keen sense of collective, antagonistic interest. This class consciousness, which led the spinners to be among the leaders in general unionism, should not be mistaken for either the sectional reformism of new industrial labor nor simply one of a multitude of equally collective identities. For the spinners of the district, class was a central compelling fact of life. In the following chapters, we shall see how it colored the politics of the district, was articulated in their discourses of contention and guided their actions in the bitter dispute of the winter of 1830–1831.

CHAPTER EIGHT

Class Structure, Class Cultures, and Social Lives

> A really humane man, will not be a practical cotton manufacturer, very few such men will embark capital in such concerns, the scenes of wretchedness which in the one case he would be compelled to witness; and those in the other case which he could not avoid hearing of the images these would raise in his imagination, would be continually present, and make him unhappy.... The manufacturer looks only to his immediate profit and cares little or nothing for what may be the profits of his successor, and it is vain to expect that any other should be the dominant feeling.
> —Francis Place to John Doherty, April 7, 1829

As we saw in the Spitalfields case, the class process was deeply insinuated into the political and cultural life of the district. The weavers constructed a class identity through a cultural understanding of themselves in relation to other workers, the petite bourgeoisie who ran the parishes, and the lines of capitalist power that led from the city to the East End. Class neither simply originated in the workshop or warehouse, nor was it inscribed by discourse as part of the imaginary of social life. Rather, class was the frictional process of power and resistance realized in everyday practices, manifested in the complex of relationships between the silk weavers' ways of life and those who played determinant roles in it. A critical field of force for this friction was the cultural life of the community, where collective actors played out their identities and fashioned a stock of discursive practices for domination or resistance.

Such was the case in the Ashton-Stalybridge district as well, where class was broadly and firmly etched across the terrain. The relationships between mill owners and factory workers defined the boundaries of class experience, but that experience and its representation happened in starkly different ways for each group. As I demonstrate below, the cultural divide between the classes provided additional friction for the incendiary sparks of open conflict.

As we have seen, spinners stood at the nexus of the production process. But just how did the spinners perceive themselves and structure their collective identities within the community? Scholars provide widely differing views of both their self-proclaimed and historically defined status. As highly paid skilled operatives, spinners are often depicted as part of an emergent nineteenth-century labor aristocracy (Kirby and Musson 1975, p. 15; Cohen 1985, p. 56; Foster 1974, p. 231; Turner 1962, pp. 93–96). Labor aristocrats were often defined as social exclusives, a concomitant attribute of superior status and pay. From this vantage point, the insular world of the spinning room begat a larger circumscribed social sphere (Catling 1970, p. 165).

Perhaps this was true in the industrial metropolis, but the evidence for the Ashton area reveals that they were integrated into an independent and combative proletarian culture. The spinners were the largest adult male section of the factory labor force, although given the region's integrated mills they constituted only about 12 to 15 percent of the factory labor force. By the mid-1830s, there were over seven hundred in Ashton and six hundred in Stalybridge (Manchester Statistical Society, 1838, app., pp. xii, Table #5).[1]

As a group they were demarcated by superior domesticity, housed in more comfortable dwellings embellished with the trappings of a higher status such as clocks and chests of drawers (Manchester Statistical Society 1838, p. 7; Coulthart 1844, pp. 32–33). Spinners generally were noted for their greater preoccupation with this household order and comfort, reflecting their status as superior male breadwinners (Kay 1970 [1832], pp. 25–26).

Yet in Ashton there is no evidence that this domestic distinctiveness signaled social exclusivity. Living in compact towns and villages, the spinners had few barriers to separate them from their factory kin. To the extent that dwellings were appendages of the mills, spinners were grouped with their compatriots. Rounds of daily existence were played out within this limited social space, and its rhythm was largely defined by demands of the mill. Contemporary observers often keenly noted that factory life pressed workers into closer ties.

Common life struggles fostered a culture of mutuality, and often nurtured bonds against the "tyrants" of the mill and the polity (Kirk 1985, pp. 60–61; Sykes 1982, v. 1, p. 74). Ure viewed this sociability with cir-

---

[1] Piecers, the spinners' assistants and de facto apprentices, formed an additional 22.6 percent of the workforce for the three towns (ibid.).

cumspection and warned his readers of its more invidious features: "Manufactures naturally condense a vast population within a narrow circuit; they afford every facility of secret cabal and co-operative union among the work-people; they communicate intelligence and energy to the vulgar mind" (Ure 1835, p. 407). Although there were significant minorities of other trade groups in the region, their similar travails helped forge broad cohesion.[2] Hatters, colliers, machine-makers, handloom weavers, and other groups experienced parallel conflicts with large employers. Additionally, with many workers moving through numerous mills over their working lives, the trials of the factory were part of a wide stock of shared experience (Gadian 1986, p. 39).

Conversely, a circumscribed social space made the construction of social barriers problematic. Without a robust petitbourgeois group to intercede between and complicate capitalist-worker antagonism, fundamental class conflict was woven into the fabric of shared experience. The Ashton area spinners experienced this conflict in a common arena of the factory, and it diffused outwards into a combative working-class identity and culture.

A Shared Culture

The region's community life was composed of two dominant, but distinct universes. A self-confident bourgeoisie constructed a culture of wealth, Dissent, and utilitarian liberalism. In opposition, the working class forged a feisty and insulated culture, cultivating an independent identity and sense of collective worth.

In the 1790s and early nineteenth century, the larger towns in the area began to witness the proliferation of social and cultural organizations, including literary societies, which fostered a strong tradition of dialect poetry (Harrop 1980, pp. 13–18). More vital to the growth of a cohesive male working-class culture was the rise of the fraternal club and the sick and burial society. Ashton and Stalybridge abounded with fraternal lodges by the 1820s, and they diffused beyond the pale of town life into the manufacturing villages. (Bowman 1960, p. 556; Butterworth 1842, p. 153; *MT*, June 11, 1829, Nov. 13, 1831; Baines 1824, v. 2, p. 557).

Lodges found venues in the center of male working-class social life, the public house. As the region's market town, Ashton was the predominant home of public houses and inns. As I noted in Chapter 2, beer shops and the male sociability and free discussion they offered were less common in the outlying mill villages dominated by mill owners. While pubs anchored

---

[2] According to the Statistical Society survey, factory hands constituted 61.9 percent of the working population of Ashton, 69 percent of Stalybridge, and 54.9 percent of Dukinfield. Illustrative of the dominance of factory production is the fact that the next largest outside occupational grouping was warehouse workers (Manchester Statistical Society 1838, app., p. xiii).

male social life in the towns, a variety of outdoor activities punctuated the flow of sociability for the region as a whole, and some integrated women. Gaming, cock-fighting, and pugilism were prized working-class entertainment. Bull-baiting was a spirited community recreation. All excited contempt and annoyance in the local elite, who unsuccessfully sought to suppress them (Bowman 1960, pp. 52–53; *MT*, Oct. 31, 1828, Oct. 24, 1829). On a more elaborate level, wakes were a particularly popular source of amusement, containing an array of vivacious sport and cheer. Lancashire was known for its wakes and fairs, which were replete with rush carts, morris dancers, high spirits, and saturnalian splendor (Walton and Poole 1982). Throughout the district, wakes were an integral part of the calendar. The Ashton wakes had existed since the sixteenth century, while the more celebrated July Bridge wakes of Stalybridge dated from the mid-eighteenth (Bowman 1960, pp. 299–307; Butterworth 1842, pp. 152–153). Despite the consternation of the mill owners, factory hands would bypass the mill gates in July for a week of high frivolity. The *Voice of the People* announced the event in bacchanalian terms: "Those who derive amusement from hurdy gurdy grinders, cat-gut scrapers; drums and ginger bread, noise and dirt, gin and penny-whistles, beef and pudding, ale and spice-cake, broken heads and bloody noses, terminating in empty pockets, blood-shot eyes, and comfortable lodgings in the lock-ups, to have ample means of gratification at the exhibition y'cleped the wakes" (July 23, 1831, p. 2). The radical Richard Carlile was struck by the debauchery of the festival. He lamented, "Drunkenness, of course, is the finishing characteristic of this carnival, and nothing more to spend is a signal among the working people to leave the rush-cart and go back to work. There are many to be found who are advocates of these sports and pastimes" (*Lion*, v. 1, no. 4, Jan. 25, 1828, pp. 103–104).

The Black Lad

Although wakes and fairs were contrapuntal to the solemnity of mill town life, their significance lay deeper than simple unfettered enjoyment. Such festivities could also serve as venues for proletarian countertheater, burlesques that mocked established power. The carnivalesque was a process of transgression and a "catalyst and site of actual and symbolic struggle" (Stallybrass and White 1986, p. 14). As James Scott suggests, "carnival is, par excellence, an occasion for recriminations of subordinate groups presumably because normal power relations operate to silence them. . . . What is so striking historically about carnival is not how often it contributed to the maintenance of existing hierarchies, but how frequently it was the scene of open social conflict" (1990, p. 174, 181; also cf. Cresswell 1994, p. 43; Stallybrass and White, passim.; E. P. Thompson

1991, p. 524). Carnivalesque festivities, through their inversions, parodies, and playful hybridity, portray willful misrule and often pose explicit challenges to existing hierarchies. The carnivalesque does not so much present alternatives as much as it serves as a vehicle of collective critique, creating possibilities for more open power struggles (Bristol 1985, p. 52; Cresswell 1994, p. 57; Stallybrass and White 1986, p. 18, 43).

Two features of the carnivalesque are important in understanding the Riding of the Black Lad as a signifying and unifying event of a working-class culture. First, carnivalesque festivities take as their site the marketplace and create a plebeian territoriality, a possessive transformation of territory and place (Bakhtin 1984, pp. 10, 154, 255; LaCapra 1983, p. 301; Stallybrass and White 1986, p. 27). In this sense, the democratizing and leveling aspects of the carnivalesque were subversive of increasing capitalist control of quintessential public space. As Stallybrass and White suggest, the marketplace was the cross-section and hybridization of the communal and the commercial, work and play, the civil and the pleasurable: bourgeois culture sought to disassociate and isolate these features (1986, pp. 30–31). As collective action, the carnivalesque presented a very concrete challenge to the capitalist transformation and control of space.

This transgressive possession was not only realized by physical presence but by the debasing and degrading forms of speech and interaction with which its participants engaged all who found themselves within this realm. Through debasing language and laughter, working people could highlight the dualities of class power. This appropriation of space, however temporary, can thus be viewed as an act of both ideological *and* spatial counter-hegemony (Bakhtin 1984, pp. 10–12, 16, 151–153, 432–433; Cresswell 1994, p. 55).

Second, women are integral to both the action and symbolism of the carnivalesque. The disorderly female was central in symbolically validating the subversive and riotous behavior of men and women alike (Davis 1975, pp. 131, 147; Russo 1986, pp. 214–215).[3] In his analysis of carnival, Bakhtin argued that the symbolism of degradation and dirt was ambivalently connected with the female image, conjuring up both a potentially inferior status but also a link to life-giving and renewal (1984, p. 240; see also Stallybrass 1985, pp. 122–125). This incorporation of women as central actors likely attenuated the gender divisions constructed in the factory and pub, helping to sustain a more cohesive class culture.

In Ashton, the occasion known as the "Riding of the Black Lad" was such

---

[3] Russo is also quick to emphasize that the marginal status of women in the normative world, coupled with the suspension of order during these periods, could make the carnival a dangerous space for women (ibid., p. 216).

an event. Its origins are obscure, but folklore attributes its origin to the ignominious fifteenth-century reign of a lord of the neighboring manor of Middleton, Sir Ralph Assheton.[4] Henry VI awarded him the life privilege of guld riding in Ashton parish, a yearly practice of riding through the tenantry's fields to police their weeding of the flowers that hampered cultivation. Recalcitrant peasants were liable for stiff fines, and lore had it that Sir Ralph dispensed these with relish. Every year around Easter, he would ride through the fields in a suit of black armor exacting his heinous toll. Upon his death, scornful relatives were said to have abolished the practice and reserved a small amount of estate money to annually memorialize the dreaded visits.

The Black Lad originated in mocking plebeian theater, but by the nineteenth century the denizens of Ashton had given it a distinctly working-class hue. The essential preparations for the festivities were made prior Easter Monday, the day of the event. A pit was dug on a lane above the old cross in the marketplace and filled with water, and an effigy of the Black Lad prepared. An eyewitness provided this account of the event in 1826.

> A singular custom prevails at this town on Easter Monday. Every year on that day a rude figure of a man made of an old suit of clothes stuffed with rags, hay, &c., is carried through all the streets. The people who attend it call at every public-house, for the purpose of begging liquor for its thirsty attendants, who are always numerous. During its progress the figure is shot at from all parts. When the journey is finished, it is tied to the market cross, and the shooting is continued till it is set on fire, and falls to the ground. The populace then commence tearing the effigy to pieces, trampling it in mud and water, and throwing it in every direction. This riot and confusion are increased by help of a reservoir of water being let off, which runs down the streets, and not unfrequently persons obtain large quantities of hay, rags, &c. independent of that which falls from the effigy. The greatest heroes at this time are of the coarsest nature. (Hone 1827, v. 2, c. 468)

The mid-1820s brought increasing participation, and thousands of workers crowded the main thoroughfares. As businessmen sought to traverse the space that they had reconstructed as an area of modern commerce, working people appropriated it as arena for degradation. Fine attire and proper manners mingled helplessly among disorderly men and women and the egalitarian effects of dirt. As the elite moved about town, they fell prey to "dowsing," those on the street pelting them with mud and

---

[4] Numerous accounts and explanations exist for the Black Lad ceremony. Among these are Axon 1870; Bamford 1967 (1841), v. 1, pp. 141–143; Baines 1825, v. 1, pp. 493–494; Harland and Wilkinson 1882, pp. 285–294; Hone 1827, v. 2, c. 467–469; Roby 1872, v. 1, pp. 95–105; Wright 1936, pp. 115–116.

refuse-soaked wads of straw and rags called bass. The 1829 *Manchester Times* observed in distress that this practice had reached unprecedented heights, with both men and women being assailed by dowsers who engaged in "the most unjustifiable assaults; several highly respectable individuals are abused and one has obtained warrants" (*MT*, April 25, 1829, p. 219). The latter was dissuaded from following through on his prosecution only when a local magistrate promised more thorough policing at subsequent rituals (*MT*, May 2, 1829, p. 230).

The Riding of the Black Lad exhibited all of the billingsgate and degradation that, Bakhtin argued, are the hallmarks of carnival. In the context of class formation, we can also see how it was a ritual that contested bourgeois control of social space and expression. The working people who clogged Ashton's streets freely dowsed their superiors, those who normally defined proper conduct within both factory and public spaces. As Samuel Bamford reflected in his reminiscences of the event, it was "expressive of hatred and contempt" through its open mocking of local authority (1967, v.1, p. 142). Through their overwhelming numbers, and much to the consternation of the local elite, working people usurped authority, and as they did so the wheels of commerce ground to a halt. The Riding, in these senses, briefly but broadly challenged the mill owners' order, and served as an important expression of class solidarity.

The Capitalists: Cotton Lords and the Shopocracy

The Ashton-Stalybridge district was the kingdom of cotton, and on the throne sat the mill owner. The "cotton lords," as they were referred to by the factory hands, were an ascendant bourgeoisie. By the 1820s, they were a maturing power, both locally and nationally, who actively sought to recreate the world in their own vision. The smoke that spewed from their chimneys and blanketed surrounding towns palpably marked the boundaries of their growing empires.

Within this kingdom, the petite bourgeoisie were the lesser subjects. A host of merchants, publicans, and grocers rose to meet the needs of the expanding population. They formed a "shopocracy," whose fortunes followed the larger economy uncertainly and whose politics often accommodated a Painite radicalism. Sandwiched between the rulers and the ruled, they largely reacted to rather than directed the district's affairs. In this section, I first survey the sphere of the lords and then turn to the vassals.

Across a broad spectrum of ideas, social activities, and background, the mill owners distinguished themselves as a distinct breed of a new bourgeois order. As Anthony Howe, a historian of the group, has observed, "The distinctiveness of the cotton masters, as a group, was the product not only of their particular social and economic formation, but also of their relationship to the dominant aristocracy and the nascent working class. . . .

As a middle class—in terms of wealth, power, status, and culture—the cotton masters developed a separate identity and their own specific organizations" (1984, p. v).

By the 1830s, entrants to this rising class came primarily from within their own ranks (Howe 1984, p. 10). This self-generation reinforced ties of family and marriage that overlay existing trade solidarity (Kirk 1985, p. 41). Geographic concentration also served as a social glue. By the 1830s, the mill owners had emerged as a "strongly hereditary group," confident in their ascendancy (Howe 1984, p. 311).

Social cohesiveness was solidly buttressed by the twin pillars of an expanding bourgeois ideology—political economy and Dissent. During the 1820s, a mechanistic political economy became the touchstone of the mill owners' creed (Sykes 1982, v. 1, p. 92). Through this discourse, the cotton lords constructed a Liberalism that attacked government interference, protectionism, and corruption.

Charles Hindley, an M.P. for the district and a Dukinfield mill owner, was a shining exemplar of this class consciousness. A champion of bourgeois Liberalism and an ardent reformer, Hindley was a vanguard member of the mill owners' community and a product of entrepreneurial Manchester. In his inaugural address for the Ashton Mechanics' Institution in 1825, he revealed his implacable liberal optimism. Hindley spoke of the beatific progress of modern industry: "Within the last five and twenty years, we have seen the most astonishing improvements in Machinery, and yet, so far from the demand for labour being diminished, we are all aware, that it never was known to be so great and so constant, as it has been for the last two years. It is the natural effect of Mechanical improvement to lower the price of comforts and conveniences of life, and thus bring them within the reach of a larger proportion of the human population" (Hindley 1825, p. 7).[5] In an enthusiastic charge to his audience, Hindley challenged them to participate in the bounties of individual moral and intellectual improvement. His words confirmed the capitalists' lack of responsibility for the workers' plight, the individuated nature of the workers' fortunes, and their status as an appendage to a much larger technical juggernaut. These constructions were hallmarks of bourgeois hegemonic discourse: "Determine, like them, to resist those inclinations to sensual indulgences which debase and destroy you, and seek to improve those facilities which you have received for your individual benefit, and the welfare of your fellow creatures. It depends upon yourselves what station you will occupy. It will be your own fault if you are contented to occupy the place of mere Machines, instead of the situation of intelligent beings" (ibid., p. 11).

---

[5] Hindley was, however, willing to admit in a casual aside that "it is true that every material alteration in Machinery must produce a temporary inconvenience to individuals" (ibid.).

Hindley's halcyon future was built upon an unflappable faith in the virtues of free trade. Unfettered commerce, guided by the eternal truths of humanistic Dissent, was his panacea for a troubled world. In a speech delivered in 1830, Hindley elucidated this gospel: "The question of free trade appears to me to lie in a small compass, and to be involved in the question whether there shall be unrestricted freedom given to commercial pursuits, or an entire prohibition to the interchange between man and man. Between the two courses I do not see any middle ground" (Hindley 1841, pp. 3–4). He continued with an impassioned plea for the enlightened path and ended with a clarion call: "And in the name of common sense, which refuses to return to the destitution of a barbarous and savage age—in the name of reason, which proves the restrictive system to be absurd—in the name of experience, which has found it to be impossible—in the name of morality, which deprecates falsehood, and abominates slavery and war—and, above all, in the name of religion, which teaches us that God has made of one blood all the families of the earth—in the name, I say, of common sense, reason, experience, morality, and religion, I propose unrestricted free trade. . . . 'Free Trade all over the World'" (ibid., pp. 15–16, 24). For Hindley, the truths of political economy were both self-evident and sanctified: industrial competition was a great machine with other worldly powers. Although its dictates could chafe various interests, the motion of the machine could not be stilled or substantively altered. It was, after all, common sense.

This political economy was morally covered by a vibrant Dissenting tradition, particularly among such Nonconformist sects as the Wesleyan Methodists, Independents, and Congregationalists. Distilled from the Dissenting tradition was a hospitable message: "Business was God-given but wealth was not pursued in its own right; wealth attained was thus wealth legitimized and honourable and lawful" (Howe 1984, p. 66). These discourses of Dissent added a humanistic veneer to the utilitarian tenets of political economy. The two were spun together into a single thread of faith, and the yarn used as binding in the moral packaging of power. The cotton lords constructed a collective identity as earnest and virtuous entrepreneurs, whose exercise of control promoted the interests of the entire community. Although it gained perhaps only modest limited credence from the working class, this discourse added assurance to the mill owners as they extended control outward over the district.

The Mill Owners of the Ashton-Stalybridge District: Social and Economic Ties

Surveying the environs of Ashton in the later 1830s, Samuel Robinson remarked, "The circumstances of this neighborhood are somewhat singular. In so large a population it is rare to find property so immensely concentrated in the hands of so few individuals" (quoted in Cotton 1977, p. 7). A few years later another observer suggested that the mill owners had succumbed to an insular world of wealth and privilege: "As a body, the manufacturers are wealthy—clever—have extensive business connexions; but their political interest is the most feeble of that of all branches of commercial industry, for they have allowed their riches to entomb them. They have huge factory-like houses within the sounds of their machinery, dinners of puzzling variety, equipages, servants, every thing of the costliest and best to administer to their sensuous wants; but no where are there any indications of a refined and generous liberality. The yearly stagnation of their incomes generates nothing but a noxious desire to have a higher chimney or a bigger mill than their neighbors" (quoted in Butterworth 1842, p. 145). In their regnant position, the mill owners' cohesion was subject to few abrasions, although their authority was at times contested by the Earl of Stamford and Warrington. The 1820s formed a watershed period for their consolidation of power. The process was considerably facilitated by common origins, and by shared social institutions and ideology. This decade was an interregnum, a transitional time when many mill founders passed the torch of authority to their offspring. These Young Turks of capitalism had shared upbringings, similar schooling, and a tight, common circle of relationships among the major families. Although they were to diverge in the Victorian decades, in these years the mill owners of the district formed a fairly cohesive order.

The first generation of mill owners had roots in a relatively small set of shared family backgrounds. Several families had lineages in the old local wool and cotton broadcloth trades, including the Harrisons, the Halls, and the Sidebottoms of Stalybridge, the Ashtons and Hindleys of Hyde, and Hegginbottoms of Ashton. These families were among the pioneers of the new industry, forming partnerships in the 1790s that served as a bedrock for future expansion.

Yet another pathway lay in the land. Several of the more prosperous families traced their lines back to some of the district's more affluent yeomanry of the eighteenth century. Included in this group were the Cheethams, Leeches, Bayleys, and Wilkinsons (Birch 1959, p. 11; Bowman 1960, p. 456; Follows 1951, p. 10; Hill 1902, pp. 241, 244, 249, 251, 254, 260, 265, 271; Middleton 1932, pp. 447–452, 459–460, 465–466).

A final set of common backgrounds lay broadly in the skilled trades. Local men schooled in rudiments of smithing, carpentry, and machine working found their knowledge readily adaptable to the demands of the nascent factory system. The father of the great magnate Thomas Mason was a joiner, and the young Mason was apprenticed as a spinner at the age of eight. Others from the Lees, Wilkinson, and Wagstaffe families had similar backgrounds (Birch, 1959, p. 11; Bowman 1960, pp. 247, 459; Hill 1902, pp. 252, 268, 272; Holland 1974, p. 9).

Several of these capitalist pioneers rose in tandem through partnerships and trade. John Leech, George Cheetham, Thomas Harrison, and John Lees pooled their capital in 1794 to form a spinning partnership. Their spindle supplier was Luke Wagstaffe, father of John and James of Wagstaffe & Sidebottom (Hill 1902, pp. 241, 248, 268, 270). Throughout the first several decades of the nineteenth century these entrepreneurial families played musical chairs with joint ventures, successively pooling their capital and dissolving partnerships in their quest for fortunes.

Characteristic of these early entrepreneurs was a drive for success and a resolve for sacrifice. Most entered the trade with modest capital and small shops. Thomas Mason was an archetypal example of this breed, whose bootstrap philosophy and unending exertion paid back enormous dividends. Along with his friends John Booth and Edward Hulton, he purchased a pair of mules, and the trio rented a small portion of a mill in Crookbrook. Mason served the firm simultaneously as carder, clerk, and salesperson. Eventually, he broke off from the partnership to rent part of the Reyner Brothers' Albion Mills, which later became part of the family's spinning empire. By the time of his retirement in 1862, he presided over one of the great industrial clans of Lancashire (Ashmore and Bolton 1975, passim; Holland 1974, p. 9; Bowman 1960, p. 460).

Partnerships between families were cemented and dissolved with the fortunes of business, but clan connections were enduring ties of the community elite. At times, they assumed an almost incestuous character. The Cheethams of Stalybridge were at the nexus of many of these relations. George, the founder of the family empire married Sarah Lees, the sister of mill owner John Lees. His son in turn married Emma Reyner, daughter of the mill owner Thomas Reyner. One of Cheetham's daughters, Amy, was wed to William, the son of Thomas Harrison, and her cousin. George's eldest daughter, Jane, married Joseph Bayley, Jr., offspring of the Bayley dynasty founder. The Bayleys also formed an important nodal point for kin ties among the Cheethams, Harrisons, and Reyners. Many other families, such as the Buckleys of Ashton, established similar if less dense alliances (Hall 1991, p. 89).

Although the bourgeoisie of the district did have substantial business ties in Manchester, social life was still relatively insular. Within the limited confines of these bourgeois circles, the mill families dominated. Bonds of blood and business thus served as the foundation for a strong and enduring solidary structure. Shared leisure enhanced these ties through ongoing cultural and recreational activities, and also forged links with the traditional power brokers, the landowners.

On the whole, the bourgeoisie seem to have been little enamored with erudite culture, although they did appreciate the status trappings of refined entertainment. The pinnacle of leisured life was found in the blue-blood recreation of the hunt. The district's elite were unabashed enthusiasts of both the chase and pigeon shooting (Bowman 1960, p. 550; *SA*, Sept. 7, 1829). The hunt was a stepping stone to the aristocratic pretensions that captured so many of the mill owners. Participation in patrician sport represented the bourgeoisie's social arrival; the recognition by the gentry of their legitimation as gentlemen. These and other leisure activities served as luster for a group often castigated for their tarnished graces.

If leisure provided a social bridge between two elite worlds, religion raised a wall of intolerance and contention. The hostility "was particularly intense in Ashton, where the division between Anglican and Dissenter made itself felt in every part of the town's social life" (Rose 1974, p. 60). Large landowners were the Anglican Church's natural constituency. The Earl of Stamford, with the tradition-hardened heart of a High Tory, viewed the parish as a perquisite of his station. The living for the parish vicarage of St. Michael was his aristocratic dispensation, which he handed to his nephew George Chetwode in 1816. Chetwode's absence and his 2000 pound income were a repugnant sign of the mill owners' vassalage. To a group self-sanctified by its successful independence, St. Michael's was a symbol of rotten privilege that stoked a reactive truculence (Bowman 1960, p. 186; Cotton 1977, pp. 34–35; Rose 1974, pp. 61–62).

Many of the bourgeoisie sought salvation in freer quarters initially found in the meeting rooms of the New Connexion Methodists.[6] In 1815, a small group of Congregationalists emerged and over the ensuing decade and a half the sect slowly drew mill owners away from the Methodists. Bringing with them their considerable resources and a keen desire to create a wholly independent sanctuary of worship, they lifted the chapel into affluence (Bowman 1960, p. 231; Glover 1884, pp. 251–252, 254, 278, 284, 298; Hall 1991, p. 75; Howe 1984, p. 65; Rose 1969, pp. 4, 10, 19; Rose 1974, p. 61).[7]

Independency was shorn of all vestiges of spiritual dictation, and the Reverend Sutcliffe, through his weekly sermons, sanctified the mill owners' ideology. By 1834, with the consecration of the Albion Chapel, the Congregationalists had become the dominant religious force in Ashton. Their trustees incorporated a full array of mill owners, including Abel, James, and Joseph Buckley, John Cheetham, James Lord, Frederick

[6] In a discussion of divisions among the mill owners' ranks, Robert Hall observes that the 1843 report of the factory inspector Leonard Horner shows that mill ownership in terms of numbers (although not size) was actually dominated by Anglicans over Dissenters, 36 to 27 mills (1991, p. 92); however, we may wonder if this was a result of an Anglican revival of the 1830s. Additionally, it might be possible that some of these Churchmen were landowners whose coal mines had led them to invest in small mills (ibid., p. 92).

[7] Robert Hall notes that the Independents actively recruited from a wide spectrum of Ashton society, seeking to cut across class lines. By his calculations, 57 percent of all baptisms during the period 1818–1837 were of children of weavers, spinners, and other factory workers (1991, pp. 78, 282).

Reyner, and William Swindell (Cotton 1977, p 51; Glover 1884, p. 256; Howe 1984, p. 67).

In the region's other towns and villages, other Dissenting sects similarly won the mill owners' hearts and pockets. In Stalybridge, mill owners followed the course charted by their Ashton peers. Starting with the establishment of the New Connexion, the opulent and powerful gravitated in increasing numbers to the nearby Dukinfield Old Chapel, a long-time bastion of Dissent whose patron was the landowner and magistrate Francis Astley (Butterworth 1842, p. 150; Cotton 1977, pp. 52–53). In the smaller industrial villages, the local cotton lords defined the tenor of religious activity. In Hyde, for example, under the hegemonic supervision of the great mill owner Thomas Ashton, Unitarianism held sway (Rose 1969, p. 33).

Whatever the activity, the district's mill owners sought to engage it on their own terms. By the 1820s, through familial, economic, and social ties they had woven a network of relationships that sustained their power. Moreover, their cohesion was well evident to the working people of the district. While the mill owners sat at the pinnacle of the market system, a small group of merchants and trades people operated below in the mundane world of pettier transactions.

The Petite Bourgeoisie

In the fissures between capital and labor was a modest petite bourgeoisie, secondary actors wedged in the middle of the more fundamental struggles. Sometimes supine, and frequently defensive and re-active, this class struggled to maintain its socioeconomic and political foothold within the communities of the district. A brief analysis of their intermediary role highlights the nature of class conflict in the district.

Shopkeepers, publicans, drapers, bakers, and a host of other essential merchants formed a collectivity that contemporaries often characterized as the "shopocracy." In a region so overwhelmingly working-class, the majority of small retailers were sellers of necessities. Their fortunes rose or fell with the fullness of the proletarian pocket. Additionally, some, such as the green grocer Timothy Higgins, were ex-spinners or perhaps relatives of operatives whose sympathies clearly lay with the factory workers (Baines 1825, v. 1, pp. 496–501; v. 2, pp. 557–559, 733–735; Epstein 1994, p. 159, n. 58; Hall 1991, p. 94).

Their quest for steady economic security took several forms, and often positioned the shopocracy awkwardly between the two major classes. In one such scheme, shopkeepers facilitated the mill owners' practice of paying workers with large bank notes every five to six weeks to avoid handling small currency, and realized a small return on conversion to smaller notes (Shapiro 1967, pp. 14–15, 141; *SA*, Nov. 6, 1829). To supplement their shop incomes, a number may have also invested in real estate during the building boom of the early 1820s. There is fragmentary evidence in the Ashton Parish rate books suggesting that some of the petite bourgeoisie, such as innkeepers, were participants in this speculation.[8]

The economic symbiosis between the worker and the shopkeeper was much stronger than that with the mill owner. Driving this class alliance was consternation with the truck system. The system encompassed several wage-payment schemes, including paying workers in kind, or the establishment of in-house shops where workers received their pay in the form of goods and necessities (Hilton 1957, 1958). Although such practices were illegal, policing was lax, and employers were rarely prosecuted. Under either system, the mill owner not only solved his payroll problem, but also was able to pad his coffers by exacting above-market prices on necessities. The *United Trades' Co-operative Journal* charged that many mill owners raised their profits by 20 to 25 percent in such dens of extraction (Apr. 17, 1830, pp. 52–54). Vociferous complaints from the region's workers and shopkeepers suggest the practice was widespread (*MT*, Oct. 23, Dec. 18, 1830; *SA*, May 25, 1830; *UTCJ*, May 29, 1830, pp. 99–100).

The truck system squeezed the mercantile arteries of the petite bourgeois economy, constricting particularly hard when commerce was slack (precisely the same periods when mill owners sought to boost their sagging profits). Bankruptcies were not infrequent among small merchants, and truck may well have made the difference for many. In early 1831, the region's shopkeepers, aided by working-class activists, formed the Protection Society to promote witnesses testifying to truck to stop the slow bleeding by this system (*MT*, Jan. 1, 1831; *WMC*, Jan. 8, 1831).

Truck and trade thus were magnetic forces within the class structure, pulling workers and the shopocracy together. The alliance was not a complete melding of interests, but the ties were highly resilient, especially in radical politics. Such a political pairing probably lies behind the radical republican activism in the post-Peterloo years. Led by Charles Walker and Joshua Hobson, a group of stalwart radicals publicly commemorated such events as Peterloo, Paine's birthday, and the imprisonment of Hunt and Carlile in the early 1820s until suppressed by the local authorities. They continued to be supporters of Carlile throughout his imprisonment in the later 1820s (Epstein 1994, p. 157–159; *Republican*, March 8, 1822, pp. 302–307, May 24, 1822, pp. 657–660, Jan. 17, 1823, pp. 85–87, Aug. 12, 1824, pp. 183–184, Aug. 4, 1826, pp. 109–110). This resurfaced in the early 1830s, with events such as the radical reform meeting in January 1831 spearheaded by shopkeepers and attended by two thousand.

---

[8] The analysis was a cross-tabulation of the listings found in Baines' *Lancashire Directory* (1825), with the remnants of the Ashton Parish rate book for 1831 (L.C.R.O. PR2576). Most of the individuals listed in the eleven extant pages of the rate book were not identifiable in Baines (the total sample was thirty persons).

There, the speeches and resolutions plunged Painite swords into the body of Old Corruption with classic form. Resolutions condemning the corn laws, church tithes, military expenditures, and the lack of a free press were warmly received, and through these shared discourses of radical politics alliances were cemented (*MT*, Jan. 29, 1831). These common discourses allowed for a shared identity as aggrieved citizens. As we shall see, however, this popular radicalism did not preclude the development of a distinctive class consciousness among working people of the district. Rather, populist radical discourse created potentials for cross-class alliances, which were sometimes realized in shared travails.

Conflicts between the mill owners and workers could cast shopkeepers in the role of sometimes reluctant but inescapable participants because of kin and friendship networks. Victualers and innkeepers who lacked political or kin ties could find themselves in an uncomfortable middle ground. For shopkeepers, a placid community fostered prosperity, while civil disturbance disrupted trade and could also mean parish expenditures for the billeting of troops. During such actions, shopkeepers also found themselves under the power of the weak. Workers scrimped to get by and depended on the shopkeeper's generous credit for the duration of a turnout. They often enforced this benevolence through "exclusive dealing," promising future customer loyalty if shopkeepers supported them during their troubles.

Precisely such an entanglement occurred with the massive strike of December 11, 1830, when the spinners of fifty-two firms turned out in reaction to piece-rate reductions imposed by the mill owners (which I will analyze in greater detail) (Cotton 1977, p. 224). The shopocracy quickly found themselves pressed from all sides; local magistrates entreated them to serve as special constables with little success. In addition, they were threatened by mill owners desiring the early closure of public houses and, of course, by workers who promised exclusive dealing (H.O. 40/26, f. 162, Foster to Melbourne, Dec. 6, 1830; Cotton 1977, p. 224; *MT*, Dec. 25, 1830). In the end, they reluctantly cast their lot with the spinners, calling at one meeting for "an interference betwixt man and master by way of mediation" to fend off their ultimate ruin (H.O. 52/12, ff. 242-4, Samuel Collins to Derby, Jan. 11, 1831; *MT*, Jan. 1, 1831).

The role of the petite bourgeoisie in local class struggle highlights the fundamental nature of the district's capitalist-worker conflict. The shopocracy was rarely the initiator or chief protagonist in the area's class conflicts. Signal actions were the venue of the powerful or the numerous, and frequently the prerogative of the mill owners. In the realm of politics in particular, the large capitalists sought to ensure that their diminutive counterparts were little more than bit players, as we shall see in the next chapter.

More generally, we have observed that class in the district was well defined by shared experiences and common cultures. Popular recreation, family ties, religion, and ideology intertwined with economic position to produce distinctive collective experiences among the mill owners, working people, and shopkeepers. The accretion of these was increasingly divergent class cultures, which were given shape through discourse. As we have seen in the example of Charles Hindley, the dominant formation of the mill owners was one of political economy and Dissent. But as much as Hindley and other mill owners believed their words to encapsulate the will of the people, as much as this discourse provided their collective identity, it did not speak to the shared experiences of their workers. In the bifurcated world of the district, the price of insularity was increasing hostility.

CHAPTER NINE

Local Political Culture: The Stranglehold of Wealth

As we have seen, historians within the linguistic turn argue that the political often ran against the grain of class in processes of identity formation and consciousness. Indeed, they argue that popular politics more often than not precluded class consciousness. In examining the case of the Spitalfields weavers, however, we noted that local politics often reinforced both class alliances and divisions in the complex matrices of daily life and parish governance. Politics and economics were inseparably intertwined, as ties of mutual dependence between the petite bourgeoisie and the weavers fostered a sense of community status and aided the development of a consciousness of class among the latter. A process of nurturing class consciousness occurred as well in the Ashton-Stalybridge district, although in this case local politics mainly served to strengthen the antagonisms between mill owners and factory workers. Additionally, the ferment of the reform crisis coupled with these deepening local antagonisms and infused radical popular politics into the process of class formation (Sykes 1988, p. 193). Indeed, as James Epstein observes, "the People" in radical discourse by the 1830s was synonymous with the "working classes" within the district (1994, p. 288). To understand how such populist political discourse took on this class dimension, we need to investigate how local politics was imbricated with other aspects of class formation. Local political struggles meshed with divergent class discourses to solidify divisions. Thus, in a different way from the Spitalfields situation community and class were mutually reinforcing.

District politics was as bifurcated as every other aspect of life. There were the rulers and the ruled—the unflappable bourgeois liberals and the implacable working-class radicals—with little middle ground. In this chapter, I survey the capitalists' successful efforts to gain control of town governance and their more modest attempts at hegemony. The latter efforts, with the possible exception of Sunday schools, were frequently lackluster and often fruitless, and stood in contrast to the vibrant radical culture among the district's working class. Even more than among the silk weavers, radical politics within the Ashton-Stalybridge district reinforced class identity, creating a more encompassing understanding of oppression and exploitation as the years passed.

Seizing the Reins of Authority

The cotton lords ruled inside the mill gates, but they also desired control in the towns beyond them. To gain this, they often put religious differences aside and negotiated mutually propitious power sharing with the Earl of Stamford and Warrington. Additionally, they fended off the endeavors of disgruntled factions of the petite bourgeoisie and the radical working class to frustrate their efforts. By the end of the 1820s, they had realized their desires.

In 1820, substantial authority lay in the hands of the earl, the parish being part of his great and highly valued preserve. Up to the latter 1820s, it was governed through two traditional institutions, the court leet, controlled by the earl, and the parish vestry (Bowman 1960, pp. 628, 633; Cotton 1977, p. 184; Midwinter 1968, pp. 9–10).[1] The court leet administered many traditional parish functions, and its officers sought to maintain order in both town and countryside. The division of responsibility between the court and the parish vestry was clearly demarcated and mutually recognized. Mill owners reached an utilitarian accord on the court's role with His Lordship, affirming the legitimacy of the institution for their own ends (Cotton 1977, p. 185; Coulthart 1844, p. 12 n., p. 13 n.; Howe 1984, pp. 134–135). In return for their bow to the earl's authority, they received a share of the administrative apparatus. John Standring, a favorite of the mill owners, was consistently reappointed as deputy constable throughout the late 1820s. In addition, cotton lords were often appointed to the constabulary. This harmony allowed mill owners to marshal their forces for the more contentious terrain of the parish vestry in their quest for local political ascendancy.

---

[1] The administration of Stalybridge, most of which lay in the Hartshead division of the parish, was the responsibility of the parish officers (Bowman 1960, p. 633).

Within the parish, the arena of acrimony was the vestry meeting. Participation mandated property qualifications, and those who did not contribute to the poor rates or whose property was not rated were excluded. Parish residents rated at under 50 pounds were given one vote, and an additional vote (up to a maximum of six) was added for every additional 25 pounds of rated property (Cotton 1977, p. 186). The system naturally favored large landowners and mill owners.

Property qualifications excluded a substantial portion of the working class, although many of the petite bourgeoisie met the criteria. The mill owners thus found that both the traditional landed upper crust and the shopocracy exhibited a feisty determination to fend off usurpation of their parish voices. Unlike their counterparts in Spitalfields, small tradesmen and artisans do not seem to have had much of a voice, and the primary lines of battle were more clearly drawn between large capital and other classes.

The struggle for vestry control was an exercise in civic sparring as the bourgeoisie tussled for power. Conflicts frequently boiled over on the legitimacy of parish expenditures, parish rates, and vestry appointments. Tenacious dissidents, largely composed of radical shopkeepers, remained undaunted by the mill owners' frequent victories (Cotton 1977, pp. 188–189, 192–193). Verbal fighting became particularly rancorous in the late 1820s and early 1830s in fights over expenditures for securing the town during strikes and the appointment and payment of officials favored by mill owners (*MM*, Sept. 28, Oct. 26, 1830; *WMC*, Sept. 25, 1830; *MT*, Oct. 2, 1830; *MG*, Oct 23, 1830; *VP*, no. 14, April 2, 1831, p. 112).

Each victory by the bourgeoisie added a measure of confidence and control, and more firmly ensconced them in power. From the mid-1820s they were especially successful at retaining favored functionaries, such as the assistant overseer Isaac Jackson. In addition, from then on they maintained a permanent presence on the board of overseers for the town division, a position that allowed them extended control over their unemployed operatives (L.C.R.O. P2565, Early Minute and Rate Book of the Ashton-under-Lyne Parish; *MT*, April 30, 1830, April 2, 1831). By the late 1820s, shopkeepers frequently fought fitful rearguard actions.

Constructing a New Order: Local Improvement Acts

The cotton lords had consolidated power, but their desire for power remained unrequited. The court leet and the parish vestry were administrative mechanisms constructed for a pastoral order long before the invention of spindles, gears, and unions. The parish had no regular petty sessions, and the town elite were uncomfortably dependent on outside magistrates. Vestry meetings themselves were often noisome and wearying exercises. Additionally, the parish had little provision for the improvement of the local infrastructure, which was sorely needed for the rise of a modern factory town (Bowman 1960, p. 440; Cotton 1977, p. 102, n. 54).

The mill owners' first action toward the construction of a modern administrative system was the steering through Parliament of the Gas and Water Act of 1825. Factories had voracious appetites for fuel and water, and their increasing numbers placed a severe strain on the town's resources. The Act solved this problem by authorizing the incorporation of the Ashton-under-Lyne Gas and Water Works Company. The Gas Company was an amicable investing arrangement among the mill owners and all other moneyed interests, including many professionals and the earl (6 Geo. IV, c. 76, pp. 1727, 1629–1330, 1632). Such shared investment strengthened alliances between landowners and mill owners.

In 1827, however, a window to power opened for mill owners rankled by vestry feuding. The earl, in need of additional authority to promote town growth, fixed on an improvement bill, which called for the establishment of a Police Commission. It also empowered the authorities to expand the market and to widen the roads for additional development, two items that swelled the earl's purse (Cotton 1977, pp. 196–197). Mill owners initially opposed the bill and its added expenditures, but it passed after the measures for additional development were withdrawn under their heavy lobbying (*MG*, March 3, June 23, 1827). With those annoyances expunged, the Improvement Act proved to be a laudable vehicle for the expansion of bourgeois control.

A yearly 35-pound rate became the benchmark for inclusion as one of the town commissioners (those eligible to participate in the local polity). This elite standard excluded as many as half of the town's freeholders, probably to the glee of the mill owners. Many of the vexatious petite bourgeoisie were excised from town governance by provisions proscribing from participation all sellers of alcohol and any merchant who benefited from trade with the Commissioners (7 & 8 Geo. IV, p. 1694). The differential system of rate assessment equally delighted Ashton's industrialists. Owners or tenants of "any Workshop, Warehouse, Manufactory, Foundry, or Mill" were to be rated at only half of their full annual rent or value (ibid., p. 1740). The commissioners were also empowered to "make such Rate or Assessment conformable to the true Intent and meaning of the Act" (ibid., p. 1744). A strong grip on fiscal power had been bought for a modest price.

Many of the duties of the commissioners centered on the sanitary and infrastructural maintenance of the town (Bowman 1960, p. 634; Cotton 1977, p. 198). The Act's heart invested the mill owners with previously elusive authority. All commissioners were sanctioned to be justices of the peace (7 & 8 Geo. IV c. 74, p. 1694). Ashton, which had suffered from a dearth of justices, found itself with a surfeit. From the middle of 1828, petty sessions were held twice weekly, with various mill owners sitting at the bench beside the local landowners such as Francis Astley (*MT*, Aug 8, 1829; Cotton 1977, p. 203). Unlike Spitalfields, employers here could control power at both the bench and in the vestry.

The enforcement provisions of the Act provided the mill owners with unparalleled power to secure their interests. Clauses for prevention of public nuisances empowered the commissioners to prosecute any individual "standing, loitering, or remaining on any such Footway or Causeway (without some reasonable or good and sufficient cause), or in any other Manner obstruct or incommode, hinder or prevent, the free Passage of any such Footway or Causeway, or prejudice, insult, jostle, or annoy any Person or Persons travelling, passing, or going thereon" (7 & 8 Geo. IV, c. 74, p. 1731). This furnished mill owners with the power to arrest and fine pickets who often formed the mainstay of factory workers' strikes. Similar provisions provided for the prohibition of demonstrations and parades, further enhancing local law as a tool of bourgeois control.[2] Lieutenant Colonel Shaw wrote with envy to his commander of this inimitable mastery: "Their police acts are such that there are no places in the Kingdom where the struggle against the Union would be more favourable to the Masters as at Ashton under Line and Staley Bridge" (H.O. 40/26, ff. 46-50, Shaw to Bouverie, Aug. 29, 1830).

In specifying procedural guidelines for the commissioners' meetings, the Act also gave the bourgeoisie mechanisms for mitigating the rancor of the vestry meetings (7 & 8 Geo. IV, pp. 1696–1697). With the bourgeoisie dominating the Police Commission's meeting, it was less a civic forum and more a controlled platform. This was not lost on the cotton lords, who at times packed the meetings with their factory hands to increase vocal support for their cause (*SA*, March 21, 1828). Meetings were not entirely cleansed of confrontation, and a faction of petty-bourgeois and landed interests kept up their vociferous challenges over the use of town funds for the billeting of troops during labor disputes (*WMC*, Jan. 8, 1831; *SA*, March 21, May 23, 1828). Most stands though were red-faced exercises in futility.

Local Administration in Neighboring Communities

The achievements of Ashton's mill owners were closely monitored by their neighboring peers, especially in Stalybridge. There, cotton lords encountered the same meddlesome resistance to the measures of their Improvement Bill (*MG*, Oct. 27, 1827). Despite such interference, the measure quickly sailed through Parliament, and by May Stalybridge too was among the ranks of the improved. The qualifications for the electorate

---

[2] A subsequent act gave the J.P.s authority to arrest any riotous people in addition to their previous authority (9 Geo. IV c. 92).

were set at an astronomical 50 pounds of ratable property, legitimating a highly select coterie to yearly elect the town's twenty-one Commissioners (9 Geo. 4, c. 27, pp. 406–407). The Act empowered the commissioners with all the powers of the Ashton measure, although they relied on the enforcement of the Ashton Petty Sessions.

In effect, the cotton lords had created a modern manor, presided over by committee. When the commissioners required capital for improvements, the mill owners were ready sources of loans; the interest accruing from such deals possibly representing a reward for their civic largesse. When the tenor of common street life became annoying, notices were promptly posted and the populace warned. When labor tension raised the specter of conflict, funds were found to expand the constabulary (T.L.L.H., IC/STA/1, Dec. 17, 1828, Aug. 15, Dec. 2, 1829, July 3, Dec. 10, 1830, Feb. 4, May 11, 1831). The crystallization of bourgeoisie power, as in the case of Ashton, had taken shape.

The industrial villages that surrounded Ashton and Stalybridge continued to function under the old constabulary system. Dominated by a few mill owners, who frequently saw the villages as their imperial territory, there was no pressing need for administrative reorganization. The village of Hyde, for example, lorded over by the mill magnate Thomas Ashton and a few of his compatriots, was notable for its tranquility.[3] The iron-fisted control exercised by Ashton and his compatriots in Hyde was no doubt replicated in the industrial villages scattered over the landscape.

In terms of civic control for the mill owners throughout the district, it was truly the best of times. Such was the nature of this control that working people's imaginations would have been pushed to the limits, even including local mill owners under the popular umbrella of "the people." This reign of the capitalists stands in marked contrast to the parish relations in Spitalfields, where petite bourgeois interests dominated and the large manufacturers remained largely outside the scope of its affairs.

Battles at the Bench: The Adjudication of Labor Disputes

Disputes between manufacturers and weavers in Spitalfields were often spun in litigious webs, with the bench serving as both a venue and force in defining just relations. In the industrial North, however, the familiar quarters of labor disputes were often the factory and the street. Occasionally, the terrain of these struggles shifted to the courts, where both mill owner and worker sought legitimation of their grievances.

---

[3] The radical lecturer and publisher Richard Carlile had the pleasure of experiencing the hospitality of the town's officers during his 1828 tour when he dealt with a "dirty ruffian" who enforced the law with "impudent officiousness," and was warned bluntly against entering altogether the following year (*Lion*, v. 1, no. 17, April 25, 1828, p. 519, v. 4, no. 5, July 31, 1829, p. 129).

The Ashton petty sessions were notorious for favoring the wealthy, since the Improvement Acts had provided the mill owners easy access to the magistracy (Greg 1837, p. 132, n.). We can see the gestation of this reputation in the disputes adjudicated between mill owners and workers at the petty sessions during 1828–1831.[4]

The overall numbers are small—for example only ten prosecutions for absenteeism and three for intimidation by factory owners and three cases of wrongful dismissal by workers during these years—and the conclusions drawn from them can be no more than suggestive. Exercising due caution, two precepts of the bench's decision-making processes emerge from their review. First, the justices had no inclination to delve into questions of common practices or trade customs. Their law was one of articulated obligations, unembellished by normative order or tradition.

This precept is exemplified in the case of a group of John Saxon's workers whom he prosecuted for absenteeism. The workers argued that they were going to the wakes, and that the festival's call was something to which all—even those in other factories—answered. The magistrates sternly rebuked and told them that their master determined "playtime," and they were summarily ordered to return to work. Four of the workers defied the order, and warrants were drawn in their names. All had to share in the payment of court expenses (*SA*, Oct. 13, 1828).[5]

The second related precept was that the breadth of the magistrates' powers was limited to the terms of the conditions of service. So long as workers were not abused, remunerated in real money, and the terms of their employment did not transgress the law, what transpired behind the factory gates was a private affair. In his own factory, the mill owner was indeed lord: his code of discipline and standards of performance were the immutable criteria of production.[6] This was true to the construction of the master-servant relationship in common law, in which the master had unquestioned control so long as his commands and activities were legal and reasonable (Orren 1991, pp. 95–98).

Several cases illustrate this precept. In late 1829, an operative at Wright's

---

[4] Tabular results are presented in Steinberg 1989, v. 2, pp. 421–422. The tabulations are of cases, not individual claims. Approximately 25% of the cases heard at the petty sessions involved more than one worker, with the extreme number being forty workers who prosecuted Orrell & Sons for back wages in 1831 (*MT*, Aug. 20, 1831). The majority of multiple-worker cases were prosecutions by mill owners, particularly cases concerning absenteeism and intimidation. Cases were compiled from area newspapers, which likely led to undercounting of the actual volume of cases.

[5] A little over a decade previously, a superior court in fact had recognized the rights of workers to participate in traditional holidays. In *Regina v. Stoke upon Trent*, 5 Q. B. 303, the court held that plate and dish-workers could absent themselves from work to attend such holidays as had customarily prevailed (Smith 1852, p. 43).

[6] As P. S. Atiyah observes, "in the magistrates' courts, where justices were, as like as not, themselves mill owners, or friends of mill owners, the working man [sic] generally got short shrift" (1979, p. 275).

mill charged an overlooker with assault. Pleading his case, the overlooker noted that the operative had been in an area where she was unauthorized, and had ignored his remonstrances to return to her station. The justices promptly dismissed her case (*SA*, Dec. 4, 1829). In the summer of 1830, an operative from John Saxon's mill summoned him to sessions for improper dismissal. She testified that while she had not arrived for work until breakfast, she had brought proof of illness as required by the factory rules. The justices ordered her reinstatement. Saxon, irked that he had been outwitted, vowed to change his regulations so that he would not have to endure a similar tribulation (*SA*, Aug. 27, 1830).

Perhaps the most telling case was that of James Donnelly employed by Charles Orrell & Sons. In April 1831, he summoned his employers to sessions for withholding 1 pound 15 shillings in wages. One of Orrell's sons appeared for the firm and argued that the money had been withheld to pay for back rent on a cottage. The justices ordered Orrell to pay the aggrieved worker, and informed him that the proper legal path to obtain the rent was to prosecute for it. A week later, Donnelly was back before the bench, this time complaining of improper dismissal. The firm's bookkeeper testified that Donnelly had neglected his work, and produced a copy of the factory rules stating that dismissal without notice was permitted for this transgression (*MT*, April 23, 30, 1831). Although Donnelly had pocketed a couple of weeks' wages, he had paid for it with his job and likely his roof as well.

From their seats at the bench, the justices, many of whom were mill owners or their peers, saw the movement of markets, machinery, and mechanics. The visible legal product of this tempest of activity was the agreement of service, a contract of a peculiar nature. The body of accumulated wisdom in English law did not recognize employment primarily as a normal contractual agreement between two equal parties. Instead, judicial understandings of the employment relationship were derived from the legacy of adjudication over the nature of servitude (Haines 1980, p. 263; Kahn-Freund 1977, p. 524; Kussmaul 1981, pp. 6–9, 60–61; Orren 1991, *passim*). In the early nineteenth century, factory workers bound themselves into service to the mill owner; they did not contract to sell their labor power. The legacy of the law was bequeathed from the rule of the household, in which a male master controlled domestic, largely female servants. This legacy allowed the justices to focus on the terms of service— what we would call the contract of employment—without broaching the mill owner's authority in the social relations of production. In some ways, the spinners' masculine work culture was crosscut by the gendering of the law in which servants answered to male authority.

Factory workers were thus caught at the intersection of two different sets of institutional practices and discourses, which reinforced the mill owner's power. The discourses of the law bound them into service, denying their rights within the mill to the extent that they were defined as generally subservient to the will of their master. The discourses of political economy, however, through which the cotton lords defined themselves and their industry (which I turn to in the next chapter) represented the factory worker as an independent individual who contracted with the mill owner for the sale of a specific commodity—labor. For the factory workers, the result was a legal purgatory, constructed from the entanglement of medieval notions of service with inklings of modern capitalism.

The local bench thus effectively upheld the primacy of the master's voice inside the factory, although it checked his potential to violate the accord that had brought the worker through the gates. Working people cleverly sought to work the system to their advantage, although more often than not they were worked upon by it. On the whole, however, it is hard to conceive that legal practices reinforced an inclusive populist understanding of local power. In their control, the mill owners seem to have been one step ahead of the large manufacturers in Spitalfields, who as we saw were seeking to legally eradicate customary practices and establish a new tenor of labor relations. For the latter, not sitting in the judges' seat, this process was more complex and protracted.

Molding the Masses: Attempts at Social Control and Hegemony

By the late 1820s, the mill owners exerted authority over production and polity. Control within the factory and town alike was reflexive confirmation of their righteousness, ardor, and faith. Yet this corroboration was largely visible only to the mill owners and their allies. For the operatives passing through factory gates in the gray fog of the early morning, the cotton lords' right to privilege was obscured just as the hulking mills.

The cotton lords had secured domination, but what they desired was legitimacy. In the late 1820s, they sought to reconstitute the divide of class cultures into an integument of community life. Through an extension of control and attempts at hegemonic incursion, the mill owners made (sometimes halting) attempts to move working people onto the terrain of political economy and Dissenting morality. In the spheres of education, religion, and justice, they acted to impress their vision of class harmony on the face of social relations. As in the Spitalfields case, however, they met with limited success in mending the tear in the social fabric.

Disciplining the Denizens: Suppression of Working-Class Activities

In the absence of deferential ties, the bourgeoisie could always turn to suppression. Town Improvement Acts provided commissioners with broad policing powers to align social life in accordance with their vision of propriety. In the same manner as they presided over the paving of Ashton's thoroughfares, the commissioners sought to resurface daily rounds of social life. Numerous prosecutions were executed against individuals for street selling, illegal carting, indecent language, and fighting (Cotton 1977, p. 206).

Popular recreations were another disdained target. Although the commissioners wisely sidestepped the wakes, they targeted bull baiting, Sunday games, and heavy drinking for eradication (*MT*, Oct. 31, 1828, Oct. 24, 1829; Cotton 1977, pp. 204–205). Sabbath drunkenness especially drew consternation, and the commissioners added a monetary incentive for the assistant constable's prosecution of such cases.

Mill owners also formed temperance societies in Ashton, Stalybridge, and Dukinfield, which not surprisingly attracted little support from workers (*MT*, July 23, 1831). In Dukinfield, a sanctimonious group organized with the intention of suppressing all Sunday amusements, but at their first attempted prosecution their lofty plans were swiftly scrapped when informed (much to their dismay) that they had no legal authority to prosecute (*WMC*, Aug. 7, 1830). In other industrial villages, cotton lords tried more subtle measures. In his empire at Hyde, Thomas Ashton erected only one pub for his entire community, making spirit acquisition a bit tougher for the spirited (Felkin 1844, p. 463). On the whole, however, such iron-fisted attempts to mold working peoples' behavior did not endear them to their superiors. In most parts of the district, the ale flowed, and Sunday continued as a day of recreation.

THE PENURY OF THE POOR HOUSE:
RELIEF AND THE PAUCITY OF SOCIAL CONTROL

Repression could not cement ties of acquiescence; those were cultivated by the outreach of the helping hand. In the case of Spitalfields, we noted how parish relief could be one means of constructing ties of deference and legitimating authority. Little record remains of the activities of the boards of overseers for Ashton's parish relief. What remains, however, suggests that relief was not an oft-used path for control, since relief seemingly did not keep pace with the swelling of the operatives' ranks. An impressionistic analysis of annual relief expenditures between 1823–1831 shows that they remained stable during these years of considerable regional growth, with due allowance for the depression of 1826–1828 (Baines 1825, v. 1, p. 493; Butterworth 1842, p. 105; P.P. 1830-1, XI, pp. 22, 35, 95).

Observers noted the factory workers' high degree of independence from the poor rates (*MT*, Dec. 16, 1829). With the proliferation of sick clubs and benefit societies by workers (such as spinners) to cushion crisis, many factory workers received proportionately less from the parish than others (Gosden 1961, pp. 24, 75; P.P. 1833, xx, D. 2, p. 45). Thus, in Ashton parish the cotton lords lacked the potential to structure such deferential relationships because of their underlings' collective resiliency, and they were forced to seek other paths.

Paving the Path of Righteousness: Religion, Charity, and the Working Class

"Considering the opulence of the town," observed Edward Baines, "Ashton is not famous for its charitable institutions" (1825, v. 1, p. 492). Most of the parish's approximately dozen charities were remnants of a different age, established by kind-hearted widows or philanthropic merchants to furnish a bit of sustenance for a few of the down-trodden (P.P. 1826–1827, IX, pp. 84–87; P.P. 1829, VIII, pp. 205–211).

The district bourgeoisie were notoriously long on advice, but short on substance. They were not blithely unconcerned with charity: Ashton did maintain a coterie of a dozen members in the Manchester Philanthropic Society (*MT*, Dec. 10, 1831). Among these gentlemen, however, talk may well have been an amenable surrogate for more active commitment. For many mill owners, political economy contained the enlightened dictums for benevolence, which argued that the poor were "in a great measure architects of their own fortunes" (Mcculloch 1827, p. 38). In Ashton, there was no legion of middle-class missionaries, as in Spitalfields, who sought to weave harmony through Christian charity.

Some mill owners, however, realized that to construct a bridge of consensus they needed a moral transom that would undergird their attempts. In many bourgeois minds, this support was found in the hand of God. In the early nineteenth century Ashton's curate was already bemoaning the lack of piety of the spinners and the spiritual debilitation of the working class in general (Rose 1969, pp. 10–11). To turn the tide of profligacy, Wesleyan Methodists were among the first to proselytize among working people, and in the late Teens and early 1820s other Dissenters purveyed their godly goods. The Primitive Methodists were the most successful in this quest. Overall, however, working-class ranks in each sect grew in proportion with their numbers (Cotton 1977, pp. 42–43, 45, 48; Hall 1991, pp. 77–79, 280).

Perhaps most working-class adults were lost in the verve of heathen life, but there was always potential to redeem the little ruffians. From the late 1810s through the 1820s, Ashton, Stalybridge, and surrounding communities experienced a proliferation of Sunday schools (Cotton 1977, p. 40; P.P. 1835, XLI, pp. 80, 87, 422). They dangled a prized commodity, education. During the week, more than half of all the district's children scuttled around the mill (Manchester Statistical Society 1838, app., p. xii). The Sunday respite provided one of the few occasions to dip into the world of knowledge. Additionally, few towns besides Ashton had even meager philanthropic alternatives to private instruction. A few paternalistic mill owners underwrote the cost of day school facilities, but this was still rare benevolence (P.P. 1835, XLI, pp. 80, 87, 422).

What largesse the mill owners did extend generally went to their Sunday schools, with the boards of these institutions directed by their guiding hands. In Ashton and Stalybridge, New Connexion mill owners dominated the growth of such schools (Rose 1969, pp. 12, 14–15; Hill 1902, pp. 110, 115–116). For many observers, the rationale behind this support was transparent. A Manchester mill owner remarked, "I think the instructions given at those Sunday-schools are for the very purpose of making those children as humble and as obedient to the wishes of the manufacturers as possible" (P.P. 1831–1832, XV, p. 327).

The idea of their children under the tutelage of mill owners and middle-class moralists may have rankled many working-class parents. As we shall see, however, there was a strong radical rationalism among the district's working people, and many thus probably placed a premium on literacy. They packed off their children in large numbers to the stern confines of the Sunday classroom. By the early 1830s, from half to over three-quarters of all Ashton children were exposed to this Sunday edification, and it became almost a communal rite of maturation for working-class youth (P.P. 1835, XLI, pp. 80, 87, 422).

After more than ten years of Bible readings and religious rearing, of catechisms and canons, working people do not seem to have been overwhelmed with piety. Table 6 shows the self-reported religious identification of working-class heads of families by the mid-1830s.

Over one-third of the family heads did not profess any religious identification. The surprisingly high allegiance to the Established Church was likely more perfunctory support than abiding faith. The earl and his adherents had opened their tightly-knotted purses for the parish and provided a pittance for education. The commitment, however, went no further than an acknowledgment. In 1830, the parish's two churches could welcome 3,200, but rarely managed to draw more souls than could fill a dozen pews in each. The parish was 6,000 pounds in debt and the south side of the rectory of St. Michael's, which had collapsed in 1821, still lay in a heap of disarray (Rose 1969, p. 64). At a charity sermon to raise funds to repair this decay in 1828, the rector had succeeded in drawing the magnanimous sum of 7 pounds in contributions (*MG*, Nov. 29, 1828). The working-class faithful, if there were more than a few, were extraordinarily subdued.

Perhaps some of the self-identified Dissenters were also more formally than fully faithful. Particularly in the industrial villages, where the cotton lords' voices took more authoritative tones, profession of proper piety might have been an act of caution. Certainly, many working people relied

Table 6. Religious identification of heads of families in Ashton, Stalybridge, and Dukinfield, c. 1835

Town	Sect	Number of heads of families
Ashton	Anglicans	1,517 (40)
	Dissenters	624 (16)
	Catholics	399 (10)
	None Stated	1,295 (34)
Stalybridge	Anglicans	769 (23)
	Dissenters	917 (27)
	Catholics	455 (14)
	None Stated	1,174 (35)
Dukinfield	Anglicans	415 (25)
	Dissenters	545 (32)
	Catholics	30 (3)
	None Stated	680 (40)
Totals	Anglicans	2,701 (30)
	Dissenters	2,086 (23)
	Catholics	904 (10)
	None Stated	3,149 (36)

Source: Manchester Statistical Society, 1838, app., p. xix.
Note: Numbers in parentheses are percentages.

on churches to ritually mark central occasions of family life, such as births and marriages, but we should be cautious in reading such records as indicators of pious commitment.

There is little wonder why Richard Carlile delighted in his trips to what in his mind was England's Eden of Infidelity. Middle-class observers who meddled, measured, and mused about the region went away with a similar picture. As in the case of Spitalfields, the altar aisle proved not to be the path to moral harmony between the classes.

OTHER AVENUES TO INFLUENCE: THE MECHANICS' INSTITUTION

Some mill owners sought other ways to influence the adult workers, believing that ties of common perspective could be forged. Led by Charles Hindley, they concentrated their efforts on imparting the axioms of success through the forum of the Mechanics' Institution, similar to the one launched in Spitalfields at the time.

Founded in the summer of 1825, the Ashton Mechanics' Institution was, in Hindley's words, "to be the Workshop of the Mind" (Hindley 1825, p. 3). Opened with considerable fanfare, supporters envisioned it to be the bedrock of betterment for their operatives. In his inaugural address, Hindley emphasized that the Institution was a hall of self-improvement, not a source of petite benevolence: "You are not to imagine that this Institution is in the common acception of the word a CHARITABLE one, that it is an offering on the part of the rich and the learned to the poor and the ignorant" (1825, p. 4). As with other such institutions governance was to be left in the hands of the working-class subscribers, although honorary members were sure to be available for valued guidance.

The Ashton Institution established a small library, which contained a collection of books mostly on scientific questions and other sedate subjects. Lecture series focused on topics such as mechanics, astronomy, and geography, the cerebral material of true working-class fascination in the opinion of Hindley and his friends. By late summer of 1825, the Institution counted 480 scholars among its ranks, and Hindley had high hopes. A year later, however, his expectations had been sorely bruised by reality. The subscription list contained only one hundred operatives and interest was rapidly waning. By 1827, the Institution was in serious fiscal straits (Tylecote 1957, p. 248–9).

Over the next few years, the Institution limped along, trying to sustain an interest in the mysteries of science and nostrums of self-improvement. By 1831, however, the founders closed its doors, packed up its library, and moved the collection to Dukinfield where it languished (Tylecote 1957, p. 249). The working people of Ashton generated no more enthusiasm for such certified knowledge than had their compatriots in Spitalfields. Reflecting on the failure, Hindley mused that the Institution's founders had opened the floodgates of knowledge too quickly for the ignorant operatives to consume: "In taking too high a ground at first . . . the artisans certainly did not understand what was given to them. The labouring classes want something more simple and pungent; they have not the leisure to pour over abstruse volumes: because they are too worn out and fatigued by the time the night comes" (quoted in Cotton 1977, p. 173).

The limited fortunes of the Ashton Institution stood in marked contrast to the modest success of its poorer cousin in Stalybridge. Opened soon after the Ashton Institution, the Society for Mutual Instruction (as it was initially titled) was a humble organization that maintained a small library in two attic rooms. Although in its early years the Institution's offices were dominated by mill owners (who subscribed as honorary members), the governing committee did contain many operatives and other manual workers, as well as bookkeepers and overlookers. The mill owners appear to have left the membership much to its own devices after the first few years of its operation, and it maintained a stable 150 subscribers.

Occasional lectures were held with small honorariums, but the heart of the Institution was the library where members gathered to exchange conversation and opinion. Fridays were designated as evenings for open discussion and newspaper readings. Although the membership was on occasion subjected to technical addresses on astronomy and geography, they also could delight in the spirited discourse of a working-class intellectual such as Rowland Detroisier (Tylecote 1957, pp. 241–242; *MT*, Nov. 14, 1828). That the Stalybridge Institution endured while its Ashton counterpart languished was probably attributable to the functions each served. The members of the Ashton Institution were subjected to carefully selected erudition; those in Stalybridge were permitted to struggle with knowledge amongst themselves.

The mill owners of the Ashton-Stalybridge district were never recognized as a group at the forefront of the new paternalism in factory relations. By the 1820s, they had largely managed to cultivate alienation and resentment rather than a hegemonic culture. Deference was not to be fostered either through the vestry or the bench. The bourgeoisie found their most accessible spheres of influence in religion and education. Although they seldom mustered an evangelical fervor that characterized their peers in other districts, their incursions were steady and sustained, particularly in the case of Sunday schools. Yet for their all efforts, they did not manage to make their underlings deferential. The cotton lords were masters of production and polity, but they had a great deal to learn about molding the masses in their own image. Not only did these languid institutions fail to construct the populist democratic imaginary in Joyce's terms, their failure allowed for the maturation of a radical political culture among working people that made the district a hotbed for Chartism in the succeeding decades. Perhaps mill owners were wiser than their peers in Spitalfields, however, for they expended less energy and achieved and equivalent result.

Working People and Radical Politics

Integral to the region's working-class culture was a deep and vibrant radical politics. "The population of Ashton," one commentator observed, "have the reputation of being turbulent and fanatical. . . . The most ultra-radical and theological opinions run riot amongst the population" (Reach 1849, p. 72). Although it had ties to middle-class radicalism, the working class moved beyond the indictment of "old corruption." Radical politics became intertwined with a burgeoning class critique, so much so that by the 1830s the "steamlords" had replaced bloated aristocrats as the incarnation of oppression (Kirk 1985, p. 61). The deep roots of radicalism in the district stand in contrast to the more measured enthusiasm of the silk weavers that we noted.

That the fiery Chartist orator Joseph Rayner Stephens found a warmly hospitable niche in the area should come as no surprise. The renowned radical, atheist, and ruling-class irritant Richard Carlile wrote appreciatively of the region's tradition: "From the days of Silvanus Hibbert to Tim Bobbin the Second, and his descendants to the present day, Ashton-under-Line has not wanted a philosopher. I found some well-informed men there, some of them young enough to have run the race of thinking with me, and others who have pursued a similar train of thought from the time of my birth" (*Lion*, Jan. 25, 1828, p. 104). The core of this radical tradition was born in the latter eighteenth century.[7] By the 1790s, a corresponding society and a radical group were active in Ashton and Stalybridge respectively. Soon after the turn of the century, local authorities expressed deep concern over insurrectionary fervor and a radical underground, and fretted again during the Luddite disturbances of 1811–1812 (Cotton 1977, pp. 76–77, 94–95; Middleton 1932, pp. 68–72; Thompson 1966, p. 474). The years 1816 to 1820 marked this radicalism's maturation. In 1817, reading societies began to proliferate in Ashton, and there were whispers of an insurrectionary spirit. During 1818, public meetings were revived as local magistrates worried about support for a general rising, watching nervously as radicals abetted the weavers in a general strike (Cotton 1977, p. 107, 109–111, 117–118; R. Hall 1989, p. 437). By the time of the Peterloo massacre in nearby Manchester, a mature radical vision had emerged. Working-class orators provided an encompassing critique of political corruption and class power, focusing much of their efforts on building a strong and effective radical organization. A Female Reform Society was also founded in Ashton, and women actively participated in radical agitation. Radicals turned their vision outward, contemplating the growth of a national movement (Cotton 1977, pp. 110–111, 119–121; Thompson 1966, p. 415). They paused after Peterloo, but by the spring of 1820 meetings were again openly held.

As we have seen in the previous chapter, Ashton was home to a lively republican contingent that cemented a petite-bourgeois and working-class alliance in local politics. A procession marked the anniversary of Peterloo from 1820 to its suppression in 1823; in 1821, it was reportedly larger than the procession for the coronation of George IV. Republican members of the Philosophical Enquiring Christians opened a Sunday School two years later, and the Republicans continued to provide a base of support for radicalism through the mid-1820s. Dinner celebrations for Paine's and Hunt's birthdays became institutionalized events. By the latter part of the 1820s, radicalism had thus sent deep roots into the Ashton-Stalybridge area (Cotton 1977, pp. 127, 138, 141, 143; Epstein 1991, pp. 274, 276, 280–283, 1994, chap. 5; *MT*, June 20, 1829; *Republican*, March 8, 1832, pp. 302–307).

The spinners were among the most astute participants in all this radical activity (Sykes 1982b, p. 182). John Bowring noted their penchant for radical language and literature. "Politicians they are all becoming. In Ashton only, 200 copies of Carpenter's Political Letter are widely sold, and a great mass of political writing is circulated and read to large num-

---

[7] This discussion on the 1790–1820 period is heavily indebted to Cotton's (1977) detailed study of popular movements in Ashton c. 1790–1832.

bers" (L.C.R.O., DDX/880/2, Bowring to Lamb, 12.30.30). Spinners also played integral roles in local political mobilization for example aiding in a counter-mobilization against Anglican opposition to the Catholic Emancipation Bill (*MT*, March 7, 1829). They were also found among the membership of local radical organizations such as the Zetetic societies which were supporters of Carlile's infidel republicanism. Among the more enthusiastic participants in the society were the future union leader, John Stewart; the secretary of the local spinners' union, John Joseph Betts; and spinners' leader Thomas Brooke (*Lion*, v. 2, no. 21, Nov. 21, p. 652; *Gauntlet*, no. 14, May 12, 1833, p. 223; Epstein 1994, p. 158; Hall 1991, p. 113, n. 53). Betts was part of the regional vanguard of militant radicals.[8] A gifted raconteur and orator, a wily tactician, and a possessor of fierce intellectual acumen, he was found at the forefront of many radical as well as union causes. His life story is a classic tale, befitting of Dickens, of a lad dragged by harsh institutions through forced apprenticeship and untold hardship (*Lion*, Feb. 29, 1828, p. 276).

By the late 1820s, it appears that Betts had forsaken the mill. With Joshua Hobson, another radical stalwart of Ashton, he was a purveyor of radical publications. He appears to have dabbled in law for some of his income, and he also used his oratorical gifts as an auctioneer (*MT* Oct. 12, 1830, July 7, 1831). Betts, along with the ex-operative George Downes and other spinners, were vocal enthusiasts of many causes. They championed a free working-class press, celebrated the revolution in France, and were even among the leaders of a local milk boycott taken against high prices (*MM*, Nov. 30, 1830; *MG*, Nov. 27, 1830; *MT*, June 27, July 18, 1828, Sept. 18, 1830). During this period, however, he was above all the leader of the local spinners union, trusted by his working-class brethren and feared by the mill owners and authorities.[9]

Leadership among union and radical political organizations frequently overlapped, creating a potent network of committed agitators. The political air in Ashton, Stalybridge, and the manufacturing villages crackled with radical fervor from all quarters of the working class (Hall 1991, *passim*; Kirk 1985, p. 58; Rose 1969, p. 6). Carlile always drew enthusiastic crowds during his tours in the late 1820s. Writing in the *Lion* in the summer of 1829, after addressing over three hundred in Ashton, he noted with exuberance, "Nothing can be better than the hopes of Infidelity here at Ashton" (*Lion*, July 24, 1829, pp. 104, 105–107, Jan. 12, 1828, no. 17, p. 76, Apr. 25, 1828, p. 517, July 31, 1829, pp. 129, 131, 137).

The July 1830 revolution in France stoked the district's fires of radicalism, and a celebration partly coordinated by Betts was held that Sep-

---

[8] For a comprehensive discussion of the area's working-class radicalism, see R. Hall (1991, chap. 4).
[9] Bowring thought that he was an intelligent and skillful secretary who had the power to keep some of the more unruly members of the union in line (L.C.R.O. DDX/880/2, Bowring to Lamb, Dec. 30, 1830).

tember (Shaw to Bouverie, 8.29.30, HO 40/26ff. 46–50; *MT*, Sept. 18, 1830). By November, tricolor handkerchiefs were being brandished at union meetings and large political demonstrations. The radicals drew five thousand for a meeting to petition Parliament for a free press. The *Manchester Guardian* was reporting rumors of possible unrest in Ashton, and in an ominous tone noted that "there is a strong political feeling amongst the people" (*MG*, Nov. 13, 27 1830; *MM*, Nov. 9, 30, 1830; *MT*, Nov. 27, 1830).

The great strike of December 1830 and January 1831 redirected the energies of the working class to the exigencies of labor antagonism, but the tumultuous parliamentary debate over the Reform Bill, however, rejuvenated an activist political spirit. With workers and the petite bourgeoisie allied, the principals attacked their common foes of Old Corruption, as well as affirming the right of a free press (*MT*, Jan. 29, 1831). Populist radical discourse created opportunities for such alliances, but not to the exclusion of class consciousness. Lectures, reading societies, and mass meetings continued to keep the pot hot throughout the year (Cotton 1977, p. 152; *MT*, Aug. 20, Nov. 26, 1831).

That local radicalism could take a decidedly working-class turn is demonstrated by the elections of 1832. As Thompson asserted in *The Making of the English Working Class*, the passage of the Reform Bill marked a watershed in working-class consciousness. In the cottages nestled near the Tame, it was clear who had gained the spoils of recent agitations. In late September, a meeting of non-electors chaired by Joshua Hobson voiced their discontent that property qualifications denied them the vote. "It is the opinion of this meeting", they declared in their first motion, "that the permanent happiness of the working classes, and the nation at large can never be accomplished until we enjoy with our fellow-countrymen, those political rights of which we are deprived, and which we certainly ought to possess" (*PMG*, Nov. 3, 1832, p. 588). Those at the meetings found the basis for their citizenship claims in their status as wealth producers, whose labor was willingly used, but whose voices were callously ignored. Their message to the cotton lords was tempered, but poignant.

> We have seen that property men, legislate not for us but for themselves, and although what is possessed by them is the product of our labour and toil (for, says Adam Smith, "the labour of the country is the wealth of the country") . . . yet, regardless of our rights and our interests, they have enacted laws that has [sic] not only almost destroyed every vestige of our liberties, but brought us to a state of poverty, degradation, and misery, the contemplations of which makes almost every man shudder for the future.
>
> To those who still hold the fallacious opinions that the labourers are to be treated as mere animated machines, we now, in the true spirit of peace, and actuated by feelings of universal benevolence, solemnly call upon them to reflect ere it is too late. (ibid., p. 589)

Led by Hobson, working-class radicals campaigned against the champion of the mill owners, Charles Hindley, electing Colonel George Williams to Ashton's first seat in the Commons. To the surprise of many, they managed to carry the day. It was a truly stunning display of power, given that Ashton contained only 422 qualifying electors and a self-assured and united bourgeoisie thirsting for their first M.P. (Cotton 1977, pp. 154–155; Bowman 1960, p. 500; R. Hall 1991, pp. 112–118).

Hindley and other Whig liberals sought patches of common ground on which they could germinate an alliance with the radicals during these years. Certainly, their shared opposition to the Anglican church represented such terrain and was the basis for a fragile 1834 alliance that secured Hindley the seat denied him two years earlier. This was a union of limited affinity, however, which collapsed in rancor over the Ten Hours Act and the New Poor law (R. Hall 1991, pp. 120–123).

It is small wonder that in later years Ashton's working class was one of the most vituperative opponents of Poor Law reform, and one of the three towns in northern England that sustained the highest level of activism during the Chartist period. Throughout the first several decades of the nineteenth century, working people developed a broad radical front, disregarding the boundaries of trade and status, and integrating it into their proletarian culture. Restive in character and oppositional in spirit, the cause was rarely dormant and certainly never neglected. The spinners were among the vanguard of organizers and organic intellectuals who constituted the movement's core, in contrast to the Spitalfields weavers who seemed to have warmed to radicalism at a later date.

Most important, the radical political populism of the district reinforced rather than mitigated the class consciousness of working people. The spinners and other factory workers found in the words of Carlile, Carpenter, and many other radicals a means of expressing their antipathy and an oppositional identity to the mill owners' liberal order. This was an active collective process, in which working people negotiated discourses in constructing worldviews and identities that spoke to their experiences. Although they warmed to Carlile's atheism and republicanism, for example, they rejected his adoption of political economy and his dismissal of unions.

In the reconstitution of town politics, in arguments before the bench, and in campaigns for parliamentary reform, working people witnessed how a language of property sanctified the cotton lords' authority. In all of these cases, the happenings of class became more deeply ingrained in the operations of the district. In this, the district provides similarities and differences to the developments in Spitalfields. Although in neither case did capitalists construct effective hegemonic relations with their workers, in Spitalfields the weavers did nurture ties of mutuality with the local vestry authorities. They in turn supported the weavers' efforts for protection. In Ashton-Stalybridge, the system was structured too antithetically for that possibility and the petite bourgeoisie and working people forged a less effective alliance against the mill owners' dominance. Yet, as in the case of Spitalfields, the history of the district demonstrates that community and class were hardly antithetical.[10] As these conflicts between the regnant capitalists and their workers deepened, the latter's fighting words reflected and refracted this accumulation of experience.

[10] The extent to which the solidarity of factory workers rested upon the networks of community life also calls into question Calhoun's characterization of their social relations. For an extended argument on this see Steinberg (1993).

CHAPTER TEN

The Vitriol of Conflict

> Fact, fact, fact, everywhere in the material aspect of the town; fact, fact, fact, everywhere in the immaterial . . . the relations between master and man were all fact, and everything between the lying-in hospital and the cemetery, and what you couldn't state in figures, or show to be purchasable in the cheapest market and saleable in the dearest, was not, and never should be, world without end, Amen.
>
> Charles Dickens, *Hard Times*

One of the fiercest actions striking factory workers took to deter persistent blacklegs was vitriol throwing. A splash of acid in the eyes was a sure corrective to crossing the picket line and a powerful deterrent for others with similar inclinations. As a tactic it was rare, but on the discursive level vitriol slinging was a commonplace of conflict. By the spring of 1830, in the Ashton-Stalybridge district fighting words were defiantly in the air.

We saw in the case of the Spitalfields weavers that discourses of contention were both determined by and determinative of processes of class formation and collective action. Systems of economic, political, and social relations in which the weavers were ensconced provided the backdrop for experiences that begged for a compelling interpretation. The cultural processes of creating such meanings of trade relations, citizenship, domestic order, and community life often pitted the weavers against manufacturers, politicians, and political economists, as they contested within a dominant discursive formation to create an intelligible and moral vision of their world. Circumstances begged interpretation, but the weavers could not create this intelligibility just as they pleased. Struggling both within and against dominant discourses, chief among them political economy, the silk weavers' representations of the world were constrained and shaped by these discourses. Their own discourses of contention emerged through dynamic processes of class, gender, and state formation. Their fighting words in turn provided the ideological rationale for their repertoires of contention. These discursive battles over economic exploitation and political oppression were part of the happenings of class.

The cotton spinners of the Ashton-Stalybridge district fought such battles too, but, true to Thompson's dictum, not quite in the same way. Throughout the formative years of industrial growth, they witnessed mill owners construct reinforcing systems of control in the mill and the community. This sturdy lamination of power accommodated landed interests, although it was largely unencumbered by past trade and community practices. The cotton lords made sense of this process through the intertwined discourses of political economy, liberal democratic politics, and institutional Dissenting faith. They fashioned a collective identity of progressive and enlightened entrepreneurs, community leaders, and national and global citizens.

In their conflicts with the mill owners, the spinners had to call into question this identity and its ideological underpinnings. As we shall see in this chapter and the next, the spinners sought to subvert and radicalize the discourses of political economy and liberal democracy from which it was spun. Their fighting words emphasized a radical popular economics and a social egalitarianism based on a labor theory of value. Coupled with radical critiques of power, they posed a strident challenge to local capitalist hegemony.

In this chapter, I discuss how spinners contested constructs of labor, value, and hierarchy within the dominant discursive formation before they seeped into daily routines, saturating them below the level of ready cognition. The spinners' fighting words fostered in this class confrontation became the common sense by which they and other factory workers adjudicated the lessons of mill and community strife.

I examine four dialogic themes that bound the development of the spinners' discourses of contention—the foundations of the social contract and basic justice, the nature of capitalism and capitalists, relations between mill owners and workers within and beyond the factory, and the utility of combinations. Parallel themes formed the nexus of the controversy regarding the Spitalfields Acts, as we have witnessed. The utterances below are not exclusively those of spinners or the mill owners. Rather they are from contemporary periodicals and tracts popular among each group, and in some instances written or edited by their members. Most of the material representative of the workers' side of the field I have derived from union periodicals—such as the *United Trades' Co-Operative Journal*, *Voice of the People*, *Poor Man's Advocate*, and *Union Pilot and Intelligencer*—which were either organs of spinners' unions or had spinners as staff members. Additionally, I also draw upon writers such as Carlile and Carpenter who were read widely in the district. All of these writers were aware of the industrial conflicts in Lancashire in the 1820s, and their words are informed by public reflections on these struggles.

These excerpts provide a sense of the discursive field and its multivocality. They are not meant to offer ideological schemata; indeed, as I have maintained, fighting words are not highly stable and elaborated ideological structures. Rather, discursive meaning is partly situational, born of the struggles that motivate it. In this case, in the friction of class formation the "political" and the "economic" became metaphorically intermeshed as working people attempted to transform and break free from grids of dominant meanings. Having roughly mapped this terrain, we turn in the next chapter to the fighting words as they were put in motion in the great strike of 1830–1831.

The Foundation of the Social Order and Its Compact

For the cotton spinners (as for the silk weavers), fundamental questions of rights and privileges morally framed conflicts. How were they to comprehend the palpable signs of inequality that were writ large in the valley? Sympathizers of the mill owners found practical wisdom in these social inequalities. Societal progress, they argued, depended on the promise of individual wealth to stimulate initiative. As Mrs. B. described to her young pupil Caroline in Jane Marcet's *Conversations on Political Economy*, "if all escaped the distresses of poverty, none would enjoy the acquisition of riches, an enjoyment which, when derived from the exercise of our talents and our industry, is a just and virtuous feeling . . . the industry of man requires the stimulus of exclusive possession and enjoyment; and will always be proportioned to the personal advantage which he derives from it" (1828, p. 50).

Social divisions of wealth and power thus greased the great wheels of societal improvement. A capitalist class was a natural outgrowth of a superior division of labor stimulated by such acquisition and was essential both to enhanced productive power and to greater civility.

> From such a state of universal toil and dreariness, one naturally turns to the more cheerful appearance which society presents, and one of whose chief advantages is derived from the circumstance that certain classes are exempt from at least the necessity of bodily labour. Now this advantage could not be possessed without a certain degree of inequality in men's fortunes; in other words, the existence of a proprietary class . . . if this capital or property did not exist, there would be no fund in reserve to maintain a class of persons occupied in what have been very inaccurately termed unproductive em-

The Vitriol of Conflict

ployments: all would be engaged in procuring food or raiment, and none could exclusively devote themselves to the pursuits of literature, science, and legislation. (Wade 1833, p. 484)

All strata intertwined in a great organic system structured on mutuality, not hostility. The lives of capitalists and workers were products of this mutual beneficence. Mrs. B. succinctly explained to her pupil the essence of the relationship: "The rich and the poor are necessary to each other; without the rich the poor would starve; without the poor the rich would be compelled to labor for their own subsistence" (1828, p. 71).

Cotton lords likely received these precepts with great sympathy. The Manchester mill magnate John Kennedy agreeably incorporated them into his own class analysis, an equilibrium model of higher, middle, and lower classes in which class divisions were fixtures: "In a prosperous country, I believe we shall find that these three classes intimately sympathize with each other; so that supposing the lower order to advance a certain number of degrees in the enjoyments and comforts of life, middle and higher classes will make a similar ascent, each preserving its original distance from the others, and *vice versa*" (1819, p. 431).

Working people were thus a piece of a larger whole, and this system of classes created a general good. Society as a whole best preserved this march of improvement if it interceded only when the short-sighted and the uninformed threatened the teleology of progress. "It is not for us to point out what may be expected from the collective exertions of *society*, to mitigate or to remove the partial and temporary evil which follows in the train even of improvement," wrote one observer. "Of one thing we are certain. Society can never interfere to stop the improvement; and if any portion of society, who feel the individual suffering, but cannot see the general good, should interfere, with an unavailing violence, to attempt to check that which must go forward, then the laws of the society must step in to protect us all, themselves amongst the number" (Knight 1831, p. 206).

To the workers, Mrs. B.'s bargain that negated on the one hand starvation, and on the other the compulsion to labor, was hardly an idyllic exercise in equity. The working-class press often depicted a world run ragged by the forced servitude of inequality. Stretching the bourgeois vocabulary used to describe the backwardness and excesses of the *ancien régime*, it frequently discussed these disparities in terms of an aristocracy of wealth: "Unhappily, though society has overgrown the state of feudal slavery peculiar to the infancy of its institutions, it has not overgrown the feeling of moral and political degradation, which was attached to the feudal slave, and which continues to be attached to the working classes. . . . An aristocracy of wealth has since arisen, and though the feudal chain and feudal collar no longer exist, taking advantage of that weakness in the labouring population which is a consequence of its great numerical extension, it has established a slavery more hideous in its effects, and has ground its victims to the extreme verge of poverty" (*VP*, Jan. 8, 1831, p. 12).

Operatives responded to the unctuous talk of a harmonious order with righteous contempt. Far from a system of mutual improvement, many saw the burgeoning industrial order crystallizing into a tightly circumscribed regime of inequity. Union leaders often drew explicit parallels between their own conditions and the slave systems of the Caribbean and the caste systems of the Indian subcontinent, which were the focus of indictment by bourgeois reformers: "Whilst increasing poverty begets increasing discontent, they hear the castes in full cry,—'*the lower orders must be kept down.*'— The result is abhorrence and contempt. Civilized England rails with pharisaical severity against the odious division into castes, which characterizes Indian society; yet how many are the circumstances which continually remind the poor man, in this country, that he is one of a caste which is permitted to exist only because it cannot be dispensed with" (*VP*, Feb. 12, 1831, p. 52).

The factory workers' calculus of social justice contained antithetical formulas for societal betterment. Drawing upon the discourse of a radical such as William Carpenter, they could argue that the natural rights constructed within liberal democratic discourse were inverted by the possessive individualism of political economy. "There is a fundamental error, which has unhappily found its way into the frame of every society," explained Carpenter. "This error is, that *the interest of each individual has been placed, in almost every circumstance and situation, in direct opposition to the interests of other individuals, and to the interests of society*" (*CMPM*, p. 316).

The measure of improvement, and of the worth of the social contract, was the level of debasement endured by its lowest classes. The organic nature of the social system was interpreted as requiring intervention to moderate inequality. John Doherty declared, "Another principle from which we shall reason is, that human life and personal liberty, and even individual happiness, is of far more importance than the accumulation of wealth in the hands of a few.... The fundamental or main one we take to be this,—that no part of society, shall be permitted to benefit itself at the expense of, or to the injury of any other part of the community" (*PMA*, 1832, Intro., p. v). Positive rights were marshaled to oppose the negative ones purveyed by political economy. Partly echoing the silk weavers, the spinners argued that at base the social contract was a covenant in which "Government and Law is, or ought to be founded upon the PRINCIPLES of *defending the weak and honest, against the powerful and unjust*; and every well regulated community is a Combination for that purpose." (P.C., set 16, v. 2, "Cotton," f. 51). The operatives did not seek a leveling of the system, but they did maintain that their contributions justified moral limits on material inequality: "It is a simple principle of natural justice, that when one part of the community are wallowing in wealth, which they can scarcely consume or find use for, every other should be at least well fed, well clothed, and comfortably lodged. No class can better deserve these things than those that produce *all* that is enjoyed by the whole" (P.C., set 16, v. 2, "Cotton," f. 72). Within this conception of natural and civil society working-class contention could be justified if an equitable balance was fundamentally violated. "Impoverish us," warned Doherty, "and you make us reckless of all consequences" (P.C., set 16, v. 2, "Cotton," f. 66).

The Spirit of Capitalism

As I have detailed, the cotton lords adopted a popularized version of political economy, compact in its simplicity, and eminently suited to their needs. As they gazed about the district, they reduced much of its social life to facts. At a rudimentary level, unfettered capitalism was depicted as a societal physic, a provider of goods and a preventative of the social ills.

> All elegant enjoyments are widely diffused, made cheap by the universal taste which exists for them, and improved at the same time in their quality by the liberal encouragement which they hence receive. . . . Such are the fruits of national wealth—of which, be it remembered, the only producing seed recognized by the political economists is labour, and its most congenial air that of liberty. Industry left free—this is indeed the whole lesson which political economy teaches . . .—and commercial freedom is the sovereign healer of national jealousies, the extinguisher of wars, and the grand diffuser of civilization. (*Penny Magazine*, v. 1, no. 14, 1832, p. 119)

Driving the bounty juggernaut was capital. True, political economists admitted, labor was the source of all value, but it lay idle until animated by capital. The logic, according to Charles Knight, was abundantly clear: "The hope of profit sets the capital to work, and capital sets the labor to work. If there is no capital there would be no labor. Capital gives the laborer power, which he has not in himself, of working for profit" (1831, p. 182). Thomas Hopkins put this logic in more concrete terms for factory operatives: "Let the journeymen weavers and spinners in any district consider what would be their situation if capital which is now employed in setting them to work, were to be entirely withdrawn, and then they will have some conception of the important service that profit renders them in preventing such withdrawal" (1831, p. 8). The vital lesson was that capital and labor were inseparable partners in progress, as J. R. McCulloch and many other political economists noted.

Many workers listened to these depictions of harmonious interests and thought the world had been turned upside down. To counter the nostrums of political economy, they adopted a labor theory of value, not unlike that articulated by the Spitalfields weavers, that was widely diffused by popular radical and labor publications. This radical political economy, what Carpenter termed "social economy," reconfigured social relations to place working people at the center of the system. Ashton spinners, reading their copies of *Carpenter's Monthly Political Magazine* just prior to their great turn-out could, for example, have been bolstered by the following:

> There is no species of wealth, or in other words, no article of real and substantial value, that is not, more or less, the product of labour....
>
> The labouring classes may be divided into two; namely, the producers and the distributors: the former are the agents of creation, the latter the agents of exchange and distribution. The distributors do not in any degree augment or multiply the wealth of the community; but they are, nevertheless, necessary, for the purpose of facilitating the interchange of commodities among those by whom they are produced....
>
> It is just and natural, therefore, while gradations, or subordinate or inferior states exist in society, the distributors should be dependent on the producers; and not, as now, the producers dependent on the distributors. Those who produce might subsist without those who merely distribute what they produce; but those who distribute could not subsist without those who produce....
>
> The present mode of making the distributors the *employers* and the producers the *employed*, is an inversion of the natural order of things, and is equally injurious to the consumers and the producers. Its consequence is, that the *labour* of the producers is made an article of commerce, and such as, liable to all consequences &c., undergo the imposition of several unnecessary *profits*, to the great injury of the consumers....
>
> Those persons who distribute articles of commerce by *the mere agency of others*, do not themselves, in any degree, benefit or enrich society, and are therefore impediments in the way of its prosperity. Mere *capitalists*, or persons who accumulate money by purchasing the labour of others, while they perform no labour themselves, do not add anything to the wealth of the society; but, on the contrary, generally consume much. (*CMPM*, pp. 21–22)

The labor theory of value provided working people with the means of fusing their interests with the national interest. As Doherty forthrightly proclaimed, "Labour must give value to every thing, and they who would reduce the price of labour were enemies of the country" (*SA*, Jan 30, 1829).

The capitalist was often presented as little more than a leech. One working-class writer described capital's iniquitous mechanics in the following terms:

> Capital—is therefore the means whereby an individual can appropriate to himself the value of other men's labour, by merely providing them with the necessaries of life, during the time that these were working for the individual in question.
>
> Capital—therefore increases the wealth of the wealthy, and leaves the poor *wealth producers* as poor as before. . . .
>
> Capital—has a tendency to collect itself into large heaps; and it says to the useful working population, "you shall work for my advantage only."
>
> Capital creates a monopoly in some cases, and in others it feeds an excessive and ruinous competition. It gives an undue advantage to its possessor and destroys every thing in the shape of a fair remuneration for industry. (*Lancashire and Yorkshire Co-operator*, Nov. 12, 1831, pp. 4–5)

The labor theory of value provided a vehicle by which working people could transform discourses of rights and justice. As Carpenter explained, because property was derived from industry, it was the latter and not the former upon which a system of fundamental rights must be predicated: "Industry is the original basis of property, or rather the right of property. Mere power gives no such right. . . . The *right*, therefore, of all property resolves itself, as we have said, into industry. But industry is the birth-right of all men, and in this view of the case it may be justly viewed as property. . . . Although the *existence* of the right of property should be conceded to be necessary, in an absolute sense, the arbitrary application of the produce of property is so far from being an *absolute right*, that it may be in certain cases a crime of a high character against natural and moral justice, and should be restrained by legal enactment to keep up the equipoise between the right of property and the right of industry" (*CMPM*, p. 231). The spinners through various conflicts had sought to shift the construction of their disputes from the internal trade affairs by manufacturers to public questions of the rights of working people. As John Doherty argued, "the act of stripping men of large portions of their property by violence," could not be considered "*a mere matter of private business*" (*PMA*, 1832, Intro., p. iii).

Through the discourse of a popular radical economy, working-class writers countered that political economy promoted human degradation. By a discursive twist similar to that exercised by the silk weavers, the factory workers of Lancashire inverted the ordering of importance between capital and labor, and made the state of the latter a collective and public concern. Political economy, they argued, erroneously conflated labor and the commodities that it created. The result was a "system which confounds the blood and bones, soul and sinews, of human beings with the 'spindles and pullies,' the wood and iron of the proud and prodigal cotton lord" (*PMA*, April 7, 1832, p. 60). To those subscribing to an alternative radical economics the "blood-stained code of private property" had penetrated insidiously the body politic, infecting the whole tenor of the social order:

"The system altogether forms a fit accompaniment or counterpart to the greatest principle of modern legislation, which is, 'perish the people, that property may be preserved'" (*PMA*, March 3, 1832, p. 50).

The Mill: Social and Technical Relations

The mill was the palpable, daily incarnation of all the talk of labor, production, and the capitalist order. For its champions, the mill held the answer to the drudgery of labor, the limitations on production, and even the morality of the masses. None penned more glowing tributes than Andrew Ure, who envisioned the factory system as "the great minister of civilization to the terraqueous globe" and the "grand palladium" of comfort for the working class (1835, pp. 18, 329). As the mill owner Wentworth patiently explained to a group of skeptical workers in Harriet Martineau's didactic melodrama on the foolishness of turn-outs, *A Manchester Strike*, the mill and its machinery were the life force of British economic dominance: "We owe it to these machines, and the mule-jenny, and the power-loom that came in afterwards, that though we have to bring our cotton from thousands of miles off, and though the wages in India are, as I said, only 3d. a day, we have beaten them in competition, and carry back their cotton five thousand miles, made into a cheaper fabric than they can afford. Such powers as these make our capital grow" (1833, p. 106).

The system of modern manufacture, argued sympathizers, decreased the toil for workers and offered increasing opportunities for those on the outside. Moreover, by providing a secure economic base for family life and instilling regularity and discipline, factory work fostered virtuousness. The Manchester mill owner, Holland Hoole, was eager to dispel the fiction that factories brought with them moral and physical pollution: "If the degree of knowledge and information possessed by a given number of individuals, forms a correct standard of morality, the case would be decided at once in favour of the Factory people against the mere hand labourers, or even against the agricultural peasantry. The regular habits created by the uniform occupation of Factory Children, render them some of the best attendants of Sunday Schools, and by consequence some of the best recipients of instruction" (1832, p. 10). Ure approvingly quoted the factory inspector Edward Tufnell on the moral virtues of factory labor: "It is my firm belief, that there is not a better or more certain mode of benefiting a country village than by establishing a cotton-factory in it" (1835, p. 342).

Moral progress was in part due to the superior conditions of labor and in part a product of the mill owner's beneficent superintendence. Factory machines were liberators, allowing operatives to draw on powers of the mind rather than the body. The mill owner supervised this emancipation, based in his benevolence, familial concern, and spiritual kindness for his operatives. "The slightest inquiry on the spot, the most superficial ocular inspection, would have satisfied any candid mind, that the owners, from regard to pecuniary interest, as well as to humanity and reputation, always set their faces against every species of oppression within their premises" (Ure 1835, p. 290). In a less idyllic vein, Edward Baines also saw many mill owners as "men of enlarged minds and humane feelings" who through vigilant superintendence might "make a factory a school of virtue rather than vice" ([1834] 1966, pp. 482–483).

Apart from such ebullience, enthusiasts were willing to concede that for some factories brought temporary disruption and distress. Yet as Charles Knight reminded his readers, any change of such social import was bound to affect some in its wake, and the progress of the many could not be halted to save a few unfortunate victims. Knight sought to assure his readers that those who suffered the worst were the sediment of society that inevitably would be washed away by the currents of change. Agitators were thus identified as societal dross: "Who, on the contrary, is always the first and last to suffer every change in the demand for labor? The unskilful workman, the drunken workman, the unthrifty workman . . . the workman, in a word, who would die in a ditch whether he lived in a country with machines, or without the power of the intellectual exertion, and possesses not the best thing which that power gives, moral conduct" (1831, pp. 211–212).

Factory workers countered this discourse of progress with one of exploitation. The obsession with profit, and the pre-occupation of the mill owner with his precious machines, made the worker a mere cog in production. Factory workers often returned to the comparison between themselves and the slaves who were a favorite object of liberal bourgeois reform. Ashton's J. J. Betts found that the advantages lay wholly with the slave.

> The only real difference is, that the negroes are slaves in *name*, while hundreds of thousands of our poor countrymen, here, are slaves in *reality*. There the slaves are comfortably housed, wholesomely fed, worked to the best economy of their health and strength, and I dare say sometimes overworked. Here, the slaves are miserably lodged, starved, beggarded, abused, despised, neglected, and overworked, always, and at all times without pity, without mercy, without hope. . . . The most humane manufacturers would never think of estimating humanity as equal to machinery. Their reasoning is, that machinery is expensive, but humanity—is—(oh it is!)—dust and ashes. (*UTCJ*, May 8, 1830, p. 78)

Playing on the idea of the importance of fixed capital to the mill owner, a worker ingeniously explained why the slaves were in a superior position. The "free" labor of the market was transformed into a system of enslavement: "The proprietor of the slave has an interest in his welfare. The return required on the capital sunk in the purchase, will induce him to feed and clothe him in such a way as to get the greatest amount of profit from his labour.... But there is no such motive to influence the conduct of the British capitalist. Those who employ thousands of 'free-born' British artizans have no interest in their welfare beyond their labour of the day" (*UTCJ*, April 3, 1830, p. 98).

Although there were many tracts deriding machinery, the spinners clearly differentiated between the technology of the system as such, and the manner in which it was harnessed. They did not strenuously object to machinery itself, but to the way its benefits were socially distributed.

> If machines should be so improved as to perform all that we have been supposing them to do, those only, under the existing regulations of this head, who possess the machines, would derive benefit from their employment; because those who have nothing to give in exchange for the produce of the machines but labour, and that labour was not granted, could not, of course, get any portion of the produce. So that all those who now subsist by labour, would be entirely cut off from all honest means of subsistence, or become wholly dependant on the will or caprices of those who own the machines.... This, then, is the great object, with regard to machinery, for which the workman ought to direct his attention, namely, *to secure to himself and his family,* A FULL SHARE OF THE PRODUCE OF EVERY MACHINE that is or may be introduced. (*VP*, Feb. 5, 1831, p. 44)

The operatives decried the owners' control of both working people and machines. They did not deny the mill owner his right to expect dependable and industrious labor. What they did roundly reject was the conflation of their labor with all other commodities over which the mill owner exercised power by controlling wealth. Seizing on the essence of the relationship as an exchange between free individuals, the factory workers maintained that what was transferred was value equity, not control over body and soul. By drawing on bourgeois notions of independence, workers constructed discourses delegitimating the mill owner's authority and justifying resistance: "The master's 'right,' and 'duty' too, is to give value for what he receives; the workman's 'duty,' founded on right is to insist upon having value for what he gives; to know that he is the property of no man; and that, when he performs his contract with the employer, he stands a free agent in society, perfectly independent of every man, except in the discharge of the mutual obligations which society has imposed upon us all. And these obligations, to be binding, must be just" (*PMA*, Feb. 18, 1832, p. 34). By drawing on these liberal constructions of freedom, workers questioned the bases of the mill owners' authority: "Large masses of wealth have been drawn together, which have given the possessors a power and influence highly dangerous to the well being and independence of the productive classes. The owner of an English manufactory possesses and exercises a power which would not be tolerated by the most despotic government in the world. . . . The master unites in his own single person, all the functions of the legislator, judge, jury, and executioner: he makes, administers, and executes the law" (*UTCJ*, May 8, 1830, pp. 73–74).

The most searing indictments of the system were reserved for the mill owners, for they had some power to mitigate its harshness. Indeed, argued many workers, this had once been the case, but their wealth had made them into "a new race," holding "proud haughty and arrogant assumptions," and who had been corrupted beyond conscience (*PMA*, May 19, 1832, p. 139). The cotton lords' mind-set was spelled out in a ribald attack by an Ashton worker entitled "The Cotton Spinners and Power-Loom Weavers' Lesser Catechism." The "Catechism" depicts the mill owner as thoroughly imbued with a wicked and maniacal acquisitiveness: "*Question.*—What is thy duty towards thyself? *Answer.*—My duty towards myself is to take all advantages, whether by falsehood or truth, by which I shall be enabled the more readily to make a fortune; to worship nothing but money; to give thanks to no one; and to serve (except myself), no one all the days of my life" (*UTCJ*, June 12, 1830, p. 115). The mill owners' principles were founded in this creed and the maintenance of class privilege.

> *Q.* Rehearse the articles of thy belief?
> *A.* I believe in the omnipotent power of the steam engine, the prime mover of all machinery . . . I believe in the holy combination of Masters, the holy rules by which they are held together—the communion that exists among them—the forgiveness of none who transgress their laws—heedless of the resurrection of life to come.
> *Q.* What dost thou chiefly learn in these articles of belief?
> *A.* First, I learn to believe in the power of wealth, which giveth to me all that I covet and not so to the rest of the world; —secondly, in the accumulation of wealth by the application of other people's industry to my own ends. (*UTCJ*, May 22, 1830, p. 92)

And the mill owners' commandments were a wanton inventory of hedonism, despotism, and cultured savagery.

> 1. Thou shalt have no other god but Mammon. 2. Thou shalt not make unto thyself any image in the likeness of any machinery that is not turned by power.—Thou shalt not employ any hands except to assist machinery to do their work, for the masters with which thou art united are jealous masters, visiting the sins of the fathers upon the children and the sins of the children upon the fathers unto the third and fourth generation. 3. Thou shalt not use the names of the masters irreverently, for they will not hold him guiltless that

so useth their names. 4. Remember that whist others keep holy the Sabbath day, after six days of labour, and in it do no manner of work—thou and thy son and thy daughter, thy man servant and thy maid servant, thy cattle and the stranger that is within they gates shall all be fully employed,—some cleaning thy boilers and retort-flues, some inspecting thy steam-engine, thy horizontal shaft, joints, and boxes, and some posting thy accounts or preparing a balance sheet of thy week's gainings. Thou, in the mean while, must see thy friends at dinner, or go out to dine with them. . . . 6. Thou shalt not do open murder. 7. Thou shalt not commit adultery, except thy pleasure and thy profit is increased by doing so. . . . 10. Thou shalt covet thy neighbor's house; thy neighbor's wife, and his servant, and his maid, and his ox, and his ass, and everything that is his, if by doing so thy profit and advantage is further secured. (*UTCJ*, May 22, June 12, 1830, pp. 92–93, 114)

Although Ashton mill owners wed Christian morality to political economy, the barbs of this worker exposed this marriage as one of base convenience.

As nefarious as the mill owners could be, organic intellectuals such as Doherty emphasized that the system was the ultimate enemy of working people. By counterpoising their radical economics to the mill owners' political economy, they moved beyond distinctions of character between individual mill owners. It was the system that propelled mill owners into ruinous competition and the flagrant abuse of their workers: "It is not a single act of oppression that we are warring against, but the entire system. . . . And as our object is, not only to expose the cruelty and injustice of the system, but at the same time to excite a spirit of discontent and *of resistance* to anything so grossly unjust, and so destructive of that spirit of national independence, which is essential to the exercise of institutions, to be necessary in order to destroy the pernicious idea that such restrictions and exactions are essential to, and form a part of the manufacturing system" (*PMA*, no. 2, Feb. 4, 1832, p. 19).

Wages and Combinations

Although the war was against the system, its battles, such as the strike of 1830–1831, were conducted around issues of wages and combinations. Much of this contention centered around the mill owners' ability to pay a just wage and the operatives' capacity to force them to do so. Struggles over just remuneration as we saw were central to the Spitalfields weavers as well.

Mill owners reminded workers that an assured level of profit, the lifeblood of capital, ultimately guaranteed employment. In a variety of ways, they naturalized a minimum return on investment and the variability of wages. John Kennedy enunciated one such dispassionate argument by which he and other mill owners determined wages: "The price of labour will and must vary from a variety of circumstances, but this most frequently arises from a redundant or scanty supply of manufactured products; and the capitalist will naturally and reasonably calculate to receive at least the ordinary interest which such capital would yield, if employed in agriculture, or which he could obtain by lending the same to those who might wish to borrow" (1831, p. 34).

Wage reductions were not the caprice of the mill owners, but were dictated by the ineluctable forces that balanced capital and labor. Within this logic, the level of wages was outside of the responsibility of capitalists. Martineau, in her lessons for the working class, annunciated a pithy Malthusian calculus: "The rate of wages in any country depends, therefore not on the wealth which the country contains, but on the proportion of population to capital" (1834, p. 44). In *A Manchester Strike*, the mill owner Wentworth explained the principle more engagingly: "'Such power as there is rests with those who take, not with those who give wages. Not such power as tips our friend's tongue there,' nodding at Clack, 'not such power as you gain by the most successful strike, not such power as combination gives you, be it peaceable or threatening: but a much more lasting power which cannot be taken from you. The power of the masters is considerable, for they hold the administration of capital; but it is not on this that the rate of wages depends. It depends on the administration of labour; and this much greater power is in your hands'" (Martineau 1833, p. 34).

Mill owners allowed that other factors affected wages, but with the caveat that these too were beyond their (at least immediate) control. A Stalybridge mill owner rankled over the Stockport strike and the denseness of the factory worker's mind that could not comprehend these economic forces.

> The very system of carrying our manufactures to such an enormous extent has been the cause of annihilating the profits of the manufacturer and reducing the wages of the workman.... A temporary turn-out can do no good, there must either be a permanent reduction in the quantity manufactured, or prices cannot rise. Is it not, therefore, madness for the operatives to attempt to get what is out of everybody's power to give them? Do they suppose their masters are made of money, and can give them as much as they demand?
>
> Trade is uncontrollable either by masters or men: and the Cotton Trade is one from which capital sunk in mills and machinery cannot be withdrawn, and as long as it is had from no cause whatever but overproduction, it will be a long time before it can recover from its depression. (*SA*, Jan. 23, 1829)

Workers, they maintained, believed otherwise because of the warped influence of combinations. According to Tufnell, "One of the worst results of combinations is the delusion, which they sanction, that wages are not subject to the general laws of supply and demand, but are dependent on the pleasures of the employers" (1834, pp. 95–96). Disgruntled and ignorant minds were easy prey for wily, self-interested union orators, who tethered workers to destructive ignorance. The district mill owner Aaron Lees explained to the Factory Inquiry Commission that union leaders ignited strikes for their own furtive machinations: "I have had great experience in turn-outs, and my father too; I am confident that the real ground of every turn-out is not the benefit of the working classes, but they are only used as a cloak for other designs. What design?—Political, as well as private animosity, but never the real welfare of the workpeople, who are only made the tools of more designing heads" (P.P. 1833, XX, pt. D.2, p. 91).

The obvious corollary was that turn-outs were entirely destructive. Not only were they rarely successful, they also exacted dear costs in lost wages, served as a magnet to draw more workers into the overstocked labor pool, induced mill owners to more rapidly replace workers with machinery, and disrupted the flow of capital and goods at great loss to the entire trade. Charles Knight proposed a strikingly ingenuous alternative to "tyranny of the mob." If workers found a crowded labor market they should simply hop the fence and seek their fortunes on the other side.

> There is a glut of laborers in the market. If you continue in the market of labor during the glut, your wages must fall. What is the remedy? To go out of the market. . . . Endeavour to acquire the same power yourselves. Become capitalists. When there is too much labor in the market, and wages are low, do not combine to raise wages; do not combine with the vain hope of compelling the employer to pay more for labor than there are funds for the maintenance of labor: but go out of the market. Leave the relations between wages and labor to equalize themselves. You can never be permanently kept down in wages by the profits of capital; for if the profits of capital are too high, the competition of other capital immediately comes in to set the matter right. But you may be kept down, and you are being kept down, by yourselves. (1831, p. 209)

Not surprisingly, operatives did not rush en masse to become entrepreneurs, nor did they accept these attributions of blame. Having established themselves as the true wealth creators through their labor theory of value, factory workers' representatives laid culpability for long-term wage decline squarely at the mill owners' feet. If capitalists were largely conduits for the wealth produced by workers, then the language of necessary profits was in reality a shroud for greed. "The masters," announced a spinners' union paper, "betray no more symptom of being satisfied, at this day, than they did on that day in which the contest began, nor will they, until they have wrung the last farthing from the hands of those who have toiled for it. Acquisition is their God—a God to whom attributes of justice and mercy do not belong—and that God only will they serve" (*UPCI*, March 10, 1832, pp. 99–100). Similarly fallacious was the idea that wages could drop no further than a base subsistence level. "Let no man tell us, that there is a point, on this side of starvation, where blood-sucking avarice will cease to grasp the vitals of the manufacturing labourers," proclaimed the committee of Stockport factory workers (P.C., set 16, v. 2, "Cotton," f. 51). In these words, they echoed those of the Spitalfields weavers.

Where factory owners envisioned the invisible hand of the marketplace, workers in turn saw the all too visible hand of power wielded by their employers. Wages would be continually whittled away because the factory owners possessed overpowering advantages to dictate. The calculus of the struggle was simple: the cotton lord's vast wealth made him infinitely more powerful than any operative. The collective force of all workers was necessary to level the field of play. As a pamphlet produced by the Manchester spinners in their strike of 1829 maintained,

> the laws by which we are governed, are made, not by the advice and council of those whose lives and conduct they are to bind, not by the poor and defenceless workmen, but by those who rule, the rich and powerful. In the framing of the laws, the workman's interests and wishes are never consulted. They are invariably made to suit the convenience, and to promote the interests, not of the employed, but the employer. . . . A master can, and too often does succeed in attempts to reduce wages, not because it is necessary to reduce, but because the men are not united. The master, in his individual capacity, singly and alone, possesses as much power at least, as all the men he employs collectively. The workman lives by his own individual labour; the master lives *and fattens* on the labour of all that work for him. So that it is only when all the men in the employment of any master refuses [*sic*] to work for him, that he is placed in the same situation as the poor man whom he discharges, and at once deprives of all means of subsistence. It is only by uniting with, and assisting each other, that workmen can hope to be a match for their employers. (P.C., set 16, v. 2, "Cotton," f. 96)

Many of the factory workers who contributed to working peoples' journals envisioned combinations as the singular solution to this oppression. In a world where organized force and amassed wealth were the true measures of power, only the mass exertion of working people was potent enough to stand up to the cotton lords: "Without Combination the exercise of right is impossible; the very same as the right to fly; for a right of impossibilities can be no right at all" (P.C., set 16, v. 2, "Cotton," f. 51). The government would provide no redress for their grievances; solutions depended on the workers themselves. As Doherty emphasized, "The master's capital is secured and hemmed round by innumerable acts of parliament, while there is not one solitary act to protect the workman's labour.... The workmen have nothing to hope for from any power but their own. They have been, and ever will be plundered, until they themselves, by one unanimous and simultaneous effort, free themselves from the galling yoke under which they have ever groaned" (*PMA*, May 2, 1832, p. 109).[1]

Unity was thus essential, and apathy and inertia were considered two of the principal foes of working people. As the *United Trades' Co-operative Journal* proclaimed, "The man of wealth imagines that he has a right to rule, uncontrouled, the conduct of his workmen, and to fix the value of labour of those who have the commodity to sell him.... [U]nited we shall possess a power that... will be defiance to all the machinations of monopoly and wealth" (*UTCJ*, May 1, 1830, pp. 65–67).

In seeking to organize a general union in the year following the Ashton strike, the Manchester Trades' Committee was to reiterate a point made many times by the spinners in the group on the necessity of unionism as the only effective form of class action. "To whom" it asked rhetorically of the workers of the region, "then, are you to look for benefits? Is it to the justice of the government? Did you ever know the government to be just, particularly to the poor? Is it to the generosity or disinterestedness of the employers? What shall make men generous or disinterested, that were not before? To whom, then, shall you look? *To yourselves*, O operatives; every class for itself is the ruling maxim of society, and it must be yours" (*UPCI*, v. 1, no. 9, March 10, 1832, p. 100). And one of its predecessors the N.A.P.L. had a trenchant warning for all those who willfully ignored their message: "Injustice and oppression should at all times be punished; and the working classes, whose rights are thus invaded and outraged, would be fully justified in leveling their whole force against the man who dares to trench on their inherent and unquestionable rights" (*UTCJ*, Sept. 25,

---

[1] The discourse of many leaders of the National Association for the Protection of Labour specifically discounted efforts to seek political solutions for economic ills. The N.A.P.L. was a spinners-led attempt to form a national trades' union, with John Doherty as its secretary (Kirby and Musson 1975). Many of its activists argued that if government was rotten, so was its potential for benevolence. At a mass meeting of the N.A.P.L. in Accrington, a small cotton town north of Manchester, Thomas Oates offered such an analysis of politically generated change: "Mr. Oates concluded by showing that unless some protecting power interposed between employers and their hands, the relief to be derived from reform, a repeal of the corn laws, or any other ministerial measure, would be a mere chimera—it would only be transferring the rod of oppression from the hands of the boroughmongers to those of the employers. Because, if any amelioration of the public burthens enabled workmen to live at a cheaper rate, the circumstance would be laid hold of by the employers as a justification for fresh reductions in the wages of their workers" (*VP*, July 16, 1831, p. 4). The meeting echoed these sentiments when it passed the following resolution: "That for the foregoing reasons, the people have no reason to expect relief from a retrenchment of the public expenditures—from the removal of the corn laws—the extinction of all existing monopolies, or any other ministerial measure. The productive classes are imperatively called upon to originate, amongst themselves, some efficient measures for the protection of their own interests, and the amelioration of their present impoverished condition" (ibid.).

1830, pp. 49–50). The precise meaning of the threat was to be displayed in full glory and horror in the strike of the Ashton-Stalybridge spinners in late 1830.

The conflicts that animated this friction of discourses not only transformed the fighting words on each side, they also changed how these words structured the silences and exclusions of those who did not speak. As I have argued, discourse cannot hermetically preclude people from social action because its heteroglossic character provides the possibility for alternative meanings and interpretations. However, the passages it leaves ajar and the ease of entrance by which these can be negotiated can be substantially affected. The development of these discourses of contention held perhaps subtle but significant import for the ways in which women could include themselves in these stories of conflict. As we have noted, women and children constituted a majority of a factory's workforce, although they were essentially excluded from the spinner's role in the district. Although we have examined the spinners' fighting words, they significantly shaped the discourses of contention of factory workers throughout the Pennines.

As Deborah Valenze observes, with the gendering of spinning as a male occupation associated with skill and technical rationality, "women's work" in the factory became increasingly demarcated as inferior (1995, pp. 183–184). But as Valenze also notes, equally important to the marginalization of women was the transformed characterization of the worker in political economy. Earlier corporatist discourses had provided the industrious poor with a collective identity as dependent members of the society but essential to national prosperity. Political economy, however, with its emphasis on the independent worker and breadwinner relegated women to the periphery. Partly, as we have seen, it did so by emphasizing the autonomy and free will of the worker, a status not attributable to women, who were legally and socially dependents. Partly too, it envisioned working women through the emerging model of the housewife of the middling ranks (pp. 129–130, 136–139).

From a dialogic perspective, increasing frictions between male workers and mill owners can also be viewed as contributing to the structuring of women's silence. For in engaging the discourses of political economy, male workers partly sought to appropriate and collectivize its individualistic constructions of autonomy, freedom, and property. Carpenter and many others had cast the livelihood gained from labor as a form of inalienable property, "the birth-right of all men"; and Doherty had insisted that as such the worker was "the property of no man; and that, when he performs his contract with the employer, he stands a free agent in society, perfectly independent of every man, except in the discharge of the mutual obligations." These were not attributes that could be ascribed to women workers.

As both the model of the primary wage earner for the household, and discursively representing themselves as free agents in control of their labor, spinners produced an early typification of the male breadwinner. In their future conflicts with the cotton lords, they would specifically construct their claims as such, and they also actively agitated for Short Time legislation to limit the hours of women and children in the factory.[2] The discursive struggles of the 1820s, however, remind us that this construction of the male breadwinner was not just an exercise in misogyny, but a result of the ways in which class and gender formation intersected at a particular conjunctures and through specific conflicts.

The conflicts in the 1820s thus vitally shaped the discourses of contention through which the factory workers constructed their collective identity, gave moral substance to their grievances, and fashioned the intelligibility for their collective actions. Engaging the discourse of political economy, the spinners and their allies responded with fighting words that both spoke and shaped their consciousness of class conflict.

In drawing on a labor theory of value and developing a radical economics, the factory workers produced fighting words with themes similar to the Spitalfields weavers. Part of what linked these two and other trades groups was precisely this dialogic struggle within the discourse of political economy. Commonalties in discursive struggle served as a bridge for drawing conclusions about more general shared interests. Indeed, while the ground-level battles of the cotton spinners and silk weavers differed in many respects, we can see that they both sought to expose the class interests that were supported by notions of free markets, the commodification of labor and the construction of relations between capital and labor as a contractual relationship of mutual benefit between free individuals. Divergences in responses arose from their particular circumstances. For the silk weavers, for whom state intervention was vital, the role of the state took on much greater weight. For the cotton spinners, who concerned themselves with independent and internal organization against mill owners, unions seemed the more effective ways of addressing rights issues. In this sense, we can see how the material concerns can shape discursive struggle.

The male factory workers' discourse of contention thus was part of a vibrant class culture, and the workers of these Lancashire factory towns were certainly present in its making. When in the bleak winter days of 1830 workers streamed from the mills and collectively voiced their defiance to the cotton lords, these words echoed about the valley narrating a tempestuous and violent conflict.

---

[2] For an analysis of the gendering of factory labor through Short Time agitation, see Clark 1995, Gray 1993, and Rose 1992.

CHAPTER ELEVEN

Class War:
The Spinners' Strikes of 1830–1831

> Utilitarian economists, skeletons of schoolmasters, Commissioners of Fact, genteel and used-up infidels, gabblers of many dog's-eared creeds, the poor you will always have with you. Cultivate in them, while there is yet time, the utmost graces of the fancies and affections to adorn their lives so much in need of ornament; or, in the day of your triumph, when romance is utterly driven out of their souls, and they and a bare existence stand face to face, Reality will take a wolfish turn and make an end of you.
>
> Charles Dickens, *Hard Times*

*A*s factory production developed, the Ashton district emerged as an active arena of working-class formation. The growth of a muscular industrial infrastructure, the maturation of a propriety group of capitalists set on ordering a world in their own image, and the fostering of relatively insular class cultures and social spheres produced increasing friction between mill owners and their employees. In a previous series of fractious strikes, spinners and cotton lords developed mounting enmity. Class struggle was, in Thompson's terms, fomenting class consciousness.

This ever-closer engagement, as in the case of the silk weavers, brought matters to a head by the end of the decade. In both cases, the discourses of political economy significantly defined the ideological boundaries of these contests. In both cases, this struggle led to an articulation of rights partly through a labor theory of value. The increasingly bitter regional battles over piece rates, however, produced distinctive dialogic responses and repertoires of collective action. Where the silk weavers partly defended their labor through class claims of citizenship, the cotton spinners framed their grievances as a direct confrontation with the power of capital. Past struggles provided both a narrative logic and a set of collective actions in which collective rights were defined in terms of collective might. The state largely entered into this narrative through the barrel of a rifle. Class and class consciousness did happen, but not in the same way.

In the analysis below, I focus on how the spinners fused a radical analysis of power with an equally radical refutation of political economy to narrate their struggles.[1] Unlike the Spitalfields weavers, the cotton spinners early on produced a creative fusion between radical "political" and "economic" discourses to critique their exploitation by the cotton lords. These discourses of contention colored their contest in stark terms. Understanding the meanings of the fighting words that morally legitimated their actions provides a key to the progressive escalation of the conflict. In several respects, the times were not propitious for a protracted struggle. The Ashton spinners' campaign came on the heels of significant losses in other districts. Winter was generally the trough in the production cycle for spinning, the industry had not long ago emerged from an extended slump, and neither the local union nor the federation had accumulated substantial resources for a prolonged turn-out. The spinners' fighting words, however, provided a powerful contextual narrative as demanding redress through forceful and sometimes violent means. They reveal that part of the logic of the spinners' actions must be sought in the collective understandings of class antipathy that had been nurtured over the years. In the analysis below then, we will see how these discourses framed the spinners' understanding of the conflict, and how the strike itself was part of the white heat of class formation.

"The struggle is a struggle of strength and 'the weakest must go to the wall.' Whatever the people either gain or lose, is gained or retained,

---

[1] The strikes of 1830–1831 have been analyzed by Kirby and Musson (1975, pp. 119–138), Cotton (1977, pp. 211–234), and R. Hall (1991, pp. 101–112). Kirby and Musson explicate the events principally within the context of the demise of the cotton spinners' Grand National Union, focusing much of their attention on the problematic links between the Manchester headquarters and the hinterlands. Their analysis concentrates on the strikes as pivotal "industrial" disputes. Cotton rightly criticizes the two authors for an overly economistic and organizational approach. He argues that the local class tensions in which the strikes are embedded are essential to an understanding of their dynamics. He also suggests that they have missed what he characterizes as the political features of the strike activity entirely. Cotton's emphasis on the local context is a vital corrective, but his discussion of an explicitly political facet seems to be a partial misreading of the discourses of contention. As I will illustrate, the spinners drew on events in France and radical discourses surrounding them as a point of reference for their own resolutions to oppression. They did not incorporate this discourse to critique the polity: class tyranny was the central issue. The radical political discourse that they employed offered a ready means of framing this oppression. Hall suggests that the strike should be seen as part of the backdrop for the rapid rise of Chartism in the district. He observes that it became a central point of the workers' collective memory and provided a legacy for subsequent class politics.

and must always be gained or retained by power," Francis Place wrote to John Doherty on April 7, 1829 (16, v. 2, "cotton," f. 92). By the spring of 1830, the district's spinners were feeling the cold damp of the wall pressing against their backs. Their peers in Stockport, Hyde, Dukinfield, and surrounding communities had recently suffered an ignominious defeat at the hands of the cotton lords. That loss had followed on the heels of the bitter and unsuccessful campaign of the fine spinners in Manchester for piece-rate equalization. With the markets still languid, factory owners again focused on piece-rate reductions to shore up profit margins. The spinners had come to understand the cotton lords' motivations for such reductions as founded in greed and the illicit prerogatives of wealth's power. The bleak vista of increased grinding called for action.

In an attempt to forestall any further reductions, the spinners of the Ashton-Stalybridge region embarked on a series of preemptive strikes. The efforts were inaugurated by limited actions against selected mill owners in Stalybridge, following their repertoire of the rolling strike. Partial victories there stoked the fires of broader class conflict, which culminated in the general turn-out against fifty-two firms in the region in December. The strike, which endured for over ten weeks, was one of the most encompassing and rancorous conflicts in which the spinners had ever engaged.

In the analysis below, I follow the course of the strikes in three stages. The first stage is the limited actions in the spring and summer months that preceded the strike of December. The second stage covers the mobilization efforts prior to the strike, and the third stage is the great turn-out.

The Prelude

By the spring, the reductions suffered in Manchester and Stockport the previous year hung ominously above the districts' spinners. Local mill owners grumbled about the lack of uniformity in piece rates. Large disparities existed most notably between Ashton and Stalybridge, where the top rates for a thousand hanks were said to be 4 shillings tuppence, and 3 shillings 5 pence respectively (Cotton 1977, p. 213; H.O. 40/26, ff. 46–50, Bouverie to Peel, Aug. 29, 1830). The mill owners saw a reduction as the most appropriate path toward equalization; the spinners hoped for a parity.

In March, J. J. Betts, the secretary of the local union, made some initial attempts at reconciliation, but he was firmly rebuffed. In April, the local union embarked on a strategy of raising piece rates at the mills with the lowest rates. The first target of the spinners' mobilization was William Hegginbottom of Ashton. Hegginbottom was an object of caustic derision for his use of truck, excessive deductions, and low piece rates (*UTCJ*, May 29, 1830, pp. 99–100). The strike commenced during the middle part of April, and Hegginbottom quickly responded by recruiting recently unemployed spinners from Stockport. The spinners saw his actions as a wanton disregard for their grievances and hunkered down for a hard-edged battle. Over the next two months, they responded with an escalating series of actions, including showering his house with stones and pelting blacklegs at the factory with mud, sticks. and stones (leading to five convictions). The attacks sufficiently alarmed the local authorities and the military that two units were detached to keep the peace (*MM*, June 15, 22, 1830; *MT*, April 24, 1830; *SA*, April 30, 1830; *WMC*, April 24, May 1, 5, 1830; H.O. 40/27, ff. 268–273, Bouverie to Phillips, May 18, 1830).

At the end of May, the spinners' vanguard inaugurated a branch of the recently formed general union, the National Association for the Protection of Labour, with representatives from each of the local trades. This served as a palpable sign of community working-class solidarity. The strike wore on in a tense stasis as attacks on the blacklegs continued. In the second week of June, however, the Hegginbottoms received an unexpected package, left for a servant to open. Fortunately for the servant and the family the package—a jerry-built bomb containing nine pounds of gunpowder—failed to explode. The union, fearful of a fierce backlash, forcefully censured the action and offered a 250-pound reward for information on the perpetrators. Nonetheless, fiery denunciations of the union rapidly filled the region's newspapers (*MG*, June 12, 26, 1830; *MM*, June 22, 1830; *MT*, April 29, June 12, 1830; *UTCJ*, May 29, 1830).

Little more than a week later, Hegginbottom unceremoniously announced piece-rate advances, although he steadfastly refused to rehire any strikers. Hegginbottom's apparent triumph over the strikers perhaps signaled the mill owners to press again for reductions. On July 14, they concurred on a rate of 3 shillings 9 pence per 1,000 hanks for #40s, higher than they had proposed in April, but well below the spinners' expectations. The cotton lords had not quite thrown down the gauntlet, but they were clearly indicating that the status quo could not last (Cotton 1977, p. 213; *MG*, June 26, 1830).

Undaunted, the union pressed ahead in Stalybridge. Those mills were logical targets, since they maintained the lowest piece rates. If the union could force the hand of the Stalybridge mill owners, they had a chance of abating reductions in Ashton. In an open letter, J. J. Betts exhorted the towns' spinners and rovers to action.

> The time has at length arrived when it has become your duty, as well as your interest, to know your own importance in society, and to exempt yourselves from that state of vassalage to which you have been long subjected, by men possessing wealth accumulated by your industry.—For years you have been sinking deeper into the mire of adversity, and in proportion as you have sunk, your employers have advanced in prosperity . . . when we see our

cheerful cottages converted into abodes of misery—when we see our offspring exhibit a mass of rags; when we witness them perambulating the streets in appearance mere walking skeletons; when knowing that indolence has no share in producing such wretchedness;—when we reflect on the length of the days we are compelled to toil;—when we reflect too, on the nature of our employment;—when we contemplate the contraction of our earnings in the shape of fines;—when we think in the projects of our employers in erecting cottages and compelling us to pay enormous rents for the same; when we know that to mention any one act of oppression to our employers with a view to better our condition would throw us out of employment; when we see our masters amplificating their establishments, and building whole streets of houses;—when we know that our wages are from 30 to 40 per cent. under the average wages paid in the united kingdom for spinning the same Nos. of yarn in this place;—knowing these things . . . is it a matter of surprise to see us thus advert to the possessions of our employers, who not content with their present title of "Cotton Lords," are aspiring to be "COTTON KINGS." (*UTCJ*, July 24, 1830, pp. 185–186)

The feudal metaphor communicated the scope of the mill owners imperious domination and effectively counterposed their reign to the emasculation of the spinners who could not provide for their families. It also served as a bridge to link radical "economic" and "political" discourses in their discursive repertoire.

Shortly after Betts's rousing appeal four thousand spinners and operatives met to oppose stirrings by two firms that had proclaimed their intentions to initiate the recently proposed reductions. Although talk of a possible turn-out was rife, the meeting decided to try compromise, appointing Betts and two Manchester officials to meet with a delegation of factory owners. Although voting for conciliation, the spinners' resolutions were forthright reminders of their fundamental opposition to reductions, denouncing them as based upon "principles of avarice" and as "a direct robbery of the comforts of the working classes" (*MT*, July 31, 1830; *MM*, Aug. 3, 1830). A halting truce was finally realized when mill owners agreed to postpone the proposed reductions to allow the union to equalize piece rates (*MG*, July 31, 1830; *UTCJ*, Sept. 11, 1830, p. 13). The fate of the spinners was firmly, if ephemerally, in their own hands.

On August 7, seven thousand operatives gathered in Stalybridge with the usual cast of union leaders on hand to foment enthusiasm. Again, through the metaphor of regal power fighting words depicted the cotton lords as duplicitous thieves of the spinners' labor. The mill owner Jeremiah Lees was singled out for rebuke as a man who "had been called a 'cotton lord' and a 'cotton king,' but he thought he would not be satisfied with either, for he wanted to be a cotton emperor. . . . He (Mr. Johnson) had once seen Mr. Lees at a charity sermon where he gave 5 pounds. He saw him put it in the box. But he could not help thinking that his poor workmen must pay for that. In fact it was not his, but theirs" (*UTCJ*, Aug. 14, 1830, p. 220). The spirit of the messages signaled impending redress (*WMC*, Aug. 14, 1830; *MG*, Aug. 14, 1830).

The contest commenced the following week, first with the turn-out at the Orrell mill, and soon after with Lee's factory; the battle for wage equalization was in full swing. A few blacklegs were quickly ushered into the struck establishments, but strikers just as quickly drove them out. Worried magistrates canvassed for volunteers for a special constabulary, and an aide to Lieutenant Colonel Shaw expressed anxiety at strikers' bold depictions of the events in terms of a political rebellion: "The excitement caused by the Revolution in France is greater than I could have anticipated; they talk a great deal of their power of putting down the Military and the Constable. . . ." (H.O. 40/27, f. 305, Shaw to Bouverie, Aug. 24, 1830; *SA*, Aug. 20, 1830; *MT*, Aug. 21, 1830). In an attempt to keep the home fires at a slow burn, Shaw persuaded Orrell and Lees to forestall the further introduction of the detested blacklegs, since he realized that if the union was to carry through with its rolling strike it would "have completely the power of ruining the whole of the Manufacturers of that place" (H.O. 40/26, ff. 46–50, Bouverie to Peel, Aug. 29, 1830).

A thorough picket, part of the spinners' instrumental repertoire, was set up around the mills and on major roads to dissuade potential blacklegs and proved an unmitigated success (H.O. 40/27, f. 520, Shaw to Clerk, Sept. 2, 1830). In the meanwhile, turn-outs received 10 shillings per week from the union, and their piecers were allotted half that sum (*UTCJ*, Sept. 11, 1830, p. 13). Within several weeks, Orrell and Lees succumbed, and the spinners accommodated a settlement by accepting a piece rate of 3 shillings 11 pence, halfway between their original demand and the cotton lords' offer. The civil and military authorities were relieved but fretted about the spinners' increasing strength and resolve (H.O. 40/26, ff. 65–66, Shaw to Bouverie, Aug. 4, 1830, ff. 69–70, Peel to Bouverie, Aug. 6, 1830; Cotton 1977, p. 213, n. 84).

Interlude

In the oft bleak valley of the Tame, the spinners had achieved a rare moment in the sun. The new piece rates were instituted by most other Stalybridge mill owners, and it was reported that in addition six hundred spinners in Ashton, Dukinfield, and Hyde were receiving an added 6 shillings per week. The *United Trades' Co-operative Journal* warmly praised the Stalybridge spinners for their "manly" determination against reduction, which, they argued, would also save mill owners from their own ruinous competition (Sept. 11, 1830, p. 13; *MM*, Oct. 5, 1830). Masculinity and class resolve went hand in hand.

Despite the glow, there was no permanent accord; the threat of reductions remained menacingly evident. Betts, Downes, and other union activists continued their mobilization efforts, and by early October the *Guardian* was reporting that union meetings were being held almost weekly in the district (*UTCJ*, Sept. 25, 1830, p. 55; *MG*, Oct. 2, 1830; M.C.L., MSS. Coll., Misc/323, Peel to Foster, Oct. 30, 1830).

With Ashton, Stalybridge, and Glossup within the fold, the union decided to test its mettle in Dukinfield. In mid-October, Messrs. Lees & Sons, the largest of the town's mills was turned out. Additionally, in a curious twist, the piecers at Hindley & Hyde's also turned out shortly thereafter (*WMC*, Oct. 23, 1830; *MG*, Oct. 23, 1830).[2]

As October shaded into November, both sides continued along a collision path. In the first week, the mill owners threw down the gauntlet, announcing that in one month they would institute new piece rates of 3 shillings 9 pence per thousand hanks of #40s throughout the district. This was below the recently won increases in Stalybridge and far short of the 4 shillings tuppence the spinners demanded. They also presented a unified front, each indemnifying their participation in the contest with a bond for 500 pounds (*MG*, Nov. 6, 1830; H.O. 40/26, ff. 131–132, Bouverie to Peel, Nov. 14, 1830).

Betts and other union leaders systematically continued mobilization for an impending turn-out. Meetings were held at Ashton, Dukinfield, Hurst and Audenshaw during the first days of November, with one newspaper reporting that "the Trades' Union is in great vogue amongst the operatives of this place" (*MM*, Nov. 9, 1830; *MG*, Nov. 6, 1830). At Dukinfield, ten thousand operatives gathered (many of them armed) to hear virulent denunciations of the mill owners. A minor excise officer wrote fearfully of the proceedings at Audenshaw to the Home Office, having furtively observed part of the meeting.

> Betts observed that Trades Unions and Political Ones were now so intimately blended together that they must be looked upon as one. He proceeded to state that we lived under the Worst, the most Rascally, Despotic, Tyrannical Government that ever existed. He told the meeting of the Glorious Victory that had been achieved in France by only 8000 Men over Tyranny and said there were more than 80,000 men ready for a similar proceeding in England. He then sat down apparently exhausted by the Efforts he had made and was followed by a person of the name of Buckley who resides in North Street near this place. He informed the Meeting that he was the chief cause of the Repeal of the Combination and Conspiracy Acts. He stated that every

---

[2] At the time of the Messrs. Lees strike, virtually all of the colliers of that town turned out in parallel with similar actions in Bury, Oldham, Rochdale, and Stockport, and the evidence clearly demonstrates the organizational strength of the district union. By early November, twenty-eight firms had agreed to a 33% wage increase and most pit owners admitted defeat shortly thereafter (*WMC*, Oct. 23, 1830; *MM*, Oct. 26, Nov. 2, 1830; *MG*, Oct. 23, Nov. 11, 13, 1830; Cotton 1977, p. 149; Kirby and Musson 1975, p. 181).

Master was a Tyrant, that they had a right to participate in whatever property any Man had, that they must down with the Cotton Lords who had no right to any such profits, that they were Omnipotent in power, that if they would be United no Force could stand against them and that they must repel Force by force; they must rouse from their Apathy and let their Despotic Tyrannical Masters know theirs was the power and that they would use it. Betts again addressed them assuring them he fully concurred in the Sentiments of the last Speaker, he told them that this and other Meetings in the Villages were only preparatory to the great Meeting which would be held shortly in Staley Bridge or Ashton. He told them to recollect their Power was Omnipotent that they must shortly use it, that Petitions were of no use, they might write to the Ministers but they must write in such a way that the Writer should never be known. He knew that ever writing would be of no use. He hoped that they would be united, that they would be determined to be Free. Let Liberty or Death be their Cry and Spreading out a small Flag with various Devices on it, told them that that was the Tricoloured Flag under which they must Act, that they must be Firm or this Opportunity would be Lost, and concluded with hoping that they would be united and All attend the meeting at Staley Bridge or Ashton as placards were to inform them, that all the Factories would Stop on that Day, and on that Day he intimated a Decisive Step would be taken. . . . I have heard that after my departure that Buckley delivered an inflammatory Speech about the Bishops and Clergy of every Denomination, condemned the Bible, opprobriously stigmatized Religion and all who professed it. (H.O. 40/27, ff. 338-339, Nightingale to the Home Office, Nov. 8, 1830)

In these heady days, Continental rebellions provided the spinners with a metaphor for and an exemplar of success. They reasoned their contest was analogous to these revolutions, and the eighty thousand members of the N.A.P.L. were spiritual kin to their rebellious brothers and sisters in France. The intertextual nature of the radical discourses through which the spinners critiqued their situation allowed for a fertile hybridization. The spinners' fight was against despotism *tout court*. What was most important to understand was the common thread of oppression tying all of its incarnations—political, economic and religious—into a package of monstrous power. Eventually, all rotten institutions had to crumble under the weight of popular redress, and the tricolor served as a cogent symbol of their purpose. This was a discourse of and on power; power that robbed working people of their property and freedom, and the power they could mobilize to liberate themselves.

These fighting words reflected the spinners' sense of social justice and pathways for redress. The most immediate, palpable, and incessant source of their oppression sat in the throne of manufacture—the "cotton lords." Storm their palaces of production first; perhaps later Windsor and Buckingham would be confronted as well. The spirited unionist Thomas Oates had articulated this vision earlier at the inaugural meeting of the N.A.P.L. in Ashton: "There was a class of men, which he was disposed to rank even lower in degree of crime, than the detested boroughmongers; men who raised a loud cry of 'stop thief' against the boroughmongers, had their own hands in the poor man's pocket, and were recklessly plundering him. Unless by their own exertions or otherwise, the working classes obtained an advance in wages, they would find radical reform itself ineffectual to relieve them" (*MT*, May 29, 1830). Oates voiced a key component of the discursive repertoire that was to serve as the narrative frame of the strike: cotton lords were stealing the workers' property, and only direct collective action could rectify this injustice.

Although almost fully mobilized by mid-November, the spinners convinced mill owners to consent to a one-month delay in the reductions to try to establish an equitable district-wide list. Within ten days, however, Doherty received a terse message from the mill owners of the accord's sudden collapse: they would institute the previously proposed piece rates on December 11 (*MG*, Nov. 13, 1830; *VP*, Jan. 8, 1831, p. 13). All hopes of a settlement were thoroughly dashed.

The pace of events quickened. Within a week after the announcement, the Ashton N.A.P.L. convened a meeting to address the embattled spinners. A week later, the self-styled champion of the working classes, Charles Hindley, discharged all of his operatives for attending the event. Two days after that, Stalybridge mill owners scotched a union meeting that was to be held at the Wesleyan Methodist chapel: they had no stomach to see a house of religion transformed, even temporarily, into a den of class antagonism (*MT*, Nov. 27, 1830; Kirby and Musson 1975, p. 120). That same day, the infamous fifty-two firms issued the following proclamation along with their proposed list of piece rates: "We the undersigned, in conformity with the above Resolution, do hereby give notice to all hands in our employ, that we shall commence paying according to the above list in Fourteen days from this date, and, from that period shall give nor require further notice" (H.O. 40/26, f. 146, Bouverie to Melbourne, Dec. 2, 1830).

War

At the start of December, the following placard was liberally posted throughout the district:

> Labour and Wages Important to the Working Classes
> In consequence of a determination on the part of the Renowned Fifty Two to effect an irretrievable ruin amongst the Operative Cotton Spinners of Ashton, Dukinfield, Mossley, and Staley Bridge we deem it requisite that the

whole of the Working Classes of the above places should hold a public meeting to consult and devise some legal means by which the nefarious intention of the Master Spinners may be fully defeated.

Notice is hereby given that a public meeting of the Working Class will be held in a Meadow belonging to Mr. Edward Cheetham near Buck Inn Dukinfield side of Staley Bridge on Saturday the 4th day of December 1830 at 10 o'clock at morn when deputies from Manchester and the neighboring districts will address the meeting and exhibit the fallacy of the Master Spinners reasons for proposing the reduction they now offer.

By order of the Operative Spinners
John Joseph Betts
Secretary

(H.O. 40/27, f. 349-350, Foster to Melbourne, Dec. 4, 1830)

As Betts depicted the meeting, this was a matter for "the whole of the Working Classes." At noon on that Saturday, the mills disgorged their workers, and the roads swelled with operatives. A procession formed in Stalybridge, with hundreds of boys leading the parade. A band of music displaying the tricolor and a sardonic banner with the words "Free Trade" marched several steps behind. Male workers, many openly armed, were arrayed ten to twelve abreast, with another tricolor at the rear. The tricolor had become a generalized symbol, a radical mark of defiance against oppression. Hundreds of women and children, many with tricolored ornaments, swelled the ranks. The women were decently dressed, many in their second-best outfits, their garb perhaps connecting aggrieved males to models of virtue and family. At a couple of the factories along the parade route, workers forcefully entered to turn out working hands. At its height, the procession was said to have stretched more than a mile (*MG*, Dec. 11, 1830; *MT*, Dec. 11, 1830; *WMC*, Dec. 11, 1830; *MM*, Dec. 14, 1830; H.O. 40/27, ff. 160-163, Foster to Melbourne, Dec. 6, 1830; H.O. 40/26, ff. 178-180, Astley to Melbourne, Dec. 9, 1830).

With at least twenty thousand assembled, Betts, with a large tricolored ribbon resplendently hung across his chest, mounted the hustings. After strongly admonishing the crowd against any unruly activity he launched into praise for their justness and sensibility:

> Gentlemen, all we ask is that we may enjoy the fruits of our labour without penury or oppression. . . . The masters of Ashton have now coalesced with the masters at Stalybridge. . . . But let not this discourage us. Their union is made up of the most repulsive materials; and, if you today conceded to their demands, the very next day they would become disunited, and melt away like "the baseless fabric of a vision," leaving "not a wreak behind." . . . Look at this beautiful valley, and up to the bosom of yon hills, and you will see

nothing but evidences of your labour. Yet you have no chance left, save that combining with your fellow creatures, in order to share the happiness that heaven has decreed to you, but of which your insolent masters would willingly deprive you. (*MM*, Dec. 14, 1830)

Betts had articulated familiar themes in their discursive repertoire: the workers' right to their property (labour), the baseless robbing of it by the cotton lords, and the absolute necessity of cohesive class action to secure justice. Those who succeeded him on the hustings amplified these axioms of social justice. A Mr. Grundy validated the righteousness of their demands against the prescriptions of political economists: "The spinners are said to be the best paid of any trade in the union, but the king receives thirty-four thousand more per annum than fifteen thousand of the best paid workmen in his dominion. They talk about the *honour and dignity* of the crown, but I would ask you, what *honour and dignity* there is when they come to take the poor man's bed from under him to support it.—(Bravo, bravo.) They tell us we 'breed too fast' too; the drones tell us we are 'too many;' and propose to transport us in order that they may keep our share of the money to themselves" (*MM*, Dec. 14, 1830). The polymorphous nature of "they" at first makes us pause on these fighting words. *They* designated the powerful, in much the same way that Betts and Buckley had posed the foundations of their oppression at the November meeting. The populist plasticity of these radical discourses allowed for the equation of aristocrats, political economists and mill owners. *They* robbed the working man's hard-gotten honor, dignity and material rewards.

Doherty next chronicled the union's good-faith negotiations, and proceeded to expose the cotton lords' true motivation—their desire to crush the union. He responded that "we will let them see that no power on earth can put us down," and closed with a plain demand for equity and honor that was a standard feature of their discursive repertoire: "All we want is proper remuneration for our labour; and that the operatives shall no longer be the slaves of masters and tyrants" (*MG*, Dec. 11, 1830).

Slater of the Ashton union followed, painting their struggle as a grand crusade and reiterating the threat of just retribution in the protection of their labor. "They wanted a regulated list for all places, that they may refer to as a great charter; they wanted security and protection for their labour. The property of the masters was protected by the pistol, the carbine, and the sword; but the operatives were so numerous that when united they could protect themselves. He should not wish for violence, but let it be understood that they would have no further reduction" (ibid.). The figurative analogy of the contract to a magna carta to protect their "property" suggests the fundamental nature of their rights claims. As with basic rights of capitalists, violence legitimately could be marshaled to protect their property.

Hodgins of Manchester, with characteristic fire, expounded on justifiable redress, focusing his attack on the toll exacted by the mill owners. He echoed previous analogies to revolutionary action and cast collective violence as masculine righteousness.

> He rose for the purpose of declaring his opinion, that if the masters persevered in their list, the consequences would fall on their own heads. He did not mean to say that it was their duty to riot, but he did mean to say, that in all cases, and in all countries, there was an evident boundary, beyond which oppression could not be borne: and when it had reached that point, those who were the cause of that oppression were the first to suffer. He did believe that the masters of Ashton and Stalybridge intended to bring about a revolution; if they did not, they must be mad indeed. It was not for the purpose of effecting a reduction that they put forth the list, but for fear the operatives should have the strength to take possession of their mills. They would prefer their list, even when they knew it would bring distress to the neighborhood. Had the operatives ever attempted to take their mills by storm?—(No, no.) Had they not laboured in them as many hours as were allowed by act of parliament?—(We have.) The masters said they would take possession of the mills. Had the operatives ever been guilty of insubordination?—(No.) Insubordination among the slaves in the West Indies meant, kicking when the master put too heavy a burden on their backs, and he did hope that they would kick most manfully if the burden became too great. He hoped that it would be such kicking as would kick the burden away. (Ibid.)

At the conclusion of Hodgins's speech, a stir came over the crowd as Charles Hindley appeared. The crowded quieted and Hindley, ever the politician, launched into an impassioned self-vindication. "There is not an honest man in the neighborhood who does not wish that masters and workmen may live in harmony with each other, since they must undoubtedly stand or fall together," he proclaimed to the assembly. After detailing his actions as a mediator, he promised, "I will do all in my power to procure a reconsideration of your claims—(cheers)" (*MG*, Dec. 11, 1830; *MM*, Dec. 14, 1830). Having resurrected his honor he took leave: no one could ever accuse Hindley of lacking bravado.[3]

---

[3] Hindley always maintained that "he loved the labouring classes, and his desire was to endeavour to alleviate their sufferings" (*MT*, March 12, 1831). As a self-styled champion of working-class interests he was one of the most active members of the master manufacturers of Manchester, which sought to enforce current legislation on child labour, and he maintained a high profile as a people's advocate for factory legislation (Follows 1951, p. 193). For all his vociferousness, some workers skeptically saw a robber baron draped in the garb of a benevolent prince. Hindley's mill was one of the first to be prosecuted by the factory inspectors for violating child labor laws. He disclaimed responsibility, laying blame on a wayward relative, but suspicions were piqued (Ward 1958, p. 96). The firm of Hindley & Hyde was party to a vicious union-busting campaign in an attempt to break the 1830 Stockport spin-

As twilight descended upon the vast assembly, the proceedings rapidly concluded. The meeting passed a resolution "That the reduction was not necessary, but was the result of restless avarice" (*MM*, Dec. 14, 1830). The band led the way back towards Stalybridge, and as the multitude marched by a mill or cotton lord's house, cries of "Four and twopence, or swing" rose from their midst (ibid.; Hill 1902, p. 69). The cry was clearly a borrowing from the collective violence of rural laborers in the South, who under the mythical guidance of Captain Swing burned thrashing machines that threatened their employment (Hobsbawm and Rudé 1968). Rural laborers had viewed bargaining by riot as a legitimate means of protecting their labor. It was a clarion message for the mill owners, foreshadowing the grim struggle ahead.

The day's fighting words exemplify the discursive repertoire of the spinners' strike. The analogies to both slavery and revolution, the defense of labor as property and of masculine honor, the labor theory of value and the depiction of low piece rates as thievery, and the shaded articulation of violence as just retribution—as we have seen, all these themes were developed in dialogic struggle with the mill owners. These strident assertions provided a compelling rationale for subsequent actions.

Over the next few days, spinners paraded through Ashton and Stalybridge. Scattered acts of window breaking at several mills in response to their premature closure, heightened the authorities' anxieties. The magistrates, lacking a sufficient special constabulary, informed Lieutenant Colonel Shaw on December 6 that military assistance was essential. Bouverie chafed at employing his troops to quell the area, believing them pawns for mill owners so "that they can succeed in reducing the Men to their terms." With the urging of the prime minister, the services of two regiments were reluctantly offered (H.O. 40/26, ff. 170–173, 176–177, 181–182, Melbourne to Foster, Dec. 9, 1830; *WMC*, Dec. 11, 1830). All sides were now fully mobilized. Shopkeepers visited the mill owners the eve of the turnout in the vain hope of an eleventh-hour compromise, but the owners were in no mood for concessions. The walls of Ashton, scrawled with slogans such as "Liberty or Death" and "Four and twopence or swing," presaged the struggle ahead (*MG*, Dec. 11, 1830).

On December 11, two thousand spinners turned out, idling some eighteen thousand other operatives, and affecting some thirty thousand people dependent upon the trade. During the first week, the spinners exhibited an almost military discipline. On December 13, between fifteen hundred and two thousand workers assembled to the call of a bugle in

---

ners' turnout (*MT*, March 13, 1830). Although he preached a strong line on factory reform, some believed that he buckled in the heat of battle. Such actions earned him an unsavory reputation among workers and with the factory reformer Richard Oastler who likened Hindley with the "Devil's Legate" (Ward 1965–1966, p. 193). Betts accused him of being a "modern Janus" during this strike (Hall 1991, p. 106). As we have seen, radicals successfully mobilized against his candidacy for M.P. in 1832.

Ashton's town square and forming a column with a band of music, a tricolor, and banners such as "Liberty or Death," "He that killeth by the sword shall also be killed by the sword," "The labour of the nation is the wealth of the nation," and "Bread or Blood," marched off to Staley Wood to turn out the mill hands. The eclectic slogans exemplify how recognizable fighting words from other major conflicts could be deployed as potent symbols of fundamental conflict. The following day, spinners assembled along the main thoroughfares to cajole the mill owners on their weekly trip to the Manchester Exchange. Wednesday and Friday brought a march to Hyde and Oldham to drum up enthusiasm for their cause. Despite the dark fears of the magistrates, all was peaceable (*WMC*, Dec. 18, 1830; *MM*, Dec. 21, 1830; H.O. 40/26, ff. 131–132, Bouverie to Peel, Dec. 14, 1830; P.C., set 16, v. 2, "Cotton," f. 108).[4]

These initial demonstrations were symbolically important in several respects. First, the massive show of support gave credence to the spinners' claims of fighting a working-class battle against the cotton lords' oppression. Festooned with tricolors and radical banners, this revolutionary imagery provided the trappings of fundamental conflict. Second, the almost universal turn-out signaled both to the fifty-two mill owners and the General Union their determination and organization.[5] The strikers were well studied in their repertoire. Third, the daily parading, in the presence of a weak civil force, symbolically demonstrated the real power in the district. The cotton lords had demarcated the district as their dominion, as they gained effective control of local government and invested ever greater amounts of capital. Yet without violence the spinners had effectively usurped local control, defining the district as their space and demarcated a moral territory of righteous grievance. Finally, since the presence of women is not mentioned by observers (as it generally was in public demonstrations), we can see how these collective actions may well have been a means of asserting masculine honor in the face of wage reductions that threatened the spinners' domestic status (see also Steinberg 1998b).

This symbolism begged a response. The mill owners, fearing the loss of the moral high ground, issued a statement proclaiming their offer to be "a fair average of the price paid in the immediate surrounding districts," open to "public examination" (*MT*, Dec. 18, 1830). The magistrates followed closely on their heels, issuing a strong pronouncement banning all further demonstrations for the sake of the public peace. The following day, a parade of soldiers with heavy artillery, ceremoniously headed by Bouverie and Shaw, marched through Ashton and Stalybridge to symbol-

---

[4] Concurrently the card room hands of the turn-out factories capitalized on events and won a new list of prices and demands, while the silk weavers of Ashton's largest manufacturer, William and Thomas Wanklyn, lost a week-long turn-out over wages (T.L.L.H., Stalybridge Constable's Log Book, Dec. 1830–Jan. 1831, Dec. 16, 1830; *MG*, Dec. 11, 18, 1830).
[5] Workers at Hyde were threatened with dismissal if they were found to be union members (Middleton 1932, pp. 80–81).

ically reclaim the district and disrupt the spinners' smooth-running repertoire. The show of force was lost on many of the spinners, three to four thousand of whom were marching to Glossup to extend the turn-out. The two parties finally faced off in the evening with the spinners' return, as they filed into town singing "Rule Britannia" and letting out occasional shouts of "Liberty or Death." In the spinners' minds, regardless of uniform, there was no question as to who should lay claim to the title of true Britons (H.O. 40/27, ff. 356–359, Astley to Melbourne, Dec. 21, 1830; H.O. 40/26, ff. 225–227, Bouverie to Phillips, Dec. 21, 1830; *MG*, Dec. 18, 1830; *MT*, Dec. 18, 1830).

Seeing both the intransigence of the mill owners and the determination of the spinners, the delegates at a meeting of the General Union in Manchester decided to forge ahead with their own uniform list of piece rates. They unanimously proclaimed that for the good of both fair mill owners and spinners a general strike for all receiving less than 4 shillings tuppence per 1,000 hanks would commence on December 27 (H.O. 40/27, ff. 353–355, Foster to Melbourne, Dec. 18, 1830). To regional authorities, the notice had the resonance of Gabriel's horn, conjuring up nightmarish visions of an impending industrial Armageddon.

The second week of the strike heightened anxieties. Faced with large military forces, the spinners paraded about the towns in small, unarmed groups. A shot fired at parading troops in Stalybridge was the only event that fractured the temporary quiet. During this repose, John Bowring warned the Home Office, "In many districts there is a disposition to violence—that disposition has been checked by the heads of the party—but it is certain that a most inflammatory spirit exists and that proposals have been made for a sudden attack on the military for the purpose of disarming them" (L.C.R.O., DDX/880/1, Bowring to Lamb, Dec. 24, 1830; *MG*, Dec. 25, 1830; H.O. 40/27, ff. 356–359, Astley to Melbourne, Dec. 21, 1830).

It rapidly became clear to all that the call for a general strike was more an act of support than of substance. On December 27, the spinners of twenty mills in Glossup responded along with about a dozen mills in nearby Longendale. A few scattered turn-outs were also reported in Manchester and other towns, but in most areas the call went unheeded (*MT*, Jan. 1, 1831; *MG*, Jan. 1, 1831).

Any hope of victory now rested solely on the shoulders of the spinners in Ashton and Stalybridge, who were approaching a state of severe distress. On the same day as the Glossup turn-out, they received their first payment from the local strike fund. Married spinners were doled 5 shillings and their single counterparts 3, far less than the stated policy of the general union. The vestry had issued an edict that none of the strikers should be issued relief, and the treasury of the N.A.P.L. was too meager to assist. By the end of December, Bowring was reporting that, "Alienation and hatred between the two interests are getting intense—and terror is becoming the weapon both among operatives and their employers" (L.C.R.O., DDX/ 880/2, Bowring to Lamb, Dec. 30, 1830).

With the new year, reality took a wolfish turn upon the mill owners. On the evening of January 3, Thomas Ashton, the eldest son of cotton magnate Samuel Ashton, was assassinated on his way home from the mill. The assailants apparently mistook him for his younger brother, a much-hated manager of the Ashton complex. Invective poured forth from the local papers, accusing the union of masterminding the murder, and calling for a stern response from the authorities. Betts vigorously denied union involvement, and an inquest held several days after the shooting failed to unearth the culprits (*MG*, Jan. 8, 1831; *WMC*, Jan. 8, 1831; *VP*, Jan. 8, 15, 1831).[6] Several days after the murder, a reward of 1,500 pounds and a royal pardon were offered for information leading to the conviction of the assassins. Placards appeared about Ashton with the spinners' contumely response: "Whe don't want £500, whe only want 4s. 2d." (Kirby and Musson 1975, p. 129). A 5-pound reward was also sardonically offered for the murder of the magistrates whose names graced the reward placard (*SA*, Jan. 21, 1831). The budding class hatred noted by Bowring was in full bloom.

Thomas Ashton's murder signaled the increasingly violent turn of the strike. On the following day, five to six hundred spinners attacked Sidebottom's mill in Millbrook. Blacklegs were dragged from the building, and the wages "3s. 9d." were chalked on their backs. The spinners also proceeded to another Sidebottom mill and warned the operatives that the same fate awaited them if they remained (*MT*, Jan. 8, 1831; *MG*, Jan. 8, 1831; T.L.L.H., Stalybridge Constable's Log Book, Dec. 1830–Jan. 1831, Jan. 4, 1831; Cotton 1977, p. 227).

By the end of the week, worried authorities in Manchester convened a meeting of the mill owners to discuss the escalating violence (*MG*, Jan. 15, 1831). The Stalybridge mill owners memorialized the government for strong military intervention. They presented themselves as honorable citizens besieged by a ruthless working-class conspiracy: "That we know the disposition of many of the turn-outs to be for violent and revolutionary measures from the quantity of fire arms they have procured, as also from the menacing language used towards their own employers, and threatening letters received by them" (H.O. 52/13, ff. 231–232, Stalybridge manufacturers to H.O., Jan. 8, 1831).

The spinners too sought assistance from outsiders. Slater of Ashton was

---

[6] Three men were eventually convicted of the murder in the spring of 1834. One who turned king's evidence and was pardoned alleged that a union activist had paid them to commit the murder, but this was never corroborated (Kirby and Musson 1975, pp. 130–131; Middleton 1932, pp. 86–92; *PMG*, Aug. 23, 1834, pp. 228–229, Oct. 25, 1834, p. 300, Nov. 8, 1834, pp. 316–317).

sent on a fund-raising tour of the Midlands. In Manchester, a public meeting was convened on January 8 to rally moral and material support for the beleaguered spinners. Some seven hundred operatives were treated to the same harsh critiques of the mill owners that had launched the contest. John Hynes attacked the factory owners for their cold-blooded attempt to annihilate the union. Betts offered up a lambasting of the cotton lords with his usual panache, accusing them of entering into "a conspiracy against the men" in order to break up the N.A.P.L. (*VP*, Jan. 8, 1831, p. 13). As a result of all these efforts, a small but steady flow of money began to accumulate, although the union's strike fund remained frightfully short. The spinners pressed on, despite disgruntlement with the Manchester leaders, with increasing boldness.

On January 10, a crowd of five to six hundred spinners, many openly armed, marched off to a mill near Glossup for a routine turn-out of blacklegs. The next day, a similar mission of sixty on their way to another nearby mill was intercepted by a large military patrol. Eleven were arrested for riot and tumultuous assembly and bound over for the assizes (*SA*, Jan. 14, 1831).

The increasingly forceful response of the military did not quiet the spinners, although it did seemingly force a modification in strategy. On the twelfth, James Howard of Stalybridge was shot and slightly wounded while in the counting house at his mill (for the spinners no doubt a perfectly ironic venue for the attack). Two days later, a blunderbuss blasted the window of Charles Kershaw's house in Mossley, causing a considerable fright but no injury. That same day, a party of spinners visited the home of William Thornley in Dukinfield, bluntly threatening him that unless they received 4 shillings tuppence, he too would be shot. A shopkeeper in Hyde was mistaken for the much-reviled James Ashton and had a harrowing brush with an assassin's bullet. As with the Ashton murder, a considerable hue and cry was raised and substantial rewards offered, but no assailants were ever identified (*MT*, Jan. 22, 1831; *MG*, Jan. 15, 1831; *SA*, Jan. 21, 1831).

Class tension now enveloped the district like factory smoke. A few outlying mills were turning out, and there seemed to be no quick end to the confrontation. Some mills were arming their blacklegs, determined to prevent further assaults. Reports circulated that Glossup mill owners were considering entering into a similar bond as their Ashton and Stalybridge peers (*SA*, Jan. 21, 1831; *MT*, Jan. 22, 1831).

The local authorities, determined to stamp out these assaults, took action. The deputy-constable of Ashton, Standring, with the assistance of two police officers on loan from Worship St. in London, conducted a late-evening raid of several operatives' houses. Without warrants, they forced their way in, rifling through chests and cupboards in search of arms. For their efforts, they were rewarded with the discovery of several pistols and a tricolored flag (*MT*, Jan. 22, 1831). Several days later, six spinners were committed to the Chester assizes for their part in the earlier assault on the Longendale mills (*MG*, Jan. 22, 1831). For all parties, force and terror were now the ruling order.

With anxiety seizing the district, a last-ditch effort was made at negotiations, with union leaders contacting Charles Hindley. A general meeting of the operatives ratified this willingness for discussion, and the two sides met on January 20 (Kirby and Musson 1975, p. 132). The mill owners maintained an intransigent stand, although they consented to cooperate with the spinners in determining a district average based on the number of spindles worked by each spinner. The spinners roundly refused what they saw as a backhanded tactic, since this would legitimize the discounts on larger mules that so rankled them. They offered instead to abide by an average of the piece rates (*MG*, Jan. 22, 1831; Cotton 1977, p. 229). Having reached an impasse, the two sides separated to plot negotiating strategy. In an effort to salvage the talks, the spinners sent word that they would be willing to accept 4 shillings 1 penny, but this was summarily rejected by the mill owners. In a futile attempt to reach an accord, the spinners bent still further to 4 shillings, but the cotton lords had already silently dispersed.

Contempt and recrimination spewed forth from sympathetic presses of each side. The *Stockport Advertiser*, a paper that took special glee in savaging the spinners' union and Doherty, depicted the strike as a rebellion directed by a cabal that controlled unwitting workers.

> Only one thing is certain, that speedy and decisive measures must be adopted to crush the germ, which, in its full expanse, embraces rebellion, revolution, and treason. A few individuals (how appointed we know not) direct the movements of thousands—*their will is the law of the multitude*—the price, the time, the *when and how they shall work*, is decided by this junta of import. . . . [T]hat a whole district should be kept in a state of commotion by the orders of such men, is really too bad; and if the law as it now stands cannot prevent this, a fresh law is called for. (*SA*, Jan. 21, 1831)

In turn, Doherty in the *Voice of the People*, fired an acrimonious salvo, accusing mill owners of deceitful grandstanding to win public sympathy. He articulated the familiar theme from the discursive repertoire of the defense of the workers' property:

> They had an object, however, to attain; and that object was to appear well with the public. They felt that their attempted reduction was a dirty affair. They knew that, unless they could cheat the public into a belief that they were acting with some degree of fairness, they would be viewed as a set of greedy, unfeeling, and unprincipled fellows, who wished to wring the last farthing, which could possibly be extorted from the incessant toil of their exhausted and unhappy workmen, to add to their already great gains. . . . Gold

> is the god of its idolatry. In its eye, the rich man, do what he will, cannot be wrong, while the poor man can do nothing right. . . . The workman's property, and his rights too, are subservient to the pride and prodigality of his employer. In fact, as a workman, he is considered to have no rights whatever, but such as the master may generously cede to him. (*VP*, Jan. 29, 1831, p. 36)

As the fighting words flowed, the turn-out dragged on. The spinners enjoyed a brief hopeful moment when a few mills agreed to reopen at 4 shillings 1 penny, contingent on the outcome of the contest. As spinners relished this small victory, however, the turn-out in Glossup was collapsing. Meanwhile, the local authorities continued to press. Nine spinners were brought before Derbyshire magistrates on the capital offense of attacking machinery for the mill assault on January 10. The spinners were clearly besieged on all sides (*SA*, Jan. 28, 1831; *MG*, Jan. 29, 1831).

At the start of February, a confident group of fifty-two mill owners met. With the turn-out crumbling around the edges, they sensed victory. They announced that the mills would re-open on February 3 under their proposed list (*SA*, Feb. 4, 1831; *WMC*, Feb. 5, 1831; *MG*, Feb. 5, 1831). The union attempted to put a heartening face on the imminent defeat and urged the spinners to maintain the spirit of the struggle. The *Voice of the People* cheerfully announced that several mills had returned at full price and others at a fraction below: a speedy settlement was finally possible (*VP*, Feb. 5, 1831, p. 44). In reality, this was a wishful bit of fantasy.

By the end of the first week of the re-opening, all but a few Stalybridge mills were once again abuzz, and twelve mills in Ashton were busily at work. Some mills accepted back old hands, but others opened only to those without strike connections. A few firms, such as Hindley & Hyde, had great difficulty in obtaining a sufficient workforce during the first weeks of the re-opening, but they too eventually returned to full production (*SA*, Feb. 14, 1831; *WMC*, Feb. 15, 1831; *MT*, Feb. 19, 26, 1831; *MG*, Feb. 12, 19, 1831). On February 19, the *Voice of the People* unassumingly printed the obituary of the once robust contest, noting in a somber tone: "A number of hands have been thrown out of employment, and left martyrs of their laudable determination not to submit willingly to an unprincipled spoliation of their industry. We hope the situation of those deserving men will not escape the attention of those who have so generously assisted them during the contest" (p. 61).

The masters showed little grace in victory. Reports circulated that at least one mill in Stalybridge was fining its spinners 30 shillings for their strike participation. Even more disparaging for the hapless losers, the mill owners established a blacklist that contained perhaps three hundred names. There was brief, wistful talk of establishing a co-operative mill to support the banned. A fund was established to underwrite their emigration to America, and by the end of April twenty spinners had in fact crossed the Atlantic (*MT*, Feb. 12, 26, April 23, 1831; *MG*, April 23, 1831;

VP, Feb. 12, 1831, March 5, 1831, p. 75). For the rest, however, the future portended nothing but a threadbare existence. Doherty, commenting on the blacklisting observed that "there is a new process of putting men to death, that is depriving them of all means of subsistence" (*VP*, v. 2, July 2, 1831, p. 1).

By the end of February, the cotton lords rested triumphantly in the unquestioned seat of authority. The heated battles of the turn-out were over. Disgruntled spinners subsequently left the union, believing that the central committee in Manchester had failed to deliver expected support (Kirby and Musson 1975, p. 138). Reflecting on the strike some months later, Doherty found a morsel of ironic solace in the outcome and the behavior of the cotton lords: "They rushed to combat—they fought—they conquered; and, like barbarians, they gave no quarter, at least history records the fact" (*VP*, v. 2, July 2, 1831, p. 1). In the silence of their defeat, the spinners no doubt sullenly concurred.

In both the daily routines and extraordinary events of the district in the early nineteenth century, class was very much about. Class palpably manifested itself in the molding of town and village environs, in the sharp bifurcation of their populations, in the circulation of living and stored labor, and in the distinctive cultures of workers and capitalists. In polity and politics, class left unquestionably clear who held the power of the vestry and the bench.

In Ashton and Stalybridge, Dukinfield and Mossley, Glossup and Mottram, class happened in life-defining ways. For the spinners particularly, the happenings of class created a crisis by the later 1820s. The possibility of the mill owners' wresting control of their station of male privilege in the mill, the looming degradation of their trade and economic security, and the assaults on their union threatened a carefully constructed way of life and gendered identity. The spinners had carved out a niche of a skilled male bread-winner in an industrial environment increasingly defined by female and child labor. Through their control over the spinning room and comparatively high wages, they had fashioned some sense of just recompense for their labor and an identity as family providers. By dint of law and economic muscle, mill owners threatened to denude them of independence, power, and dignity and to emasculate their work culture.

This continual class jostling reached a peak in the great turn-out of 1830–1831. A surface reading of the contest marks it as a struggle over wages or perhaps as a strike entangled in the radical politics of the time. A more extensive analysis, however, particularly through its fighting words, reveals it to have been an affray over fundamental issues of social justice, broadly supported by the working people of the district. The workers' central goals were to stem the tide of degradation, preserve their rights as the sole producers of wealth, and to face down the increasing tyranny of the cotton lords. These concerns were deeply rooted in the spinners' fighting words, fashioned through available discourses, which critiqued the forces of oppression that they saw arrayed against them. Their discourses represented their own type of the Liberty Tree nurtured in local soil. Its branches contained graftings of radical republican politics and a radical economics, and they had broadened its branches over decades of struggle.

The endurance of the spinners over two months in the dead of winter, lacking sufficient funds and facing increasing repression, cannot be explained solely by the organizational cohesion of their ranks and of their communities. Nor can their use of violence against ignominious mill owners be construed as acts of frustration or calculated desperation. A contextual reading of the spinners' discursive repertoire reveals the larger logic of their contest, the moral bases for their cohesion and the principled foundations upon which violence was justified.

The spinners' discursive repertoire unquestionably demarcated these concerns as the nexus of the fight. The issues were framed in terms of inherent rights and basic social equity. Four shillings tuppence was the symbolic condensation of these quintessential rights, not the sole goal. Both factory owners and spinners shared this fundamental understanding, as must we if we are to wholly understand the course of the conflict.

Ultimately, the source of the spinners' defeat was located in the very imbalance of power that they tenaciously fought to redress. It too was certainly part of the happening of class. The mill owners' wealth and the military's might proved to be a powerful twin phalanx, and indeed spinners' fighting words reveal their own troubled recognition of it. But these fighting words also suggested that to accept such odds was indeed the only chance they had for shifting the balance in the long term. To do any less would have been to succumb to perpetual tyranny, to void their abiding vision of a justly constituted society, and to sink into the smoke and oil-stained abyss of slavish emasculated automatons. Surely, in the smoke-shrouded light of the early morning on February 5, 1831, class was plainly visible to the spinners, even if it is obscured to some who now write their history.

> But the sun itself, however beneficent generally, was less kind to Coketown than hard frost, and rarely looked intently into any of its regions without engendering more death than life. So does the eye of Heaven itself become an evil eye, when incapable or sordid hands are interposed between it and things it looks upon to bless. (Dickens, *Hard Times*)

CONCLUSION

CHAPTER TWELVE

Class Formation, Collective Action, and the Role of Discourse

*D*uring this investigation, our analytic ambling has been much like that of a contemporary popular radical making a circuit tour of the English populace. We have trod the packed streets of London's Spitalfields district, through silk weavers' enclaves scourged by distress. We have hiked through the Lancashire Pennines and into the smoke-infused towns along the river Tame, past rows of factory cottages and the six-story monuments to an emerging industrial society. Much like the political itinerant, we have witnessed the considerable happenings of class and the conflicts that gave rise to it.

The purposes of this journey have been those of both affirmation and amendment. I have argued that despite recent critiques from the linguistic turn, theories of historical class formation and of political process and resource mobilization provide essential windows on fundamental processes that have been and continue to be part of great transformations in the modern world. I have also maintained, however, that the critics raise compelling issues concerning the centrality of discourse in class formation and collective action. Although rejecting the linguistic turn's alternatives, I have proposed revising Thompson's perspective on class and the political process/resource-mobilization model of contentious action with discourse as a critical intervening process. Rather than choose between material and discursive analyses, we need to conjoin the explanatory powers that each perspective offers.

The cases of the Spitalfields silk weavers and Ashton district cotton spinners have offered two case studies in how material and discursive processes are intimately bound together in the processes of class, collective action, and gender relations. In picking two examples that offer a series of contrasts in terms of the organization of production, polity, and public life, I have demonstrated how these distinctive configurations reveal common underlying processes. In addition, through these cases I have detailed how common processes of class formation and collective action do yield distinctive outcomes, because of the uniqueness of the conditions in each case. Finally, these studies have explicated how discourse bounded the ways in which the material conditions of social, economic, and political life could be made intelligible and acted upon by working people.

In this conclusion, I return to these principal theoretical concerns by way of reviewing the findings of the case studies. I first address issues of class formation and then discuss revisions in the analysis of collection action.

Talking Class: Class Formation and the Role of Discourse

Over twenty-five years ago, E. P. Thompson observed that "sociologists who have stopped the time-machine, and with a great deal of conceptual huffing and puffing, have gone down into the engine-room to look, tell us that nowhere at all have they been able to locate and classify class. They can only find a multitude of people with different occupations, incomes, status hierarchies and the rest. Of course they are right, since class is not this or that part of the machine, but the way the machine works once it is put in motion—not this interest and that interest, but the friction of interests—the movement itself, the heat, the thundering noise . . . class itself is not a thing, it is a happening" ([1965] 1978, p. 295). A remarkably similar denial of class has been reborn in the historical revisionism of the linguistic turn. Recently, historians and sociologists have dug about in the history of nineteenth-century England and found a curious absence of class consciousness and struggle. They have unearthed trade consciousness, political populism and melodrama, reformism, and (now and again) industrial conflict. In the process, they have concluded that class-conscious working people, however, are phantoms of a predisposed historical imagination. There were no self-conscious pronouncements concerning the overthrow of the capitalist system among these working people, and no constellation of meanings constituting working people as the cohesive destined agents of a new antithetical order.

Of course they are right, since class consciousness is not represented through this discourse or that, but through the friction of discourses produced in struggle, the "thundering noise" as Thompson so aptly described it. We cannot so easily separate class from the political or the popular, because the friction as often as not happens within dominant formations rather than as some opposing force from outside. The messy realities of collective life rarely if ever neatly circumscribe and demarcate such frictions into tidy packages of politics and economics. Rather, they kinetically spark intermittently in arenas of conflict, which often cross-cut the two as groups experience opposition.

Nonetheless, discourse is a critical part of the open-ended process of working-class formation because within and through it working people create and share the commonalties of their experiences of inequality in their relations with other groups in particular places and times. English working people frequently struggled within the limitations imposed by a dominant discursive formation to expose the class-interested foundations of what was presented as a natural narrative of their world (Somers 1994a,b). In the process of questioning, appropriating, and reframing meaning within this hegemonic system, they fashioned a moral critique of their oppression and exploitation, a collective identity as an aggrieved group with opposing interests, and a vision of a more just social order, a culture of solidarity.[1] Discourse mediated between the experiences imposed by a shared material existence and the cultures of solidarity that manifested class consciousness. It thus both bounded the potential for working-class formation and provided opportunities for agency within these imposed constraints.

In this sense, Thompson's critics within the linguistic turn have perceptively argued that he failed to theorize adequately how the particular experiences of class led to a more general working-class culture. What they have not appreciated is that dialogic theory provides the analytic tools for bringing discourse explicitly into class-formation analysis. It allows us to strengthen Thompson's understanding of how the ever-closer engagement of classes in struggle involved conflict within moral language. It also empowers us to detail how working people constructed a class consciousness from their local experiences and collective memories of struggles. For while their conflicts germinated in concrete relationships of employment, the parish, the household, popular culture, and the law, the dialogues of conflict stretched far beyond their immediate territory. Discourse, although embedded in the daily patterns of social life, was neither simply born of nor constrained by local culture. The language of power can never be just local. Dominant discursive formations legitimize control, normalize inequality, and justify the oppression necessary for their maintenance through general narratives that naturalize these conditions (Ewick and

---

[1] As Margaret Somers argues from a narrative perspective on class identity, "the language of rights embraced both politics and class; it was the explanatory prism through which class issues and other aspects of social distress were mediated and made sense of" (Somers 1992, p. 613).

Silbey 1995, pp. 211–214).[2] Rulers achieve hegemony when they speak an encompassing monologue of possibilities.

Mill owners, silk warehousers, members of Parliament, and bourgeois scribes sought to create such a monologue through the discourses of political economy, Whiggish nationalism, Christian (and often Dissenting) pietism, and liberal democracy. Their narratives were particular to their aspirations and struggles, but their attempts at hegemony through this dominant discursive formation linked these local affairs to national processes. These capitalists and their allies did not engage in this process in a cynical, calculating, or even wholly conscious manner. They were privileged people, but not positioned beyond the limitations discourse imposes on all actors: discourse does not mediate between consciousness and experience selectively.

Working people, through the production of their fighting words, thus in turn dialogically produced responses that were part local and part national. The cultural processes of class struggle and thus of class formation surpassed the confines of their immediate circumstances precisely because the discourses of contention always spoke beyond them. Contrary to Calhoun's conclusions, then, this perspective shows us that class formation and consciousness are simultaneously local and national. Working people are no less involved in the process of class if they are not nationally organized, for in local struggles they are still talking back. In this back talk, the particular ways in which they struggle can take shape in more shared concerns, larger mutual understandings, and a greater consciousness. This consciousness in turn provides a window on the processes of capitalist transformation and state building, which many historians and sociologists argue are hallmarks of nineteenth-century working-class formation. At the same time, this discourse projects onto working men and women gendered meanings that deeply inform their relations with one another and their actions against those they see as the oppressors.

In the case studies of the weavers and the spinners, we saw how the material processes of class formation and discursive struggles conjointly produced both these particular, conjunctural outcomes along with a greater class consciousness. Both the weavers and spinners faced threats from their employers to their economic and social security, and developed discursive repertoires that spoke clearly and passionately of their exploitation and oppression. Starting in the early 1820s, the weavers confronted a determined and increasingly powerful coalition of large manufacturers, members of Parliament, and political economists—a wrecking crew of their tenuous security and community status. The process of dismantling

---

[2] As Ewick and Silbey note, hegemony is often achieved by a discourse's capacity to maintain a local vision of power: "Insofar as particular and subjective narratives reinforce a view of the world made up of autonomous individuals interacting only in immediate and local ways, they hobble collective claims and solutions to inequality" (1995, p. 217).

their modest insurance against degradation occurred on many fronts. The most visible and fearsome was the repeal of the Spitalfields Acts, the legal moorings that preserved the weavers' way of life. But the web of relations that supported it was also woven deep in the community, in their symbiotic relations with petty-bourgeois parish vestry officials, and cultivation of respect from other local authorities, who recognized the weavers as generally peaceable. Under the Acts, male weavers affirmed their independent role as masters of a workshop and could harbor, however wishfully, some hopes of becoming a small master. Internal trade divisions and the importance of fancy goods signaled the skill and independence that made possible these dreams and the characterization of silk weaving as an honorable trade. Their history of trade societies kept alive this sense of solidarity and provided the organization necessary for mobilization.

In their battle against repeal and their subsequent campaigns for protection and to halt the hemorrhaging of piece rates, the weavers exemplify the particulars and generalities of the class formation process. Their struggle to preserve the Spitalfields Acts and their subsequent focus on protection colored their experiences of degradation with a distinctive hue. These experiences led the weavers to understand their plight and its resolution partly in terms of a balancing of interests by and in the polity. Yet at the same time the silk weavers recognized that their degradation was only one swatch of a much larger cloth and that the rise of large capital, free markets, and the internationalization of trade affected working people throughout the country.

Their struggles from the start were not simple reactions to these institutional transformations, but were always mediated by discursive repertoires. In particular, the weavers articulated concepts of rights, justice and citizenship, trade and production, male authority, and a collective identity as working people in a dialogic conflict with the discourse of political economy. Their fighting words crystallized around a labor theory of value, a moral argument for the protection of labor as property, and a concept of citizenship rights as wealth producers. Positioning themselves within and against the dominant formation, the weavers also creatively appropriated liberal political theory and Christian morality into their discursive repertoire. Through these fighting words, they sought to expose the partial and class-interested nature of the discourse used to champion free trade in the name of freedom and prosperity. In these ongoing struggles, the silk weavers' consciousness stretched beyond the confines of their enclave, encompassing a vision of how working people in diverse trades were threatened by the gnawing consumption of exploitation and degradation and ultimately by impoverishment for the riches of a few.

The particulars of the cotton spinners' plight distinguish their conflicts from the weavers in terms of the organization of trade and production, power and authority in the parish and town, historical bases and the role of the state. Yet beneath these differences we saw the bridging generalities of class formation. Spinners were an elite male enclave in factory production, but their claims to privilege never rested secure. In the 1820s, the intensification of the labor process, a growing reserve army of labor and the specter of replacement by women, their underling piecers, and fully automated spinning mules all loomed as menaces to their control, relative affluence, and status as male breadwinners. The spinners faced off against mill owners, who had sunk great sums of capital, caught in the shifting forces of vast markets. The imperatives of control on both sides fostered increasing divisiveness that punctuated the industry with high-profile conflicts.

The cotton spinners lived these large shifts and conflicts, but did so in a corner of Lancashire within their communities. In the political order of their towns, the control mill owners sought over the workers' leisure and cultural lives, the often fractious divisions of national politics, and the material manifestations of wealth etched into their landscape, the spinners experienced the echoes of class fissure. The reverberations of these echoes produced a cohesive and insular culture among working people of the district, uniting the spinners with their less privileged factory compatriots in both symbolic and real politics against the mill owners. Across the district in late 1820s, class tensions percolated in a series of contests between spinners and mill owners, culminating in the massive contest in the gray winter of 1830–1831.

The spinners structured an encompassing understanding of these experiences and a vision of a just world through a fusion of radical economic and political discourses. Pitted against a dominant formation anchored in the discourse of political economy, the spinners, much like the silk weavers, dialogically produced a concept of their position through a labor theory of value. Starting from that supposition, they constructed a collective vision of the factory system in which operatives were the chattel of cotton lords and capitalists. Capital was illegitimately accumulated wealth produced by wage slaves, who were given less respect and attention than the machines to which they were tethered. Inside the factory, the cotton lord was "legislator, judge, jury, and executioner", while outside he was allied to others "in the holy combination of Masters" to construct a monolithic system of exploitation and despotism. The mill owners' power was metaphorically conceptualized through a discourse of popular political radicalism, which cast the mill owners as an imperious and corrupt ruling order that denied fundamental rights. In the mobilizations and strikes of 1830–1831, the spinners creatively incorporated the symbols and slogans of revolt to frame the justice of their cause and the necessity of their actions.

Both the silk weavers and the cotton spinners thus faced the exigencies of capitalist transformation that, as we noted, unevenly but broadly threatened many groups of working people in these decades. Parallel experiences however are not themselves sufficient for the germination of class consciousness. For these and other working people, what marked the commonalty of their struggles as exemplary of class conflict were the cultural ways in which these experiences could be shared. If the union leaders of the weavers and spinners, William Hunter and J. J. Betts, had shared a few pints in the Crown and Anchor they would have had much to discuss, and a bridgeable set of discourses by which they could do so. Both had conceptions about how labor was the origin of wealth and about how that wealth was robbed from the worker; both had understandings of labor as the workers' property; both maintained that the economic system was fundamentally misaligned in the interests of wealth and power; both articulated beliefs in the fundamental rights of the laboring classes; both provided compelling arguments for why determined collective action was necessary to rectify their penury and misery. And though it may have taken a few pints, I am confident that in their respective discourses there was plenty of foundation for mutual understanding: such was the nature of their class consciousness.

Experience never comes in neat analytic packages, and as workers faced the vagaries of class they were also deeply intertwined with gender processes. We have seen how class conflict threatened systems of patriarchal workplace and household order for both the male silk weavers and cotton spinners. The degradation of weaving eroded the status of male weavers in the workshop and household, as they progressively lost their grip on an independent base of production, which undercut their stature. In the spinning room, the potential employment of women and piecers and the deskilling of the spinning process through automation were direct affronts to patriarchal independence and control. Moreover, as one of the few groups of factory workers earning sufficient wages to assume the status of a male breadwinner, the downward pressure on piece rates threatened their household authority.

Women in both trades and communities allied with these male workers because the bonds of class, household, and community partly mitigated these divisions of gender. They appeared in public rallies and marches as stalwart defenders of the rights articulated by their male compatriots. As Anna Clark (1995) argues, the pragmatics of survival were compelling reasons for common cause. But bonds of unity and demarcations of differences were also products of the discursive contention fashioned in the trials with mill owners and warehousers. The gendering in political economy discourse thus called forth and explicitly configured a masculine discursive response that paralleled the implicit presumptions of masculine independence imbedded in liberal social-contract theory. In addition, the rising discourse of separate spheres within the middle class provided a cogent logic for the maintenance of piece rates and the concept of a living wages. Class struggle was thus a catalyst in solidifying a model in which men were the active claimants of citizenship rights on behalf of their households and women were the moral supporters of their efforts as defined by their domestic responsibilities. If, as Clark argues, the concept of the male breadwinner surfaces as part of the articulated rationale for wage demands in the late 1820s, then we can find its origins in the intersection of these threats to class and gender position. As the history of working people demonstrates for subsequent decades, this emergent model was to resound in the reconfigured marginalization of women both in the household and the public sphere.

Collective Action and the Role of Discourse

The struggles of the Spitalfields weavers and Ashton district cotton spinners also demonstrate the ways in which discourse critically mediates the processes of mobilization and contentious action. A group's sense of agency, its members' shared consciousness of the moral precepts that justify their actions, and their vision of a desired future are all constructed through the fighting words that accompany their repertoire of instrumental action. A dialogic analysis of ideology, identity, and interest demonstrates how contests over social meaning are both part of the struggle and a power dynamic that shapes other aspects of conflict. Aggrieved groups must develop a shared understanding of injustice to legitimize their claims, interests, and actions. Such understandings are nested in discursive repertoires that are themselves produced in sustained interactions between powerholders and subordinates. Situated in the give and take of regularized interactions, and subject to powerholders' hegemony, subordinates construct ways of articulating their claims against the powerful and reasons for surmounting their dictates. They do so within specific discursive formations that provide the materiel for the fight. Repertoires always bear the marks of hegemony, with the meanings produced within them being dominated by powerholders. Conversely, because of the multivocality of language, hegemonic formations are always prey to resistance and appropriation. A dialogic perspective suggests that a challenging group's discursive repertoire is significantly produced by reacting to and appropriating powerholders' discourse, creating the ideological legitimacy necessary for legitimating interests and action. Discursive and instrumental action repertoires are recursively linked, and over the course of conflict, they can create a sustaining system of action and legitimation. But discourse imposes limits as well; for in providing intelligibility and justification, it also fixes the ways in which people can construct their claims and the calculus they use to seek redress.

Discursive repertoires make collectively interpretable the identities and interests upon which contention is founded. Groups do not simply enter a social situation, confront the deliberations and vagaries of power, and realize their interests. Rather, a group fashions a repertoire of fighting words through which they analyze the nature of the inequality they confront, the collective disadvantages that accrue to them because of this, and what they can and should demand to change their collective condition. Through their discursive repertoires challenging groups link contemporary experiences and struggles to a usable past, creating larger historical narratives for immediate claims. Partly, this construction process is conducted during consensus mobilization; partly it takes place within the dynamics of sustained contention itself. Partly anchored in past usage, partly keyed to situational struggle, and partly cobbled together from different genres, these repertoires are more aptly depicted as loosely coupled ensembles than as frames (Steinberg 1998a). Such links between situated action and enduring formations also provide a unique window on the relationship between the macro and micro dynamics of collective contention. We can follow how larger systems of meaning are put in motion and are sometimes transformed in local contexts; and how these local uses potentially reflect back on these systems as they are collectively reassembled in national and regional formations.

The weavers' and spinners' development of discursive repertoires illustrates these processes. We have seen how these groups discursively constructed interests in this process of resistance and counterhegemony, and the way in which the process shaped the course of conflict. As the 1820s gradually shaded into the 1830s, the discourse of political economy had become the predominant discourse of economic power. Political economy was not gospel, but its ascendancy within the halls of power and the mainstream press provided its users the opportunity to define issues of economy and polity. To discuss any matter of trade and industry was to react to the theory of political economy, and both the weavers and spinners did so with concerted effort.

The weavers sought to legitimize their claims by appropriating and transforming concepts of property, freedom, rights, and the national good. Although certainly predicated on discourses produced by both their indigenous community and by London's artisans more generally in preceding generations, their repertoire was nonetheless developed in reaction to the onslaught of the warehousers and free traders. Large capitalists and their political allies depicted a natural fissure between economy and polity; they defined rights and freedoms from the perspective of an atomized economic actor and property owner; they discussed labor and property as equivalent commodities in the great motions of commerce; and they measured the common good through aggregate economic indicators. The silk weavers and their sympathizers responded with fighting words, emphasizing a labor theory of value, an understanding of freedom based in communal and group rights of wealth producers, a conception of state regulation emphasizing legal reins on market optimization, and a notion of the common good that placed a premium on an equitable distribution of wealth for the continued expansion of the national economy.

Through the development of this repertoire, the silk weavers articulated an abiding sense of injustice, legitimizing both the state and the manufacturers as targets of redress, and providing, as Somers argues, a narrative for their continuing collective actions. They produced this discursive repertoire within a web of relations that gave its meaning a quotidian substance that was verified by their experiences with small masters, shopkeepers, and (more unsteadily) the local magistrates. National formations and local processes conjoined to infuse discourse with meaning. Over the course of their prolonged struggles, oscillating between the state and capital, their discursive and instrumental repertoires were mutually reinforcing. Ultimately, we can fully comprehend the purposiveness behind the contrapuntal patterning of their actions, and their sustained efforts to realize a set of well-articulated interests in the face of repeated defeats, only if we understand the justifying role of their fighting words.

The Ashton district cotton spinners also found themselves squaring off against champions of political economy. By the 1820s, the mill owners' self-confident prognostications depicted an economic order that was to capture the globe. It was an order in which factory workers benefited from the power and wealth of their employers, free-flowing capital gave life and purpose to labor, mill owner and machinery exercised efficiency and beneficence in organizing factory work, and the workers' economic well-being was wedded to the fortunes of these profit generators. The spinners, embroiled in a deepening battle over work control, responded with a discursive repertoire spun with radical political critiques of power. Through their dialogic response, the spinners described an economic system in which value was based on their sweat and that of their fellow workers, cotton lords were unproductive leeches on their labor, machinery and factory discipline became tools to enslave and rob them, and cotton lords conspired to create an empire of greed, sparing none in their efforts. Revolutionary metaphors from the radical republicanism fostered in their ranks provided a vocabulary and symbolism to frame mill owners as despots. This discursive repertoire reflected both the heated battles over control between the spinners' union and the mill owners in the 1820s, and the frictions of class within these communities. It too exemplifies how regional and national struggles conjoin with the particularly local to vivify discourse.

As with the weavers, the exigencies of the spinners' material circumstances conjoined with the discourses of contention to shape their purposiveness. Gazing beyond the imposing forms of the factory to the mansions above, encountering the legal logic of local order, watching the town being transformed by the logic of compulsive accumulation, the district's spinners everywhere experienced an imposed world of bourgeois facts. And in the end, to comprehend why, in the dead of winter and tight economic circumstances, twenty thousand workers marched out of the factory gates with tricolors flying to challenge the power of the cotton lords, we must both critically examine material forms of exploitation and listen to their collective voice.

The processes by which both the weavers and the spinners constructed their discursive repertoires provide exemplary detail for the theoretical cases I have made concerning counterhegemony and resistance. In both cases, these workers bored from within as much as they attacked from without. Conceptions of freedom and the value of labor were turned about and made weapons of the weak. In workers' hands, the sacrosanct status of property justified and ennobled their fierce protection of their labor. Adam Smith and the Bible gave their imprimaturs for a "living" wage. The boundaries of the dominant formations limited opportunities for resistance and channeled counterhegemonic strategies. They did not mandate content or meaning, however, nor did they constitute the workers as resisters. For the weavers and the spinners, fighting words were imbricated in their social and material lives rather than serving as impresarios.

I also have argued that challenging groups construct a collective identity providing a license for legitimate action. Such identities not only mark a group's status within a social structure and patterned past, they also assert a bundle of rights, the bases for internal solidarity, a recognized history, and the potential rationale for support by outsiders. These collective identities are the adversarial "we" of claims and actions, the bedrock of collective resistance. They derive from positions in the social structure and collective experiences, but are never their simple reductive products. As all else that is performative in contention, identities are the conjoined product of discourse and material experience, a relational and sometimes unstable product of contention (J. Gamson, 1995; Valverde 1991).

In both cases, identities were negotiated in relation to others—manufacturers, Parliament, overlookers, magistrates, parish officers, charity workers, troops, and other trades—and the outcomes were cultures of solidarity that helped sustain collective action. The silk weavers fashioned themselves productive citizens, creating a socio-political status in the polity and community by which they laid claim to protection. They structured a collective identity as honorable artisans and wealth producers, rate-payers, and loyal defenders of the empire; and each facet added currency to their status as claimants on both the state and the manufacturers. While large portions of the weavers were not far above simple shuttle cock throwers, and many were women and children, the identity the male weavers constructed was one of a respectable artisanate, whose skill and craft set them beside London's finer trade brethren and made them authorities in household and workshop. This identity was both articulated and enacted in their parish relations and was essential in mobilizing potential supporters in their political battles for protection. Moreover, it helped sustain a protracted series of campaigns for trade protection and wage increases in the face of increasing impoverishment, growing dispersion within the district, and even the occasional disapprobation of other workers for impolitic actions in the name of protectionism.

The cotton spinners made few such claims to being members of a trade elite. Instead, they painted a collective portrait of themselves as part of an exploited class, reduced by capitalists and their system to little more than wage slaves. Indeed, part of their collective identity was in the absence of their self-constitution. They were unfree men, tethered to the imperious dictates of machines and mill managers, and to wages too meager for an honorable man to support his family. Such freedom could only be won through the collective exercise of combination. Moreover, this collective identity dovetailed with the radical politics favored by many spinners, allowing for the incorporation of some of its discourse in their repertoire. Vassals overthrew despots, and the force of tyranny had to be answered by the cry of liberty or death. In Ashton and Stalybridge, factory workers built this rebellious identity with sturdy materials, ones that left it standing quite serviceable for the Chartist cause in the late 1830s and 1840s.

In the articulation of identities and the rights they foster—at the conjoining of fighting words, contentious action and social structure—we can see how the situationally-expressed meets the durable and the national finds expression in the local. In each discursive repertoire, we find a dynamic, although enduring, conceptualization of rights, duties, obligations, and statuses held by each group. These understandings were anchored in experiences of past struggle, the friction of conflict produced by hierarchy and division, and the enactment of power. Discursive repertoires translated durable interests into usable cultural constructions—narratives of rights, principles, matters of justice and equity—and in so doing made the durable a palpable collective reality upon which to be acted. The silk weavers and cotton spinners never fought simply for pounds and pence, nor for some abstract class power or location. Their collective visions of interests always captured the past and projected the future.

In sum, the analysis of fighting words helps to provide a more extensive purposive account of collective contentious action. Discourse mediates the processes of mobilization and action by bounding the ways in which challenging groups can formulate, share, and articulate their collective identities and interests. Fighting words are a vehicle of power to the extent that they both facilitate and inhibit ideologies that provide efficacy, identities that solidify a sense of agency, and interests that are nested in larger moral visions of rights and justice. Ultimately, however, this power is tied to their use in concrete social situations, to ossified remains of past actions, and to the challengers who pursue change or power-holders intent on suppressing it. Fighting words are necessary for conflict but they are not sufficient; for it is people who make the cause and not the words themselves.

Final Thoughts

The focus of many scholars in recent years has been on the uneasy and often conflicting analytical balance between materialist and discursive processes. In this book, I have argued for a slightly different course from what is often articulated, one that refuses to give up on the materialist perspective, but fully acknowledges the quintessential role of discourse to which those in the linguistic turn and new social movement perspective have alerted us. I have argued for a more relational approach, one that focuses on group action embedded in networks of larger interactions, and views the material and the discursive, the cultural and the structural as mutually constitutive processes and products (Emirbayer 1997; Somers 1994b; Tilly 1995). I have sought to demonstrate that the weavers and spinners were neither the simple constructs of their and others' discourses, nor were they reactors to an obvious set of oppressive and compelling conditions. They were neither symbols, nor automatons, but people. They faced life conditions whose origins reached far beyond their words for describing them, yet they needed those words to make sense of their lives. This took place in the fusion of the material and discursive, the dynamic give and take of material realities and symbolic processes, in which the problematics of life arose and were confronted. People live their lives in the intersection of these processes, and in these junctures we find them facing both constraints and opportunities in the thick of their own making. We are always, as Thompson maintained, part victims and part agents. If we wish to wholly understand how and why people find their lives sculpted into durable collective structures, how they make sense of these contours and morally define the curves of their existence, and how occasionally with great purpose they act to refashion the lines of both the present and future, then this is precisely where our analyses should focus as well. To reach back into these histories is to understand how both processes and people conjoin, and how in this conjoining social change is born.

APPENDIX ONE

Spitalfields weavers' collective actions, c. 1825–1831

Date	Action	Target	Goal
1825			
July 20	General meeting of broad silk weavers	Government	Prevention of re-enactment of Combination Laws
Sept. 30	General meeting	Weavers	Formation of Weavers' Society
Oct. 9	General meeting	Government	Import protection
Dec. 18	General meeting	Government	Import protection
Winter	Shop strikes against reducing masters	Masters	Prevention of wage reductions
1826			
Early Jan.	Weavers' committee meets with ministers to discuss imports threats	Government	Import protection
Jan. 12	Memorialize government to reconsider import protection	Government	Import protection
Jan. 27	Presentation of memorial to Board of Trade	Government	Import protection
Jan. 27	Meeting of engine silk weavers	Masters	Wage reductions
Jan. 31	Meeting of engine weavers to discuss proposed reductions	Masters	Wage reductions
Feb. 20	Meeting to petition Parliament	Government	Import protection
April 6	Reaffirmation of weavers' committee lobbying efforts	Government	Import protection

Date	Action	Target	Goal
May	Organization of General Protection Society to create strike fund	Masters, weavers	Prevention of wage reductions
June 12	General meeting	Weavers, masters	Formation of Protection Society; prevention of wage reductions
July 24	Election of committee to negotiate wages	Masters	Wage stabilization
Aug. 14	Meeting with masters on piece rates	Masters	Prevention of wage reductions
Aug. 29	Meeting to discuss negotiations with masters and petition for royal patronage	Masters, royal family	Prevention of wage reductions
Oct. 4	Petitioning of royal family	Royal family	Promotion of consumption of domestic silk
Oct. 19	Delivery of petition to king by delegation	King	Patronage
Oct. 23	Meeting of General Protection Society	Masters	Prevention of wage reductions
Oct. 30	Meeting of General Protection Society	Masters	Prevention of wage reductions
Dec.	Organizing of ribbon weavers' co-operative	Weavers	Employment and stability
Feb.	Mobilization for the General Association of Trades	Weavers, government	Law for wage arbitration and stabilization
March 20	Meeting to petition for wage protection	Government	Wage protection
March 25	General strike	Masters	Prevention of wage reductions
March 26	Processions to request wage increases	Masters	Wage increases
March 27	Processions to request wage increases	Masters	Wage increases
March 28	Processions to request wage increases	Masters	Wage increases
March 31	Meeting to discuss masters' responses	Masters	Wage increases
April 2	Meeting to discuss strike settlement	Masters	Price list agreement
May	Opening of National Silk Weavers' Society	Weavers	Co-operation, stable employment, education
May 23	Meeting to petition Parliament	Government	Wage protection bill
1828			
Feb. 20	Petition Parliament for wage protection	Government	Wage protection
April 21	General meeting of broad silk weavers	Government	Imports and wage protection
April 28	General meeting of broad silk weavers	Government	Imports and wage protection
May 12	General meeting of broad silk weavers	Government	Import protection
July	Campaign for tariff protection	Government	Import protection

Date	Action	Target	Goal
Nov. 3	General meeting	Government	Import protection
(Spring through Autumn)	Formation of co-operatives	Weavers	Stable employment
Feb.	Campaign against tariff reductions	Government	Import protection
March	Campaign against tariff reductions	Government	Import protection
April	Trade meetings and petitioning of Board of Trade	Government	Import protection
April 13	Picket of Parliament to support wages protection bill	Government	Wage protection
April 15	Meeting with delegates from Macclesfield and Manchester on trade protection and tariff	Government	Import protection
April 16	General trade meeting to discuss parliamentary rejection of petition	Government	Trade protection
May 5	Silk cutting	Masters	Prevention of wage reductions
May 7	Meeting, procession, and petitioning of House of Lords	Government	Relief
May 8	Silk cutting, meeting to discuss wage demands	Masters	Wage stabilization
May 9	Silk cutting	Masters	Wage stabilization
May 20	General trade meeting	Masters	Wage stabilization
May 21	Shop meetings on wage demands	Masters	Wage stabilization
May 23	Loom sealing	Masters	Wage stabilization
May 24	Loom sealing	Masters	Wage stabilization
May 27	Assault on employer's foreman and patrolmen	Masters	Wage stabilization
May 31	Silk cutting (Moore's looms)	Masters	Wage stabilization
June 1	Silk cutting	Masters	Wage stabilization
June 2	Mob threat against weaver for unsealing loom	Weaver	Maintain strike
June 22	Meeting to discuss petition for emigration	Government	Finding secure employment
July 1	Silk cutting	Masters	Wage stabilization
July 7	Meeting to discuss subscriptions for emigration plans and petitioning government	Government, patrons	Finding secure employment
July 15	Meeting to discuss emigration proposals	Government	Finding secure employment
July 31	Meeting to discuss patronage	Royal family	Finding secure employment
Aug. 7	General meeting on emigration	Royal family	Finding secure employment
Aug 12	General meeting on emigration	Royal family	Finding secure employment
Sept. 24	Silk cutting	Masters	Wage stabilization
Oct. 1	General meeting	Royal family	Patronage

Appendix 1

Date	Action	Target	Goal
Oct. 18	General meeting	Royal family	Patronage
Oct. 25	Silk cutting	Masters	Renewal of wage advances
Nov.	Renewed attempt at bargaining with masters	Masters	Wage stabilization
1830			
Jan. 26	General meeting to discuss wage protection bill	Government	Wage protection
First quarter	Initiation of co-operative production through B.A.P.C.K.	Weavers	Wages/employment
First quarter	Meetings to discuss formation of trade union	Masters	Wage stabilization
May	Meeting to discuss weavers' committee report on bargaining with masters	Masters	Wage stabilization
Oct. 1	Memorialize royal family for relief	Royal family	Relief, patronage
Oct. 18	Memorialize royal family for relief	Royal family	Relief, patronage
1831			
Jan. 22	Meeting to discuss formation of union and petitioning for a wage protection bill	Masters	Wage stabilization
March 7	Meeting to petition Commons to investigate distress	Government	Relief
March 26	Meeting to petition king	Royal family	Relief, patronage

APPENDIX TWO

Ashton and Stalybridge spinners' collective actions, April 1830 – January 1831

Date	Action	Target	Goal
1830			
Mid-April	Strike	Firm of Hegginbottom	Raise wages
Mid-April	Assault	Strikebreakers	Prevent replacement
Late April	Attack	Hegginbottom house	Raise wages
Mid-June	Attempted bombing	Hegginbottom	Raise wages
Mid-July	Mass meeting	Mill owners	Equalize wages
August 7	Mass meeting	Mill owners	Stabilize wages; unionization
Mid-August	Strike	Firm of Orrell	Equalize wages
Mid-August	Strike	Firm of Lee	Equalize wages
Mid-August	Assault	Strikebreakers	Prevent replacement
Late Sept.	Meeting	Workers	Unionization
Mid-Oct.	Strike in Dukinfield	Firm of Lees & Sons	Equalize wages
Mid-Oct.	Strike by piecers	Firm of Hindley & Hyde	Wage increase
Early Nov.	Mass meeting in Ashton	Spinners	Strike mobilization
Early Nov.	Mass meeting in Dukinfield	Spinners	Strike mobilization
Early Nov.	Mass meeting in Audenshaw	Spinners	Strike mobilization
Nov.	Mass meeting in Hurst	Spinners	Strike mobilization
Nov.	Union delegates' meeting with mill owners delegates	Mill owners	Equalize wages
Dec. 4	Mass meeting	Factory workers	Strike
Dec. 6–7	Mass parading of discharged spinners	Mill owners	Equalize wages; strike
Dec. 11	Mass strike	52 Firms	Equalize wages

247

Date	Action	Target	Goal
Dec. 13	Mass parading of striking spinners	Mill owners	Equalize wages
Dec. 14	Demonstration	Mill owners	Equalize wages
Dec. 15	Mass parade to turn out spinners in Hyde	Spinners	Extend strike
Dec. 16	Mass parade to Oldham	Public	Publicize strike
Dec. 17	Mass parade to Glossup	Spinners	Extend strike
Dec. 20	Turn-out of spinners in Glossup	Mill owners	Equalize wages
1831			
Jan. 3	Assassination	Thomas Ashton	Pressure mill owners
Jan. 4	Mass assault on factories	Firm of Sidebottom	Turn out knobsticks
Jan. 8	Rally in Manchester	Spinners; public	Support for strike
Jan. 10	Mass assault on factory	Firm in Hayfield	Turn out knobsticks
Jan. 12	Shooting	James Howard	Pressure owners
Jan. 14	Shooting	House of Charles Kershaw	Pressure
Jan. 14	Threatened shooting	William Thornley	Pressure
Jan. 14	Attempted shooting	James Ashton	Pressure
Mid-Jan.	Mass meeting to discuss negotiations	Mill owners	End strike; equalize wages
Jan. 20	Spinners' delegates meet owners' delegates	Mill owners	End strike; equalize wages

References

Archives

British Library, London.
  Add. MSS. 27799, 27803, 27804, 27805 (Place Papers).
  Francis Place Collection of Newspaper Clippings and Pamphlets.
Lancashire Country Record Office, Preston.
  Letters of Dr. John Bowring, to the Right Honourable George Lamb, M.P., Under-Secretary of State for the Home Office, about Attempts of the Masters to Reduce the Wages of the Spinners in the Ashton Area and the Organization of the Spinners into a Trades Association (DDX/880/1-2).
  Early Minute and Rate Book of the Ashton-under-Lyne Parish (P2565).
  Ashton Parish Rate Book, 1831 (PR2576).
London School of Economics, British Library of Political and Economic Science.
  Sidney and Beatrice Webb, Collected Papers, Section A. Manuscript Sources, v. XL, ff. 83-170, "Silk Manufacture: Historical Extracts, etc.".
Manchester Central Library, Local History Collection.
  Ashton-under-Lyne Parish, St. Michael's Church, Misc. Papers 1631-1894.
Manchester Central Library, Manuscripts Collection.
  Letters from Robert Peel as Home Secretary to John Fred. Foster, Stipendiary Magistrate of Manchester (Misc/333).
  Henry Romilly MSS. Collection.
Oldham Public Library, Local History Collection.
  Edwin Butterworth MSS Collection.
British Public Record Office (Kew Gardens), Home Office Papers.
  H.O. 40/23-27. Correspondence, Civil Disturbances.
  H.O. 44/18. Correspondence, George IV.
  H.O. 52/12-13. Correspondence, Counties.

H.O. 54/4. Petitions and Addresses.
H.O. 61/1. Correspondence, Metropolitan.
H.O. 62/1–7. Metropolitan Police Reports. Reports of the Proceedings at Several Police Offices.
Tameside Library (Stalybridge), Local History Collection.
Stalybridge Constable's Log Book, December 1830–January 1831.
Stalybridge Improvement Commissioners Records, Minute Books, June 1828–April 1833 (IC/STA/1).
Stalybridge Rate Book, 1830 (IC/STA/11).
Tower Hamlets Library (London), Local History Collection.
Christ Church, Spitalfields, Vestry Minute Books, 1828–31.
Old Artillery Ground Trustees Minutes Book, 1828–31 (S.46).
Old Artillery Ground Treasurer's Account Book for Disbursements on Behalf of the Poor, 1826–36 (S.73).
Old Artillery Ground Pauper Examination Books, 1826–36 (S.80).

British Parliamentary Debates, Papers, and Reports

House of Commons Journal, v. 55. 1800.
Hansard's Parliamentary Debates. Second Series.
Hansard's Parliamentary Debates. New Series.

HOUSE OF LORDS SELECT COMMITTEE REPORTS

L.S.P. 1823, (57) CLVI, Minutes of Evidence Taken Before the Lords Committees on The Bill, intitled, "An Act to repeal certain Acts of His late Majesty relating to the Wages of Persons employed in the Manufacture of Silk, and of Silk mixed with Other Materials," House of Lords Sessional Papers.

HOUSE OF COMMONS SELECT COMMITTEE REPORTS

P.P. 1814–1815 (473) III. Report of the Committee on the State of Mendicity in the Metropolis.
P.P. 1817 (642) VI. Report of the Select Committee on the Poor Laws.
P.P. 1817 (283) VII. Report of the Committee on the State of the Police in the Metropolis.
P.P. 1818 (134) IX. Report of the Committee on Silk Weavers' Petitions.
P.P. 1818 (211) IX. Second Report of the Committee on Silk Weavers' Petitions.
P.P. 1819 (83) X. Reports from the Commissioners on Charities in England for Education of the Poor.
P.P. 1824 (51) V. Reports from the Select Committee on Artizans, Machinery and Combinations. First Report.
P.P. 1826–1827 (22) IX. 17th Report of the Commissioners for Inquiries Concerning Charities.
P.P. 1828 (533) VI. Report of the Select Committee on the State of the Police in the Metropolis.
P.P. 1828 (576) XIX. An Account of the Quantity of Raw and Thrown Silk, and Also of the Quantities Entered for Home Consumption, in Each of the Last Five Years.
P.P. 1829 (349) VIII. 22nd Report of the Commissioners for Inquiries Concerning Charities.
P.P. 1830 (590) X. Report of the Select Committee Appointed to Consider the Means

of Lessening the Evils Arising from the Fluctuations of Employment in Manufacturing Districts.

P.P. 1830–1831 (30) XI. An Account of the Money Expended for the Maintenance and Relief of the Poor . . . 1825–1829.

P.P. 1831–1832 (706) XV. Report of the Select Committee on the Bill to Regulate the Labour of Children in Mills and Factories.

P.P. 1832 (678) XIX. Report of the Select Committee on the Silk Trade.

P.P. 1833 (690) VI. Report of the Select Committee on the Present State of Manufactures, Commerce, and Shipping in the United Kingdom.

P.P. 1833 (60) XVIII. 25th Report of Commissioners on Charities connected with Education.

P.P. 1833 (681) XIX. 26th Report of Commissioners on Charities Connected with Education.

P.P. 1833 (450) XX. Report of the Royal Commission on the Employment of Children in Factories. First Report of the Central Board.

P.P. 1834 (465) VII. Report from the Select Committee on Education in England and Wales.

P.P. 1834 (556) X. Report from the Select Committee on Handloom Weavers' Petitions.

P.P. 1834 (44) XXIX. Report from the Assistant Poor Law Commissioners, pt. III.

P.P. 1834 (36) XXXV. Appendices to the Report of the Poor Law Commissioners. Appendix B.2. Answers to Questions Circulated by the Commissioners in Towns.

P.P. 1835 (572) VII. Report from the Select Committee on the State of Education in England and Wales.

P.P. 1835 (62) XLI. Abstract of the Answers and Returns Relative to the State of Education in England and Wales.

P.P. 1836 (40) XXXIV. Report on the State of the Irish Poor.

P.P. 1837–1838 (485) VIII. First Report from the Select Committee on Combinations of Workmen.

P.P. 1839 (169) XIX. First Report of the Commissioners Appointed to Inquire as the Best Means of Establishing an Efficient Constabularly Force in the Counties of England and Wales.

P.P. 1840 (43–1) XXIII. Reports from the Assistant Handloom Weavers' Commissioners. Report from J. Mitchell, Esq. LL.D., on the East of England.

ACTS OF PARLIAMENT

An Act for lighting with Gas the Town of Ashton-under-Lyne and the Neighborhood thereof, in the County Palatine of Lancaster, and the Township of Dukinfield, in the County Palatine of Chester; and for supplying with Water the said Town of Ashton-under-Lyne and the Neighborhood thereof. (6 Geo. IV, c. 67).

An Act for lighting, cleansing, watching, and otherwise improving the Town of Ashton-under-Lyne in the County Palatine of Lancaster, and for regulating the Police thereof. (7 & 8 Geo. IV, c. 76).

An Act for lighting, watching, and otherwise improving the Town of Stalybridge in the Counties Palatine of Lancaster and Chester, and for regulating the Police thereof; and for establishing and regulating a Market, and erecting a Market Place, within the said Town. (9 Geo. IV, c. 27).

An Act for altering and amending an Act passed in the last Session of Parliament, intituled *An Act for lighting, cleansing, watching, and otherwise improving the Town of Ashton-under-Lyne in the County Palatine of Lancaster, and for regulating the Police thereof*, and also for regulating the Market and erecting a Market Place within and for the said Town. (9 Geo. IV c. 92).

Newspapers and Periodicals

Annual Register
Carpenter's Monthly Political Magazine
The Co-operative Magazine and Monthly Herald
Eclectic Review
Edinburgh Review
European Magazine
Gentlemen's Magazine
Gauntlet
Lancashire and Yorkshire Cooperator
Lion
London Magazine
London Quarterly Review
Manchester Guardian
Manchester Mercury
Manchester Times
Morning Chronicle
Penny Magazine
Philanthropist
Poor Man's Advocate
Poor Man's Guardian
The Stocking Makers' Monitor
Stockport Advertiser
The Times
Trades' Newspaper and Mechanics' Weekly Journal
Trades' Weekly Free Press
Union Pilot and Co-operative Intelligencer
United Trades' Co-operative Journal
Voice of the People
Weekly Free Press
Westminster Review
Wheelers' Manchester Chronicle

Contemporary Literature

An Account of the Proceedings of the Committees of the Journeymen Silk Weavers of Spitalfields; In the Legal Defence of the Acts of Parliament, Granted to their Trade, in the 13th, 32nd, and 51st Years of the Reign of his late Majesty, King George the Third. London: E. Justins, 1823.

Armitage, Arthur. n.d. "The Spitalfields Weaver." [Tower Hamlets Library, Local History Collection, L. P. 1644 680.2].

Badnall, Richard. 1828. *A View of the Silk Trade; With Remarks on the Recent Measures of Government in Regard to the Branch of Manufacture*. London: John Miller.

Baines, Edward. 1835 (1966). *History of the Cotton Manufacture in Great Britain*. London: Frank Cass.

———. 1824. *History, Directory and Gazetteer of the County Palatine of Lancashire*. 2 vols. Liverpool: Wm. Wales & Co.

Bamford, Samuel. 1841 (1967). *The Autobiography of Samuel Bamford*. 2 vols. Edited with an Introduction by W. H. Chaloner. London: Frank Cass.

Bayley, Edward W. 1829. *Londinina*. v. 4. London: Hurst, Chance.

Brock, Irving. 1817. *A Letter to the Inhabitants of Spital-Fields, On the Character and Views of Modern Reformers*. London: F. C. and J. Rivington.

Burn, William. 1820. *The Justice of the Peace, and Parish Officer.* 23d ed. Edited by George Chetwynd. London: A Strahan.

Butterworth, Edwin. 1842. *An Historical Account of the Towns of Ashton-under-Lyne, Stalybridge, and Dukinfield.* Ashton: A. Phillips.

———. 1841. *A Statistical Sketch of the County Palatine of Lancaster.* London: Longman.

Cobbett, William. 1830 (1912). *Rural Rides.* v. 2. London: J. M. Dent & Sons.

Cooke-Taylor, William. 1842 (1968). *Notes of a Tour in the Manufacturing Districts in Lancashire.* 3d ed. Introduction by W. H. Chaloner. London: Frank Cass.

Coulthart, John Ross. 1844. *A Report on the Sanitary Condition of the Town of Ashton-under-Lyne; With Remarks on the Existing Evils, and Suggestions for Improving the Health, Comfort, and Longevity of the Inhabitants.* Ashton-under-Lyne: Luke Swallow.

"Coventry Freeman." 1824. *Animadversions on the Repeal of the Act for Regulating the Wages of Labour among the Spitalfields Weavers; and in the Combination Law.* London: R. Brown.

Dickens, Charles. 1854 (1961). *Hard Times.* New York: New American Library.

Dodd, George. 1851. "Spitalfields." In *London.* v. 2. Edited by Charles Knight. London: Henry G. Bonn. 385–400.

Dodd, William. 1842 (1968). *The Factory System.* Illustrated. Introduction by W. H. Chaloner. London: Frank Cass.

Doherty, John. 1829. *A Report of the Proceedings of a Delegate Meeting of the Operative Spinners of England, Ireland and Scotland, Assembled at Ramsey, Isle of Man, On Saturday, December 5, 1829, and Three Following Days.* Manchester: M. Wardle.

Engels, Friedrich. 1842 (1968). *The Condition of the Working Class In England.* Translated and edited by W. O. Henderson and W. H. Chaloner. Stanford: Stanford University Press.

Gorton, John. 1831. *Topographical Dictionary of Great Britain and Ireland.* London: Chapman & Hall.

Greg, Robert H. 1837. *The Factory Question, Considered in Relation to Its Effects on the Health and Morals of Those Employed in the Factories, and the "Ten Hours" Bill, in Relation to Its Effects upon the Manufactures of England, and Those of Foreign Countries.* London: James Ridgway & Sons.

Gurney, W. B. 1819. *The Trials at Large of Joseph Merceron, Esq. for Fraud, as the Treasurer of the Poor Rate Funds of St. Matthew, Bethnal Green; and Also for Corrupt Conduct as a Magistrate; in Re-Licensing Disorderly Public Houses, His Property.* 2 vols., London: W. Wright.

Hale, William, 1822. *An Appeal to the Public, in Defence of the Spitalfields Act: with Remarks on the Causes Which Have Led to the Miseries and Moral Deterioration of the Poor.* London: E. Justins.

———. 1806. *A Letter to Samuel Whitebread, Esq., M.P., Containing Observations on the Distresses Peculiar to the Poor of Spitalfields, Arising From Their Local Situation.* London: William & Smith.

Henson, Gravenor, and George White. 1823. *A Few Remarks on the State of the Laws, at Present Regulating Masters and Work-People, Intended as a Guide for the Consideration of the House, In Their Discussions on the Bill for Repealing Several Acts Relating to Combinations of Workmen, and for More Effectually Protecting Trade, and for Settling Disputes between Masters and Servants.* London: Private printing.

Hindley, Charles. 1841. *Free Trade. Speech of Charles Hindley, Esq., Now M.P. for Ashton-under-Lyne, at the Public Dinner Given in Saddleworth, to Lord Morpeth and Henry Brougham, Esq., September 25, 1830. On Their Election for the County of York.* London: James Ridgway.

———. 1825. *An Address Delivered at the Establishment of the Mechanics' Institution, Ashton-under-Lyne. June 22, 1825.* Ashton-under-Lyne: Thomas Cunningham.

Hone, William. 1827. *The Everyday Book; or Everlasting Calendar of Popular Amusements,*

Sports, Pastimes, Ceremonies, Manners, Customs, and Events, Incident to Each of the Three Hundred and Sixty Five Days, in Past and Present Times. . . . v. 2. London: William Hone.

Hoole, Holland. 1832. *A Letter to the Right Honourable Lord Viscount Althorp, M.P., Chancellor of the Exchequer; in Defence of the Cotton Factories of Lancashire.* Manchester: T. Sowler.

Hopkins, Thomas. 1831. *Wages; Or Masters and Workmen.* Manchester: Alexander Wilson.

Kay, James Phillips. 1832 (1970). *The Moral and Physical Condition of the Working Classes Employed in the Cotton Manufacture in Manchester.* 2d ed. Edited by W. H. Chaloner. London: Frank Cass.

Kennedy, John. 1831. "Observations on the Influence of Machinery upon the Working Classes of the Community." *Memoirs of the Literary and Philosophical Society of Manchester.* Second series, 5: 25–35.

———. 1819. "Observations on the Rise and Progress of the Cotton Trade in Great Britain, Particularly in Lancashire and the adjoining Counties." *Memoirs of the Literary and Philosophical Society of Manchester.* Second series, 3: 115–137.

Knight, Charles. 1831. *The Results of Machinery; Namely, Cheap Production and Increased Employment, Exhibited; being an Address to the Working-Men of the United Kingdom.* Boston: Stimpson & Clapp.

Letters, Taken from Various Newspapers, Tending to Injure the Journeymen Silk Weavers of Spitalfields, with an Attack against the Acts of Parliament, Regulating the Prices of Their Work. . . . *Also, the Answers, by the Journeymen and Their Friends.* London: E. Justins. 1818.

Lewis, Samuel. 1831. *A Topographical Dictionary of England.* . . . 4 vols. London: S. Lewis.

A List of Prices in Those Branches of the Weaving Manufactory, Called Strong Plain, Foot Figured and Flowered Branches. London, 1769.

Lovett, William. 1867 (1967). *The Life and Struggles of William Lovett.* v. 1. London: MacGibbon & Kee.

Lysons, Daniel. 1811. *The Environs of London,* v. 2. London: T. Cadell & W. Davies.

Manchester Statistical Society. 1838. *Report of the Committee of the Manchester Statistical Society, on the Condition of the Working Classes, in an Extensive Manufacturing District, in 1834, 1835, and 1836.* London: James Ridgway & Son.

Marcet, Jane. 1828. *Conversations on Political Economy; in Which the Elements of that Science are Familiarly Explained.* Boston: Bowles & Dearborn.

Martineau, Harriet. 1834. *Illustrations of Political Economy. No. VII. A Manchester Strike.* 3d ed. London: Charles Fox.

———. 1833. *Illustrations of Political Economy. No. XVII. The Loom Lugger.* Part 1. London: Charles Fox.

McCulloch, John R. 1837. *A Statistical Account of the British Empire: Exhibiting Its Extent, Physical Capacities, Population, Industry, and Civil and Religious Institutions.* 2 vols. London: Charles Knight.

———. 1834. *A Dictionary, Practical, Theoretical, and Historical, of Commerce and Commercial Navigation.* 2d ed. London: Longman, Rees, Orme, Brown, Green, and Longman.

———. 1827. "On the Rise and Progress of Cotton Manufacture in Great Britain." *Edinburgh Review.* 46: 1–39.

Montgomery, James. 1833. *The Theory and Practice of Cotton Spinning; or The Carding and Spinning Master's Assistant.* 2d ed. Glasgow: John Niven.

More, Hannah. 1819a. "The Delegate; with Some Account of Mr. James Dawson of Spitalfields." In *Cheap Repository Tracts.* London: F., C. & J. Rivington.

———. 1819b. *The Contented Spital-Fields Weaver; Jeremiah Nott, His Address to His Brother Artificers, Respecting the Smithfield Meeting, and Other Matters.* 8th ed. London: Howard.

Nightingale, Joseph. 1815. *London and Middlesex; or An Historical, Commercial, and Descriptive, Survey of the Metropolis of Great Britain.* v. 3. London: Vernor, Hood & Sharpe.

Observations on the Ruinous Effects of the Spitalfields Acts to the Silk Manufacture of London: to Which is Added a Reply to Mr. Hale's Appeal to the Public in Defence of the Act. 1822. London: John and Arthur Arch.

Parliamentary Gazetteer of England and Wales, Adapted to the New Poor-Law. Franchise, Municipal, and Ecclesiastical Arrangements, and Compiled with Special Reference to the Lines of Railroad and Canal Communication, as Existing in 1842–3. 1844. London: A. Fullarton.

Partington, Charles F. 1825. *A Course of Three Lectures Illustrative of the Rise and Progress of Science, in Mechanics, Pneumatics, and the General History of the Steam Engine Occasioned by the Formation of the Spitalfields Mechanics' Institution.* London: S. Teulon.

Pigot and Co.'s London and Provincial New Commercial Directory For 1822–3. London: J. Pigot & Son.

Pigot and Co.'s London and Provincial New Commercial Directory For 1828–9. London: J. Pigot & Son.

Pigot and Son's General Directory of Manchester, Salford, &c. For 1828. Manchester : J. Pigot & Son.

Pigot and Son's General Directory of Manchester, Salford, &c. For 1829. Manchester : J. Pigot & Son.

Porter, G. R. 1831. *Treatise on the Origin, Progressive Improvement, and Present State of the Silk Trade.* London: Longman, Rees, Orme, Brown & Green.

Powell, John. 1824. *A Letter Addressed to Weavers, Shopkeepers, and Publicans, on the Great Value of the Principle of the Spitalfields Acts: In Opposition to the Absurd and Mischievous Doctrines of the Advocates for their Repeal.* London: E. Justins.

Prentice, Archibald. 1851. *Historical Sketches and Personal Recollections of Manchester.* Manchester: J. T. Parkes.

——. 1829. *An Address on the State of the Cotton Trade, to the Master Spinners and Weavers of Lancashire.* Manchester: James Whittle.

Prout, John. 1829. *Practical View of the Silk Trade. . . .* Macclesfield: J. Swinnerton.

Pymlot, J. 1826. *Strictures on the Wisdom and Policy of the Present Measures Relative to the Importation of Silk.* Macclesfield: Philip Hall.

Reach, Angus. 1849 (1972). *Manchester and the Textile Districts in 1849.* Edited by C. Aspin. Rossendale: Helmshore Local Historical Society.

Remarks upon Mr. Hale's Appeal to the Public, in Defence of the Spitalfields Act. . . . 1822. London: Steuart & Panton.

Report Adopted at a General Meeting of the Journeymen Broad Silk Weavers, held in Saint John Street Chapel, Brick-lane, Spitalfields, On Wednesday, the 20th of February, 1828, to take into their Consideration the Necessity of Petitioning the Legislature for a Wage Protection Bill and such other purposes as may arise out of the same. To which is Appended, The Petition. 1828. London: W. C. Mantz.

Rose, Henry. 1825. *Manual Labour versus Brass and Iron: Reflections in Defence of the Body of Cotton Spinners, Occasioned by a Perusal of the Description of Mr. Robert's Self-acting Mule.* Manchester: J. Pratt.

Senior, Nassau. 1865. *Historical and Philosophical Essays.* v. 2. London: Longman, Green, Longman, Roberts & Green.

Sholl, Samuel. 1812. *A Short Historical Account of the Silk Manufacture In England, From Its Introduction to the Present Time. . . .* London: M. Jones.

Smith, Charles Manley. 1852. *A Treatise on the Law of Master and Servant, Including Therein Master and Workmen in Every Description of Trade and Occupation; With an Appendix of Statutes.* Philadelphia: T. & J. W. Johnson.

Spitalfields Benevolent Society. 1812. *First Report of the Spitalfields Benevolent Society, Instituted in the Year MDCCCXI for Visiting and Relieving Cases of Great Distress, Chiefly among the Numerous Poor of Spitalfields and its Vicinity.* London: Ellerton & Henderson.

Spitalfields Soup Society. 1813. *Report of the Committee of the Spitalfields Soup Society for 1811–12.* London: Darton, Harvey.

Tufnell, Edward C. 1834. *Character, Object and Effects of Trades' Unions; with Some Remarks on the Law Concerning Them.* London: James Ridgway & Sons.
Ure, Andrew. 1836. *The Cotton Manufacture of Great Britain.* 2 vols. London: Charles Knight.
———. 1835. *The Philosophy of Manufactures: or An Exposition of the Scientific, Moral, and Commercial Economy of the Factory System of Great Britain.* London: Charles Knight.
"Verax." 1822. *Review of the Statements in Hale's Appeal to the Public on the Spitalfields Acts.* London: J. Hudson.
Wade, John. 1833. *History of the Middle and Working Classes; with a Popular Exposition of the Economic and Political Principles Which Have Influenced the Past and Present Condition of the Industrious Order.* London: Effigham Wilson.
Walpole, Horace. 1845. *Memoirs of the Reign of King George III.* v. 1. Philadelphia: Lea & Blanchard.
Whatley, Richard. 1832 (1966). *Introductory Lectures on Political Economy.* 2d ed. New York: Augustus M. Kelley.

Data Sets

Great Britain Study. New School for Social Research. Charles Tilly, Principal Investigator.

Modern Historical Studies

Alexander, Sally. 1984. "Women, Class, and Sexual Difference in the 1830s and 1840s: Some Reflections on the Writing of Feminist History." *History Workshop.* 17: 125–149.
———. 1976. "Women's Work in Nineteenth-Century London: A Study of the Years 1820–50." In *The Rights and Wrongs of Women.* Edited by Juliet Mitchell and Ann Oakley. Harmondsworth: Penguin. 59–111.
Anderson, Michael 1971. *Family Structure in Nineteenth-Century Lancashire.* Cambridge: Cambridge University Press.
Ashmore, Owen. 1974. "The Industrial Archaeology of Ashton-under-Lyne." In *Victorian Ashton.* Edited by Sylvia A. Harrop and E. A. Rose. Ashton-under-Lyne: Tameside Libraries and Arts Committee. 86–107.
———, and Trevor Bolton. 1975. "Hugh Mason and the Oxford Mills and Community, Ashton-under-Lyne." *Transactions of the Lancashire and Cheshire Antiquarian Society.* 78: 38–50.
Aspinall, Arthur. 1949. *The Early English Trade Unions: Documents from the Home Office Papers in the Public Record Office.* London: Batchworth Press.
Atiyah, P. S. 1979. *The Rise and Fall of Freedom of Contract.* Oxford: Oxford University Press.
Axon, William E. A. 1870. *The Black Knight of Ashton.* Manchester: John Heywood.
Barr, Kenneth. 1980. "Long Waves and the Cotton-Spinning Enterprise, 1789–1849." In *Processes of the World System.* Edited by Terence K. Hopkins and Immanuel Wallerstein. Beverly Hills: Sage. 84–100.
Bateman, John. 1879. *The Great Landowners of Great Britain and Ireland.* 3d ed. London: Harrison.
Batt, John. 1986. "United to Support but Not Combined to Injure: Public Order, Trade Unions and the Repeal of the Combination Acts of 1799–1800." *International Review of Social History.* 31: 185–203.
Behagg, Clive. 1990. *Politics and Production in the Early Nineteenth Century.* London: Routledge.
———. 1988. "The Democracy of Work, 1820–1850." In *British Trade Unionism 1750–1850: The Formative Years.* Edited by John Rule. London: Longman. 162–177.

———. 1984. "Masters and Manufacturers: Social Values and the Smaller Units of Production in Birmingham, 1800–50." In *Shopkeepers and Master Artisans in Nineteenth-Century Europe.* Edited by Geoffrey Crossick and Heinz-Gerhard Haupt. London: Methuen. 137–154.

———. 1982. "Secrecy, Ritual and Folk Violence: The Opacity of the Workplace in the First Half of the Nineteenth Century." In *Popular Custom and Culture in Nineteenth-Century England.* Edited by Robert D. Storch. New York: St. Martin's Press. 154–179.

———. 1979. "Custom, Class and Change." *Social History.* 4: 455–480.

Belchem, John C. 1994. "'Freedom and Friendship to Ireland': Ribbonism in Early Nineteenth-Century Liverpool." *International Review of Social History.* 39: 33–56.

———. 1990. *Industrialization and the Working Class: The English Experience, 1750–1900.* Portland: Areopagitica Press.

———. 1988. "Radical Language and Ideology in Nineteenth-Century England: The Challenge of the Mass Platform." *Albion.* 20: 247–259.

———. 1981. "Republicanism, Popular Constitutionalism and the Radical Platform in Nineteenth-Century England." *Social History.* 6: 1–32.

———. 1978. "Henry Hunt and the Evolution of the Mass Platform." *English Historical Review.* 93: 739–773.

Berg, Maxine. 1993. "What Difference Did Women's Work Make in the Industrial Revolution?" *History Workshop.* 25: 22–44.

———. 1988. "Women's Work, Mechanisation and the Early Phases of Industrialisation in England." In *The Historical Meanings of Work.* Edited by Patrick Joyce. Cambridge: Cambridge University Press. 64–98.

———. 1980. *The Machinery Question and the Making of Political Economy.* Cambridge: Cambridge University Press.

Birch, A. H. 1959. *Small-Town Politics: A Study of Life in Glossup.* Oxford: Oxford University Press.

Bland, A. E., P. A. Brown, and R. H. Tawney. Editors. 1919. *English Economic History: Select Documents.* New York: Macmillan.

Blaug, Mark. 1961. "The Productivity of Capital in the Lancashire Cotton Industry during the Nineteenth Century." *Economic History Review.* Second Series. 13: 358–381.

Bohstedt, John. 1983. *Riots and Community Politics in England and Wales 1790–1810.* Cambridge: Harvard University Press.

Bowman, Winifred M. 1960. *England in Ashton-under-Lyne.* London: John Sherratt & Son.

Boyson, Rhodes 1970. *The Ashworth Cotton Enterprise.* Oxford: Oxford University Press.

Bretano, Lujo. 1870. *On the History and Development of Gilds, and the Origin of Trade Unions.* London: Trubner.

Brewer, John. 1976. *Party Ideology and Popular Politics at the Accession of George III.* Cambridge: Cambridge University Press.

Bristol, Michael D. 1985. *Carnival and Theater: Plebeian Culture and the Structure of Authority in Renaissance England.* New York: Methuen.

Bruland, Tine. 1982. "Industrial Conflict as a Source of Technical Innovation: Three Cases." *Economy and Society.* 11: 91–121.

Bythell, Duncan. 1978. *The Sweated Trades: Outwork in Nineteenth-Century Britain.* New York: St. Martin's Press.

———. 1969. *The Handloom Weavers.* Cambridge: Cambridge University Press.

Canning, Kathleen. 1992. "Gender and the Politics of Class Formation: Rethinking German Labor History." *American Historical Review.* 92: 736–768.

Carson, W. G. 1974. "Symbolic and Instrumental Dimensions of Early Factory Legislation." In *Crime, Criminology and Public Policy.* Edited by R. Hood. London: Heinemann. 107–138.

Catling, Harold. 1978. "The Development of the Spinning Mule." *Textile History.* 9: 35–57.
———. 1970. *The Spinning Mule.* Newton Abbot: David & Charles.
Chapman, S. D. 1972. *The Cotton Industry in the Industrial Revolution.* London: Macmillan.
Chapman, S. J. 1904. *The Lancashire Cotton Industry: A Study in Economic Development.* Manchester: Manchester University Press.
Claeys, Gregory. 1987. *Machinery, Money, and the Millennium: From Moral Economy to Socialism, 1815–1850.* Cambridge: Polity.
Clapham, J. H. 1916. "The Spitalfields Acts 1773–1824." *Economic Journal.* 26: 459–471.
Clark, Anna. 1995. *The Struggle for the Breeches: The Making of the British Working Class, 1780–1850.* Berkeley: University of California Press.
———. 1992. "The Rhetoric of Chartist Domesticity: Gender, Language, and Class in the 1830s and 1840s." *Journal of British Studies.* 31: 62–88.
———. 1990. "Queen Caroline and the Sexual Politics of Popular Culture in London, 1820." *Representations.* 31: 46–68.
Clark, Peter. *The English Alehouse: A Social History, 1200–1830.* London: Longman, 1983.
Clark, Sylvia. 1978. "Chorlton Mills and Their Neighbors." *Industrial Archaeology Review.* 2: 207–239.
Cohen, Isaac. 1985. "Workers' Control in the Cotton Industry: A Comparative Study of British and American Mule Spinning." *Labor History.* 26: 53–85.
Cole, G. D. H. 1953. *Attempts at General Union.* London: Macmillan.
Coleman, D. C. 1969. *Courtlands: An Economic and Social History.* v. 1. Oxford: Oxford University Press.
Colley, Linda. 1986. "Whose Nation? Class and National Consciousness in Britain 1750–1830." *Past and Present.* 113: 97–117.
Collier, Frances. 1964. *The Family Economy of the Working Classes in the Cotton Industry, 1784–1833.* Edited by Robert Fitton. Manchester: Manchester University Press.
Corrigan, Philip, and Derek Sayer. 1985. *The Great Arch: English State Formation as Cultural Revolution.* Oxford: Basil Blackwell.
Cotton, Nicolas. 1977. "Popular Movements in Ashton-under-Lyne and Stalybridge before 1832." Unpublished M.Litt. thesis in History, University of Birmingham.
Creighton, Colin. 1992. "Richard Oastler, Factory Legislation and the Working-Class Family." *Journal of Historical Sociology.* 5: 292–321.
Cronin, James. 1993. "Neither Exceptional nor Peculiar: Towards the Comparative Study of Labor in Advanced Society." *International Review of Social History.* 38: 59–75.
———. 1986. "Review Essay: Language, Politics and the Critique of Social History." *Journal of Social History.* 20: 177–183.
Cuca, James R. 1977. "Industrial Change and the Progress of Labour in the English Cotton Industry." *International Review of Social History.* 22: 241–255.
Cunningham, Hugh. 1981. "The Language of Patriotism, 1750–1914." *History Workshop.* 12: 8–37.
———. 1980. *Leisure in the Industrial Revolution, c. 1780–c. 1880.* London: Croom Helm.
Daniels, G. W. 1920. *The Early English Cotton Industry.* Manchester: Manchester University Press.
Darvall, Frank O. 1934 (1969). *Popular Disturbances in Regency England.* New York: Kelley.
Davidoff, Lenore. 1986. "The Role of Gender in the 'First Industrial Nation': Agriculture in England, 1780–1850." In *Gender and Stratification.* Edited by Rosemary Crompton and Michael Mann. Cambridge: Polity Press. 190–214.

Davis, Natalie Zemon. 1975. *Society and Culture in Early Modern France*. Stanford: Stanford University Press.
Dean, Mitchell. 1991. *The Constitution of Poverty: Toward a Genealogy of Liberal Governance*. London: Routledge.
Derry, T. K. 1931. "The Repeal of the Apprenticeship Clauses of the Statute of Apprentices." *Economic History Review*. Second Series. 3: 67–87.
Diamond, A. S. 1932. *The Law of the Relation between Master and Servant*. London: Stevens & Sons.
Dinwiddy, John. 1979. "Luddism and Politics in the Northern Counties." *Social History*. 4: 33–63.
Dobson, C. R. 1980. *Master and Servant*. London: Croom Helm.
Edwards, M. M. 1967. *The Growth of the British Cotton Trade, 1780–1815*. Manchester: Manchester University Press.
———, and R. Lloyd-Jones. 1973. "N. J. Smelser and the Cotton Factory Family: A Reassessment." In *Textile History and Economic History*. Edited by N. B. Harte and K. G. Ponting. Manchester: Manchester University Press. 309–319.
Eley, Geoff. 1992. "Nations, Publics and Political Cultures: Placing Habermas in the Nineteenth Century." In *Habermas and the Public Sphere*. Edited by Craig Calhoun. Cambridge: MIT Press. 289–339.
———. 1990. "Edward Thompson, Social History, and Political Culture: The Making of a Working-Class Public, 1780–1850." In *E. P. Thompson: Critical Perspectives*. Edited by Harvey J. Kaye and Keith McClelland. Philadelphia: Temple University Press. 12–49.
Epstein, James. 1994. *Radical Expression: Political Language, Ritual, and Symbol in England, 1790–1850*. New York: Oxford University Press.
———. 1988. "Radical Dining, Toasting and Symbolic Expression in Early Nineteenth-Century Lancashire: Rituals of Solidarity." *Albion*. 20: 271–291.
———. 1986. "Rethinking the Categories of Working-Class History." *Labour/Le Travail*. 18: 195–208.
———. 1982. *The Lion of Freedom: Feargus O'Connor and the Chartist Movement, 1832–1842*. London: Croom Helm.
———, and Dorothy Thompson, editors. 1982. *The Chartist Experience: Studies in Working-Class Radicalism: 1830–1860*. London: Macmillan.
Farnie, D. A. 1979. *The English Cotton Industry and the World Market, 1815–1896*. Oxford: Oxford University Press.
Fentriss, James, and Chris Wickham. 1992. *Social Memory*. Oxford: Blackwell.
Finn, Margot. 1992. "'A Vent Which Has Conveyed Our Principles': English Radical Patriotism in the Aftermath of 1848." *Journal of Modern History*. 64: 637–659.
Follows, John W. 1951. *Antecedents of the International Labour Organization*. Oxford: Clarendon Press.
Fong, H. D. 1930. *Triumph of the Factory System in England*. Tientsin: Chihli Press.
Foster, Derek. 1974. "Class and County Government in Early Nineteenth-Century Lancashire." *Northern History*. 9: 42–61.
Foster, John. 1985. "The Declassing of Language." *New Left Review*. 150: 29–45.
———. 1974. *Class Struggle and the Industrial Revolution*. New York: St. Martin's Press.
Fox, Alan. 1985. *History and Heritage: The Social Origins of the British Industrial Relations System*. London: George Allen & Unwin.
Fraser, Peter. 1961. "Public Petitioning and Parliament before 1832." *History*. 47: 195–211.
Freifeld, Mary. 1986. "Technological Change and the Self-Acting Mule: A Study of Skill and the Sexual Division of Labour." *Social History*. 11: 319–343.
Gadian, D. S. 1986. "Class Formation and Class Action in North-West Industrial Towns,

1830–50." In *Class, Power and Social Structure in British Nineteenth-Century Towns*. Edited by R. J. Morris. Leicester: Leicester University Press. 24–66.

———. 1978. "Class Consciousness in Oldham and Other North-West Industrial Towns 1830–1850." *Historical Journal*. 21: 161–172.

Gash, Norman. 1979. *Aristocracy and People: Britain, 1815–1865*. Cambridge: Harvard University Press.

Gatrell, V. A. C. 1977. "Labour, Power, and the Size of Firms in Lancashire in the Second Quarter of the Nineteenth Century." *Economic History Review*. Second Series. 30: 95–139.

George, M. Dorothy. 1962. *England in Transition*. Harmondsworth: Penguin.

———. 1927. "The Combination Laws Reconsidered." *Economic History*. 1: 214–228.

———. 1925. *London Life in the 18th Century*. London: K. Paul, Trench & Trubner.

Glenn, Robert. 1984. *Urban Workers in the Industrial Revolution*. London: Croom Helm.

Glover, William. 1884. *History of Ashton-under-Lyne and the Surrounding District*. Ashton-under-Lyne: J. Andrews.

Goodway, David 1984. *London Chartism, 1838–1848*. Cambridge: Cambridge University Press.

Goodwin, Albert. 1979. *The Friends of Liberty: The English Democratic Movement in the Age of the French Revolution*. Cambridge: Harvard University Press.

Gordon, Barry. 1979. *Economic Doctrine and Tory Liberalism, 1824–1830*. London: Macmillan.

Gosden, P. H. J. H. 1961. *The Friendly Societies in England, 1815–1875*. Manchester: Manchester University Press.

Gray, Robert. 1993. "Factory Legislation and the Gendering of Jobs in the North of England, 1830–1860," *Gender and History*. 5: 56–80.

———. 1988. "The Language of Factory Reform in Britain, c. 1830–1860." In *The Historical Meanings of Work*. Edited by Patrick Joyce. Cambridge: Cambridge University Press. 143–179.

———. 1986. "The Deconstruction of the English Working Class." *Social History*. 11: 363–373.

Haines, Brian W. 1980. "English Labour Law and the Separation from Contract." *Journal of Legal History*. 1: 262–246.

Hair, P. E. H. 1965. "The Binding of the Pitmen of the North-East, 1800–1809." *Durham University Journal*. 43: 1–13.

Hall, Catherine. 1992. *White, Male and Middle-Class: Explorations in Feminism and History*. New York: Routledge.

———. 1990. "The Tale of Samuel and Jemima: Gender and Working-class Culture in Nineteenth-century England." In *E. P. Thompson: Critical Perspectives*. Edited by Harvey J. Kaye and Keith McClelland. Philadelphia: Temple University Press. 78–102.

Hall, Robert G. 1991. "Work, Class and Politics in Ashton-under-Lyne, 1830–1860." Unpublished Ph.D. dissertation in History. Vanderbilt University.

———. 1989. "Tyranny, Work and Politics: The 1818 Strike Wave in the English Cotton District." *International Review of Social History*. 34: 433–470.

Hammond, J. L., and Barbara Hammond. 1967 (1919). *The Skilled Labourer, 1780–1832*. New York: August M. Kelley.

———. 1975 (1917). *The Town Labourer, 1780–1832: The New Civilization*. Gloucester, Mass.: Peter Smith.

Hanagan, Michael. 1993. "Commentary: For Reconstruction in Labor History." In *Rethinking Labor History: Essays on Discourse and Class Analysis*. Edited by Lenard R. Berlanstein. Urbana: University of Illinois Press. 182–199.

———. 1989. *Nascent Proletarians: Class Formation in Post-Revolutionary France*. Oxford: Basil Blackwell.

Handley, Robin. 1986. "Public Order, Petitioning and Freedom of Assembly." *Journal of Legal History*. 7: 123–155.

Harland, John, and T. T. Wilkinson. 1882. *Lancashire Folk-lore*. Manchester: John Heywood.

Harrison, J. F. C. 1969. *Quest for the New Moral World: Robert Owen and the Owenites in Britain and America*. New York: Charles Scribner & Sons.

Harrison, Mark. 1988. *Crowds and History: Mass Phenomena in English Towns, 1790–1835*. Cambridge: Cambridge University Press.

Harrop, Sylvia. 1980. "Community Involvement in Education in North-East Cheshire in the Late Eighteenth and Early Nineteenth Centuries." *Transactions of the Lancashire and Cheshire Antiquarian Society*. 80: 1–21.

———. 1974. "Nineteenth-Century Housing in Ashton." In *Victorian Ashton*. Edited by Sylvia A. Harrop and E. A. Rose. Ashton-under-Lyne: Tameside Libraries and Arts Committee. 29–49.

Hay, Douglas, et al. 1975. *Albion's Fatal Tree: Crime and Society in Eighteenth-Century England*. New York: Pantheon.

Haynes, M. J. 1977. "Class and Class Conflict in the Early Nineteenth Century: Northampton Shoemakers and the Grand National Consolidated Trades' Union." *Literature and History*. 5: 73–94.

Hedges, R. Y., and Allan Winterbottom. 1930. *The Legal History of Trade Unionism*. London: Longman, Green.

Henderson, W. O. 1976. "The Labour Force in the Textile Industries." *Archiv fur Sozialgeshcichte*. 16: 283–324.

Hertz, Gerald B. 1898. "The English Silk Industry in the Eighteenth Century." *English Historical Review*. 24: 710–727.

Hill, Frank. 1860. "Abstract of the Minutes of Evidence Taken before a Select Committee of The House of Commons Appointed in 1825, to Inquire into the Effect of the Repeal of the Combination Laws on the Conduct of Workmen and Others in Different Parts of the United Kingdom." In *National Association for the Promotion of Science. Trades' Societies and Strikes: Report of the Committee on Trades' Societies, Appointed by the National Association for the Promotion of Science*. London: John W. Parker & Son. 373–384.

Hill, Harold. 1927. "Mill Construction." *Journal of the Textile Institute: Special Issue, Official Record of the Annual Conference of the Textile Institute*. 18: 41–70.

Hill, Samuel. 1902. *Bygone Stalybridge*. Private Printing.

Hilton, Boyd. 1977. *Corn, Cash, Commerce: The Economic Policies of the Tory Governments, 1815–1830*. Oxford: Oxford University Press.

Hilton, George W. 1958. "The Truck Act of 1831." *Economic History Review*. Second Series. 10: 471–479.

———. 1957. "The British Truck System in the Nineteenth Century." *Journal of Political Economy*. 65: 237–256.

Hobsbawm, Eric J. 1984. "Artisan or Labour Aristocrat?" *Economic History Review*. Second Series. 37: 355–373.

———. 1983. "Introduction: Inventing Traditions." In *The Invention of Tradition*. Edited by E. J. Hobsbawm and Terrence Ranger. Cambridge: Cambridge University Press. 1–14.

———. 1952. "The Machine Breakers." *Past and Present*. 1: 57–70.

———. 1951. "The Tramping Artisan." *Economic History Review*. Second Series. 3: 299–320.

———, and George Rudé. 1968. *Captain Swing*. New York: Norton.

Holland, John. 1974. "Hugh Mason: Cotton Master, Puritan and Father Figure." In *Victorian Ashton*. Edited by Sylvia A. Harrop and E. A. Rose. Ashton-under-Lyne: Tameside Libraries and Arts Committee. 7–15.

Hollis, Patricia. 1970. *The Pauper Press: A Study of Working-Class Radicalism of the 1830s*. Oxford: Oxford University Press.

———, editor. 1973. *Class and Class Conflict in Nineteenth-Century Britain, 1815–1830*. London: Routledge & Kegan Paul.

Hone, J. Ann. 1982. *For the Cause of Truth: Radicalism in London, 1796–1821*. Oxford: Clarendon Press.

Howe, Anthony. 1984. *The Cotton Masters, 1830–1860*. Oxford: Clarendon Press.

Huberman, Michael. 1991. "How Did Labor Markets Work? More Evidence on Prices and Quantities in Cotton Spinning, 1822–1852." *Explorations in Economic History*. 28: 87–120.

———. 1986. "Invisible Handshakes in Lancashire: Cotton Spinning in the First Half of the Nineteenth Century." *Journal of Economic History*. 46: 987–998.

Jaffe, James. 1991. *The Struggle for Market Power: Industrial Relations in the British Coal Industry, 1800–1840*. Cambridge: Cambridge University Press.

Jewkes, John. 1930. "The Localisation of the Cotton Industry." *Economic History*. 2: 91–106.

Johnson, Christopher H. 1993. "Lifeworld, System, and Communicative Action: The Habermasian Alternative in Social History." In *Rethinking Labor History: Essays on Discourse and Class Analysis*. Edited by Lenard R. Berlanstein. Urbana: University of Illinois Press. 55–89.

Jones, S. R. H. 1987. "Technology, Transaction Costs, and the Transition to Factory Production in the British Silk Industry, 1700–1870." *Journal of Economic History*. 47: 71–96.

Jones, Stuart. 1978. "The Lancashire Cotton Magnates' Move into Banking, 1826–1850." *Textile History*. 9: 90–111.

Jordan, W. M. 1931. "The Silk Industry in London, 1760–1830, with Special Reference to the Conditions of the Wage-Earners and the Policy of the Spitalfields Acts." Unpublished M.A. thesis in History, University of London.

Joyce, Patrick. 1995. "The End of Social History," *Social History*. 20: 73–91.

———. 1994. *Democratic Subjects: The Self and the Social in Nineteenth-Century England*. Cambridge: Cambridge University Press.

———. 1993. "The Imaginary Discontents of Social History: A Note of Response to Mayfield and Thorne, Lawrence and Taylor." *Social History*. 18: 81–85.

———. 1992. "A People and a Class: Industrial Workers and the Social Order in Nineteenth-Century England." In *Social Orders and Social Classes in Europe since 1500: Studies in Social Transformation*. Edited by M. L. Bush. London: Longman. 199–217.

———. 1991. *Visions of the People*. Cambridge: Cambridge University Press.

———. 1990. "Work." In *The Cambridge Social History of Britain, 1750–1950: People and Their Environment*. v. 2. Edited by F. M. L. Thompson. Cambridge: Cambridge University Press. 131–194.

———. 1988. "The Historical Meanings of Work: An Introduction." In *The Historical Meanings of Work*. Cambridge: Edited by Patrick Joyce. Cambridge University Press. 1–30.

———. 1980. *Work, Society and Politics*. Atlantic Highlands: Harvester.

———. 1975. "Factory Politics in Lancashire in the Later Nineteenth Century." *Historical Journal*. 18: 525–553.

Kahn-Freund, Otto. 1977. "Blackstone's Neglected Child: The Contract of Employment." *Law Quarterly Review*. 93: 508–522.

Kaye, Harvey J. 1990. "E. P. Thompson, the British Marxist Tradition, and the Contemporary Crisis." In *E. P. Thompson: Critical Perspectives*. Edited by Keith McClelland and Harvey J. Kaye. Philadelphia: Temple University Press. 252–275.

———. 1984. *The British Marxist Historians*. Oxford: Polity Press.

Keith-Lucas, B. 1952. *The English Local Government Franchise, A Short History*. Oxford: Basil Blackwell.

Kenmitz, Thomas M., and Jacques Fleurage. 1974. "J. R. Stephens and the Chartist Movement." *International Review of Social History*. 19: 211–227.

Kirby, R. G., and A. E. Musson. 1975. *The Voice of the People: John Doherty, 1798–1854*. Manchester: Manchester University Press.

Kirk, Neville. 1987. "In Defense of Class: A Critique of Revisionist Writing upon the Nineteenth-Century English Working Class." *International Review of Social History*. 32: 2–47.

———. 1985. *The Growth of Working-Class Reformism in Mid-Victorian England*. London: Croom Helm.

Koditschek, Theodore. 1990. *Class Formation and Urban-Industrial Society: Bradford, 1750–1850*. Cambridge: Cambridge University Press.

Kussmal, Ann. 1981. *Servants in Husbandry in Early Modern England*. Cambridge: Cambridge University Press.

Lawrence, Jon, and Miles Taylor. 1993. "The Poverty of Protest: Gareth Stedman Jones and the Politics of Language—A Reply." *Social History*. 18: 1–15.

Lazonick, William. 1981. "Production Relations, Labor Productivity, and Choice of Technique: British and U.S. Cotton Spinning." *Journal of Economic History*. 41: 491–516.

———. 1979. "Industrial Relations and Technical Change: The Case of the Self-acting Mule." *Cambridge Journal of Economics*. 3: 231–262.

Lee, Clive H. 1972. *A Cotton Enterprise, 1795–1840: A History of M'Connel & Kennedy Fine Cotton Spinners*. Manchester: Manchester University Press.

Lees, Lynn. 1980. "The Study of Social Conflict in English Industrial Towns." In *Urban History Yearbook 1980*. Edited by David Roeder. Leicester: Leicester University Press. 34–43.

Linebaugh, Peter. 1992. *The London Hanged: Crime and Civil Society in the Eighteenth Century*. Cambridge: Cambridge University Press.

———. 1985. "(Marxist) Social History and (Conservative) Legal History: A Reply to Professor Langbein." *New York University Law Review*. 60: 212–243.

———. 1982. "Labour History without the Labour Process: A Note on John Gast and His Times." *Social History*. 7: 319–328.

Lloyd-Jones, Roger, and A. A. Le Roux. 1980. "The Size of Firms in the Cotton Industry: Manchester, 1815–1841." *Economic History Review*. Second Series. 33: 72–82.

Lown, Judy. 1990. *Women and Industrialization: Gender at Work in Nineteenth-Century England*. Minneapolis: University of Minnesota Press.

Malcolmson, Robert W. 1973. *Popular Recreations in English Society, 1700–1850*. Cambridge: Cambridge University Press.

Manchee, W. H. 1913. "Memories of Spitalfields." *Proceedings of the Huguenot Society of London*. 10: 298–345.

Mann, Julia de Lacy. 1958. "The Textile Industry: Machinery for Cotton, Flax, Wool, 1760–1850." In *A History of Technology*. Edited by Charles Singer et al. Oxford: Clarendon Press. 277–307.

Mayfield, David, and Susan Thorne. 1993. "Reply to 'The Poverty of Protest' and 'The Imaginary Discontents.'" *Social History*. 18: 219–233.

———. 1992. "Social History and Its Discontents: Gareth Stedman Jones and the Politics of Language." *Social History*. 17: 165–188.

McCalman, Iain. 1989. *Radical Underworld: Prophets, Revolutionaries and Pornographers in London, 1795–1840*. Cambridge: Cambridge University Press.

———. 1987. "Ultra-Radicalism and Convivial Debating-Clubs in London, 1795–1838." *English Historical Review*. 102: 309–333.

———. 1984. "Unrespectable Radicalism: Infidels and Pornography in Early Nineteenth-Century London." *Past and Present*. 104: 74–110.
McCann, Phillip. 1977. "Popular Education, Socialization, and Social Control: Spitalfields 1812–1824." In *Popular Education and Socialization in the Nineteenth Century*. Edited by Phillip McCann. London: Methuen. 1–40.
McClelland, Keith. 1989. "Some Thoughts on Masculinity and the 'Representative Artisan' in Britain, 1850–1915." *Gender & History*. 1: 164–177.
McKendrick, Neil. 1961. "Josiah Wedgewood and Factory Discipline." *Historical Journal*. 4: 30–55.
Middleton, Thomas. 1932. *The History of Hyde and Its Neighborhood*. Hyde: Higham Press.
Midwinter, E. C. 1968. *Law and Order in Early Victorian Lancashire*. York: St. Anthony Press.
Moher, James. 1988. "From Suppression to Containment: Roots of Trade Union Law to 1825." In *British Trade Unionism 1750–1850: The Formative Years*. Edited by John Rule. London: Longman. 74–97.
——— et al. 1984. "Conference Report. From Suppression to Containment: Trade Union Law 1799–1825." *Bulletin for the Society for the Study of Labour History*. 49: 7–22.
Morgan, Carol E. 1992. "Women, Work and Consciousness in the Mid-Nineteenth-Century English Cotton Industry." *Social History*. 17: 23–41.
Morris, R. J. 1983. "Voluntary Societies and British Urban Elites, 1780–1850: An Analysis." *Historical Journal*. 26: 95–118.
———. 1980. "What Happened to the British Working Class, 1750–1850?" *Bulletin of the Society of the Study of Labour History*. 41: 13–18.
———. 1972. *Class and Class Consciousness in the Industrial Revolution, 1780–1850*. London: Macmillan.
Munby, Lionel. 1971. "The Luddites in the Period 1779–1830." In *The Luddites and Other Essays*. Edited by Lionel Munby. London: Michael Katanka. 33–56.
Munger, Frank. 1981a. "Contentious Gatherings in Lancashire, England, 1750–1830." In *Class Conflict and Collective Action*. Edited by Louise A. Tilly and Charles Tilly. Beverly Hills: Sage. 73–109.
———. 1981b. "Suppression of Popular Gatherings in Lancashire, England, 1800–1830." *American Journal of Legal History*. 25: 111–140.
Musson, A. E. 1972. *British Trade Unions, 1800–1875*. London: Macmillan.
———. 1958. "The Ideology of Early Co-operation in Lancashire and Cheshire." *Transactions of the Lancashire and Cheshire Antiquarian Society*. 68: 117–138.
Oliver, W. H. 1964. "The Consolidated Trades' Union of 1834." *Economic History Review*. Second Series. 17: 77–95.
———. 1958. "The Labour Exchange Phase of the Co-operation Movement." *Oxford Economic Papers*. New Series. 10: 355–367.
Orren, Karen. 1991. *Belated Feudalism: Labor, the Law and Liberal Development in the United States*. Cambridge: Cambridge University Press.
Orth, John V. 1987. "English Combination Acts of the Eighteenth Century." *Law and History Review*. 5: 175–211.
———. 1980. "The Legal Status of English Trade Unions, 1799–1871." In *Law-Making and Law-Makers in British History*. Edited by Alan Harding. London: Royal Historical Society. 195–207.
Palmer, Bryan D. 1994. "Homage to E. P. Thompson, Part II," *Labour/Le Travail*. 33: 13–68.
———. 1993a. "Critical Theory, Historical Materialism, and the Ostensible End of Marxism: The Poverty of Theory Revisited." *International Review of Social History*. 38: 133–162.
———. 1993b. "Homage to E. P. Thompson, Part I," *Labour/Le Travail*. 32: 10–71.
———. 1990a. "The Eclipse of Materialism: Marxism and the Writing of Social History in

the 1980s." In *The Socialist Register 1990*. Edited by Ralph Miliband, Leo Panitch, and John Saville. London: Merlin. 111–146.

———. 1990b. *Descent into Discourse: The Reification of Language and the Writing of Social History*. Philadelphia: Temple University Press.

———. 1987. "Response to Joan Scott." *International Labor and Working-Class History*. 31: 14–23.

———. 1976. "Most Uncommon Men: Craft and Culture in Historical Perspective." *Labour/Le Travailleur*. 1: 5–31.

Parssinen, T. 1972. "Association, Convention and Anti-Parliament in British Radical Politics, 1771–1848." *English Historical Review*. 86: 504–533.

Patterson, A. Temple. 1948. "Luddism, Hampden Clubs, and Trade Unions in Leicestershire, 1816–17." *English Historical Review*. 93: 170–188.

Peacock, A. J. 1971. "Luddism and the Early Trade Unions." In *People for the People*. Edited by David Rubinstein. London: Ithaca Press. 45–52.

Peel, Frank. 1968 (1895). *The Rising of the Luddites, Chartists and Plug-Drawers*. 4th ed. New York: August M. Kelley.

Pelling, Henry. 1963. *A History of British Trade Unionism*. London: Macmillan.

Pinchbeck, Ivy. 1969. *Women Workers and the Industrial Revolution, 1780–1850*. London: Virago.

Plummer, Alfred. 1972. *The London Weavers' Company, 1600–1970*. London: Routledge & Kegan Paul.

Pollard, Sidney. 1965. *The Genesis of Modern Management*. London: Arnold.

———. 1964. "The Factory Village in the Industrial Revolution." *English Historical Review*. 79: 513–531.

———. 1963. "Factory Discipline in the Industrial Revolution." *Economic History Review*. Second Series. 16: 254–271.

Poovey, Mary. 1988. *Uneven Developments: The Ideological Work of Gender in Mid-Victorian England*. Chicago: University of Chicago Press.

Price, Richard. 1984. "Conflict and Co-operation: A Reply to Patrick Joyce." *Social History*. 9: 217–224.

———. 1983. "The Labour Process and History." *Social History*. 8: 57–75.

Prothero, Iowerth. 1979. *Artisans and Politics in Early Nineteenth-Century London: John Gast and His Times*. London: Methuen.

Randall, Adrian. 1991. *Before the Luddites: Custom, Community and Machinery in the English Woollen Industry, 1776–1809*. Cambridge: Cambridge University Press.

———. 1990. "New Languages or Old?: Labour, Capital and Discourse in the Industrial Revolution." *Social History*. 15: 195–216.

———. 1986. "The Philosophy of Luddism: The Case of the West of England Woolen Workers, ca. 1790–1809." *Technology and Culture*. 27: 1–17.

———. 1982. "The Shearmen and the Wiltshire Outrages of 1802: Trade Unionism and Industrial Violence." *Social History*. 7: 283–304.

Ratcliffe, Barrie M., and W. H. Chaloner, editors and translators. 1977. *A French Sociologist Looks at Britain: Gustave d'Eichthal and British Society in 1828*. Manchester: Manchester University Press.

Roberts, David. 1979. *Paternalism in Early Victorian England*. New Brunswick: Rutgers University Press.

Roby, John. 1872. *Traditions of Lancashire*. Manchester: John Heywood.

Rodgers, H. B. 1960. "The Lancashire Cotton Industry in 1840." *Institute of British Geographers: Transactions and Papers*. 28: 135–154.

Rose, A. E. 1974. "Ashton Churches and Chapels." In *Victorian Ashton*. Edited by Sylvia A. Harrop and E. A. Rose. Ashton-under-Lyne: Tameside Libraries and Arts Committee. 60–75.

———. 1969. *Methodism in Ashton-under-Lyne, Part II*. Ashton-under-Lyne: Andrews.

Rose, Sonya O. 1993. "Gender and Labour History: The Nineteenth-Century Legacy." *International Review of Social History.* 38: 145–162.

———. 1992. *Limited Livelihoods: Gender and Class in Nineteenth-Century England.* Berkeley: University of California Press.

———. 1991. "'From Behind the Women's Petticoats': The English Factory Act of 1874 as a Cultural Production." *Journal of Historical Sociology.* 4: 32–51.

———. 1988. "Gender Antagonism and Class Conflict: Exclusionary Strategies of Male Trade Unionists in Nineteenth-Century Britain." *Social History.* 13: 191–208.

———. 1987. "Gender Segregation in the Transition to the Factory: The English Hosiery Industry, 1850–1910." *Feminist Studies.* 13: 167–184.

———. 1986. "'Gender at Work': Sex, Class and Industrial Capitalism," *History Workshop.* 21: 113–131.

Rothstein, Natalie. 1977. "The Introduction of the Jacquard Loom to Great Britain." In *Studies in Textile History.* Edited by Veronica Gervers. Toronto: Royal Ontario Museum. 281–304.

Rowe, D. J. 1967. "Chartism and the Spitalfields Weavers." *Economic History Review.* Second Series. 20: 482–493.

Rudé, George. 1981. *The Crowd in History 1730–1848.* Revised Edition. London: Lawrence & Wishart.

———. 1962. *Wilkes and Liberty.* Oxford: Oxford University Press.

Rule, John. 1988. "The Property of Skill in the Period of Manufacture." In *The Historical Meaning of Work.* Edited by Patrick Joyce. Cambridge: Cambridge University Press. 99–118.

———. 1986. *The Labouring Classes in Early Industrial England, 1750–1820.* London: Macmillan.

———. 1985. "Artisan Attitudes: A Comparative Survey of Skilled Labour and Proletarianization before 1848." *Bulletin for the Society for the Study of Labour History.* 50: 22–31.

———. 1981. *The Experience of Labour in Eighteenth-Century Industry.* London: Croom Helm.

Sabel, Charles, and Jonathan Zeitlin. 1985. "Historical Alternatives to Mass Production: Politics, Markets, and Technology in Nineteenth-Century Industrialization." *Past and Present.* 108: 133–174.

Samuel, Raphael. 1992. Reading the Signs: II. Fact-grubbers and Mind Readers." *History Workshop.* 33: 220–251.

———. 1991. "Reading the Signs." *History Workshop.* 32: 88–109.

———. 1977. "Workshop of the World: Steam Power and Hand Power in Mid-Victorian England." *History Workshop.* 2: 6–72.

Sanderson, Michael. 1967. "Education and the Family in the Industrial Revolution." *Economic History Review.* Second Series. 20(2): 266–279.

Saville, John. 1971. "J. E. Smith and the Owenite Movement, 1833–1834." In *Robert Owen: Prophet of the Poor.* Edited by Sidney Pollard and John Salt. London: Macmillan. 115–144.

Schwarz, L. D. 1982. "Social Class and Social Geography: The Middle Classes in London at the End of the Eighteenth Century," *Social History.* 7: 167–185.

———. 1979. "Income Distribution and Social Structure in London in the Late Eighteenth Century," *Economic History Review.* Second Series. 32: 250–259.

Scott, J. H. 1896. *Spitalfields, 1197–1896. Past and Present.*

Scott, Joan W. 1991. "The Evidence of Experience." *Critical Inquiry.* 17: 773–797.

———. 1988. "Women in The Making of the English Working Class." In *Gender and the Politics of History.* New York: Columbia University Press. 67–90.

———. 1987. "On Language, Gender, and Working-Class History." *International Labor and Working-Class History.* 31: 1–13.

Seed, John. 1993. "Capital and Class Formation in Early Industrial England." *Social History*. 18: 17–30.

———. 1982. "Unitarianism, Political Economy and the Antimonies of Liberal Culture in Manchester, 1830–50." *Social History*. 7: 1–25.

Sewell, William. 1993. "Toward a Post-materialist Rhetoric for Labor History." In *Rethinking Labor History*. Edited by Lenard R. Berlanstein. Champaign: University of Illinois. 15–38.

———. 1990. "How Classes are Made: Critical Reflections on E. P. Thompson's Theory of Working-Class Formation." In *E. P. Thompson: Critical Perspectives*. Edited by Harvey J. Kaye and Keith McClelland. Philadelphia: Temple University Press. 50–78.

———. 1988. "Uneven Development, the Autonomy of Politics, and the Dockworkers of Nineteenth-Century Marseilles." *American Historical Review*. 93: 604–637.

Shapiro, Seymour. 1967. *Capital and the Cotton Industry in the Industrial Revolution*. Ithaca: Cornell University Press.

Sharpin, Steven, and Barry Barnes. 1977. "Science, Nature, and Control: Interpreting Mechanics' Institutes." *Social Studies of Science*. 7: 31–74.

Shelton, Walter J. 1972. *English Hunger and Industrial Disorders*. Toronto: Toronto University Press.

Simon, Daphne. 1954. "Master and Servant." In *Democracy and the Labour Movement*. Edited by John Saville. London: Lawrence & Wishart. 160–200.

Smail, John. 1991. "New Languages? Yes Indeed: A Reply to Adrian Randall." *Social History*. 16: 217–222.

———. 1987. "New Languages for Labour and Capital: The Transformation of Discourse in the Early Years of the Industrial Revolution." *Social History*. 12: 49–72.

Smart, William. 1964. *Economic Annals of the Nineteenth Century 1821–1830*. v. 2. New York: Augustus M. Kelley.

Smiles, Samuel. 1881. *The Huguenots: Their Settlements, Churches and Industries in England and Ireland*. London: John Murray.

Smith, Roland. 1963. "Manchester as a Centre for the Manufacture and Merchanting of Cotton Goods, 1820–30." *University of Birmingham Historical Journal*. 4: 47–65.

The Spitalfields Acts. Six Pamphlets, 1818–1828. Advisory Editor Kenneth E. Carpenter. New York: Arno Press. 1972.

Stallybrass, Peter. 1985. "'Drunk with the Cup of Liberty': Robin Hood, the Carnivalesque, and the Rhetoric of Violence in Early Modern England." *Semiotica*, 54: 113–145.

Stansell, Christine. 1987. "A Response to Joan Scott." *International Labor and Working-Class History*. 31: 24–29.

Stedman Jones, Gareth. 1991. "The Changing Face of 19th-Century Britain." *History Today*. 41: 36–40.

———. 1984. "The Mid-Century Crisis and the 1848 Revolutions." *Theory and Society*. 12: 505–520.

———. 1983. *Languages of Class: Studies in English Working-Class History, 1832–1982*. Cambridge: Cambridge University Press.

———. 1982. "The Language of Chartism." In *The Chartist Experience: Studies in Working-Class Radicalism: 1830–1860*. Edited by James Epstein and Dorothy Thompson. London: Macmillan. 3–59.

———. 1975. "Class Struggle and the Industrial Revolution." *New Left Review*. 40: 35–69.

Steinberg, Marc W. 1996a. "'The Labour of the Country Is the Wealth of the Country . . .': Class Identity, Consciousness and the Role of Discourse in the Making of the English Working Class." *International Labor and Working-Class History*. 49: 1–25.

———. 1996b. "Culturally Speaking: Creating a Dialogue between Post-Structuralism and the Thompsonian Perspective." *Social History*. 21: 193–214.

———. 1995a. *See* Social Science and Other Theoretical Literature section.
———. 1995b. "'The Great End of All Government': Working Peoples' Construction of Citizenship Claims in Early Nineteenth-Century England and the Matter of Class." *International Review of Social History*. Supplement 3. 40: 19–50.
Stevenson, John. 1979. *Popular Disturbances in Britain 1700–1870*. London: Longman.
Storch, Robert, editor. 1982. *Popular Culture in Nineteenth-Century England*. London: Croom Helm.
Styles, John. 1983. "Embezzlement, Industry and the Law in England, 1500–1800," In *Manufacture in Town and Country before the Factory*. Edited by Maxine Berg, Pat Hudson, and Michael Sonenscher. Cambridge: Cambridge University Press. 173–210.
Survey of London. 1957. *Spitalfields and Mile End New Town*. General Editor F. H. W. Sheppard. v. 27. London: Athelone Press.
Sykes, Robert A. 1988. "Trade Unionism and Class Consciousness: the 'Revolutionary' Period of General Unionism, 1829–1834." In *British Trade Unionism, 1750–1850: The Formative Years*. Edited by John Rule. London: Longman. 178–199.
———. 1982a. "Popular Politics and Trade Unionism in Southeast Lancashire, 1829–1842." v. 1. Ph.D. diss., University of Manchester.
———. 1982b. "Early Chartism and Trade Unionism in South-East Lancashire." In *The Chartist Experience: Studies in Working-Class Radicalism: 1830–1860*. Edited by James Epstein and Dorothy Thompson. London: Macmillan. 152–193.
———. n.d. "Physical Force Chartism: The Cotton District and the Chartist Crisis of 1839." Unpublished manuscript.
Taylor, A. J. 1949. "Concentration and Specialization in the Lancashire Cotton Industry, 1825–1850." *Economic History Review*. Second Series. 1: 114–122.
Taylor, Barbara. 1983. *Eve and the New Jerusalem: Socialism and Feminism in the Nineteenth Century*. New York: Pantheon.
Taylor, Miles. 1992. "John Bull and the Iconography of Public Opinion in England c. 1712–1929." *Past and Present*. 134: 93–128.
Thomis, Malcolm I., editor. 1972. *Luddism in Nottinghamshire*. Thoronton Society Record Series. v. 26. London: Phillimore.
———. 1970. *The Luddites*. New York: Shocken.
Thompson, Dorothy. 1987. "The Languages of Class." *Bulletin of the Society for the Study of Labour History*. 52: 54–57.
———. 1984. *The Chartists*. New York: Pantheon.
Thompson, Edward P. 1994a. "Hunting the Jacobin Fox." *Past and Present*. 142: 94–140.
———. 1994b. "Agenda for a Radical History." In *Making History: Writings on History and Culture*. New York: New Press. 358–364.
———. 1993a. "The Making of a Ruling Class." *Dissent*. 40: 377–382.
———. 1993b. *Witness against the Beast: William Blake and the Moral Law*. Cambridge: Cambridge University Press.
———. 1991. *Customs in Common: Studies in Traditional Popular Culture*. New York: New Press.
———. 1981a. "The Politics of Theory." In *People's History and Socialist Theory*. Edited by Raphael Samuel. London: Routledge & Kegan Paul. 396–408.
———. 1981b. "A Letter to America." In *Protest and Survive*. Edited by E. P. Thompson and Dan Smith. New York: Monthly Review Press. 3–52.
———. 1978a (1965). "The Peculiarities of the English." In *The Poverty of Theory and Other Essays*. New York: Monthly Review Press. 245–301.
———. 1978b. "Eighteenth-Century English Society: Class Struggle without Class?" *Social History*. 3: 133–165.
———. 1977a. "Folklore, Anthropology, and Social History." *Indian Historical Review*. 3: 247–266.

———. 1977b. "Caudwell." In *The Socialist Register 1977*. Edited by Ralph Miliband and John Saville. London: Merlin. 228–276.
———. 1976. "The Grid of Inheritance: A Comment." In *Family and Inheritance: Rural Society in Western Europe, 1200–1800*. Edited by Jack Goody, Joan Thirsk, and E. P. Thompson. Cambridge: Cambridge University Press. 328–360.
———. 1974a. "Patrician Culture, Plebeian Society." *Journal of Social History*. 7: 382–405.
———. 1974b. "Time, Work-Discipline, and Industrial Capitalism." In *Essays in Social History*. Edited by M. W. Flinn and T. C. Smout. Oxford: Oxford University Press. 39–77.
———. 1971. "The Moral Economy of the Crowd in the Eighteenth Century." *Past and Present*. 50: 76–136.
———. 1968. *The Making of the English Working Class*. 2d ed. Harmondsworth: Penguin.
———. 1966. *The Making of the English Working Class*. New York: Vintage.
———. 1961a. "The Long Revolution." *New Left Review*. 9: 24–33.
———. 1961b. "The Long Revolution II." *New Left Review*. 10: 34–39.
———. 1960a. "Revolution." *New Left Review*. 3: 3–9.
———. 1960b. "Revolution Again! Or Shut Your Ears and Run." *New Left Review*. 6: 18–31.
———. 1960c. "Homage to Tom Maguire." In *Essays in Labour History*. Edited by Asa Briggs and John Saville. London: Macmillan. 276–316.
———. 1959. "Commitment in Politics." *Universities and Left Review*. 6: 50–55.
———. 1957a. "Socialist Humanism: An Epistle to the Philistines." *New Reasoner*. 1: 105–143.
———. 1957b. "Socialism and the Intellectuals," *Universities and Left Review*. 1: 31–36.
Thompson, Noel W. 1988. *The Market and Its Critics: Socialist Political Economy in Nineteenth-Century Britain*. London: Routledge.
———. 1984. *The People's Science: The Popular Political Economy of Exploitation and Crisis, 1816–34*. Cambridge: Cambridge University Press.
Trimberger, Ellen Kay. 1984. "E. P. Thompson: Understanding the Process of History." In *Vision and Method in Historical Sociology*. Edited by Theda Skocpol. Cambridge: Cambridge University Press. 211–243.
Tucker, Rufus J. 1936. "Real Wages of Artisans in London, 1729–1935." *Journal of the American Statistical Association*. 31: 73–84.
Turner, Herbert A. 1962. *Trade Union Growth, Structure and Policy: A Comparative Study of the Cotton Unions*. London: George Allen & Unwin.
Tylecote, Mabel. 1957. *The Mechanics' Institutes of Lancashire and Yorkshire before 1851*. Manchester: Manchester University Press.
Valenze, Deborah. 1995. *The First Industrial Woman*. New York: Oxford University Press.
Valverde, Marianna. 1988. "'Giving the Female a Domestic Turn': The Social, Legal and Moral Regulation of Women's Work in British Cotton Mills, 1820–1850." *Journal of Social History*. 21: 619–34.
Vernon, James. 1994. "Who's Afraid of the 'Linguistic Turn'? The Politics of Social History and Its Discontents." *Social History*. 19: 81–97.
———. 1993. *Politics and the People: A Study in English Political Culture, c. 1815–67*. Cambridge: Cambridge University Press.
von Tunzelman, G. N. 1978. *Steam Power and British Industrialization before 1860*. Oxford: Clarendon Press.
Walby, Sylvia. 1990. "From Private to Public Patriarchy: The Periodization of British History." *Women's Studies International Forum*. 13: 91–104.
Walton, John K., and Robert Poole. 1982. "The Lancashire Wakes in the Nineteenth Century." In *Popular Culture and Customs in Nineteenth-Century England*. Edited by Robert D. Storch. London: Croom Helm. 100–124.
Warburton, W. H. 1931. *The History of Trade Union Organization in the North Staffordshire Potteries*. London: George Allen & Unwin.

Ward, J. T. 1965–1966. "The Factory Movement in Lancashire, 1830–1835." *Transactions of the Lancashire and Cheshire Antiquarian Society*. 75–76: 186–210.

——. 1958. "Revolutionary Tory: The Life of Joseph Rayner Stephens of Ashton-under-Lyne (1805–1879)." *Transactions of the Lancashire and Cheshire Antiquarian Society*. 68: 93–116.

Warner, Frank. 1921. *The Silk Industry in the United Kingdom: Its Origin and Development*. London: Drane's.

Wearmouth, R. F. 1949. *Methodism and Working-Class Movements of England, 1800–1850*. London: Epworth.

Weaver, Stewart. 1988. "The Political Ideology of Short Time: England, 1820–1850." In *Worktime and Industrialization: An International History*. Edited by Gary Cross. Philadelphia: Temple University Press. 77–102.

Webb, Sidney, and Beatrice Webb. 1920. *The History of Trade Unionism*. Revised Ed. London: Longman & Green.

——. 1906. *English Local Government from the Revolution to the Municipal Corporations Act: The Parish and the County*. London: Longman, Green.

Weekley, C. M. 1950. "The Spitalfields Silkweavers." *Proceedings of the Huguenot Society of London*. 18: 284–291.

Wells, E. A. 1972. *The British Hosiery and Knitwear Industry: Its History and Organization*. New York: Barnes & Noble.

Wiener, Joel H. 1983. *Radicalism and Freethought in Nineteenth-Century Britain: The Life of Richard Carlile*. Greenwood Press.

Wolf, Wayne. 1978. "The Radical Movement in Clerkenwell and Spitalfields, 1820–1850: A Comparative Study." Master's thesis, University of London.

——. 1975. "The Spitalfields Silk Weavers: Their Place in the London Radical Movement and the Decline of Their Community, 1820–1850." Bachelor's thesis, University of Sussex.

Wood, George H. 1910a. "The Statistics of Wages in the United Kingdom during the Nineteenth Century (Part XV.) The Cotton Industry. Section I." *Journal of the Royal Statistical Society*. New Series, 73: 39–58.

——. 1910b. "The Statistics of Wages in the United Kingdom during the Nineteenth Century (Part XV.) The Cotton Industry. Section II." *Journal of the Royal Statistical Society*. New Series. 73: 128–163.

——. 1910c. "The Statistics of Wages in the United Kingdom during the Nineteenth Century (Part XV.) The Cotton Industry. Section III." *Journal of The Royal Statistical Society*. New Series. 73: 283–315.

——. 1910d. "The Statistics of Wages in the United Kingdom during the Nineteenth Century (Part XVIII.) The Cotton Industry. Section IV." *Journal of the Royal Statistical Society*. New Series. 73: 411–432.

——. 1910e. "The Statistics of Wages in the Nineteenth Century (Part XIX.) The Cotton Industry. Section V. Changes in the Average Wage of All Employed, with Some Account of the Forces Operating to Accelerate or Retard the Progress of Industry." *Journal of the Royal Statistical Society*. New Series. 73: 585–633.

Wright, A. R. 1936. *British Calendar Customs, England, Volume I: Moveable Festivals*. Edited by T. E. Jones. London: Folk-lore Society.

Yeo, Eileen 1971. "Robert Owen and Radical Culture." In *Robert Owen: Prophet of the Poor*. Edited by Sidney Pollard and John Salt. London: Macmillan. 84–114.

——, and E. P. Thompson, editors. 1975. *The Unknown Mayhew*. New York: Schocken.

Social Science and Other Theoretical Literature

Aminzade, Ronald. 1993a. *Ballots and Barricades: Class Formation and Republican Politics in France, 1830–1871*. Princeton: Princeton University Press.

———. 1993b. "Class Analysis, Politics, and French Labor History." In *Rethinking Labor History: Essays on Discourse and Class Analysis*. Edited by Lenard R. Berlanstein. Urbana: University of Illinois Press. 90–113.

Bakhtin, Mikhail M. 1986. *Speech Genres and Other Late Essays*. Translated by Vern W. McGee. Edited by Caryl Emerson and Michael Holquist. Austin: University of Texas Press.

———. 1984. *Rabelais and His World*. Translated by Helene Iswolsky. Bloomington: Indiana University Press.

———. 1981. *The Dialogic Imagination*. Edited by Michael Holquist. Translated by Caryl Emerson and Michael Holquist. Austin: University of Texas Press.

Bernard-Donals, Michael F. 1994. *Mikhail Bakhtin: Between Phenomenology and Marxism*. Cambridge: Cambridge University Press.

Biernacki, Richard. 1995. *The Fabrication of Labor: Germany and Britain, 1640–1914*. Berkeley: University of California Press.

Brandist, Craig. 1996a. "Gramsci, Bakhtin and the Semiotics of Hegemony." *New Left Review*. 216: 94–109.

———. 1996b. "The Official and the Popular in Gramsci and Bakhtin." *Theory, Culture and Society*. 13: 59–74.

Briggs, Charles L., and Richard Bauman. 1992. "Genre, Intertextuality, and Social Power." *Journal of Linguistic Anthropology*. 2: 131–172.

Buechler, Steven M. 1993. "Beyond Resource Mobilization: Emerging Trends in Social Movement Theory." *Sociological Inquiry*. 34: 217–235.

Calhoun, Craig. 1995. "'New Social Movements' of the Early Nineteenth Century." In *Cycles and Repertoires of Collective Action*. Edited by Mark Traugott. Durham: Duke University Press. 173–216.

———. 1993. "Who Was That Masked Post-Marxist? A Response to Steinberg." *Political Power and Social Theory*. 8: 277–295.

———. 1992. "Postmodernism and Pseudohistory." *Theory, Culture and Society*. 10: 75–96.

———. 1991. "The Problem of Identity in Collective Action." In *Macro-Micro Linkages in Sociology*. Edited by Joan Huber. Newbury Park: Sage. 51–75.

———. 1987. "Class, Place and Industrial Revolution." In *Class and Space: The Making of Urban Society*. Edited by Nigel Thrift and Peter Williams. London: Routledge & Kegan Paul. 51–72.

———. 1983a. "The Radicalism of Tradition: Community Strength or Venerable Disguise and Borrowed Language?" *American Journal of Sociology*. 88: 886–914.

———. 1983b. "Industrialization and Radicalism: British and French Workers' Movements and the Mid-Nineteenth-Century Crisis." *Theory and Society*. 12: 485–504.

———. 1982. *The Question of Class Struggle: Social Foundations of Popular Radicalism during the Industrial Revolution*. Chicago: University of Chicago Press.

———. 1980a. "Transition in Social Foundations for Collective Action: Communities in Southeast Lancashire Textile Regions in the 1820s and 1830s." *Social Science History*. 4: 419–452.

———. 1980b. "Community: Toward a Variable Conceptualization for Comparative Research." *Social History*. 5: 105–129.

Cohen, Jean. 1985. "Strategy or Identity: New Theoretical Paradigms and Contemporary Social Movements." *Social Research*. 52: 663–716.

———. 1983. "Rethinking Social Movements." *Berkeley Journal of Sociology*. 28: 97–113.

———, and Andrew Arato. 1992. *Civil Society and Political Theory*. Cambridge: MIT Press.

Cresswell, Timothy. 1994. "Putting Women in Their Place: The Carnival at Greenham Common." *Antipode*. 26: 35–58.

Eley, Geoff. 1996. "Is All the World a Text? From Social History to the History of Society Two Decades Later." In *The Historic Turn in the Human Sciences*. Edited by Terrence J. McDonald. Ann Arbor: University of Michigan Press. 193–244.

Emirbayer, Mustafa. 1997. "Manifesto for a Relational Sociology." *American Journal of Sociology.* 103(2): 281–317.
Epstein, Barbara. 1991. *Political Protest and Cultural Revolution: Nonviolent Direct Action in the 1970s and 1980s.* Berkeley: University of California Press.
Evans, F. 1990. "Language and Political Agency: Derrida, Marx, and Bakhtin." *Southern Journal of Philosophy.* 27(4): 505–523.
Ewick, Patricia, and Susan Silbey. 1995. "Subversive Stories and Hegemonic Tales: Toward a Sociology of Narrative." *Law and Society Review.* 29(2): 197–226.
Fantasia, Rick. 1988. *Cultures of Solidarity.* Berkeley: University of California Press.
Femia, Joseph V. 1981. *Gramsci's Political Thought: Hegemony, Consciousness, and the Revolutionary Process.* Oxford: Oxford University Press.
Ferree, Myra Marx. 1992. "The Political Context of Rational Choice: Rational Choice Theory and Resource Mobilization." In *Frontiers in Social Movement Theory.* Edited by Aldon Morris and Carol Mueller. New Haven: Yale University Press. 29–52.
Fireman, Bruce, and William A. Gamson. 1979. "Utilitarian Logic in the Resource Mobilization Perspective." In *The Dynamics of Social Movements.* Edited by Mayer N. Zald and John D. McCarthy. Cambridge: Winthrop. 8–44.
Fraser, Nancy, and Linda Gordon. 1994. "Civil Citizenship against Social Citizenship? On the Ideology of Contract-versus-Charity." In *The Condition of Citizenship.* Edited by Bert Van Steenbergen. London: Sage. 90–107.
Gamson, Joshua. 1995. "Must Identity Movements Self-Destruct: A Queer Dilemma." *Social Problems.* 42(3): 390–407.
Gamson, William A. 1992a. *Talking Politics.* Cambridge: Cambridge University Press.
———. 1992b. "The Social Psychology of Collective Action." In *Frontiers in Social Movement Theory.* Edited by Aldon Morris and Carol Mueller. New Haven: Yale University Press. 53–76.
———. 1988. "Political Discourse and Collective Action." *International Social Movement Research.* 1: 219–244.
———. 1985. "Goffman's Legacy to Political Sociology." *Theory and Society.* 14: 605–622.
———, Bruce Fireman, and Steven Rytina. 1982. *Encounters with Unjust Authority.* Homewood, Ill.: Dorsey Press.
Gardiner, Michael. 1992. *The Dialogics of Critique: M. M. Bakhtin and the Theory of Ideology.* London: Routledge.
Gastil, John. 1992. "Undemocratic Discourse: A Review of Theory and Research on Political Discourse." *Discourse and Society.* 3: 469–500.
Gramsci, Antonio. 1971. *Selections from the Prison Notebooks.* Edited and translated by Quintin Hoare and Geoffrey N. Smith. New York: International Publishers.
Grossberg, Lawrence, editor. 1986. "On Postmodernism and Articulation: An Interview with Stuart Hall." *Journal of Communication Inquiry.* 10: 45–60.
———, Cary Nelson, and Paula A. Treicher, editors. 1992. *Cultural Studies.* London: Routledge.
Hall, Stuart. 1985. "Signification, Representation, Ideology: Althusser and the Post-Structuralist Debates." *Critical Studies in Mass Communication.* 2: 91–114.
Hirschkop, Ken. 1989. "Introduction: Bakhtin and Cultural Theory." In *Bakhtin and Cultural Theory.* Edited by Ken Hirschkop and David Shepherd. Manchester: Manchester University Press. 1–38.
———. 1986. "Bakhtin, Discourse and Democracy." *New Left Review.* 160: 91–111.
Hitchcock, Peter. 1994. *Dialogics of the Oppressed.* Minneapolis: University of Minnesota Press.
Hodge, Robert, and Guenther Kress. 1988. *Social Semiotics.* Ithaca: Cornell University Press.
Holquist, Michael. 1990. *Dialogism: Bakhtin and His World.* London: Routledge.

Hunt, Alan. 1990. "Rights and Social Movements: Counter-Hegemonic Strategies." *Journal of Law and Society.* 17: 309–328.

Jenkins, J. Craig. "Resource Mobilization Theory and the Study of Social Movements." *Annual Review of Sociology.* 9: 527–553.

Johnston, Hank, Enrique Laraña, and Joseph R. Gusfield. 1994. "Identities, Grievances, and New Social Movements." In *New Social Movements: From Ideology to Identity.* Edited by Enrique Laraña, Hank Johnston, and Joseph R. Gusfield. Philadelphia: Temple. 3–35.

Johnston, Hank, and Bert Klandermans, editors. 1995. *Social Movements and Culture.* Minneapolis: University of Minnesota Press.

Katznelson, Ira. 1992. *Marxism and the City.* Oxford: Clarendon Press, 1992.

——. 1986. "Working-Class Formations: Contrasting Cases and Comparisons." In *Working-Class Formation: Nineteenth-Century Patterns in Western Europe and the United States.* Edited by Ira Katznelson and Aristide R. Zolberg. Princeton: Princeton University Press. 3–41.

Klandermans, Bert. 1992. "The Social Construction of Protest and Multiorganizational Fields." In *Frontiers in Social Movement Theory.* Edited by Aldon Morris and Carol Mueller. New Haven: Yale University Press. 77–103.

——. 1988. "The Formation of Mobilization and Consensus." *International Social Movement Research.* 1: 173–196.

——. 1984. "Mobilization and Participation: Social Psychological Expansions of Resource Mobilization Theory." *American Sociological Review.* 49: 583–600.

LaCapra, Dominick. 1983. *Rethinking Intellectual History: Texts, Contexts, Language.* Ithaca: Cornell University Press.

Lackoff, George, and Mark Johnson. 1979. *Metaphors We Live By.* Chicago: University of Chicago Press.

Laclau, Ernesto, and Chantal Mouffe. 1987. "Post-Marxism without Apologies." *New Left Review.* 166: 106.

——. 1985. *Hegemony and Socialist Strategy: Toward a Radical Democratic Politics.* London: Verso.

Macdonnell, Diane. 1986. *Theories of Discourse: An Introduction.* Oxford: Basil Blackwell.

Martin, Patricia Yancey. 1990. "Rethinking Feminist Organizations." *Gender & Society.* 4: 182–206.

McAdam, Doug. 1988. "Micromobilization Contexts and Recruitment to Activism." *International Social Movement Research.* 1: 125–154.

——. 1982. *Political Process and the Development of Black Insurgency, 1930–1970.* Chicago: University of Chicago Press.

——, Sidney Tarrow, and Charles Tilly. 1996. "To Map Contentious Politics." *Mobilization.* 1(1): 17–34.

——, John D. McCarthy, and Mayer Zald, editors. 1996. *Comparative Perspectives on Social Movements: Political Opportunities, Mobilizing Structures, and Cultural Framings.* Cambridge: Cambridge University Press.

McNall, Scott. 1988. *The Road to Rebellion: Class Formation and Kansas Populism, 1865–1900.* Chicago: University Chicago Press.

McNally, David. 1995. "Language, History and Class Struggle." *Monthly Review.* 47(3): 13–31.

Meiksins, Peter. 1987. "New Classes and Old Theories: The Impasse of Contemporary Class Analysis." In *Recapturing Marxism.* Edited by Rhonda Levine and Jerry Lembcke. New York: Praeger. 37–63.

Meiksins Wood, Ellen. 1990. "Falling through the Cracks: E. P. Thompson and the Debate on Base and Superstructure." In *E. P. Thompson: Critical Perspectives.* Edited by Harvey J. Kaye and Keith McClelland. Philadelphia: Temple University Press. 125–152.

———. 1986. *The Retreat from Class*. New York: Verso.

———. 1982. "The Politics of Theory and the Concept of Class: E. P. Thompson and His Critics." *Studies in Political Economy*. 9: 45–75.

Melucci, Alberto. 1996. *Challenging Codes: Collective Action in the Information Age*. Cambridge: Cambridge University Press.

———. 1989. *Nomads of the Present*. Philadelphia: Temple University Press.

Meszaros, Istvan. 1989. *The Power of Ideology*. New York: New York University Press.

Moore, Barrington. 1978. *Injustice: The Social Bases of Obedience and Revolt*. New York: Sharpe.

Mouffe, Chantal. 1990. "Radical Democracy or Liberal Democracy?" *Socialist Review*. 2: 57–66.

———. 1988. "Hegemony and New Political Subjects: Towards a New Concept of Democracy." In *Marxism and the Interpretation of Culture*. Edited by Cary Nelson and Lawrence Grossberg. Urbana: University of Illinois Press. 89–104.

———. 1979. "Hegemony and Ideology in Gramsci." In *Gramsci and Marxist Theory*. Edited by Chantal Mouffe. London: Routledge and Kegan Paul. 168–204.

Offe, Claus. 1987. "Challenging the Boundaries of Institutional Politics: Social Movements since the Sixties." In *Changing Boundaries of the Political*. Edited by Charles S. Maier. Cambridge: Cambridge University Press. 63–105.

———, and Helmut Wiesenthal. 1980. "Two Logics of Collective Action: Theoretical Notes on Social Class and Organizational Form." *Political Power and Social Theory*. 1: 67–115.

Oliver, Pam. 1989. "Bringing the Crowd Back In: The Nonorganizational Elements of Social Movements." *Research in Social Movements, Conflict and Change*. 11: 1–30.

Pateman, Carole. 1988. *The Sexual Contract*. Stanford: Stanford University Press.

Pred, Allan. 1992. "Capitalisms, Crises, and Cultures II: Notes on Local Transformation and Everyday Cultural Struggles." In *Reworking Modernity*. Edited by Allan Pred and Michael J. Watts. New Brunswick: Rutgers University Press. 106–117.

———. 1989. "The Locally Spoken Word and Local Struggles." *Environment and Planning D: Society and Space*. 7: 211–233.

Purvis, Trevor, and Alan Hunt. 1993. "Discourse, Ideology, Discourse, Ideology, Discourse, Ideology . . ." *British Journal of Sociology*. 44: 473–499.

Russo, Mary. 1986. "Female Grotesques: Carnival and Theory." In *Feminist Studies/Critical Studies*. Edited by Teresa de Lauretis. Bloomington: Indiana University Press. 213–229.

Sampson, Edward E. *Celebrating the Self: A Dialogic Account of Human Nature*. Boulder: Westview.

Sayer, Derek. 1987. *The Violence of Abstraction: The Analytic Foundations of Historical Materialism*. Oxford: Basil Blackwell.

Scott, James. 1990. *Domination and the Arts of Resistance: Hidden Transcripts*. New Haven: Yale University Press.

———. 1985. *Weapons of the Weak: Everyday Forms of Peasant Resistance*. New Haven: Yale University Press.

Shorter, Edward, and Charles Tilly. 1974. *Strikes in France, 1830–1968*. Cambridge: Cambridge University Press.

Smelser, Neil. 1959. *Social Change in the Industrial Revolution*. Chicago: University of Chicago Press.

Snow, David A., and Robert Benford. 1992. "Master Frames and Cycles of Protest." In *Frontiers in Social Movement Theory*. Edited by Aldon Morris and Carol Mueller. New Haven: Yale University Press. 133–155.

———, and Robert D. Benford. 1988. "Ideology, Frame Resonance, and Participant Mobilization." *International Social Movement Research*. 1: 197–217.

———, E. Burke Rochford Jr., Steven K. Worden, and Robert D. Benford. 1986. "Frame Alignment Processes, Micromobilization, and Movement Participation." *American Sociological Review.* 51: 464–481.

Somers, Margaret. 1994a. "Rights, Relationality, and Membership: Rethinking the Making and Meaning of Citizenship." *Law and Social Inquiry.* 63–112.

———. 1994b. "The Narrative Constitution of Identity: A Relational and Network Approach." *Theory and Society.* 23: 605–649.

———. 1993. "Law, Community, and Political Culture in the Transition to Democracy." *American Sociological Review.* 58: 587–620.

———. 1992. "Narrativity, Narrative Identity, and Social Action: Rethinking English Working-Class Formation." *Social Science History.* 16: 591–631.

———. 1989. "Workers of the World, Compare!" *Contemporary Sociology.* 18: 325–329.

———. 1986. "The People and the Law." Ph.D. diss., Harvard University.

———, and Gloria D. Gibson. 1994. "Reclaiming the Epistemological 'Other': Narrative and the Social Construction of Identity." In *From Persons to Nations: The Social Constitution of Identities.* Edited by Craig Calhoun. London: Basil Blackwell. 37–99.

Spohn, Willfried. 1990. "Toward a Historical Sociology of Working-Class Formation." *Critical Sociology.* 17: 75–90.

Stallybrass, Peter, and Allon White. 1986. *The Politics and Poetics of Transgression.* Ithaca: Cornell University Press.

Stam, Robert. 1988. "Mikhail Bakhtin and Left Cultural Critique." In *Postmodernism and Its Discontents.* Edited by E. Ann Kaplan. London: Verso. 116–145.

Steinberg, Marc. 1998a. "Tilting the Frame: Considerations on Collective Action from a Discursive Turn." *Theory and Society.* 27(b): 845–872.

———. 1998b. "Riding the Black Lad and Other Ritualistic Actions: Toward a Spatialized and Gendered Analysis of Nineteenth-Century Repertoires." In *Challenging Authority: The Historical Study of Contentious Politics.* Edited by Michael P. Hanagan, Leslie Page Moch, and Wayne te Brake. Minneapolis: University of Minnesota Press. 17–35.

———. 1997. "'A Way of Struggle': Reformations and Affirmations of E. P. Thompson's Class Analysis in Light of Postmodern Theories of Language." *British Journal of Sociology.* 48(3): 471–492.

———. 1996. "Culturally Speaking: Finding a Commons between Post-Structuralism and the Thompsonian Perspective." *Social History.* 21(2): 193–214.

———. 1995a. "The Roar of the Crowd: Repertoires of Discourse and Collective Action among the Silk Weavers in Nineteenth-Century London." In *Cycles and Repertoires of Collective Action.* Edited by Mark Traugott. Durham: Duke University Press. 57–88.

———. 1995b. *See Modern Historical Studies section.*

———. 1994. "The Dialogue of Struggle: The Contest over Ideological Boundaries in the Case of the Silk Weavers in the Early Nineteenth Century." *Social Science History.* 18: 505–542.

———. 1993. "New Canons or Loose Cannons? The Post-Marxist Challenge to Neo-Marxism as Represented in the Work of Calhoun and Reddy." *Political Power and Social Theory.* 8: 221–270.

———. 1989. "Worthy of Hire: Discourse, Ideology, and Collective Action among English Working-Class Trade Groups, 1800–1830." 2 vols. Ph.D. diss., University of Michigan.

Tarrow, Sidney. 1994. *Power in Movement: Social Movements, Collective Action and Politics.* Cambridge: Cambridge University Press.

———. 1992. "Mentalities, Political Cultures, and Collective Action Frames: Constructing Meanings through Action." In *Frontiers in Social Movement Theory.* Edited by Aldon Morris and Carol Mueller. New Haven: Yale University Press. 174–201.

Taylor, Verta, and Nancy Whittier. 1995. "Analytic Approaches to Social Movement Culture: The Case of the Women's Movement." In *Social Movements and Culture*. Edited by Hank Johnston and Bert Klandermans. Minneapolis: University of Minnesota Press. 163–187.

———. 1992. "Collective Identity in Social Movement Communities: Lesbian Feminist Mobilization." In *Frontiers in Social Movement Theory*. Edited by Aldon D. Morris and Carol McClurg Mueller. New Haven: Yale University Press, 1992. 104–129.

Terdiman, Richard. 1986. *Discourse/Counter-Discourse: The Theory and Practice of Symbolic Resistance in Nineteenth-Century France*. Ithaca: Cornell University Press.

Therborn, Goran. 1984. "Why Some Classes Are More Successful than Others." *New Left Review*. 138: 37–55.

———. 1980. *The Power of Ideology and the Ideology of Power*. London: Verso.

Thomson, Clive. 1989. "Bakhtin and Contemporary Anglo-American Feminist Theory." *Critical Studies: A Journal of Critical Theory, Literature and Culture*. 1(2): 141–161.

Tilly, Charles. 1995a. "Contentious Repertoires in Great Britain, 1758–1834." In *Cycles and Repertoires of Collective Action*. Edited by Mark Traugott. Durham: Duke University Press. 15–40.

———. 1995b. *Popular Contention in Great Britain, 1758–1834*. Cambridge: Harvard University Press.

———. 1986. *The Contentious French*. Cambridge: Harvard University Press.

———. 1985. "Models and Realities of Popular Collective Action." *Social Research*. 52: 717–747.

———. 1982. "Britain Creates the Social Movement." In *Social Conflict and Political Order in Modern Britain*. Edited by James Cronin and Jonathan Schneer. London: Croom Helm. 21–51.

———. 1978. *From Mobilization to Revolution*. Reading, Mass.: Addison-Wesley.

———, Louise Tilly, and Richard Tilly. 1975. *The Rebellious Century, 1830–1930*. Cambridge: Harvard University Press.

Tilly, Louise, and Charles Tilly, editors. 1981. *Class Conflict and Collective Action*. Beverly Hills: Sage.

Todorov, Tzvetan. 1984. *Mikhail Bakhtin: The Dialogic Principle*. Minneapolis: University of Minnesota Press.

Valverde, Marianne. 1991. "As If Subjects Existed: Analysing Social Discourses." *Canadian Review of Sociology and Anthropology*. 28(2): 173–187.

Vogel, Ursula. 1991. "Is Citizenship Gender-Specific?" In *The Frontiers of Citizenship*. Edited by Ursula Vogel. New York: St. Martin's Press. 58–85.

Volosinov, V. N. 1986. *Marxism and the Philosophy of Language*. Translated by Ladislav Matejka and I. R. Titunik. Cambridge: Harvard University Press.

———. 1983. "Literary Stylistics." In *Bakhtin School Poetics*. Edited by Ann Shukman. Oxford: RPT Publications. 93–152.

Whipp, Richard. 1985. "Labour Markets and Communities: An Historical View." *Sociological Review*. 33: 768–791.

Whittier, Nancy. 1995. *Feminist Generations: The Persistence of the Radical Women's Movement*. Philadelphia: Temple University Press.

Zald, Mayer. 1996. "Culture, Ideology and Strategic Framing." In *Comparative Perspectives on Social Movements: Political Opportunities, Mobilizing Structures, and Cultural Framings*. Edited by Doug McAdam, John D. McCarthy, and Mayer Zald. Cambridge: Cambridge University Press. 261–274.

Index

absenteeism, prosecution for, 173
agreements of service, 174
Albion Chapel, 162
Albion Mills, 161
Alexander, Sally, 11, 55–56n. 8
America, emigration to, 224
Ames & Atkinson (silk manufacturers), 122
Anglican Church. *See* Church of England
apprenticeships: control of, 24, 28; in cotton industry, 138; in silk industry, 52, 55, 60n. 9; women in, 55, 60n. 9
aristocracy: support for, 83; of wealth, 190–191
Armitage, Arthur, 59–60
artisans: collectivism of, 24–25; defined, 24; gender of, 24; ideologies of, 53; organizational structure of, 25–26; as preservationists, 25; reactionary radicalism of, 10. *See also* silk weavers
Ashton, Col. George Williams, 185
Ashton, James, 222
Ashton, Thomas, 145; assassination of, 221; control of Hyde by, 172, 176; housing constructed by, 43; productivity of mills owned by, 42, 144; reaction to strikes, 148–149; tenure of spinners of, 139

Ashton Female Reform Society, 182
Ashton Mechanics' Institution, 158, 179–181
Ashton Parish: description of, 37; poor relief in, 176–177
Ashton-Stalybridge district (Lancashire): canals in, 40; description of, 36–46; development of, 37–38, 39–40; economy of, 38–39, 129, 163–166, 167–186; local improvements in, 169–171, 175–176; location of, 37; number of mills, 134–135; number of pubs in, 44; piece rate in, 140; population of, 42–43; proportion of working class in, 41, 42; recreation and leisure activities in, 153–157, 176; social geography of, 41–43, 129, 151–153, 189–192
Ashton-under-Lyne (Lancashire). *See* Ashton-Stalybridge district (Lancashire)
Ashton-under-Lyne Gas and Water Works Company, 170
assaults, prosecution for, 30, 174
Assheton, Sir Ralph, 156
Astley, Francis, 163, 171
Atiyah, P. S., 173n. 6
Audenshaw (Lancashire): development of, 42; prestrike meeting in, 212

277

Australia, emigration to, 123
authority, in cotton mills, 135–136, 138, 146, 168, 225
automation, of cotton industry, 145–146, 235

Baines, Edward, 130, 140, 145, 177, 196
Bakhtin, Mikhail M., 14–15, 14n. 11, 17, 155, 157
Ballance, John, 84n. 12
Bayley, Jane Cheetham, 161
Bayley, Joseph, Jr., 161
Behagg, Clive, 58
Bell, William, 82
benevolent societies, 176
Benford, Robert, 7
Bethnal Green (London): development of, 39; number of pubs in, 43–45; N.U.W.C. (radical politics) in, 84–85. *See also* Saint Matthew's Parish, Bethnal Green
Betts, John Joseph, 41, 140, 183, 196, 208–216, 221, 222, 235
binding arbitration, in silk industry, 52
Birkbeck, Dr. (founder of mechanics institutions), 80
Black Lad, Riding of the, 154–157
blacklisting, 224–225
Board of Trade, 109, 118
bombazines, protectionism for, 53n. 5
Booth, John, 161
Bouverie, Maj. Gen. Henry, 140, 218, 219
Bowring, John, 140, 182, 220
broadcloth (plain weave): payments for, 105; piece rate for, 62, 105; production of, 60–61
brocades, production of, 54
Brock, Irving, 78
Brooke, Thomas, 183
Brutton, Robert, 65, 72, 106
Buckley, Abel, 162
Buckley, James, 162
Buckley, Joseph, 162
Bunn, James, 106
burial societies, 44, 153–154
Butterworth, Edwin, 40, 42

Calhoun, Craig, 67, 130, 186n. 10, 232; *The Question of Class Struggle*, 10
capitalists: attempts to control courts (magistrates), 76–77; characterized as parasitic nonproducers, 33, 115–116, 117, 189–190, 193–194; as "cotton lords," 157–163; interest in increased productivity, 27; opposition to wage protectionism, 89–90; political economy of, 192–195; setting of wages by, 199–200; workers' conflicts with, 23–24, 26, 27
Carlile, Richard, 154, 164, 172n. 3, 179, 181–182, 183, 185, 189
carnival, in Lancashire, 154–157
Caroline, queen of England, 84
Carpenter, William, 185, 189, 191, 193, 194, 204
Carpenter's Monthly Political Magazine, 193
Catholic Emancipation Bill, 183
Charles Orrell & Sons (cotton manufacturers), 174, 211
Chartism, 100, 181, 185, 207n. 1, 240
Cheetham, Edward, 215
Cheetham, Emma Reyner, 161
Cheetham, George, 161
Cheetham, John, 162
Cheetham, Sarah Lees, 161
Chetwode, George, 162
Christ Church Parish, Spitalfields: development of, 37, 39, 40–41; governance of, 69–70; poor relief in, 69–70, 71n. 4, 72; watch (police) and lamp in, 70
Christian virtues, social control through, 69, 77–79, 106
Church of England, 162, 232; opposition to, 185
civic virtue, 124
Clark, Anna, 11, 19, 60, 100, 111, 143, 235–236
class: formation of, xiv, 2, 3–6, 23, 36, 67–68, 100, 101, 125, 130, 229; as historical, 5; Marxist theory of, xiv, 5; as relational, 5, 14. *See also* petite bourgeoisie; working class, English
class consciousness: of cotton spinners, 150, 151–153, 167, 206–207, 225–226; formation of, xiv, 2, 4, 7, 17–18, 100, 230–236; of silk weavers, 87–88, 125
class struggle, identification of, 24
cloth, destruction of (silk industry), 51, 119, 120, 121, 122
coarse spinning (of cotton), 131, 132, 142
Cobbett, William, 83
collective action: causes of, 50; changes in types of, 29, 30–31, 107–109; and construction of new collective identities, 13, 88, 101, 114, 239–240; frequency of, 31–32; models of, xii, 3, 6–14; targets of, 108. *See also specific types of actions*

278 *Index*

Combination Laws: opposition to, 29, 84; repeal of (1824), 25, 28, 33, 83, 148
combinations, 202–203
Commission on the Silk Trade (1932), 84n. 12
Committee for the Distressed Weavers of Spitalfields, 80
common good, support of, 94
community: class consciousness within, 5, 21, 67–68, 85–86; political participation in, 82; reciprocity in (silk weavers), 69–77
Congregationalists, 162
consciousness, xii. *See also* class consciousness
Constitutionalism, 96
contention, discourses of: defined, xi, 14–21; dialogic processes of, 14–15, 88, 125, 129–130, 187–188, 236–241; justification for, xii; transformation of genres into, 17
contentious action, repertoires of, 20, 34–35
cooperation, between workers and employers, 50
cooperatives, development of, 34
Corn Laws: opposition to, 89n. 1; support for, 83
Cotton, Nicolas, 207n. 1
cotton fustian trade, 38
cotton industry: automation of, 145–146, 235; collective actions in, 142, 145, 146, 147, 165, 184, 199, 200, 201, 204, 206–226, 247–248 (table); fluctuations in, 131, 132, 142; free trade in, 92; growth of, 130, 131; intensification of, 143–145; mill economy and production in, 132–35, 234; mill social and technical relations, 195–199; number of mills, 134–135; organization of authority in, 135–136; productivity of, 38, 42, 130, 131, 134, 144; role in national and global economy, 130–132; shared culture of, 153–154; unionization of, 146–150, 183, 203, 212–214
cotton manufacturers (mill owners): authority (hegemony) of, 168–169, 171–181, 188, 197–199, 225, 234; bankruptcy of, 131; reaction to strikes, 148–149, 206–226; shopocracy of, 157–159, 163; social and economic ties of, 159–163
cotton spinners: age of, 139–140; competition from women, 142–143, 234; description of, 36–46; exploitation of, 196–199, 240; national and ethnic identity of, 23–24n. 1; opposition to reorganization of, 27; organizational alliances of, 28, 33; potential replacement of, 141–146, 234; productivity for, 136–139; protectionism for, 29; status of, 141, 152, 234; struggle for control of, 26, 233–234; tenure of, 139, 141–142; workplace particulars of, 22, 136–139. *See also* Ashton-Stalybridge district (Lancashire)
"Cotton Spinners and Power-Loom Weavers' Lesser Catechism, The," 198
Coulthart, John R., 41
courts: capitalist control of, 30, 106–107; control over cotton spinners, 172–175; control over silk weavers, 72, 122
Coventry: ribbon merchants of, 104; ribbon weavers of, 53, 114n. 1
"Coventry Freeman," *Animadversions on the Repeal of the Act for Regulating the Wages of Labour among the Spitalfields Weavers*, 94–95, 97, 98
crafts (handicrafts), control of, 26
Crookbrook, cotton mill in, 161
culture, xii; defined, 4
"cutting." *See* cloth, destruction of

Dawson, James, 79
democratic representation, in silk weavers' unions, 65
demonstrations (public and nonviolent), 29; prohibition of, 171; by silk weavers, 51, 118
Detroisier, Rowland, 134, 136, 181
discourse: ambiguity in, 15; defined, 14; function of, xiii, 2, 15–16, 229–230, 231, 241; multivocality of, 15, 19, 88. *See also* contention, discourses of; language
Dissenters, 158, 159, 162–163, 177, 178, 232
Dodd, George, 41n. 3
Doherty, John, 132, 136, 139–141, 146, 148, 191–194, 199, 202–204, 214, 216, 223–225
donkeying, 30
Donnelly, James, 174
Downes, George, 183, 211
Duce, Isaac, 121
Duff & Brooks (silk manufacturers), 122
Dukinfield (Lancashire): attack on mill

Index 279

Dukinfield (Lancashire) (*continued*)
owners in, 222; cotton industry in, 132; cotton spinners' strikes in, 208; development of, 42–43; prestrike meeting in, 212; suppression of Sunday amusements attempted in, 176
Dukinfield Old Chapel, 163
Dunn, Henry, 81

East London Auxiliary Sunday School Union, 81
East London Bible Association, 79
Eastman & Hill (silk manufacturers), 122
education, social control through, 81, 168, 177–178, 181, 182
Eichtal, Gustave d', 45
Eley, Geoff, 9n. 6
embezzlement: prosecution for, 72, 73, 74; punishment for, 122; rise in incidence of, 105, 107
emigration: to America, 224; to Australia, 123
employment law, 174
Epstein, James, 96, 167
ethnicity, 23–24n. 1
Evangelicalism, 69, 77–79, 81, 93, 106, 232
Ewick, Patricia, 232n. 2

factories. *See* cotton industry
Factory Inquiry Commission, 201
factory workers, reformist consciousness of, 10
fancy goods (silk): demise (destruction) of producers, 104; piece rate for, 62, 105; production of, 54, 61–62
Fantasia, Rick, 8
Ferree, Myra Marx, 11
fighting words. *See* contention, discourses of
fine spinning (of cotton), 131–132
foreign silk. *See* French silk goods
framing (frame analysis), 7, 19–20, 88
fraternal societies, 44, 153–154
free press, petition for, 184
free trade: in cotton industry, 92, 159; inhibition of, 54; support for, 89, 92–93; workers' reaction to, 96, 97, 102, 118–119
French revolution (1830), 183, 213
French silk goods, import of, 51, 58–59, 99n. 5, 103, 109
French silk weavers, settlement in London, 37, 51
Fyler, Thomas, 103

Gamson, William, 7
Gas and Water Act of 1825, 170
gender differences: in cotton occupations, 136–137, 141; models of, 11–12; overlooked by Thompson, 10–11; reinforcement of, 19. *See also* patriarchy; women
General Association, 28
General Protection Society, 111
general strikes. *See* strikes
General Trade Union (silk weavers), 65, 108
General Union (cotton spinners), 219, 220
genres, defined, 15
Gibson, Thomas, 57, 80, 82
Glossup (Lancashire): cotton spinners' strikes in, 220, 222, 224; development of, 42
government: intervention by, 94; within parishes, 69. *See also* Parliament
Gramsci, Antonio, 4n. 3
Grand National Union, 207n. 1
Great Britain, nineteenth-century labor struggles in, 23–35. *See also* collective action; strikes
Grundy, Mr. (cotton spinner), 216

Hale, William, 37, 45, 54–55, 83n. 8, 89, 96, 107
Hall, Catherine, 11
Hall, Robert G., 162nn. 6, 7, 207n. 1
Hall, Stuart, 14n. 12, 15–16n. 13
Harrison, Amy Cheetham, 161
Harrison, Thomas, 161
Harrison, William, 161
hegemony: of cotton mill owners, 168–69, 171–181, 188, 197–199, 225, 234; defined, 16n. 14; and discourse, 16, 231–232; struggle for in silk weavers' community, 69, 77–82, 232–233
Hegginbottom, William, 208–209
Higgins, Timothy, 163
Hindley, Charles, 44, 158–159, 166, 179–180, 185, 214, 217, 223
Hindley & Hyde (cotton manufacturers), 212, 217–218n. 3, 224
Hobson, Joshua, 164, 183, 184, 185
Hodgins, Mr. (of Manchester), 217
Hoole, Holland, 195
Hopkins, Thomas, 192
Horner, Leonard, 162n. 6
household, rule of the, 174
housewives, emergence of, 204
Howard, James, 222

Howe, Anthony, 157
Huguenot silk weavers, settlement in London, 37, 51
Hulton, Edward, 161
Hume, Joseph, 91, 99
Hunt, Robert, 122
Hunter, Isaac, 119
Hunter, William, 120, 235
Hurst (Lancashire), development of, 42
Huskisson, William, 92, 93, 99, 103
Hyde (Lancashire): attack on mill owners in, 222; cotton industry in, 132; cotton spinners' strikes in, 145, 148, 208; development of, 42; number of mills in, 135; number of pubs in, 176; political control of, 172; religion in, 163
Hynes, John, 222

ideology, defined, 15–16n. 13
individualism, 191, 204
industrial capitalism, 9
inequality, reactions to, 1–2. *See also* social justice
intellectual societies, 45
interests, formulation of, 8
interventionism, 94
intimidation, prosecution for, 173
Irish laborers, in Lancashire, 42, 43

Jackson, Isaac, 169
Johnson, Christopher, 9n. 6
Johnson, Mark, 17n. 15
Jones, Mr. (silk weaver), 110
Joyce, Patrick, 12–13, 19, 50, 67, 130, 181; *Democratic Subjects*, 13; *Voices of the People*, 13
justice: as locally defined, 30n. 3, 69, 72; narratives of, 12
just wage. *See* living wage; wages

Katznelson, Ira, 8, 9, 68
Kennedy, John, 190, 199–200
Kershaw, Charles, 222
Kirby, R. G., 207n. 1
Knight, Charles, 192, 196, 201
"knobsticks" (strikebreakers), 30
Koditschek, Theodore, 67

labor market: in Ashton-Stalybridge district, 141–142, 201; effects of protectionism on, 53
labor theory of value. *See* value, labor theory of
labor unions. *See* unions
Lackoff, George, 17n. 15

Laclau, Ernesto, 13
laissez faire, 89. *See also* free trade
Lancashire: carnival in, 154–157; development of weaving in, 58; distribution of pubs in, 153–154; powerloom riots in (1826), 32; wakes in, 154. *See also* Ashton-Stalybridge district (Lancashire)
language: appropriation of, 17; in construction of social meaning, 12–13, 14–15, 16. *See also* discourse
larceny, prosecution for, 73
Lea & Wilson (silk wholesalers), 56
Leech, John, 40, 161
Lees, Aaron, 201
Lees (Lancashire), development of, 42
Lees, Jeremiah, 210, 211
Lees, John, 161
liberal democracy, 232
liberty, of workers, 76, 111–112, 116
Linebaugh, Peter, 73
Lion, 183
literacy, value of, 178
Liverpool, cotton dealers and agents in, 131
living wage: in cotton industry, 199–205, 238; in silk industry, 52, 108–109, 111, 119
London: masons of, 53. *See also* Spitalfields district (London)
London Corresponding Society, 45, 82–83
Longendale (Lancashire), cotton spinners' strikes in, 220, 223
looms: brokering of, 105; changes in, 104; warping of, 61. *See also* machines, breaking of
Lord, James, 162
Lovett, William, 105
Luddites, 31, 32, 182
lustres, production of, 54

Macclesfield, silk industry in, 58, 111, 114n. 1, 118
machines, breaking of: in cotton industry, 224; description of, 30–31; punishment for, 32; in silk industry, 51
macklers, 56
magistrates. *See* courts
Manchester: cotton industry in, 131, 140, 142, 208; cotton manufacturers in, 161; cotton spinners' strikes in, 145, 202, 220; development of, 37; meeting of mill owners in, 148–149; silk industry in, 53, 58, 114n. 1, 118;

Index 281

Manchester (*continued*)
  support for striking spinners in, 222;
  traffic to Ashton from, 38
Manchester Guardian, 145, 184, 212
Manchester Philanthropic Society, 177
Manchester Statistical Society, 41, 44
Manchester Times, 157
Manchester Trades' Committee, 203
manufacturers. *See* cotton manufacturers; silk manufacturers
Marcet, Jane, *Conversations on Political Economy*, 189
Martineau, Harriet, 59, 60, 200; *A Manchester Strike*, 195, 200
Marx, Karl, 3, 23, 145
Marxist theory of class, xiv, 5
Mason, Thomas, 160, 161
Master Manufacturers of Manchester, 217–218n. 3
master weavers: organization under, 54–55, 57–58; return to 1824 prices by, 111
materialism, xii, 2, 21, 229–30, 241
Mayfield, David, 18n. 16
Mayhew, Henry, 45n. 4
McCann, Phillip, 79n. 7, 81
McConnel cotton mill, 143
McCulloch, J. R., 130, 192
McNall, Scott, 8
mechanization, 27. *See also* automation
Meiksins Wood, Ellen, 4n. 1
Merceron, Joseph, 39, 44
mercers, 56
Messrs. Lees & Sons (cotton manufacturers), 212
Messrs. Remington, Wilson & Mills (silk manufacturers), 75
Messrs. Tarrant & Co. (silk manufacturers), 121
Mile End New Town (London), 39
Millbrook (Lancashire), attack on Sidebottom's mill at, 221
mills. *See* cotton industry
mobilization, 9; of cotton spinners, 149, 183, 208, 211–214, 215, 218; of silk weavers, 65–66, 107–108, 233. *See also* resource mobilization model; unions
Moore, Ambrose, 53n. 6, 57, 103, 105, 118, 121; attacks on cloth owned by, 122
moral language, 18–19
More, Hannah, 79
Mossley (Lancashire): attack on mill owners in, 222; development of, 42

Mouffe, Chantal, 13
Murray, George, 142–143n. 3
Musson, A. E., 207n. 1

narrative identity, 12
National Association for the Protection of Labour (N.A.P.L.), 28, 203, 203n. 1, 209, 213, 214
national identity (nationalism), 23–24n. 1, 232
National Political Union, 84–85
National Union of the Working Classes (N.U.W.C.), 84–85
negligence: in cotton industry, 140–141; defined, 74–75; in silk industry, 75–76, 107
New Connexion Methodists, 162, 163, 178
new social movements theory, xii, 13, 20
Noquet, Robert, 110, 123
Norwich, silk industry in, 114n. 1
Nott, Jeremiah, 79

Oastler, Richard, 217–218n. 3
Oates, Thomas, 203n. 1, 214
Observations on the Ruinous Effects of the Spitalfields Acts, 91
Old Corruption, 113–114, 181, 184
organization, 8
organized (collective) violence: in silk industry, 51–52, 54, 64, 119–122, 243–246 (table); threat of, 32; types of, 29, 30–31. *See also* assaults
organzine (warp thread), 55
Orrell's mill (Lancashire). *See* Charles Orrell & Sons (cotton manufacturers)

Parliament: charter of parishes by, 69; control of labor laws in, 32; petitioning of, 29, 30, 65, 108, 109, 113, 114, 123, 184. *See also* government
participation, political, 82
paternalism: of Lancashire mill owners, 43, 181; in poor relief, 70; of West End masters, 46
patriarchy, 11, 235–36; of male cotton spinners, 136–137, 142–143, 204–205, 235; of male silk weavers, 50, 52–53, 55, 60, 87, 95, 98, 111, 125, 235
patriotism: of silk weavers, 83, 97–98. *See also* national identity
Peel, Sir Robert, 149
Peterloo massacre (Manchester): com-

memoration of, 164, 182; impact on radical politics, 182
petite bourgeoisie, in Lancashire, 157, 163–166, 169, 170
Philosophical Enquiring Christians, 182
picketing, 171, 211
piece brokers, 56
piece rate
  in cotton industry: discounting of, 144, 208, 210, 212, 214, 218; equalization of, 211, 220, 223, 224; regional variation in, 140, 147, 206, 209; for women, 142–143n. 3
  in silk industry: attempts to end, 76, 90; depression of, 104–105; established, 51, 55; hierarchy in, 61–62; rate books for, 62 *See also* wages
Pigot and Co.'s London . . . Commercial Directory For 1822–3, 55
Place, Francis, 45n. 4, 82, 83, 99, 151, 208
Platt, Rev. Josiah, 77
political economy, 19; characterization of the worker in, 204; education in, 80; fear of, 94; opposition to, 29, 94, 97, 109, 117, 188, 191, 193–195, 237–238; rise of, 28, 32, 87, 88–89, 99, 158, 175, 188, 192, 232, 237
political language, solidarity through, 12–13
political process model, xii, 6–10, 229
Political Union of the Working Classes of Tower Hamlets, 85
politics, mass meetings in, 32
Poor Laws, 71, 185
Poor Man's Advocate, 188
Poor Mans' Guardian, 85
poor relief: for cotton workers, 176–177; from Evangelicals, 77–79, 81; parish administration of, 69–71, 78; for silk weavers, 71–72, 80–82, 106
poplins, protectionism for, 53n. 5
popular rights, 82
populism, 13, 165, 167, 185
post-materialism, xii, 13
Powell, John, 94, 96, 97
power looms: in cotton industry, 134, 146; development of, 27
Poyton, John, 55, 94, 98, 124
Pred, Alan, 16
Preston, Thomas, 84n. 10
Primitive Methodists, 177
production, modes of, 3
productive relations, 3–4, 21–22

productivity: capitalists' attempts to increase, 27; of cotton industry, 38, 42, 130, 131, 134, 144; of cotton spinners, 136–139; of silk weavers, 61
protectionism: in silk industry, 28, 29, 46, 50, 51–54; Tory opposition to, 89, 92. *See also* Spitalfields Acts
Protection Society, 164
public nuisances, prevention of, 171

radicalism: of cotton spinners, 181–186; of petite bourgeoisie, 165; reactionary, 10, 117; of silk weavers, 69, 82–86
rationalism, radical, 178
reading societies, 182
real estate speculation, in Lancashire, 164
reciprocity: and protection of workers, 96; in silk weavers' community, 69–77, 80
Reform Bill, 184
reformist consciousness, 10
Regina v. Stoke upon Trent, 173n. 5
religion, social control through, 69, 77–79, 81, 93, 106, 177–179
reserve labor, 26–27
resource mobilization model, xii, 6–10, 229
Reyner, Frederick, 162–163
Ricardo, David, 91
riots, 29, 31, 32
Roberts, Richard, 145
Robinson, Samuel, 159
Rose, Sonya, 11, 19
Rothstein, Natalie, 92–93n. 2
Rudé, George, 51
Rugg, Mr. (silk manufacturer), 122
Rule, John, 24, 95
Russo, Mary, 155n. 3

Saint Matthew's Parish, Bethnal Green: corruption in, 69, 70; development of, 39, 40–41; poor relief in, 65n. 10, 70, 71, 106
St. Michael's vicarage (Ashton), 162, 178
satins, production of, 54, 61
Saxon, John, 173, 174
Scott, James, 16, 154
Scott, Joan, 11n. 8, 12
self-employment, of artisans, 24
separate spheres, doctrine of, 11
Seven Years War, 51
Sewell, William, 4n. 1

Index 283

Shaw, Lt. Col., 171, 211, 218, 219
"shopocracy," 157–159, 163–166
Shoreditch, opposition to silk weavers in, 84
short-time (half work), 32, 105, 106, 205
Silbey, Susan, 232n. 2
silk industry: benefit societies in, 64; collective actions in, 51–52, 54, 64, 75, 76, 102, 108, 112–113, 119–122, 243–246 (table); demise (destruction) of, 102–104; development of, 51; fluctuations in, 71–72, 80, 102–104, 108, 124; master manufacturers (warehousers) in, 56–58, 64; masters (small masters) in, 54–55, 57–58; organization of production in, 54–59; protectionism in, 28, 29, 46, 50, 51–54; repeal of protectionism in, 102–107; unionization (organization, alliances) of, 28, 33, 50, 63–66, 108, 123; wage security in, 62–63; workshop structure of, 59–63
silk manufacturers (warehousers): development of power of, 56–58, 64, 87; increasing control of silk industry by, 104, 117; on parish boards, 70; poor relief from, 80–81; reorganization of, 27; repeal of Spitalfields Acts requested by, 89–94, 118
silkmen (warehousers), 56–58
silk weavers: attempts to convert and educate, 77–79; attempts to resurrect protectionism, 105–107, 108, 109; bankruptcy of, 104; call for "equal justice" for, 102, 117, 124; degraded skills of, 61; description of, 36–46; embezzlement by, 73, 74, 107; moral character (economy) of, 44–45, 52, 68–69, 71, 72, 77, 79, 82, 87, 92, 100, 104, 125, 239–240; national and ethnic identity of, 23–24n. 1; negligence by, 75–76, 107; opposition to reorganization of, 27; poor relief for, 71–72, 80–82; productivity of, 61; radical politics of, 10, 69, 82–86; reciprocity among, 69–77; recreation and leisure activities of, 44–46; struggle for control of, 26, 68, 69, 77–82, 232–233; use of organized (collective) violence by, 51–52, 54, 64; workplace particulars of, 22, 59–60. *See also* Spitalfields district (London)

Slater, Mr. (of Ashton spinners' union), 216, 221–222
Smith, Adam, 96–97, 117, 239
smuggling, of French silk goods, 58–59, 103
Snow, David, 7
social contract theory, 95n. 3, 96, 191–192
social control: by bourgeois charities, 69, 77–79; by cotton mill owners, 175–181; through education, 81, 168, 177–178, 181, 182; through religion, 69, 77–79, 81, 93, 106, 177–179
social economy, 116–117, 193
socialism. *See* cooperatives
social justice, 191, 213, 225–226
Society for Mutual Instruction (Stalybridge), 180–181
Somers, Margaret, 12, 231n. 1, 238
Spa Fields meetings (1816), 83
Spicer St. Lancasterian school, 81
Spitalfields Acts: collective actions triggered by repeal of, 101–126; extended to women's work, 60; maintaining, 84, 89; opposition to, 89–94; passage of (1773), 50, 51–54; productive relations defined by, 28; repeal of (1823), 28, 53n. 6, 65, 87–100, 233; repeal's effect on silk industry, 102–107; support for, 94–99
Spitalfields Association, 78, 79
Spitalfields Benevolent Society, 38, 79
Spitalfields district (London): description of, 36–46; development of, 37, 39; economy of, 38, 54; literacy in, 45–46; location of, 36–37; number of pubs in, 43–44; population of, 38; proportion of weavers in, 39, 46; recreation and leisure activities in, 44–46; social geography of, 40–41. *See also* Christ Church Parish, Spitalfields
Spitalfields Mechanics' Institution, 80, 81
Spitalfields Soup Society, 46, 77–78, 106
Stallybrass, Peter, 155
Stalybridge (Lancashire). *See* Ashton-Stalybridge district (Lancashire)
Stam, Robert, 14
Stamford and Warrington, Earl of, 39–40, 160, 168, 170, 178
Standring, John, 168, 222

state-making, 9
Statute of Apprenticeship, repeal of (1813), 28
Statutes of Apprentices and Artificers, 29
Stedman Jones, Gareth, 12
Stephens, Joseph Rayner, 181
Stewart, John, 183
Stockport, cotton spinners' strikes in, 145, 148–149, 200, 208
Stockport Advertiser, 223
strike funds, 220, 222. *See also* poor relief
strikes (turn-outs): in cotton industry, 142, 145, 146, 147, 165, 184, 199, 200, 201, 204, 206–226, 247–248 (table); description of, 29, 31, 32–33, 34; in silk industry, 75, 76, 102, 108, 112–113, 119–122, 243–246 (table). *See also* picketing
Styles, John, 72
Sunday schools, social control through, 81, 168, 177–178, 181, 182
supply and demand, laws of, 201
Sutcliffe, Rev., 162
sweatshops, rise of, 26–27
Swindell, William, 163

technology, destruction of, 30–31
temperance societies, 176
Ten Hours Act, 185
Thelwall, John, 45
Therborn, Goran, 8, 9
Thistlewood, Arthur, 83n. 9
Thompson, E. P., 230; *Customs in Common*, 4; *The Making of the English Working Class*, xiv, 3–6, 17, 21, 23, 27, 49, 67, 72, 85, 101, 130, 184, 206; *Whigs and Hunters*, 18
Thompson, William, 112, 122
Thorne, Susan, 18n. 16
Thornley, William, 222
Tilly, Charles, 20, 29
Times (London), 121
trade organizations, development of, 33–34
trades: degradation of, 26–27, 31, 49, 55–56n. 8, 61, 62; mechanization of, 27
Trades' Free Press, 83, 109
trade societies (silk weavers), 26, 111, 233
trade unions. *See* unions
tram (weft thread), 55, 61

truck system, 164
Tufnell, Edward, 195, 200–201
Twig Folly neighborhood (London), 39, 81

unemployment: after Napoleonic wars, 26; in silk industry, 62
"Unfortunates," 122
Union Pilot and Intelligencer, 188
unions: of cotton spinners, 146–150, 183, 203, 212–214; development of, 29, 33; prohibition (suppression) of, 28, 68; of silk weavers, 28, 33, 50, 63–66, 108, 123; of women in cotton industry, 142, 143
Unitarianism, 163
United Trades' Co-operative Journal, 43, 164, 188, 203, 211
Ure, Andrew, 132, 141, 146, 152, 195

Valenze, Deborah, 95, 204
value, labor theory of: of cotton spinners, 188, 193–195, 201, 205, 206, 218, 234; of silk weavers, 95, 96, 114, 115, 116–117, 233, 237
Valverde, Marianne, 15
velvets, production of, 54, 61
"Verax," *Review of the Statements in Hale's Appeal to the Public on the Spitalfields Acts*, 92
Vernon, James, 12, 13, 19, 67–68
vitriol throwing, 187
Voice of the People, 154, 188, 223–224
Volosinov, V. N., 15

wages: control of, 28, 90, 91; depression of, 104–105, 124; fixing of, 32; standards in cotton industry, 140–141; standards in silk industry, 52–53. *See also* living wage; piece rate
Wages Protection Bill (proposed), 114
Wagstaffe, Luke, 161
Wagstaffe & Sidebottom (cotton manufacturers), 161
wakes, in Lancashire, 154, 173, 176
Walker, Charles, 164
Wallis, William, 110, 124
Walters, Daniel, 122
Weavers' Company, 56
Wellesley, Arthur (duke of Wellington), 118
Wesleyan Methodists, 177, 214
White, Allon, 155
Whitechapel Parish (London), 39

Wilson, Thomas, 89
Wilson and Moore (silk wholesalers), 56
women: absence from strike reports, 219; apprenticing of (silk industry), 55, 60n. 9; in carnival, 155; class consciousness of, 235–236; in cotton industry, 142–143; excluded as artisans, 24; excluded as public (political) voices, 100; inclusion in discourse of contention, 204; as reserve labor, 26–27; unionization of, 142, 143. *See also* gender differences; patriarchy
woolen cloth, production of, 38
work: control of, 26; neglect of, 74–76, 107

workers: exploitation of, 49, 115–116, 117, 196–199, 240; liberty (freedom) of, 76, 111–112, 116; role in economy, 93–94. *See also* factory workers
workhouses, silk weavers in, 106
working class, English: formation of, xiv–xv, 5–6, 68; in Lancashire mill towns, 153–154, 167, 206, 209, 219
work stoppages: description of, 29, 30; in silk industry, 75
Wright's mill (Lancashire), 173–174
wrongful dismissal, prosecution for, 173, 174

Zetetic societies, 183